"博学而笃志,切问而近思。"
(《论语》)

博晓古今,可立一家之说;
学贯中西,或成经国之才。

复旦博学·复旦博学·复旦博学·复旦博学·复旦博学·复旦博学

主编简介

高凌云，复旦大学法学院教授，山东烟台人。华东政法大学国际法学学士，新加坡国立大学比较法学硕士，美国威拉姆特大学法学博士，美国纽约州、俄勒冈州律师，比利时根特大学、美国纽约大学、密歇根大学和哈佛大学法学院访问学者，美国凯斯西储大学、圣约翰大学法学院和东芬兰大学法商学院客座教授，出版《英美法：案例分析与法律写作》（上海人民出版社）、《英美法：合同、侵权与法律实务》（上海人民出版社）、《Chinese Business Law》（合著，美国Thomson West法律出版公司）、《被误读的信托——信托法原论》（复旦大学出版社）和《英美普通法读写教程》（上海交大出版社）等专著和教材，并在国内外法学期刊发表论文若干。主要研究和授课领域为英美法、信托法、国际金融法、国际商法和法律英语。

博学 法学系列

英美合同侵权法
（第二版）

高凌云 编著

复旦大学出版社

内容提要

本书主要介绍英美法中的合同法和侵权法。针对每一部门法的特点，分别讨论合同的成立、履行与抗辩，以及故意侵权、过失侵权与严格责任侵权等方面。除了讨论实体法内容，本书还从案例阅读与分析的角度引导读者深入学习英美法的精髓。本书的特点之一是英文语言准确，并辅以适当的中文解释和介绍；二是适应的读者群比较广泛，既可以用作法科学生的法律英语课程教材，也可以作为法科学生的英美法或比较法全英文课程的教材，还可以为其他对英美法感兴趣的读者提供全面的英美合同法与侵权法的知识。本书资料来源丰富，既有国外原版著作和判例，也包括国内学者的观点。

前　言

随着全球经济一体化的发展以及法律在我国地位的不断提升,法律英语的学习成为我国法科学生的必修课以及大多数综合性大学学生的选修课。法律英语应包括两个层面:一是以英语表达的外国法,主要以英美法为主;二是以英语表达的中国法,主要包括中国法条英译以及中国法律概念、法律文献的英译等。而要做到能够准确将我国的法条与法律文献翻译成英语,首先必须了解在英美法系和其他英语国家是否有类似的法律概念以及这些概念是否有约定俗成的表达方法,否则即便把我国的法律概念翻译成英文也可能牛头不对马嘴。因此,学习英美法是培养学生将我国法律准确翻译成英文的能力的基础。

一般而言,学习英语要同时注重听说读写,学习法律英语也是如此。

以前网络不发达,寻找原版听力材料比较困难,只能依靠国内的有声出版物或者电台。而有声出版物大多经过编辑,可能失去原汁原味;收听电台也有很多不便,诸如信号问题以及时间问题。现在我们处于网络时代,通过网络很容易找到各种音频和视频资料,英美国家的有些法院也把庭审资料放到官方网站。因此,我们有条件听到未经编删的原版资料,"听"的资源问题比较容易解决,只要我们坚持不懈就能够提高法律英语学习中的听力能力。另外,通过参加法律英语课的学习,在课堂上一直听老师和同学们用英语讨论法律问题,这本身也是提高听力的一个好办法。

"说"对于我国学生一直是一个大问题,因为缺少说的环境,并且通过上课来锻炼说的能力也很有限,因为上课时间较短,班上同学可能较多,不大可能轮到每个人发言。我建议有心练习口语的同学在课下自己组织类似"英语角"等活动,作为法科学生,更可积极组织或参加英美法模拟法庭,用英文辩论。当然,在课堂上应该主动积极用英文发言。曾有学生告诉我,他们在连续上英语课或者全英文专业课之后,到食堂打饭时都不由自主对着打饭的阿姨说起英语来。这充分说明"说"的能力是完全可以培养的。

"读"和"写"对中国学生来说相对容易,尤其是"读",我们同学的阅读能力一般都很强。可是法律英语的读和写与普通英语的不同,因为学生面对的是英文法条、判例或法律文献,里面大量的法律词汇对英语是母语的学生而言都很难。因此,学习法律英语,一定要重视读和写。英美法的特点是以判例法为主,因此读案例就成为英美律师每天最重要的功课。对于我们来说,这也是学习英美法的基本功。能够读懂一般的英语并不一定能读懂案例。"写"也是如此,即便能够用英文写信、写短文,甚至写小说,却并不一定能够写法律文书。除了特殊的法律英语词汇外,法律文书的写作有其特殊的格式与要求。

"法律专业英语"是复旦大学法学院本科生和研究生的必修课程。《英美合同侵权法》是在复旦大学法学院本科生法律专业英语课讲义的基础上编撰而成,其前身是《英美法:合同、侵权与审判实务》(上海人民出版社,2006),与《英美普通法读写教程》(上海交通大学出版社,2012)系属同一系列中的基础教材。后者着重介绍如何读英美案例,撰写案例综述,如何用英文撰写一种最重要的法律文书——法律分析报告,又叫备忘录(memorandum)。而本书则主要介绍英美合同法和侵权法的实体法内容。全书分为两大部分:第一部分关于英美合同法,第二部分关于英美侵权法。每部分自成体系,既可以单独使用,也可以综合使用。本书各章节之间逻辑性强,循序渐进、由浅入深地探讨了英美合同法和侵权法的主要内容。除了用在法律专业英语课上外,本书还可以用于英美合同法和英美侵权法的双语或全英文教学中,并可辅佐以模拟法庭来帮助学生充分理解英美法律的精髓。另外,本书中所引用法官判决书保持原有风貌,有益于学生领悟法律英语特色。

目前国内市场上有不少很好的法律英语教材,由浅入深地介绍英国或美国的各个部门法,侧重于英语语言方面的介绍和讨论,并附有词语解释和翻译练习等,适合非法科学生或者对自己的英语程度不够自信的同学使用。另外国内还出版了不少原版法律书的影印本,大都是美国法学院的教材,适合英语程度较高、对某一部门法有特殊兴趣的同学使用。我建议有志于提高法律英语能力并希望学习英美法的同学在学习本书的同时可以根据自己的英语程度购买一本或一套其他法律英语教材，不在多，而在于把书从头读到尾。因此，为了避免类似教材的重复，本书将读者定位于已经具备相当的英语知识并同时掌握了法律基础知识的人，目的在于让读者通过学习用英语编写的法律文章和案例，在提高法律英语水平的同时学到原汁原味的英美法律中部分学科的精髓。因此，本书中包含了大量未经简化的原版案例和尽量全面的有关英美合同法和侵权法的内容，以帮助学生理解原版案例的结构和推理过程，加深学生对英美法律的理解。

感谢复旦大学2002级以来的法学本科生、法学硕士生和法学博士生；他们先后都用过本书的前身做教材，在教学期间给我提出了很好的建议；他们的学习过程与进步情况对于如何进一步完善本教材、提高教学质量给了我很大的启迪。感谢复旦大学法学院民商法博士李锋对本书第一版所提出的建设性意见以及对本书的出版提供的帮助，感谢复旦大学出版社张咏梅编辑对本书第一版所做的贡献。复旦大学法学院2014届国际法专业研究生李维佳同学帮忙从本书中选定一些较难的词汇并初步翻译成中文，在此一并表示感谢。

另外，最重要的，我要感谢复旦大学出版社的张炼编辑，没有她的辛勤工作与一丝不苟的敬业精神，本书永远也不会得以及时出版与再版。

最后，由于能力与时间所限，错误在所难免，敬请指正。

高凌云

2016年5月于纽约

lygao@fudan.edu.cn

CONTENTS

PART I COMMON LAW OF CONTRACTS

CHAPTER 1   INTRODUCTION ·········· 003
   1. Contracts and Contract Law ·········· 005
      1.1   Definition of "Contract" ·········· 005
      1.2   Sources of the Law of Contract ·········· 006
   2. Classifications of Contracts ·········· 007
   3. Case 1: Hawkins v. McGee ·········· 008
   Review Questions ·········· 016

CHAPTER 2   FORMATION OF CONTRACT ·········· 017
   1. Offer ·········· 018
      1.1   Elements of Offer ·········· 018
      1.2   Case 2: Carlill v. Carbolic Smoke Ball Co. ·········· 020
      1.3   Invitation to Make an Offer ·········· 035
      1.4   Case 3: Lefkowitz v. Great Minneapolis Surplus Store ·········· 036
      1.5   Termination of Offer ·········· 040
      1.6   Case 4: Ardente v. Horan ·········· 042
   2. Acceptance ·········· 048
      2.1   Elements of Acceptance ·········· 048
      2.2   Effectiveness of Acceptance ·········· 050
   3. Consideration ·········· 051
      3.1   Elements of Consideration ·········· 051
      3.2   Case 5: Hamer v. Sidway ·········· 053
      3.3   Case 6: Harris v. Time, Inc. ·········· 063
      3.4   Invalid Consideration ·········· 065

3.5　Case 7: Slattery v. Wells Fargo Armored Service Corp. 067
　　3.6　Promissory Estoppel 071
　　3.7　Case 8: Ricketts v. Scothorn 072
　Review Questions 077

CHAPTER 3　DEFENSES 078
　1. Misrepresentation 079
　2. Mistake 080
　3. Duress 082
　4. Undue Influence 082
　5. Capacity of Parties 082
　6. Illegality 087
　7. Statute of Frauds 098
　8. The Parol Evidence Rule 104
　Review Questions 104

CHAPTER 4　SELECTED TOPICS ON COMMON LAW OF CONTRACT 106
　1. Performance 107
　2. Remedies 120
　3. Assignment of Contract Rights and Delegation of Duties 123
　4. Third Party Beneficiaries 125
　Review Questions 126

PART II　COMMON LAW OF TORTS

CHAPTER 5　INTRODUCTION TO TORT LAW 129
　1. Torts vs. Crimes 130
　2. Torts vs. Breach of Contracts 130
　3. Classifications of Torts 131
　4. Remedies 131
　Review Questions 132

CHAPTER 6   INTENTIONAL TORTS 133
　1. The General Elements of Intentional Torts 134
　2. Intentional Torts to the Person 135
　　2.1　Battery and Assault 135
　　2.2　False Imprisonment 164
　　2.3　Intentional Infliction of Emotional Distress 171
　3. Intentional Torts to Property 177
　　3.1　Trespass and Nuisance 177
　　3.2　Conversion 178
　4. Defenses to Intentional Torts 183
　　4.1　Case 19: Katko v. Briney 185
　　4.2　Case 20: Courvoisier v. Raymond 213
　5. Intentional Torts to Economic and Dignitary Interests 220
　　5.1　Defamation 220
　　5.2　Invasion of Privacy 237
　Review Questions 274

CHAPTER 7   TORTS OF NEGLIGENCE 275
　1. Duty 276
　　1.1　The General Duty 276
　　1.2　To Whom the Duty of Care Owed 276
　　1.3　Standard of Care 277
　　1.4　Duty Owed by Owners and Occupiers of Land 278
　　1.5　Affirmative Duty to Act 280
　　1.6　Case 26: Tubbs v. Argus 280
　2. Breach 284
　3. Damage 296
　4. Causation 297
　　4.1　Case 28: Lyons v. Midnight Sun Transportation Services, Inc. 298
　　4.2　Case 29: Palsgraf v. The Long Island Railroad Co. 305
　5. Defenses to Negligence 320
　Review Questions 372

CHAPTER 8   STRICT LIABILITY ··· 373
   1. A *Prima Facie* Case ·· 374
   2. Products Liability ·· 374
   3. Defenses to Strict Liability ·· 376
   Review Questions ·· 377

REFERENCES ·· 378

PART I
COMMON LAW OF CONTRACTS

CHAPTER 1
INTRODUCTION

"Common Law"的准确译法应该是"共同法"。最初英国没有统一的法律,由于环境条件制约,人们的生活与行动范围被限制在较小的、相对孤立的社区里,每个社区都形成自己的一套风俗习惯与规则,由当地法院执行。1066年诺尔曼人征服英国后,开始着手统一英国的法律,至1215年左右正式形成统一的法律规则取代以前的社区风俗习惯和规则。由于这套法律规则适用于所有的英国人,是全部英国人共同的法律,因此被称为"Common Law",亦即"共同法",后来逐渐被其他国家接受,成为目前世界上两大法系之一。其中美国承袭了英国的共同法,并对其进行了修正和发展。

由于最初将该概念引进我国的学者将其翻译成"普通法",之后被频繁引用,目前我国法学界普遍接受了"普通法"的译法,因此本书也沿用"普通法"(有时也用"英美法")来描述英美共同法。

众所周知,英美法的主要特点在于遵循先例,因此判例法为学习英美法的重点。然而,英美等国家同时也存在制定法,并且随着两大法系的日益融合,制定法在英美法系国家的地位越来越重要。因此,美国律师在谈到"Common Law"时,往往指的是判例法(并且主要是各州法律),一般不包括其制定法(当然有例外情形)。合同法和侵权法传统上属于美国判例法的内容,虽然晚近也出现了诸如《美国统一商法典》等制定法。本书着重介绍美国的合同法和侵权法中的判例法部分内容。

英美法中的合同也叫契约,其本质上是关于在将来的某一个时间做或者不做某件事情的允诺或一组允诺。根据英美法律师的观点,合同无处不在。人们买书时,和书店之间就有了合同;工作时,和单位之间也有了合同;人们用水、电、煤气时,就和这些公用事业单位订立了合同;乘公交车,又和公交公司订立了合同。根据英美法,结婚是合同,离婚协议也是合同。一个人出生时,他的父母与接生医院订立了合同;而当这个人死后,他与那些处理他后事的人也订立了合同。既然在日常生活中合同与我们每个人的关系非常密切,那么合同到底是什么?

本书第一章将介绍美国法中有关合同的定义及分类，介绍规范合同的普通法渊源，最后，还将介绍一个非常著名的美国新罕布什尔州最高法院于1929年作出的判例，来帮助读者更好地理解英美合同法的目的和宗旨，以及合同法是如何规范人们生活中的各种合同的。

1. Contracts and Contract Law

1.1 Definition of "Contract"

When talking about "contract," people may think of other words like "agreement" or "promise." Do they mean the same thing or things distinguished from each other?

"Agreement" covers much broader concept than that of "contract." Actually, we make agreements all the time. We can have an agreement that you are a law student at Fudan University School of Law. We can also have an agreement that the color of the buildings on campus is yellow. We can agree on many other issues such as the correct date and place of your birth, or the date when our spring semester will start. We can have an agreement that our friendship will last forever. We can also agree to have a lunch together, go shopping, attend a party, or engage in some other activities.

These agreements are not contracts. First, a contract must suggest a plan for future action, *i.e.* something to be done or not done in the future. An agreement on the correct color of the buildings on campus is not such a future plan. Second, a court will recognize a contract as <u>legally binding</u> and if one party <u>breaches</u> it, the court will <u>grant</u> some <u>legal remedies</u> to the <u>non-breaching party</u>. Although an agreement to have a lunch together or to be friends forever is a future plan, if somehow you decide not to go for the lunch or if you decide to break up with your friend, it seems <u>odd</u>, if not <u>absurd</u>, if the court would <u>hold</u> you <u>legally responsible</u>, because you do not expect to <u>be legally bound</u> by such an agreement. Even if the court would <u>enforce</u> the agreement and grant remedies to the non-breaching party, it is almost impossible to measure the harm caused by breaching of the friendship or lunch-together agreement. This kind of heart-broken disappointment is not <u>remediable</u> at law, not only because reasonable people do not expect such a disappointed expectation to be <u>remedied</u>, but also

legally binding（be legally bound）在法律上有约束力的,有法律约束力的

breach 违约,指合同一方当事人未能履行合同条款

grant legal remedies 给予法律救济

non-breaching party 非违约方,守约方

odd 古怪的,奇怪的

absurd 不合理的,荒谬可笑的,愚蠢的

hold someone legally responsible 裁定（或判决）某人应⋯⋯承担法律责任

enforce（enforceable）强制执行（可以被强制执行的）

remedy（remediable）救济,补救（可救济的）

because any attempt to measure such a disappointment is speculative. Thus, these social agreements are not "contracts," either.

Then what kind of agreements are contracts? For example, an agreement concerning the purchase and sale of a computer is a contract. It is about a plan for a future action and it is not a social agreement. Both the seller and buyer reasonably expect the legal consequences if either of them breaches the agreement. This is a binding agreement enforceable at law and the court could easily measure the loss caused by the breach of the agreement. If the seller breaches the computer contract, the buyer will typically purchase a similar or identical computer from another seller. If the price for the substitute computer is higher than the contract price, the court can order the breaching seller to pay the difference to the aggrieved buyer. In doing so, the buyer will get the computer at the expected price under the original contract. Thus contracts are agreements, but not all agreements are contracts.

A promise is a commitment or undertaking to do or not to do something in the future. An agreement designed to regulate future action requires such a commitment. Similarly, not all promises are contracts. Contracts may be viewed as legally binding promises.

Thus, contract may be defined as "a promise or set of promises for the breach of which the law gives a remedy, or the performance of which the law in some way recognizes as a duty." RESTATEMENT (2ND) OF CONTRACTS § 1.

1.2 Sources of the Law of Contract

The general contract law is based largely on common law and statutes. Common law is composed of previously decided cases that are binding precedents. The Uniform Commercial Code (UCC), its Article 2 in particular, is the most important statute governing contract law in the United States.

The UCC is created by two distinguished organizations: The National Conference of Commissioners on Uniform State Laws which promotes uniformity in state laws, and the American Law Institute. It is now law in all of the 50 states governing contracts for the sale of goods, which may be defined essentially as tangible, moveable property.

In addition, the United Nations Convention on Contracts for the International Sale of Goods (CISG), which is a uniform law for international sale-of-goods contracts, is also part of the sources of law in the United States. It is an official treaty of the US government; therefore, it preempts the general contract law and the contract law of the UCC.

2. Classifications of Contracts

Contracts are divided into various classes based on their characteristics; these classifications are neither all-inclusive nor all-exclusive and the same contract may fall into various different classifications depending on the characteristics which are determinative of the class in question.

A contract may be express or implied. An express contract has its terms, conditions, and promises specifically set forth in words; whereas an implied contract is one where the essential elements are not set forth in words but must be determined from the circumstances, general language, or conduct of the parties.

Contracts may be unilateral or bilateral. A unilateral contract is one in which only one of the parties makes a promise, whereas in a bilateral contract each of the contracting parties makes a promise. If A gives B a book in return for B's promise to give A $50 next week, a unilateral contract is formed. However, if A promises to give B a book in return for B's promise to give A $50 next week, the contract is a bilateral one.

Contracts may be valid or void. A valid contract is one which meets all of the legal requirements for a contract and which will be enforced by the courts. A void contract is a contract which is of no legal force or effect and therefore is really not a contract. For example, a contract to kill someone is null and void and courts will not aid in its enforcement.

Contracts may be unenforceable or voidable. An unenforceable contract is one which generally meets

tangible property 有体财产,有形财产
moveable property 动产
CISG《联合国国际货物销售合同公约》

treaty 条约
preempt 优先于

class (classification) 类型(分类)
characteristics 特性,特色,特征
all-inclusive 包括一切的
all-exclusive 排除一切的
determinative 决定性的,限定性的
in question 讨论中的,考虑中的
express contract 明示合同
implied contract 默示合同
term 合同条款
condition 合同条件
essential elements 必要元素,要素,要件
conduct 行为
unilateral contract 单方允诺合同
bilateral contract 双方允诺合同

form (a contract) 订立(合同)

valid contract 有效合同

void contract 无效合同

null (nullification) 无效的,无法律约束力的(无效)

evidence 证据;证明
voidable contract 可撤销的合同
bind 使受约束
option 选择权
withdraw from the contract 撤销合同
comply with the contract 守约,遵守合同约定
minor 未成年人
an executory contract 待履行的合同
an executed contract 已履行的合同,指双方当事人均已完全履行义务的合同

confer 给予,授予
benefit 好处或利益

injustice 不公平,非正义
retain 保留
quasi contract 准契约,准合同
recover (recovery) 获得损害赔偿,得到补救(指在诉讼或其他法律程序中获得损害赔偿或其他方式的补救)(得到赔偿)
conferrer 授予者
unjust enrichment 不当得利
beneficiary 受益人
be justified 有正当理由
consent 同意

case law 判例法

the basic requirements for valid contracts, but is forbidden by a statute or rule of law to be enforceed by the courts. For instance, under the UCC, contracts for the sale of goods with a value of more than $500 must be in writing to be enforceable. If there is no writing to evidence such a contract, the contract is unenforceable. A voidable contract is one which binds one of the parties to the transaction but gives the other party the option of either withdrawing from the contract or of insisting on compliance with the contract. For example, a contract signed between a minor and an adult is voidable to the minor's option.

Contracts may be executory or executed. A contract is said to be executory until all of the parties have fully performed their responsibilities under the contract; at that point it becomes an executed contract.

There are some situations where one person confers benefits on another person under such circumstances that it is clear they were not intended to be a gift and where the other person accepts the benefits even though he has not promised to pay for the benefits. Such a situation does not fall within the usual concept of a contract where a return promise would normally be made; yet the courts often imply a return promise in order to avoid the injustice that would result from allowing the person to retain the benefits without paying for them. It is based on the concept of "quasi contract." In such a case the recovery allowed the conferrer of benefits is the amount of the unjust enrichment that would otherwise occur. However, there can be no recovery in quasi contract if there is an express contract actually covering the situation nor can there be recovery if under the circumstances the beneficiary is justified in believing that the benefits are a gift or if the benefits are conferred without the beneficiary's knowledge or consent.

3. Case 1: Hawkins v. McGee

Common law is case law; the cases previously decided by the courts are binding to the courts themselves and the lower courts within the same jurisdiction. Therefore in common law countries, law students must read cases because they are the law! The following is a famous case decided based on the common law of contract. When we read a "case," we actually read the "opinion" written by the judge or judges. Pay attention to the format of the judicial opinion. The heading of the opinion shows the court that reviewed the case, the case name composed of the names of the two parties, the citation of the case which helps the readers to locate the text of the opinion in the case reports, and the date when the opinion was made. Then comes the main body of the opinion, starting from the name of the judge who wrote the opinion.① The party who initiated the lawsuit is called "plaintiff," while the party who was sued against is called "defendant." Read the case below and try to understand what happened to the plaintiff and whether he got any remedies for his suffering. Then think about the contract formulated in the case and summarize how Justice Branch decided the case. If you feel a little bit difficult to figure out what happened, there is an explanation of the background of this case following the opinion.

jurisdiction 具有统一法律的司法辖区(亦指管辖权)

opinion 法院(或法官)的判决意见书(内容通常包括案件事实、本案所适用的法律及判决基于的理由及附带意见等)

citation 援引,引用(这里指用以对某案例的年度、案卷、判决时间及记载页进行援引的格式参考)

case report 判例汇编
initiate lawsuit 发起诉讼,提起诉讼
plaintiff 原告
sue 起诉
defendant 被告
suffering 肉体上的痛苦;精神上的苦恼
formulate (a contract) 订立(合同);形成

figure out 明白,理解,判断

Supreme Court of New Hampshire
Hawkins v. McGee②
84 N. H. 114, 146 A. 641
June 4, 1929

Branch, J.

1. The operation in question consisted in the removal of a considerable quantity of scar tissue from the palm of the plaintiff's right hand and the grafting of skin taken from the plaintiff's chest in place thereof. The scar tissue was the result of a severe burn

---

① For more about how to read a common law case, *see* Lingyun Gao, UNDERSTANDING THE COMMON LAW: ANALYZING & WRITING AS A LAWYER (SHANGHAI JIAOTONG UNIVERSITY PRESS, 2012).

② "Hawkins v. McGee" is the case name, indicating the two parties' names and who sued whom; the following line includes two citations to this same case, which helps the readers find the original case opinion in different case reports. For more about case citations, *see* Lingyun Gao, UNDERSTANDING THE COMMON LAW: ANALYZING & WRITING AS A LAWYER (SHANGHAI JIAOTONG UNIVERSITY PRESS, 2012).

to the effect	大意是,要旨是
testimony	(证人)证言,声明,证据
to the same effect	大意类似
justify	证明合法,证明正当
finding	裁决[通常指法庭或陪审团经审议后作出的(主要针对事实方面的)结论,也指行政部门的决定]
construe	解释(法律、行为等)
disability	残疾
impose liability upon someone	判定由某人承担责任
substantial	实质性的
claim	(对一项财产、权利、救济等提出的)权利要求,权利请求,权利主张
guarantee	保证,担保,保证人承担保证责任的行为
allege	主张,申述,宣称(尤指无证据或有待证实的情况下)
be taken at their face value	从字面意思理解
proof	证明
utter (utterance)	说话,宣布
establish	证明;建立,确立
warranty	担保;保证
argue	主张,辩论
intention	意图,目的,蓄意
enter into	缔结,约定
contractual relation	契约关系,合同关系
reasonably	合理地,相当地
concede	承认
contend (contention)	(诉讼中的)主张,声称

caused by contact with an electric wire, which the plaintiff received about nine years before the time of the transactions here involved. There was evidence to the effect that before the operation was performed the plaintiff and his father went to the defendant's office, and that the defendant, in answer to the question, "How long will the boy be in the hospital?" replied, "Three or four days, not over four; then the boy can go home and it will be just a few days when he will go back to work with a good hand."① Clearly this and other testimony to the same effect would not justify a finding that the doctor contracted to complete the hospital treatment in three or four days or that the plaintiff would be able to go back to work within a few days thereafter. The above statements could only be construed as expressions of opinion or predictions as to the probable duration of the treatment and plaintiff's resulting disability, and the fact that these estimates were exceeded would impose no contractual liability upon the defendant. The only substantial basis for the plaintiff's claim is the testimony that the defendant also said before the operation was decided upon, "I will guarantee to make the hand a hundred per cent perfect hand or a hundred per cent good hand."② The plaintiff was present when these words were alleged to have been spoken, and, if they are to be taken at their face value, it seems obvious that proof of their utterance would establish the giving of a warranty in accordance with his contention.

The defendant argues, however, that, even if these words were uttered by him, no reasonable man would understand that they were used with the intention of entering "into any contractual relation whatever," and that they could reasonably be understood only "as his expression in strong language that he believed and expected that as a result of the operation he would give the plaintiff a very good hand." It may be conceded, as the defendant contends, that, before the question

---

① Do you think this statement is a promise therefore leading to a contract? Why didn't Justice Branch think so? Do you agree?
② Is there any difference between this statement and the first one? Why did Justice Branch think this one a promise which formed a contract while the first one did not? Do you agree? Why and why not?

of the making of a contract should be submitted to a jury, there is a preliminary question of law[1] for the trial court to pass upon, *i.e.* "whether the words could possibly have the meaning imputed to them by the party who founds his case upon a certain interpretation," but it cannot be held that the trial court decided this question erroneously in the present case. It is unnecessary to determine at this time whether the argument of the defendant, based upon "common knowledge of the uncertainty which attends all surgical operations," and the improbability that a surgeon would ever contract to make a damaged part of the human body "one hundred per cent perfect," would, in the absence of countervailing considerations, be regarded as conclusive, for there were other factors in the present case which tended to support the contention of the plaintiff. There was evidence that the defendant repeatedly solicited from the plaintiff's father the opportunity to perform this operation, and the theory was advanced by plaintiff's counsel in cross-examination of defendant that he sought an opportunity to "experiment on skin grafting," in which he had had little previous experience. If the jury accepted this part of plaintiff's contention, there would be a reasonable basis for the further conclusion that, if defendant spoke the words attributed to him, he did so with the intention that they should be accepted at their face value, as an inducement for the granting of consent to the operation by the plaintiff and his father, and there was ample evidence that they were so accepted by them. The question of the making of the alleged contract was properly submitted to the jury.

2. The substance of the charge to the jury on the question of damages appears in the following quotation: "If you find the plaintiff entitled to anything, he is entitled to recover for what pain and suffering he has been made to endure and for what injury he has sustained over and above what injury he

jury 陪审团
preliminary question 先决问题
question of law 法律问题(区别于事实问题)
trial court 初审法院,一审法院
impute to 归于,归因于,归咎于
interpretation 解释
hold (法院)认定,判定
decide (法院)判决,判定
erroneously 错误地
the present case 本案
argument 理由,论点
uncertainty 不确定(性)
improbability 不大可能,不大可能之事
countervailing consideration 足以与其抗争的考虑因素
conclusive 结论性的,决定性的
solicit 要求,恳求,请求
advance 提出,宣称
counsel 律师,代理律师
cross-examination 交叉询问,反询问
attribute to 被归咎于,被认为是……所造成的,是因为,起因于
inducement 诱导或怂恿某人缔约的行为
ample evidence 充分证据
damages 损害赔偿;损害赔偿金,损害赔偿额
quotation 引证(指向法庭或法官提出成文法、法庭意见、判例或其他权威言论的准确语句,以支持所提出的论点或主张)
be entitled to 有……的资格,有……的权利
pain and suffering 精神损害,痛苦与创伤(指不但有身体上的痛苦,而且有精神上的创伤)
injury 侵害,伤害,人身伤害
sustain 遭受,承受

---

[1] In common law, the court will decide the question of law while the jury will decide the question of fact.

instruction（法官）对陪审团的指示，指法官就与案件有关的法律适用问题向陪审团所作的指示，对该指示，陪审团应当接受和适用	
seasonably 合时令地，应时地	
except（exception）抗议，提出异议	
authority 权威（这里指有拘束力的制定法或判例，有时也指有说服力的判例或学术文献）	
analogy（analogous）类推，类比（类推的，类比的，类似的）	
term 术语	
compensation 补偿，赔偿	
comply with 遵守	
chattel 动产	

had before." To this instruction the defendant seasonably excepted. By it, the jury was permitted to consider two elements of damage: (1) pain and suffering due to the operation; and (2) positive ill effects of the operation upon the plaintiff's hand. Authority for any specific rule of damages in cases of this kind seems to be lacking, but, when tested by general principle and by analogy, it appears that the foregoing instruction was erroneous.①

"By 'damages,' as that term is used in the law of contracts, is intended compensation for a breach, measured in the terms of the contract." *Davis v. New England Cotton Yarn Co.*, 77 N. H. 403, 404, 92 A. 732, 733.② The purpose of the law is "to put the plaintiff in as good a position as he would have been in had the defendant kept his contract." 3 WILLISTON CONT. § 1338; *Hardie-Tynes Mfg. Co. v. Easton Cotton Oil Co.*, 150 N. C. 150, 63 S. E. 676. The measure of recovery "is based upon what the defendant should have given the plaintiff, not what the plaintiff has given the defendant or otherwise expended." 3 WILLISTON CONT. § 1341. "The only losses that can be said fairly to come within the terms of a contract are such as the parties must have had in mind when the contract was made, or such as they either knew or ought to have known would probably result from a failure to comply with its terms." *Davis v. New England Cotton Yarn Co.*, 77 N. H. 403, 404, 92 A. 732, 733, *Hurd v. Dunsmore*, 63 N. H. 171.③

The present case is closely analogous to one in which a machine is built for a certain purpose and warranted to do certain work. In such cases, the usual rule of damages for breach of warranty in the sale of chattels is applied, and it is held that the measure of damages is the difference between the value of the

---

① The court realized that there was no authority, *i.e.* binding cases, governing this case; however, the court adopted the general principles of law to decide this case. The following paragraph discusses the general principles of law regarding the issue before the court.

② The quotation was from a previously decided case. In civil law countries, lawyers and judges rely on written statutes to analyze or decide the case before them; however, in common law countries, lawyers and judges cite cases to support their reasoning.

③ After stating the rules of law by citing the cases and treatises discussing the similar issue, the opinion continues in the following paragraph to apply the general principles of law to the facts of this case.

machine, if it had corresponded with the warranty and its actual value, together with such <u>incidental losses</u> as the parties knew, or ought to have known, would probably result from a failure to comply with its terms. *Hooper v. Story*, 155 N. Y. 171, 175, 49 N. E. 773; *Adams Hardware Co. v. Wimbish*, 201 Ala. 548, 78 So. 902.

 The rule thus applied is well settled in this state.① "As a general rule, the measure of the <u>vendee</u>'s damages is the difference between the value of the goods as they would have been if the warranty as to quality had been true, and the actual value at the time of the sale, including gains prevented and losses sustained, and such other damages as could be reasonably <u>anticipated</u> by the parties as likely to be caused by the <u>vendor</u>'s failure to keep his agreement, and could not by reasonable care on the part of the vendee have been avoided." *Union Bank v. Blanchard*, 65 N. H. 21, 23, 18 A. 90, 91; *Hurd v. Dunsmore*, *supra*; *Noyes v. Blodgett*, 58 N. H. 502. We therefore conclude that the true measure of the plaintiff's <u>damage</u> in the present case is the difference between the value to him of a perfect hand or a good hand, such as the jury found the defendant promised him, and the value of his hand in its present condition, including any <u>incidental consequences</u> fairly within the <u>contemplation</u> of the parties when they made their contract. 1 SUTHERLAND, DAMAGES (4TH ED.) § 92. Damages not thus limited, although naturally resulting, are not to be given.

 The extent of the plaintiff's suffering does not measure this difference in value. The pain necessarily incident to a serious surgical operation was a part of the contribution which the plaintiff was willing to make to his joint undertaking with the defendant to produce a good hand. It was a <u>legal detriment</u> suffered by him which <u>constituted</u> a part of the <u>consideration</u>② given by him for the contract. It represented a part of

  incidental losses 附带产生的杂项损失

  vendee 买主,买方(通常用于不动产交易)

  anticipate (anticipation) 预期,预料
  vendor 卖主(尤指不动产的出卖人)

  damage 损害(包括人身伤害与财产损失)

  incidental consequences 附带后果
  contemplation 期待,预见

  legal detriment (受允诺人的)法定损害
  constitute 构成,组成
  consideration 对价

---

① Here Justice Branch drew a conclusion based on the above analysis. This conclusion can be viewed as the "law" made by the judges which would bind the lower courts in deciding similar cases in the future.
② "Consideration" is one of the most important elements of a contract, which will be discussed later in this book.

the price which he was willing to pay for a good hand, but it furnished no test of the value of a good hand or the difference between the value of the hand which the defendant promised and the one which resulted from the operation.

It was also erroneous and <u>misleading</u> to submit to the jury as a separate element of damage any change for the worse in the condition of the plaintiff's hand resulting from the operation, although this error was probably more <u>prejudicial</u> to the plaintiff than to the defendant. Any such <u>ill effect</u> of the operation would be included under the true rule of damages set forth above, but damages might properly be <u>assessed</u> for the defendant's failure to improve the condition of the hand, even if there was no evidence that its condition was made worse as a result of the operation.

It must be <u>assumed</u> that the trial court, in <u>setting aside</u> the <u>verdict</u>, undertook to <u>apply</u> the same rule of damages which he had previously given to the jury, and, since this rule was erroneous, it is unnecessary for us to consider whether there was any evidence to justify his finding that all damages <u>awarded</u> by the jury above $500 were <u>excessive</u>.

3. Defendant's requests for instructions were loosely drawn, and were properly denied. A considerable number of <u>issues</u> of fact were raised by the evidence, and it would have been extremely misleading to instruct the jury in accordance with defendant's request No. 2, that "the only issue on which you have to pass is whether or not there was a special contract between the plaintiff and the defendant to produce a perfect hand." Equally <u>inaccurate</u> was defendant's <u>request</u> No. 5, which reads as follows: "You would have to find, in order to hold the defendant liable in this case, that Dr. McGee and the plaintiff both understood that the doctor was guaranteeing a perfect result from this operation." If the defendant said that he would guarantee a perfect result, and the plaintiff relied upon that promise, any <u>mental reservations</u> which he may have had are <u>immaterial</u>. The standard by which his conduct is to be judged is not <u>internal</u>, but <u>external</u>. *Woburn Bank v. Woods*, 77 N. H. 172, 89 A. 491.

Defendant's request No. 7 was as follows: "If you should get so far as to find that there was a special contract guaranteeing a perfect result, you would still have to find <u>for the defendant</u> unless you also found that a further operation would not correct the disability claimed by the plaintiff." <u>In view of</u> the testimony that the defendant had refused to perform a further operation, it would clearly have been erroneous to give this instruction. The evidence would have justified a verdict for an amount sufficient to cover the cost of such an operation, even if the theory underlying this request was correct.

for the defendant 支持被告,被告胜诉(参照:against the defendant 反对被告,被告败诉)

in view of 根据

4. It is <u>unlikely</u> that the questions now presented in regard to the argument of plaintiff's counsel will arise at another trial, and therefore they have not been considered.

unlikely 不太可能的

New trial.

new trial 重新审判

Background of Hawkins v. McGee[①]

When George Hawkins was eleven years old, he suffered an electrical burn which left a small scar on his hand. The scar did not significantly affect the use of the hand, however, it did not look good. Dr. McGee persuaded George and his parents to allow him to perform a surgery for George, partly because he was eager to seek an opportunity to perform such kind of operations in order to improve his skills. Finally, George agreed, and the operation was performed shortly after George's 18th birthday. The skin graft was taken from George's chest. There was infection and profuse bleeding. George was hospitalized for three months. The graft covered the thumb and two fingers and soon was matted with hair. Subsequently, movement of the hand was greatly restricted and George actually became permanently disabled. George brought a lawsuit against Dr. McGee. The jury awarded George $3,000 as compensation. The case was appealed to the Supreme Court of New Hampshire who ordered a new trial, as you have read. In the new trial, the case was settled for $1,400.

---

① *See* Robert W. Hamilton, *et al*, Cases and Materials on Contracts 5 (2nd ed., West Publishing Co., 1992).

Review Questions
1. How to distinguish an agreement, a promise, and a contract?
2. If there is a conflict among the case law, Article 2 of the UCC, and the CISG, which shall prevail?
3. What is the difference between a bilateral contract and a unilateral contract? Do you think "bilateral contract" can be translated into Chinese as "双务合同" while "unilateral contract" as "单务合同"?
4. What is a *quasi* contract? Is it a contract at all?
5. What are the differences between valid, unenforceable, voidable and void contracts?
6. After reading *Hawkins v. McGee*, think about what the purpose of the law of contract is.

CHAPTER 2
FORMATION OF CONTRACT

　　合同法的目的是保护合同当事人的权益,具体而言,当合同一方违约时,另一方可以要求法院强制执行该合同,即迫使违约方补偿守约方因对方违约而遭受的损失。此时,守约方为了得到救济,必须首先证明合同已经有效成立,有时,英美律师把这叫做原告必须"初步证明"合同已然成立。本章讨论合同成立的三个要件:(1)要约,即一方允诺、承诺或保证在将来做或不做某事;(2)承诺,即收到要约的另一方允诺、承诺或保证完全接受要约里包含的所有条件;(3)对价,即双方当事人之间交换的且被法律承认的"价值"。

1. Offer

In order to have a contract there must be a <u>mutual understanding</u> between the two <u>parties</u> as to what each party will give and receive in return. Prior to the existence of a contract, the parties normally engage in <u>negotiations</u> in an effort to arrive at that mutual understanding. Usually one party may set forth a <u>proposition</u> — the <u>offer</u> — which, if accepted by the other party, will result in the <u>formation of a contract</u>.

An offer to contract is a <u>manifestation of intention</u> to be presently bound by a series of definite and specific terms, which is <u>communicated</u> to the <u>offeree</u> and creates power in the offeree to <u>accept</u>. The party making the offer is the <u>offeror</u> while the party who is intended to receive the offer is the offeree. The offeror indicates in the offer what he will do or not do, and what he demands in return.

1.1 Elements of Offer

The terms of an offer must be definite and specific, with reasonable certainty, or at least provide a basis for determining them with such certainty. If the terms are not reasonably certain, then the offer will be void. Although the <u>omission</u> of a <u>minor</u> or <u>immaterial term</u> will not affect the <u>validity</u> of the offer or contract, the omission of <u>a material term</u> or an agreement to agree later on a material term will <u>preclude</u> the making of a valid contract so that the courts will not make a contract for the parties where they did not make a valid one themselves. Under the UCC, an offer does not fail for lack of definiteness because certain terms have been omitted if the court has a basis for supplying them and granting an appropriate remedy. Actually, the UCC contains provisions for determining price, <u>time for performance</u>, and other similar terms in cases where the parties intended to <u>conclude a contract</u> but left these provisions open.

The offer must be communicated to the offeree in

---

mutual understanding（合同）双方合意
party 当事人［这里指合同双方(parties)］
negotiation 协商,谈判
proposition 慎重提议或建议（这里指要约）
offer 要约
formation of a contract 合同的成立
manifestation of intention 意思表示
communicate (communication) 传递,传达,交流
offeree 受要约人
accept（acceptance）承诺,接受要约
offeror 要约人

omission 省略；缺少
a minor term 次要条款,不重要的条款
an immaterial term 不重要的条款
validity 有效,有效性
a material term 重要条款
preclude 排除

time for performance 履行时间
conclude a contract 成立合同

order to be valid and is not effective until it has been so communicated. The communication may be written, oral, by some acts, or by any combination of these means. Disputes may arise when determining whether a particular term is included in the offer or in the contract between the parties. Sometimes the offeror prints certain of the terms of an offer on a tag or ticket attached to merchandise or given to the offeree. Have such terms been communicated so as to form part of the offer, particularly if they are in small type or included among many other terms? In such a case, a determination must be made as to whether such terms were likely to be noticed so that it is reasonable to conclude that they were communicated.

dispute（尤指引发诉讼之）争议

More importantly, an offer must appear to the ordinary, reasonable person that the offeror did in fact intend to make an offer and to be presently bound by it. The offeror's actual state of mind is irrelevant; what is important is whether the offeree is justified in believing that an offer was made.

a reasonable person 一个理性（法律拟制）的人

state of mind 心理状态
irrelevant 不相关的

In *Barnes v. Treece*, 15 Wash. App. 437, 549 P. 2d 1152 (1976), the defendant Treece was the Vice-President of a company distributing punchboards which were used in gambling. Treece made a statement before the Washington State Gambling Commission in support of the legitimacy of punchboards that "I'll put a hundred thousand dollars to anyone to find a crooked board. If they find it, I'll pay it." The statement brought laughter from the audience. Later plaintiff Barnes watched a television news report of the proceedings and heard Treece's $100,000 statement. Barnes found two fraudulent punchboards and called Treece asking whether his $100,000 statement had been made seriously. Treece said that the statement was serious, that it was firm, and that $100,000 was held safely in escrow. Barnes then produced two of the fraudulent boards for inspection as directed by Treece; however, Treece and the company refused to pay Barnes, so Barnes brought an action against Treece and his company.

legitimacy 合法性,合理性

fraudulent 欺诈的,骗人的

firm 确定的,肯定的
be held in escrow 在条件实现前暂将某物交第三者保管
produce 提出,出示,拿出
inspection 检查,调查
action 诉讼

Was the statement made by Treece an offer? The court said yes. The terms of the offer were found to be reasonably certain and there was no problem with the means of communication. Moreover, the court found an objective manifestation of mutual assent because Treece's subsequent statements would have been understood by a reasonable person in the position of Barnes as serious manifestations of assent to a particular transaction. Suppose Treece had not made the subsequent statements, would the court hold otherwise?

1.2 Case 2: Carlill v. Carbolic Smoke Ball Co.

The following is an English case decided based on the common law of contract. When reading it, use the elements of offer to analyze whether the advertisement in the case was an offer. There is another purpose for you to read this case. This is a case with multiple opinions, i.e., three judges wrote three separate opinions on the same case. Try to see the different points expressed in the different opinions and think what the judges agreed or disagreed on. Lastly, suppose this case is still good law, if lawyers want to use it as an authority, which opinion should be relied on?

Carlill v. Carbolic Smoke Ball Co.
1 Q.B. 256 (1893)

[The defendants, who were the proprietors and vendors of a medical preparation called "The Carbolic Smoke Ball," inserted in the *Pall Mall Gazette* of November 13, 1891, and in other newspapers, the following advertisement:

"£100 reward will be paid by the Carbolic Smoke Ball Company to any person who contracts the increasing epidemic influenza, colds, or any disease caused by taking cold, after having used the ball three times daily for two weeks according to the printed directions supplied with each ball. £1000 is deposited with the Alliance Bank, Regent Street, shewing our sincerity in the matter."

"During the last epidemic of influenza many thousand carbolic smoke balls were sold as preventives against this disease, and in no ascertained case was the disease contracted by those using the carbolic smoke ball."

"One carbolic smoke ball will last a family several months, making it the cheapest remedy in the world at the price, 10s., post free. The ball can be refilled at a cost of 5s. Address, Carbolic Smoke Ball Company, 27, Princes Street, Hanover Square, London."

The plaintiff, a lady, on the faith of this advertisement, bought one of the balls at a chemist's, and used it as directed, three times a day, from November 20, 1891 to January 17, 1892, when she was attacked by influenza. Hawkins, J.① held that she was entitled to recover the £100. The defendants appealed.]

Lindley, L. J.

We must first consider whether this was intended to be a promise at all, or whether it was a mere puff which meant nothing. Was it a mere puff? My answer to that question is No, and I base my answer upon this passage: "£1000 is deposited with the Alliance Bank, shewing our sincerity in the matter." Now, for what was that money deposited or that statement made except to negative the suggestion that this was a mere puff and meant nothing at all? The deposit is called in aid by the advertiser as proof of his sincerity in the matter — that is, the sincerity of his promise to pay this £100 in the event which he has specified. I say this for the purpose of giving point to the observation that we are not inferring a promise; there is the promise, as plain as words can make it.

Then it is contended that it is not binding. In the first place, it is said that it is not made with anybody in particular. Now that point is common to the words of this advertisement and to the words of all other advertisements offering rewards. They are offers to anybody who performs the conditions named in the advertisement, and anybody who does perform the condition accepts the offer. In point of law this

---

① Apparently this is the trial court judge.

advertisement is an offer to pay £100 to anybody who will perform these conditions, and the performance of the conditions is the acceptance of the offer. That rests upon a string of authorities, the earliest of which is *Williams v. Carwardine*, which has been followed by many other decisions upon advertisements offering rewards.

But then it is said, "Supposing that the performance of the conditions is an acceptance of the offer, that acceptance ought to have been notified." Unquestionably, as a general proposition, when an offer is made, it is necessary in order to make a binding contract, not only that it should be accepted, but that the acceptance should be notified. But is that so in cases of this kind? I apprehend that they are an exception to that rule, or, if not an exception, they are open to the observation that the notification of the acceptance need not precede the performance. This offer is a continuing offer. It was never revoked, and if notice of acceptance is required — which I doubt very much, for I rather think the true view is that which was expressed and explained by Lord Blackburn in the case of *Brogden v. Metropolitan Ry. Co.* — if notice of acceptance is required, the person who makes the offer gets the notice of acceptance contemporaneously with his notice of the performance of the condition. If he gets notice of the acceptance before his offer is revoked, that in principle is all you want. I, however, think that the true view, in a case of this kind, is that the person who makes the offer shews by his language and from the nature of the transaction that he does not expect and does not require notice of the acceptance apart from notice of the performance.

We, therefore, find here all the elements which are necessary to form a binding contract enforceable in point of law, subject to two observations. First of all, it is said that this advertisement is so vague that you cannot really construe it as a promise — that the vagueness of the language shews that a legal promise was never intended or contemplated. The language is vague and uncertain in some respects, and particularly in this, that the £100 is to be paid to any person who contracts the increasing epidemic after having used the balls three times daily for two weeks. It is said, When are they to be used? According to the language of the advertisement no time is fixed, and, construing the offer most strongly against the person who has made it, one might infer that any time was meant. I do not think that was meant, and to hold the contrary would be pushing too far the doctrine of taking language most strongly against the person using it. I do not think that business people or reasonable people would understand the words as meaning that if you took a smoke ball and used it three times daily for two weeks you were to be guaranteed against influenza for the rest of your life, and I think it would be pushing the language of the advertisement too far to construe it as meaning that. But if it does not mean that, what does it mean? It is for the defendants to shew what it does mean; and it strikes me that there are two, and possibly three, reasonable constructions to be put on this advertisement, any one of which will answer the purpose of the plaintiff. Possibly it may be limited to persons catching the "increasing epidemic" (that is, the then prevailing epidemic), or any colds or diseases caused by taking cold, during the prevalence of the increasing epidemic. That is one suggestion, but it does not commend itself to me. Another suggested meaning is that you are warranted free from catching this epidemic, or colds or other diseases caused by taking cold, whilst you are using this remedy after using it for two weeks. If that is the meaning, the plaintiff is right, for she used the remedy for two weeks and went on using it till she got the epidemic. Another meaning, and the one which I rather prefer, is that the reward is offered to any person who contracts the epidemic or other disease within a reasonable time after having used the smoke ball. Then it is asked, What is a reasonable time? It has been suggested that there is no standard of reasonableness; that it depends upon the reasonable time for a germ to develop! I do not feel pressed by that. It strikes me that a reasonable time may be ascertained in a business sense and in a sense satisfactory to a lawyer, in this way; find out from a chemist what the ingredients are; find out from a

to hold the contrary 作出相反的判决或决定

prevailing (prevalence) 流行的,通行的,占优势的,有影响的(流行,盛行;广泛)
epidemic 传染病,流行病
commend itself to 值得推荐,值得称赞

skilled physician how long the effect of such ingredients on the system could be reasonably expected to endure so as to protect a person from an epidemic or cold, and in that way you will get a standard to be laid before a jury, or a judge without a jury, by which they might exercise their judgment as to what a reasonable time would be. It strikes me, I confess, that the true construction of this advertisement is that £100 will be paid to anybody who uses this smoke ball three times daily for two weeks according to the printed directions, and who gets the influenza or cold or other diseases caused by taking cold within a reasonable time after so using it; and if that is the true construction, it is enough for the plaintiff.

I come now to the last point which I think requires attention — that is, the consideration. It has been argued that this is *nudum pactum* — that there is no consideration. We must apply to that argument the usual legal tests. Let us see whether there is no advantage to the defendants. It is said that the use of the ball is no advantage to them, and that what benefits them is the sale; and the case is put that a lot of these balls might be stolen, and that it would be no advantage to the defendants if the thief or other people used them. The answer to that, I think, is as follows. It is quite obvious that in the view of the advertisers a use by the public of their remedy, if they can only get the public to have confidence enough to use it, will react and produce a sale which is directly beneficial to them. Therefore, the advertisers get out of the use an advantage which is enough to constitute a consideration.

But there is another view. Does not the person who acts upon this advertisement and accepts the offer put himself to some inconvenience at the request of the defendants? Is it nothing to use this ball three times daily for two weeks according to the directions at the request of the advertiser? Is that to go for nothing? It appears to me that there is a distinct inconvenience, not to say a detriment, to any person who so uses the smoke ball. I am of opinion, therefore, that there is ample consideration for the promise.

We were pressed upon this point with the case of

Gerhard v. Bates, which was the case of a promoter of companies who had promised the bearers of share warrants that they should have dividends for so many years, and the promise as alleged was held not to shew any consideration. Lord Campbell's judgment when you come to examine it is open to the explanation, that the real point in that case was that the promise, if any, was to the original bearer and not to the plaintiff, and that as the plaintiff was not suing in the name of the original bearer there was no contract with him. Then Lord Campbell goes on to enforce that view by shewing that there was no consideration shewn for the promise to him. I cannot help thinking that Lord Campbell's observations would have been very different if the plaintiff in that action had been an original bearer, or if the declaration had gone on to shew what a *societe anonyme* was, and had alleged the promise to have been, not only to the first bearer, but to anybody who should become the bearer. There was no such allegation, and the Court said, in the absence of such allegation, they did not know (judicially, of course) what a *societe anonyme* was, and, therefore, there was no consideration. But in the present case, for the reasons I have given, I cannot see the slightest difficulty in coming to the conclusion that there is consideration.

It appears to me, therefore, that the defendants must perform their promise, and, if they have been so unwary as to expose themselves to a great many actions, so much the worse for them.

Bowen, L. J.

I am of the same opinion. We were asked to say that this document was a contract too vague to be enforced.

The first observation which arises is that the document itself is not a contract at all, it is only an offer made to the public. The defendants contend next, that it is an offer the terms of which are too vague to be treated as a definite offer, inasmuch as there is no limit of time fixed for the catching of the influenza, and it cannot be supposed that the advertisers seriously meant to promise to pay money to

promoter（公司等的）发起人,创办人
bearer 持票人,持有人
share warrant 认股权证
dividend 股息,红利,股利

societe anonyme 股份有限公司

allegation 断言,宣称,主张（当事人在诉状中对事实的肯定性陈述）

unwary 不注意的,疏忽的,不留心的

every person who catches the influenza at any time after the inhaling of the smoke ball. It was urged also, that if you look at this document you will find much vagueness as to the persons with whom the contract was intended to be made — that, in the first place, its terms are wide enough to include persons who may have used the smoke ball before the advertisement was issued; at all events, that it is an offer to the world in general, and, also, that it is unreasonable to suppose it to be a definite offer, because nobody in their senses would contract themselves out of the opportunity of checking the experiment which was going to be made at their own expense. It is also contended that the advertisement is rather in the nature of a puff or a proclamation than a promise or offer intended to mature into a contract when accepted. But the main point seems to be that the vagueness of the document shews that no contract whatever was intended. It seems to me that in order to arrive at a right conclusion we must read this advertisement in its plain meaning, as the public would understand it. It was intended to be issued to the public and to be read by the public. How would an ordinary person reading this document construe it? It was intended unquestionably to have some effect, and I think the effect which it was intended to have, was to make people use the smoke ball, because the suggestions and allegations which it contains are directed immediately to the use of the smoke ball as distinct from the purchase of it. It did not follow that the smoke ball was to be purchased from the defendants directly, or even from agents of theirs directly. The intention was that the circulation of the smoke ball should be promoted, and that the use of it should be increased. The advertisement begins by saying that a reward will be paid by the Carbolic Smoke Ball Company to any person who contracts the increasing epidemic after using the ball. It has been said that the words do not apply only to persons who contract the epidemic after the publication of the advertisement, but include persons who had previously contracted the influenza. I cannot so read the advertisement. It is written in colloquial and popular language, and I think that it is equivalent to this:

"£100 will be paid to any person who shall contract the increasing epidemic after having used the carbolic smoke ball three times daily for two weeks." And it seems to me that the way in which the public would read it would be this, that if anybody, after the advertisement was published, used three times daily for two weeks the carbolic smoke ball, and then caught cold, he would be entitled to the reward. Then again it was said: "How long is this protection to endure? Is it to go on for ever, or for what limit of time?" I think that there are two constructions of this document, each of which good sense, and each of which seems to me to satisfy the exigencies of the present action. It may mean that the protection is warranted to last during the epidemic, and it was during the epidemic that the plaintiff contracted the disease. I think, more probably, it means that the smoke ball will be a protection while it is in use. That seems to me the way in which an ordinary person would understand an advertisement about medicine, and about a specific against influenza. It could not be supposed that after you have left off using it you are still to be protected for ever, as if there was to be a stamp set upon your forehead that you were never to catch influenza because you had once used the carbolic smoke ball. I think the immunity is to last during the use of the ball. That is the way in which I should naturally read it, and it seems to me that the subsequent language of the advertisement supports that construction. It says: "During the last epidemic of influenza many thousand carbolic smoke balls were sold, and in no ascertained case was the disease contracted by those using" (not "who had used") "the carbolic smoke ball," and it concludes with saying that one smoke ball will last a family several months (which imports that it is to be efficacious while it is being used), and that the ball can be refilled at a cost of 5s. I, therefore, have myself no hesitation in saying that I think, on the construction of this advertisement, the protection was to endure during the time that the carbolic smoke ball was being used. My brother, the Lord Justice who preceded me, thinks that the contract would be sufficiently definite if you

exigency（迫切的）需要，急需

import 意味着，含有……的意思

efficacious 有效的，灵验的

were to read it in the sense that the protection was to be warranted during a reasonable period after use. I have some difficulty myself on that point; but it is not necessary for me to consider it further, because the disease here was contracted during the use of the carbolic smoke ball. ①

Was it intended that the £100 should, if the conditions were fulfilled, be paid? The advertisement says that £1000 is lodged at the bank for the purpose. Therefore, it cannot be said that the statement that £100 would be paid was intended to be a mere puff. I think it was intended to be understood by the public as an offer which was to be acted upon.

But it was said there was no check on the part of the persons who issued the advertisement, and that it would be an insensate thing to promise £100 to a person who used the smoke ball unless you could check or superintend his manner of using it. The answer to that argument seems to me to be that if a person chooses to make extravagant promises of this kind he probably does so because it pays him to make them, and, if he has made them, the extravagance of the promises is no reason in law why he should not be bound by them.

It was also said that the contract is made with all the world — that is, with everybody; and that you cannot contract with everybody. It is not a contract made with all the world. There is the fallacy of the argument. It is an offer made to all the world; and why should not an offer be made to all the world which is to ripen into a contract with anybody who comes forward and performs the condition? It is an offer to become liable to any one who, before it is retracted, performs the condition, and, although the offer is made to the world, the contract is made with that limited portion of the public who come forward and perform the condition on the faith of the advertisement. It is not like cases in which you offer to negotiate, or you issue advertisements that you have got a stock of books to sell, or houses to let, in which

---

① This is one of the points of Lord Bowen which is different from that of Lord Lindley. Try to find other different points from the opinions.

case there is no offer to be bound by any contract. Such advertisements are offers to negotiate — offers to receive offers — offers to chaffer, as, I think, some learned judge in one of the cases has said. If this is an offer to be bound, then it is a contract the moment the person fulfils the condition. That seems to me to be sense, and it is also the ground on which all these advertisement cases have been decided during the century; and it cannot be put better than in Willes, J.'s, judgment in *Spencer v. Harding*. "In the advertisement cases," he says, "there never was any doubt that the advertisement amounted to a promise to pay the money to the person who first gave information. The difficulty suggested was that it was a contract with all the world. But that, of course, was soon overruled. It was an offer to become liable to any person who before the offer should be retracted should happen to be the person to fulfill the contract, of which the advertisement was an offer or tender. That is not the sort of difficulty which presents itself here. If the circular had gone on, 'and we undertake to sell to the highest bidder,' the reward cases would have applied, and there would have been a good contract in respect of the persons." As soon as the highest bidder presented himself, says Willes, J., the person who was to hold the *vinculum juris* on the other side of the contract was ascertained, and it became settled.

  Then it was said that there was no notification of the acceptance of the contract. One cannot doubt that, as an ordinary rule of law, an acceptance of an offer made ought to be notified to the person who makes the offer, in order that the two minds may come together. Unless this is done the two minds may be apart, and there is not that consensus which is necessary according to the English law — I say nothing about the laws of other countries — to make a contract. But there is this clear gloss to be made upon that doctrine, that as notification of acceptance is required for the benefit of the person who makes the offer, the person who makes the offer may dispense with notice to himself if he thinks it desirable to do so, and I suppose there can be no doubt that where a person in an offer made by him to another person,

chaffer 讨价还价,讲价钱

ground 根据;理由

overrule 推翻先例

fulfill the contract 履行合同
tender 可供承诺及成为具约束力合约的要约

bidder 出价人

vinculum juris 法律上的约束,法律义务
to be settled 把(合同)内容最后定下来

consensus 一致同意,一致意见

gloss 注释,解释,注解

dispense with 省却,免除

expressly or impliedly intimates a particular mode of acceptance as sufficient to make the bargain binding, it is only necessary for the other person to whom such offer is made to follow the indicated method of acceptance; and if the person making the offer, expressly or impliedly intimates in his offer that it will be sufficient to act on the proposal without communicating acceptance of it to himself, performance of the condition is a sufficient acceptance without notification.

That seems to me to be the principle which lies at the bottom of the acceptance cases, of which two instances are the well-known judgment of Mellish, L. J., in *Harris's Case*, and the very instructive judgment of Lord Blackburn in *Brogden v. Metropolitan Ry. Co.*, in which he appears to me to take exactly the line I have indicated.

Now, if that is the law, how are we to find out whether the person who makes the offer does intimate that notification of acceptance will not be necessary in order to constitute a binding bargain? In many cases you look to the offer itself. In many cases you extract from the character of the transaction that notification is not required, and in the advertisement cases it seems to me to follow as an inference to be drawn from the transaction itself that a person is not to notify his acceptance of the offer before he performs the condition, but that if he performs the condition notification is dispensed with. It seems to me that from the point of view of common sense no other idea could be entertained. If I advertise to the world that my dog is lost, and that anybody who brings the dog to a particular place will be paid some money, are all the police or other persons whose business it is to find lost dogs to be expected to sit down and write me a note saying that they have accepted my proposal? Why, of course, they at once look after the dog, and as soon as they find the dog they have performed the condition. The essence of the transaction is that the dog should be found, and it is not necessary under such circumstances, as it seems to me, that in order to make the contract binding there should be any notification of acceptance. It follows from the nature of the thing that the performance of the condition is sufficient acceptance without the notification of it, and a person who makes an offer in an advertisement of that kind makes an offer which must be read by the light of that common sense reflection. He does, therefore, in his offer impliedly indicate that he does not require notification of the acceptance of the offer.

A further argument for the defendants was that this was a *nudum pactum* — that there was no consideration for the promise — that taking the influenza was only a condition, and that the using the smoke ball was only a condition, and that there was no consideration at all; in fact, that there was no request, express or implied, to use the smoke ball. Now, I will not enter into an elaborate discussion upon the law as to requests in this kind of contracts. I will simply refer to *Victors v. Davies* and Sergeant Manning's note to *Fisher v. Pyne*, which everybody ought to read who wishes to embark in this controversy. The short answer, to abstain from academical discussion, is, it seems to me, that there is here a request to use involved in the offer. Then as to the alleged want of consideration. The definition of "consideration" given in Selwyn's *NISI PRIUS*, 8TH ED. p. 47, which is cited and adopted by Tindal, C. J., in the case of *Láythoarp v. Bryant*, is this: "Any act of the plaintiff from which the defendant derives a benefit or advantage, or any labor, detriment, or inconvenience sustained by the plaintiff, provided such act is performed or such inconvenience suffered by the plaintiff, with the consent, either express or implied, of the defendant." Can it be said here that if the person who reads this advertisement applies thrice daily, for such time as may seem to him tolerable, the carbolic smoke ball to his nostrils for a whole fortnight, he is doing nothing at all — that it is a mere act which is not to count towards consideration to support a promise (for the law does not require us to measure the adequacy of the consideration). Inconvenience sustained by one party at the request of the other is enough to create a consideration. I think, therefore, that it is consideration enough that the plaintiff took the trouble of using the smoke ball. But I think also that the defendants received a benefit

elaborate 精细的,精心的,详尽的

controversy 纠纷,争议
abstain from 免于

want of consideration 对价的欠缺
nisi prius 初审(表示由法官及陪审团组成的初审法庭聆讯)

derive 获得

fortnight 两星期

from this user, for the use of the smoke ball was contemplated by the defendants as being indirectly a benefit to them, because the use of the smoke balls would promote their sale.①

Then we were pressed with *Gerhard v. Bates*. In *Gerhard v. Bates*, which arose upon demurrer, the point upon which the action failed was that the plaintiff did not allege that the promise was made to the class of which alone the plaintiff was a member, and that therefore there was no privity between the plaintiffs and the defendant. Then Lord Campbell went on to give a second reason. If his first reason was not enough, and the plaintiff and the defendant there had come together as contracting parties and the only question was consideration, it seems to me Lord Campbell's reasoning would not have been sound. It is only to be supported by reading it as an additional reason for thinking that they had not come into the relation of contracting parties, but, if so, the language was superfluous. The truth is, that if in that case you had found a contract between the parties there would have been no difficulty about consideration, but you could not find such a contract. Here, in the same way, if you once make up your mind that there was a promise made to this lady who is the plaintiff, as one of the public — a promise made to her that if she used the smoke ball three times daily for a fortnight and got the influenza, she should have £100, it seems to me that her using the smoke ball was sufficient consideration. I cannot picture to myself the view of the law on which the contrary could be held when you have once found who are the contracting parties. If I say to a person, "If you use such and such a medicine for a week I will give you £5," and he uses it, there is ample consideration for the promise.

A. L. Smith, L. J.

The first point in this case is, whether the defendants' advertisement which appeared in the *Pall Mall Gazette* was an offer which, when accepted and

demurrer 异议,抗诉

privity（指在契约当事人之间存在的对同一财产权利的）相互关系、共同关系或连续关系

superfluous 多余的,过量的,过剩的

---

① Is there any difference between Lord Bowen's analysis on consideration and Lord Lindley's? You may want to come back to read this case again after you have learned "acceptance" and "consideration."

its conditions performed, constituted a promise to pay, assuming there was good consideration to uphold that promise, or whether it was only a puff from which no promise could be implied, or, as put by Mr. Finlay, a mere statement by the defendants of the confidence they entertained in the efficacy of their remedy.① Or as I might put it in the words of Lord Campbell in *Denton v. Great Northern Ry. Co.*, whether this advertisement was mere waste paper. That is the first matter to be determined. It seems to me that this advertisement reads as follows: "£100 reward will be paid by the Carbolic Smoke Ball Company to any person who after having used the ball three times daily for two weeks according to the printed directions supplied with such ball contracts the increasing epidemic influenza, colds, or any diseases caused by taking cold. The ball will last a family several months, and can be refilled at a cost of 5s." If I may paraphrase it, it means this: "If you" — that is one of the public as yet not ascertained, but who, as Lindley and Bowen, L.J., have pointed out, will be ascertained by the performing the condition — "will hereafter use my smoke ball three times daily for two weeks according to my printed directions, I will pay you £100 if you contract the influenza within the period mentioned in the advertisement." Now, is there not a request there? It comes to this: "In consideration of your buying my smoke ball, and then using it as I prescribe, I promise that if you catch the influenza within a certain time I will pay you £100."② It must not be forgotten that this advertisement states that as security for what is being offered, and as proof of the sincerity of the offer, £1000 is actually lodged at the bank wherewith to satisfy any possible demands which might be made in the event of the conditions contained therein being fulfilled and a person catching the epidemic so as to entitle him to the £100. How can it be said that such a statement as that embodied only a

uphold 支持,维持

prescribe 规定,指示;开药,开处方

security 担保

embody 具体表达,包含

---

① Pay attention to the different writing styles of the different Lords. Lord Smith formulated the issue of the case in the beginning of the opinion.
② Note that each Lord tried to construe the language of the advertisement. Pay attention to the different constructions.

mere expression of confidence in the wares which the defendants had to sell? I cannot read the advertisement in any such way. In my judgment, the advertisement was an offer intended to be acted upon, and when accepted and the conditions performed constituted a binding promise on which an action would lie, assuming there was consideration for that promise. The defendants have contended that it was a promise in honor or an agreement or a contract in honor — whatever that may mean. I understand that if there is no consideration for a promise, it may be a promise in honor, or, as we should call it, a promise without consideration and *nudum pactum*; but if anything else is meant, I do not understand it. I do not understand what a bargain or a promise or an agreement in honor is unless it is one on which an action cannot be brought because it is *nudum pactum*, and about *nudum pactum* I will say a word in a moment.

In my judgment, therefore, this first point fails, and this was an offer intended to be acted upon, and, when acted upon and the conditions performed, constituted a promise to pay.

In the next place, it was said that the promise was too wide, because there is no limit of time within which the person has to catch the epidemic. There are three possible limits of time to this contract. The first is, catching the epidemic during its continuance; the second is, catching the influenza during the time you are using the ball; the third is, catching the influenza within a reasonable time after the expiration of the two weeks during which you have used the ball three times daily. It is not necessary to say which is the correct construction of this contract, for no question arises thereon. Whichever is the true construction, there is sufficient limit of time so as not to make the contract too vague on that account.

Then it was argued, that if the advertisement constituted an offer which might culminate in a contract if it was accepted, and its conditions performed, yet it was not accepted by the plaintiff in the manner contemplated, and that the offer contemplated was such that notice of the acceptance had to be given by the party using the carbolic ball to the defendants

---

expiration 期满, 届满; 截止

culminate 告终, 结束（这里指合同成立）

before user, so that the defendants might be <u>at liberty</u> to superintend the experiment. All I can say is, that there is no such clause in the advertisement, and that, in my judgment, no such clause can be read into it; and I entirely agree with what has fallen from my Brothers, that this is one of those cases in which a performance of the condition by using these smoke balls for two weeks three times a day is an acceptance of the offer.

It was then said there was no person named in the advertisement with whom any contract was made. That, I suppose, has taken place in every case in which actions on advertisements have been maintained, from the time of *Williams v. Carwardine*, and before that, down to the present day. I have nothing to add to what has been said on that subject, except that a person becomes a <u>*persona designata*</u> and able to sue, when he performs the conditions mentioned in the advertisement.

Lastly, it was said that there was no consideration, and that it was *nudum pactum*. There are two considerations here. One is the consideration of the inconvenience of having to use this carbolic smoke ball for two weeks three times a day; and the other more important consideration is the money gain likely to <u>accrue to</u> the defendants by the enhanced sale of the smoke balls, by reason of the plaintiff's user of them. There is ample consideration to support this promise. I have only to add that as regards the policy and the wagering points, in my judgment, there is nothing in either of them.

Appeal <u>dismissed</u>.

1.3 Invitation to Make an Offer

An offer must be distinguished from "<u>an invitation to make an offer.</u>" An invitation to make an offer is part of the process of preliminary negotiations, which refer to a period during which the parties seek to determine the bargain the other is willing to make but where no definite statement of what is offered and what is demanded in return is made. An invitation to make an offer is not an offer, it does not create power in the intended "offeree" to accept in order to form a binding contract.

Sometimes it is difficult to distinguish an offer from an invitation to make an offer. For example, advertisements pose a special problem as to whether they constitute an offer or just an invitation to make an offer. There have been lots of debates as we can see from the case *Carlill v. Carbolic Smoke Ball Co*. Normally advertisements are considered only invitations to negotiate; however, an advertisement will be held to constitute an offer if it contains a positive promise and a positive statement of what the advertiser demands in return. The offer to pay a reward is an example of an advertisement which is usually held to constitute a binding offer that can be accepted by performing the requested act.

Bids normally are considered invitations to make offers unless the bid advertisement states that the job will be let to the lowest bidder without reservation, in which case it is an offer to let the job to the lowest bidder. Likewise, auctions, unless they are stated to be without reserve, are merely invitations to make offers which may be either accepted or rejected by the auctioneer.

The following is a case decided by a U.S. court. Read it to see how U.S. courts decided the cases relating to advertisement.

1.4 Case 3: Lefkowitz v. Great Minneapolis Surplus Store

Supreme Court of Minnesota
Morris Lefkowitz, Respondent,
v.
Great Minneapolis Surplus Store, Inc., Appellant
251 Minn. 188, 86 N.W. 2d 689
Dec. 20, 1957

Murphy, Justice.

This is an appeal from an order of the Municipal Court of Minneapolis denying the motion of the defendant for amended findings of fact, or, in the alternative, for a new trial. The order for judgment awarded the plaintiff the sum of $138.50 as damages for breach of contract.

This case grows out of the alleged refusal of the defendant to sell to the plaintiff a certain fur piece which it had offered for sale in a newspaper advertisement. It appears from the record that on April 6, 1956, the defendant published the following advertisement in a Minneapolis newspaper:

> *Saturday 9 A.M. Sharp*
> *3 Brand New*
> *Fur Coats*
> *Worth to $100.00*
> *First Come First Served*
> *$1 Each*

On April 13, the defendant again published an advertisement in the same newspaper as follows:

> *Saturday 9 A.M.*
> *2 Brand New Pastel Mink 3-Skin Scarfs*
> *Selling for $89.50*
> *Out they go*
> *Saturday. Each ... $1.00*
> *1 Black Lapin Stole*
> *Beautiful,*
> *worth $139.50 ... $1.00*
> *First Come First Served*

The record supports the findings of the court that on each of the Saturdays following the publication of the above-described ads the plaintiff was the first to present himself at the appropriate counter in the defendant's store and on each occasion demanded the coat and the stole so advertised and indicated his readiness to pay the sale price of $1. On both occasions, the defendant refused to sell the merchandise to the plaintiff, stating on the first occasion that by a "house rule" the offer was intended for women only and sales would not be made to men, and on the second visit that plaintiff knew defendant's house rules.

The trial court properly disallowed plaintiff's claim for the value of the fur coats since the value of these articles was speculative and uncertain. The only evidence of value was the advertisement itself to the

ad (advertisement) 广告

house rule 店规

disallow 驳回,否决,拒绝

effect that the coats were "Worth to $100.00," how much less being speculative especially in view of the price for which they were offered for sale. With reference to the offer of the defendant on April 13, 1956, to sell the "1 Black Lapin Stole ... worth $139.50 ..." the trial court held that the value of this article was established and granted judgment in favor of the plaintiff for that amount less the $1 quoted purchase price.

The defendant contends that a newspaper advertisement offering items of merchandise for sale at a named price is a "unilateral offer" which may be withdrawn without notice. He relies upon authorities which hold that, where an advertiser publishes in a newspaper that he has a certain quantity or quality of goods which he wants to dispose of at certain prices and on certain terms, such advertisements are not offers which become contracts as soon as any person to whose notice they may come signifies his acceptance by notifying the other that he will take a certain quantity of them. Such advertisements have been construed as an invitation for an offer of sale on the terms stated, which offer, when received, may be accepted or rejected and which therefore does not become a contract of sale until accepted by the seller; and until a contract has been so made, the seller may modify or revoke such prices or terms. *Montgomery Ward & Co. v. Johnson*, 209 Mass. 89, 95 N.W. 290; *Craft v. Elder & Johnson Co.*, 38 N.E. 2d 416, 34 Ohio L.A. 603.

The defendant relies principally on *Craft v. Elder & Johnston Co.*, *id*. In that case, the court discussed the legal effect of an advertisement offering for sale, as a one-day special, an electric sewing machine at a named price. The view was expressed that the advertisement was (38 N.E. 2d 417, 34 Ohio L.A. 605) "not an offer made to any specific person but was made to the public generally. Thereby it would be properly designated as a unilateral offer and not being supported by any consideration could be withdrawn at will and without notice." It is true that such an offer may be withdrawn before acceptance. Since all offers are by their nature unilateral because they are necessarily made by one party or on one side in the negotiation of a contract, the distinction made in that decision between a unilateral offer and a unilateral contract is not clear. On the facts before us we are concerned with whether the advertisement constituted an offer, and, if so, whether the plaintiff's conduct constituted an acceptance.

There are numerous authorities which hold that a particular advertisement in a newspaper or circular letter relating to a sale of articles may be construed by the court as constituting an offer, acceptance of which would complete a contract.

The test of whether a binding obligation may originate in advertisements addressed to the general public is "whether the facts show that some performance was promised in positive terms in return for something requested." 1 WILLISTON CONTRACTS (REV. ED.) s 27.

The authorities above cited emphasize that, where the offer is clear, definite, and explicit, and leaves nothing open for negotiation, it constitutes an offer, acceptance of which will complete the contract. The most recent case on the subject is *Johnson v. Capital City Ford Co.*, La. App., 85 So. 2d 75, in which the court pointed out that a newspaper advertisement relating to the purchase and sale of automobiles may constitute an offer, acceptance of which will consummate a contract and create an obligation in the offeror to perform according to the terms of the published offer.

Whether in any individual instance a newspaper advertisement is an offer rather than an invitation to make an offer depends on the legal intention of the parties and the surrounding circumstances. We are of the view on the facts before us that the offer by the defendant of the sale of the Lapin fur was clear, definite, and explicit, and left nothing open for negotiation. The plaintiff having successful[ly] managed to be the first one to appear at the seller's place of business to be served, as requested by the advertisement, and having offered the stated purchase price of the article, he was entitled to performance on the part of the defendant. We think the trial court was correct in holding that there was in the conduct of the parties a sufficient mutuality of obligation to constitute

---

explicit 详尽的,明确的,清楚的

leave nothing open for negotiation 没有留有任何谈判的余地

consummate 作成,成立

be of the view 认为

a contract of sale.

The defendant contends that the offer was modified by a "house rule" to the effect that only women were qualified to receive the bargains advertised. The advertisement contained no such restriction. This objection may be disposed of briefly by stating that, while an advertiser has the right at any time before acceptance to modify his offer, he does not have the right, after acceptance, to impose new or arbitrary conditions not contained in the published offer. *Payne v. Lautz Bros. & Co.*, *City Ct.*, 166 N. Y. S. 844, 848; *Mooney v. Daily News Co.*, 116 Minn. 212, 133 N. W. 573.

Affirmed.

The *Lefkowitz* case formulated a test to distinguish an offer from an invitation to make an offer: "Whether in any individual instance a newspaper advertisement is an offer rather than an invitation to make an offer depends upon the legal intention of the parties and the surrounding circumstances." However, it is not easy to determine what the "legal intention of the parties and the surrounding circumstances" are.

1.5 Termination of Offer

Once made, an offer gives the offeree the power to convert it into a binding contract by accepting it. However, an offer is not valid forever. An offer may be terminated, and thus the offeree's power to accept the offer is also terminated accordingly, by a provision in the offer itself or by the expiration of a reasonable time. An offer may also be terminated by revocation, rejection, death or insanity of the offeror or offeree, destruction of the subject matter of the proposed contract, or the performance of the proposed contract becoming illegal.

If the offeror indicates in the offer that it must be accepted within a certain period of time, then it must be accepted within that time period; otherwise the offer becomes invalid and a late acceptance does not bind the offeror. If the offeror does not specify such a period of time in the offer, the offer will remain open for a reasonable time; the determination of what a reasonable time is will depend on all the facts and circumstances of the particular case.

An offer may be terminated by revocation. Normally, the offeror has the right to revoke the offer at any time before it is accepted by the offeree. In order to revoke the offer, the offeror must communicate the revocation to the offeree and generally the revocation is not effective until actually received by the offeree. Offers made to the public — as in the case of <u>rewards</u> or advertisements — may be revoked if done in essentially the same manner as the offer was originally made. However, there are exceptions to this general rule of revocation.

    reward 悬赏广告,悬赏通告

If the offeror promises not to revoke the offer <u>for a stated period of time</u> on the condition that the offeree pays consideration to keep the offer open, then an option contract has been formed which makes the offer <u>irrevocable</u> for the stated period of time. Under an option contract, the offeror <u>surrender</u>s the power to revoke in exchange for some consideration provided by the offeree. It is to be noted that under the UCC, a written promise by the offeror to leave an offer open for a stated period of time is valid and binding for a period of up to three months even though the offeree has not actually purchased an option by giving consideration to the offeror.

    for a stated period of time 在规定的时间内

    irrevocable 不可撤回的,不可撤销的
    surrender 交出,放弃

Another exception to the revocation rule is based on the <u>promissory estoppel doctrine</u>. If the offeror knows or has reason to know that the offeree will change his position in reliance on the offer, then the offer may be held to be irrevocable if the offeree does indeed change his position in reliance on the offer.

    promissory estoppel doctrine 允诺的不容否定原则(即允诺人相信对方将由于信赖其允诺作出某项实质性的作为或不作为,所受允诺人确实因此作出某项作为或不作为,此时所作出的允诺不得否定或取消,以免给对方造成损害)

Neither does the revocation rule apply if the offer was for a unilateral contract where acceptance would be made by doing the requested act, and if the offeree had already begun performance at the time of the revocation and completed his performance within a reasonable time thereafter.

An offer may be terminated by rejection made by the offeree. Once the offeree rejects an offer, the offer is terminated and the offeree cannot later on attempt to accept it. The offeree may reject an offer directly or indirectly. Both a <u>counteroffer</u> and a <u>conditional acceptance</u> are considered to be indirect rejections since both reject the terms contained in the original offer. However, an inquiry regarding the terms is not to be considered a counteroffer and does not terminate the offer.

Death or some legal <u>incapacity</u>, such as insanity, of the offeror or offeree automatically terminates an offer as does destruction of the proposed subject matter of the contract without the fault of either party. In addition, if prior to the acceptance of the offer, a statute is enacted which would make performance of the completed contract illegal, the offer is terminated. Read the following pages for cases discussing the termination of offer.

1.6 Case 4: Ardente v. Horan

Supreme Court of Rhode Island
Ardente v. Horan
117 R. I. 254, 366 A. 2d 162
Dec. 2, 1976

Doris, Justice.

Ernest P. Ardente, the plaintiff, brought this <u>civil action</u> in Superior Court to specifically enforce an agreement between himself and William A. and Katherine L. Horan, the defendants, to sell certain real property. The defendants <u>filed an answer</u> together with a motion for <u>summary judgment</u> pursuant to Super. R. Civ. P. 56. Following the submission of <u>affidavits</u> by both the plaintiff and the defendants and a <u>hearing</u> on the motion, judgment was entered by a Superior Court justice for the defendants. The plaintiff now appeals.

In August 1975, certain residential property in the city of Newport was offered for sale by defendants. The plaintiff made a bid of $250,000 for the property which was communicated to defendants by their attorney. After defendants' attorney advised plaintiff that the bid was acceptable to defendants, he prepared a purchase and sale agreement at the direction of defendants and forwarded it to plaintiff's attorney for plaintiff's signature. After investigating certain title conditions, plaintiff executed the agreement. Thereafter plaintiff's attorney returned the document to defendants along with a check in the amount of $20,000 and a letter dated September 8, 1975, which read in relevant part as follows:

> My clients are concerned that the following items remain with the real estate: a) dining room set and tapestry wall covering in dining room; b) fireplace fixtures throughout; c) the sun parlor furniture. I would appreciate your confirming that these items are a part of the transaction, as they would be difficult to replace.

The defendants refused to agree to sell the enumerated items and did not sign the purchase and sale agreement. They directed their attorney to return the agreement and the deposit check to plaintiff and subsequently refused to sell the property to plaintiff. This action for specific performance followed.

In Superior Court, defendants moved for summary judgment① on the ground that the facts were not in dispute and no contract had been formed as a matter of law. The trial justice ruled that the letter quoted above constituted a conditional acceptance of defendants' offer to sell the property and consequently must be construed as a counteroffer. Since defendants never accepted the counteroffer, it followed that no contract was formed, and summary judgment was granted.

Summary judgment is a drastic remedy and should be cautiously applied; nevertheless, where there is no genuine issue as to any material fact and the moving party is entitled to judgment as a matter of law, summary judgment properly issues. *Ladouceur v. Prudential Ins. Co.*, 111 R. I. 370, 302 A. 2d 801 (1973). On appeal this court is bound by the same rules as the trial court. *Cardente v. Travelers Ins.*

---

title conditions 权利状况（这里指不动产所有权的归属状况）
execute 签署（协议等）

enumerated items 明确列举的项目
specific performance 特定履行,实际履行,具体履行（是衡平法上对违反合同的一种救济,指强制被告实际履行其合同义务,亦即令其完全按原合同中他所担从事之事来履行清偿）
on the ground(s) 基于……原因
rule （法院）作出判决,作出决定

genuine issue 真正的争议点(指双方当事人对案件的有关事实的争执,一方当事人申请适用简易程序时必须证明案件中并无真正的争议点)
the moving party 提出动议一方当事人,提出请求方

---

① Summary judgment is a mechanism for deciding cases for which a trial is not necessary and would serve no purpose. One party may move for summary judgment asserting that there is "no genuine issue as to any material fact." If the judge grants the motion, then the case will end and no further trial will be conducted.

Co., 112 R.I. 713, 315 A.2d 63 (1974). With these rules is[sic]① mind we address ourselves to the facts.

The plaintiff assigns several grounds for appeal in his brief. He urges first that summary judgment was improper because there existed a genuine issue of fact. The factual question, according to plaintiff, was whether the oral agreement which preceded the drafting of the purchase and sale agreement was intended by the parties to take effect immediately to create a binding oral contract for the sale of the property.

We cannot agree with plaintiff's position. A review of the record shows that the issue was never raised before the trial justice. The plaintiff did not, in his affidavit in opposition to summary judgment or by any other means, bring to the attention of the trial court any facts which established the existence of a relevant factual dispute. Indeed, at the hearing on the motion plaintiff did not even mention the alleged factual dispute which he now claims the trial justice erred in overlooking. The only issue plaintiff addressed was the proper interpretation of the language used in plaintiff's letter of acceptance. This was solely a question of law. See *Cassidy v. Springfield Life Ins. Co.*, 106 R.I. 615, 262 A.2d 378 (1970); *Johnson v. Kile & Morgan Co.*, 49 R.I. 99, 140 A. 3 (1928).

It is well-settled that one who opposes a motion for summary judgment may not rest upon the mere allegations or denials of his pleading. He has an affirmative duty to set forth specific facts which show that there is a genuine issue of fact to be resolved at trial. If he does not do so, summary judgment, if appropriate, will be entered against him. *Gallo v. National Nursing Homes, Inc.*, 106 R.I. 485, 488, 261 A.2d 19, 21 (1970); *Sutter v. Harrington*, 51 R.I. 325, 154 A. 657 (1931). Accordingly, since no genuine issue of fact was presented to the trial justice, we hold that he did not err in ruling that summary judgment was appropriate.

---

① The correct wording here is "with these rules in mind," however, the author wrongfully typed it as "with these rules is mind," therefore the word "[sic]" is used following the word "is" indicating that it was originally written or typed like this.

The plaintiff's second contention is that the trial justice incorrectly applied the principles of contract law in deciding that the facts did not disclose a valid acceptance of defendants' offer. Again we cannot agree.

The trial justice proceeded on the theory that the delivery of the purchase and sale agreement to plaintiff constituted an offer by defendants to sell the property. Because we must view the evidence in the light most favorable to the party against whom summary judgment was entered, in this case plaintiff, we assume as the trial justice did that the delivery of the agreement was in fact an offer.①

The question we must answer next is whether there was an acceptance of that offer. The general rule is that where, as here, there is an offer to form a bilateral contract, the offeree must communicate his acceptance to the offeror before any contractual obligation can come into being. A mere mental intent to accept the offer, no matter how carefully formed, is not sufficient. The acceptance must be transmitted to the offeror in some overt manner. *Bullock v. Harwick*, 158 Fla. 834, 30 So. 2d 539 (1947); *Armstrong v. Guy H. James Constr. Co.*, 402 P. 2d 275 (Okl. 1965); 1 RESTATEMENT CONTRACTS § 20 (1932). See generally 1 CORBIN, CONTRACTS § 67 (1963). A review of the record shows that the only expression of acceptance which was communicated to defendants was the delivery of the executed purchase and sale agreement accompanied by the letter of September 8. Therefore it is solely on the basis of the language used in these two documents that we must determine whether there was a valid acceptance. Whatever plaintiff's unexpressed intention may have been in sending the documents is irrelevant. We must be concerned only with the language actually used, not the language plaintiff thought he was using or intended to use.

delivery 交付

in the light most favorable to 根据对……最为有利的观点

transmit 传达
overt 公开的,明显的(表现为行动的,而不仅仅停留在意图或策划的程度)

---

① The conclusion that the delivery of the agreement was an offer is not unassailable in view of the fact that defendants did not sign the agreement before sending it to plaintiff, and the fact that plaintiff told defendants' attorney after the agreement was received that he would have to investigate certain conditions of title before signing the agreement. If it was not an offer, plaintiff's execution of the agreement could itself be no more than an offer, which defendants never accepted.

execution 签署

personalty 动产

equivocal 有歧义的,模棱两可的,不确定的(反义为 unequivocal)

qualified acceptance 附条件承诺

absolute acceptance 无条件承诺

a collateral matter （与争议问题无直接关系的）间接问题,间接事实

There is no doubt that the execution and delivery of the purchase and sale agreement by plaintiff, without more, would have operated as an acceptance. The terms of the accompanying letter, however, apparently conditioned the acceptance upon the inclusion of various items of personalty. In assessing the effect of the terms of that letter we must keep in mind certain generally accepted rules. To be effective, an acceptance must be definite and unequivocal. "An offeror is entitled to know in clear terms whether the offeree accepts his proposal. It is not enough that the words of a reply justify a probable inference of assent." 1 RESTATEMENT CONTRACTS § 58, comment a (1932). The acceptance may not impose additional conditions on the offer, nor may it add limitations. "An acceptance which is equivocal or upon condition or with a limitation is a counteroffer and requires acceptance by the original offeror before a contractual relationship can exist." *John Hancock Mut. Life Ins. Co. v. Dietlin*, 97 R. I. 515, 518, 199 A. 2d 311, 313 (1964). *Accord, Cavanaugh v. Conway*, 36 R. I. 571, 587, 90 A. 1080, 1086 (1914).

However, an acceptance may be valid despite conditional language if the acceptance is clearly independent of the condition. Many cases have so held. Williston states the rule as follows:

> Frequently an offeree, while making a positive acceptance of the offer, also makes a request or suggestion that some addition or modification be made. So long as it is clear that the meaning of the acceptance is positively and unequivocally to accept the offer whether such request is granted or not, a contract is formed.
> 1 WILLISTON CONTRACTS § 79 at 261-62 (3d ed. 1957).

Corbin is in agreement with the above view. 1 CORBIN, *supra*, § 84 at 363-65. Thus our task is to decide whether plaintiff' letter is more reasonably interpreted as a qualified acceptance or as an absolute acceptance together with a mere inquiry concerning a collateral matter.

In making our decision we recognize that, as one text states, "The question whether a communication by an offeree is a conditional acceptance or counter-offer is not always easy to answer. It must be determined by the same common-sense process of interpretation that must be applied in so many other cases." 1 CORBIN, *supra* § 82 at 353. In our opinion the language used in plaintiff's letter of September 8 is not consistent with an absolute acceptance accompanied by a request for a <u>gratuitous</u> benefit. We interpret the letter to impose a condition on plaintiff's acceptance of defendants' offer. The letter does not unequivocally state that even without the enumerated items plaintiff is willing to complete the contract. In fact, the letter seeks "<u>confirmation</u>" that the listed items "are a part of the transaction." Thus, far from being an independent, collateral request, the sale of the items in question is explicitly referred to as a part of the real estate transaction. Moreover, the letter goes on to stress the difficulty of finding replacements for these items. This is a further indication that plaintiff did not view the inclusion of the listed items as merely collateral or incidental to the real estate transaction.

A review of the relevant case law discloses that those cases in which an acceptance was found valid despite an accompanying conditional term generally involved a more definite expression of acceptance than the one in <u>the case at bar</u>. *E.g.*, *Moss v. Cogle*, 267 Ala. 208, 101 So. 2d 314 (1958); *Jaybe Constr. Co. v. Beco, Inc.*, 3 Conn. Cir. 406, 216 A. 2d 208, 212 (1965); *Katz v. Pratt Street Realty Co.*, 257 Md. 103, 262 A. 2d 540 (1970); *Nelson v. Hamlin*, 258 Mass. 331, 155 N. E. 18 (1927); *Duprey v. Donahoe*, 52 Wash. 2d 129, 323 P. 2d 903 (1958).

Accordingly, we hold that since the plaintiff's letter of acceptance dated September 8 was conditional, it operated as a rejection of the defendants' offer and no contractual obligation was created.

The plaintiff's appeal is denied and dismissed, the judgment appealed from is affirmed and the case is <u>remanded</u> to the Superior Court.

gratuitous 单方受益的（指在无对价或法定约因的情况下作出的赠与或转让）

confirmation 确认

the case at bar 正在审理中的案件,本案

remand 发回重审

2. Acceptance

As indicated earlier, an offer creates a power in the offeree to accept the offer, and once accepted, the terms contained in the offer <u>are integrated into</u> a contract which binds both the offeror and the offeree.

2.1 Elements of Acceptance

An acceptance is a manifestation of intention to be presently bound by the terms contained in the offer. The acceptance must be communicated to the offeror in order to form a binding contract. In the case of a unilateral contractual offer which requests an act in return for a promise, acceptance is not complete until the act, as requested, is completed. In the case of a bilateral contractual offer which requests a promise in return for a promise, the offer is accepted by making the requested promise.

Under the traditional common law, an acceptance must be a manifestation of intention by the offeree to be presently bound by, and only by the terms contained in the offer. Put it another way, the acceptance must correspond in all respects with the offer if it is to be effective. If a purported acceptance does not so correspond is nothing more than a counteroffer or conditional acceptance, which terminates the original offer and requires acceptance by the original offeror in order for a completed contract to result. This is referred to as the "<u>*mirror image rule*</u>."

The modern law of contract does not strictly stick to the mirror image rule; instead, it focuses more on the intentions of the parties and less on the technical requirements of form that prevail under the traditional common law. For example, under the UCC, contracts can be made through the exchange of printed forms even though those forms contain <u>conflicting terms</u>. So long as the parties act as if they have a contract, then a contract exists with its terms consisting of those terms on which they agree, or which were added by one party's form without objection by the other party. Conflicting terms or those on which they disagree are <u>disregarded</u>. <u>Supplementary terms</u> supplied by the UCC or by trade usage are used to fill in terms discarded as conflicting.

A contract can be made under the UCC in any manner sufficient to show agreement even though some terms may be left open and even though the moment of the making of the contract is uncertain. Acceptance may be by any reasonable means; for example, where orders for immediate shipment are made, acceptance may be by either promptly shipping the goods or by giving notice of acceptance. If non-conforming goods are shipped and no notice is given that they are being shipped only for the buyer's convenience, then there is a breach of contract at the same time there is acceptance.

In order to be effective, an acceptance must be communicated to the offeror. The offeror is the one who initiates the offer, therefore the offeror is the master of the offer and may specify an exclusive manner and medium of acceptance. For example, the offeror may specify that the acceptance will not become effective until it reaches his home or place of business. If the offer specifies the time, place, or method of communication, then these terms must be complied with and any attempt to accept at a time, place, or manner other than that specified is a counteroffer which terminates the offer. However, if the offeror does not specify the manner, medium, or time of acceptance, then communication may be in any reasonable manner as long as it is received prior to termination of the offer.

As a prerequisite for communication of acceptance, the offeree must have knowledge about the offer, and must consent to the offer. One cannot accept an offer without knowledge of the offer. For example, in case of a unilateral contractual offer, the requested act must be done with the intent of accepting the offer. The party who coincidently performs the act without knowing the existence of the offer cannot claim a breach of contract. Occasionally courts make an exception to this rule in reward cases and allow a person to collect a reward for doing a requested act even though he did not know of the reward offer at the time he performed the act.

trade usage 商业惯例和习惯
discard 抛弃

non-conforming goods 不合格的产品或货物

initiate 发起,首先提出
exclusive 唯一的,特定的

coincidently 巧合地

A party cannot be bound to a contract without his or her express or implied consent. Thus, silence is not an effective acceptance even if the offer provides that such silence will be construed as consent, unless there is some evidence that the silence was intended by the offeree as acceptance, or prior dealings or other circumstances impose on the offeree a duty to reply. Such circumstances might well include a situation where benefits are conferred on the offeree under such conditions that it was clear they were not intended as a gift and the offeree was aware of this when accepting them.

2.2 Effectiveness of Acceptance

When the acceptance is made orally to the offeror, the contract comes into existence at that time. However, where the acceptance is by mails or telegraph, disputes may arise as to when the acceptance is effective, upon dispatch of the acceptance letter by the offeree or upon receipt of it by the offeror, because the letter notifying the offeror of the offeree's acceptance may be lost or delayed in the mail or other communication process.

The common law courts tend to adopt the mailbox rule, or dispatch rule, i.e., the acceptance letter is effective once the offeree deposits it into the mailbox. The main reason is that if the acceptance letter is not effective until it is received, a number of problems may arise. For example, the offeree would not know whether a contract was formed until he received notification that his acceptance was received. That notification, itself, may be lost in the mail. The offeror would not know whether the offeree received that notice until the offeror received notice that the offeree had received the earlier notice.

However, the mailbox rule is not flawless. Suppose the letter of acceptance is never received, an innocent offeror may assume that his offer was not accepted and proceed to make a contract for the same subject matter with another party, only to discover later that the letter of acceptance was dispatched. The offeror is then confronted with two contracts for the same subject matter, only one of which may be performable, while the other will be breached. Nevertheless, the offeror can control the risk of transmission by, for example, requiring the acceptance to be received to be effective. If the offeror chooses not to control the risk, he should assume the risk since a reasonable offeree is impliedly authorized to use the same or a similar reasonable medium of communication for acceptance.

Generally, if the mode of communication used to convey the acceptance was <u>authorized</u> by the offeror, then the carrier is considered to be the agent of the offeror and the acceptance is effective to create a contract when it is put in the hands of that agent. Where the acceptance is sent by an agency that was not specifically authorized by the offeror or by trade usage, then it is not effective until received and only then if it is received within the time it would have been received if it had been sent by the authorized method of communication. The practice of common law countries is quite different from that of the civil law countries in this regard.

After discussing the elements of acceptance, you may want to go back to read the three cases in Section 1 again, focusing on the analyses on acceptance.

authorize 授权,认可

3. Consideration

A promise is not enforceable by way of court action unless it is <u>validated</u> by consideration or <u>a substitute of consideration</u>. Consideration is a bargained-for-exchange for a legal value. Two essential elements of consideration are (1) legal value, and (2) bargained-for-exchange.

validate 使有效
a substitute of consideration
对价的替代

3.1 Elements of Consideration

The legal value may consist either in some right, interest, profit, or benefit accruing to one party, or some <u>forbearance</u>, detriment, loss, or responsibility, given, suffered, or undertaken by another. So it is usually defined as either a detriment to the <u>promisee</u> or a benefit to the <u>promisor</u>. The detriment must be a special kind of detriment — a legal detriment — which means the surrendering of a legal right or the <u>assuming</u> of a legal burden. It does not have to have any

forbearance 容忍,忍耐,克制

promisee 受允诺人
promisor 允诺人

assume 承担,承受

economic value. For example, a person has a right to seek court enforcement of claims he may have against others. If the person promises to another person not to bring suit on a claim which he reasonably believes he has, this forbearance to sue is a legal detriment to him which constitutes consideration and supports a contract. The promisor need not be the party threatened with suit, and a promise made by a third person may be supported by the promisee's forbearance to sue.

Such a detriment to the promisee usually produces a benefit for the promisor, although a detriment without any corresponding benefit is considered to constitute consideration. However, mere benefit to the promisor without corresponding detriment to the promisee does not constitute consideration. For example, if A says to B: "I will pay you $100 tomorrow if you do not enter into my apartment tonight." Assume that B has no right to enter into A's apartment at any time, there is no detriment to B in forbearing from entering into A's apartment because he has surrendered no legally recognized right in such forbearance. There is also no benefit to A since A received nothing in exchange for his promise. Here is another example: if A promises to sell his car to B for $5,000 unless A changes his mind, and B promises to buy the car for $5,000, B cannot be bound to his promise because he is receiving nothing from that promise. Since A can change his mind at his own will, A has no duty to perform; accordingly, he cannot be held to any promise made by B. B, the promisor, receives no benefit because A, the promisee, suffers no detriment.

In order to constitute consideration, the detriment to the promisee or benefit to the promisor must be bargained for and given in exchange for the promise. If it is intended as a gift, it will not constitute legal consideration. Justice Holmes stated in *Wisconsin & Mich. Ry. v. Powers*, 191 U.S. 379 (1903) that "the promise and the consideration must purport to be the motive each for the other, in whole or at least in part. It is not enough that the promise induces the detriment or that the detriment induces the promise, if the other half is wanting." Therefore, the legal value element without the bargained-for-exchange element is insufficient to find consideration.

Normally, the courts will not look into the sufficiency of the consideration as long as some legal consideration has been given. However, if the exchange is marked by gross inequality of considerations and there is evidence of unfair dealing such as fraud, duress, misrepresentation, or undue influence, the courts may refuse to enforce the contract. If a sufficient or nominal consideration is stated in the contract to have been given, but in fact has not been given, then the contract or promise will not be enforced.

sufficiency 充分
gross inequality 明显不公
unfair dealing 不公正的交易,不当交易
fraud 欺诈
duress 胁迫
misrepresentation 虚假陈述（指以语言或其他行为作出与事实情况不符的意思表示,如被他人接受,会导致错误的理解）
undue influence 不当影响
nominal 名义上的

3.2 Case 5: Hamer v. Sidway

Court of Appeals of New York
Hamer v. Sidway
124 N. Y. 538, 27 N. E. 256
April 14, 1891

This action was brought upon an alleged contract.

The plaintiff presented a claim to the executor of William E. Story, Sr., for $5,000 and interest from the 6th day of February, 1875. She acquired it through several mesne assignments from William E. Story, 2d. The claim being rejected by the executor, this action was brought. It appears that William E. Story, Sr., was the uncle of William E. Story, 2d; that at the celebration of the golden wedding of Samuel Story and wife, father and mother of William E. Story, Sr., on the 20th day of March, 1869, in the presence of the family and invited guests he promised his nephew that if he would refrain from drinking, using tobacco, swearing and playing cards or billiards for money until he became twenty-one years of age he would pay him a sum of $5,000. The nephew assented thereto and fully performed the conditions inducing the promise. When the nephew arrived at the age of twenty-one years and on the 31st day of January, 1875, he wrote to his uncle informing him that he had performed his part of the agreement and had thereby become entitled to the sum of $5,000. The uncle received the letter and a few days later and on the sixth of February, he wrote and mailed to his nephew the following letter:

executor 遗嘱执行人

mesne assignment 中间让与

refrain from 忍住,抑制,制止

BUFFALO, Feb. 6, 1875.
W. E. STORY, Jr.:

DEAR NEPHEW — Your letter of the 31st ult. came to hand all right, saying that you had lived up to the promise made to me several years ago. I have no doubt but you have, for which you shall have five thousand dollars as I promised you. I had the money in the bank the day you was [sic] 21 years old that I intend for you, and you shall have the money certain. Now, Willie I do not intend to interfere with this money in any way till I think you are capable of taking care of it and the sooner that time comes the better it will please me. I would hate very much to have you start out in some adventure that you thought all right and lose this money in one year. The first five thousand dollars that I got together cost me a heap of hard work. You would hardly believe me when I tell you that to obtain this I shoved a jackplane many a day, butchered three or four years, then came to this city, and after three months' perseverance I obtained a situation in a grocery store. I opened this store early, closed late, slept in the fourth story of the building in a room 30 by 40 feet and not a human being in the building but myself. All this I done to live as cheap as I could to save something. I don't want you to take up with this kind of fare. I was here in the cholera season of '49 and '52, and the deaths averaged 80 to 125 daily and plenty of small-pox. I wanted to go home, but Mr. Fisk, the gentleman I was working for, told me if I left then, after it got healthy he probably would not want me. I stayed. All the money I have saved I know just how I got it. It did not come to me in any mysterious way, and the reason I speak of this is that money got in this way stops longer with a fellow that gets it with hard knocks than it does when he finds it. Willie, you are 21 and you have many a thing to learn yet. This money you have earned much easier than I did, besides acquiring good habits at the same time and you are quite welcome to the money; hope you will make good use of it. I was ten long years getting this together after I was your age. Now, hoping this will be satisfactory, I stop. One thing more. Twenty-one years ago I bought you 15 sheep. These sheep were put out to double every four years. I kept track of them the first eight years; I have not heard much about them since. Your father and grandfather promised me that they would look after them till you were of age. Have they done so? I hope they have. By this time you have between five and six hundred sheep, worth a nice little income this spring. Willie, I have said much more than I expected to; hope you can make out what I have written. Today is the seventeenth day that I have not been out of my room, and have had the doctor as many days. Am a little better today; think I will get out next week. You need not mention to father, as he always worries about small matters.

Truly Yours,
W. E. STORY

P. S. — You can consider this money on interest.

The nephew received the letter and thereafter consented that the money should remain with his uncle in accordance with the terms and conditions of the letters. The uncle died on the 29th day of January, 1887, without having paid over to his nephew any portion of the said $5,000 and interest.

Parker, J.
The question which provoked the most discussion by counsel on this appeal, and which lies at the foundation of plaintiff's asserted right of recovery, is whether by virtue of a contract defendant's testator William E. Story became indebted to his nephew William E. Story, 2d, on his twenty-first birthday in the sum of five thousand dollars. The trial court found as a fact that "on the 20th day of March, 1869, ... William E. Story agreed to and with William E. Story, 2d, that if he would refrain from drinking liquor, using tobacco, swearing, and playing cards or

provoke 激起,导致

by virtue of 依……力量,依……权威,凭借
testator 立遗嘱之人
be indebted to 负债的

billiards for money until he should become 21 years of age then he, the said William E. Story, would at that time pay him, the said William E. Story, 2d, the sum of $5,000 for such refraining, to which the said William E. Story, 2d, agreed," and that he "in all things fully performed his part of said agreement."

The defendant contends that the contract was without consideration to support it, and, therefore, invalid. He asserts that the promisee by refraining from the use of liquor and tobacco was not harmed but benefited; that that which he did was best for him to do independently of his uncle's promise, and insists that it follows that unless the promisor was benefited, the contract was without consideration. A contention, which if well founded, would seem to leave open for controversy in many cases whether that which the promisee did or omitted to do was, in fact, of such benefit to him as to leave no consideration to support the enforcement of the promisor's agreement. Such a rule could not be tolerated, and is without foundation in the law. The Exchequer Chamber, in 1875, defined consideration as follows: "A valuable consideration in the sense of the law may consist either in some right, interest, profit or benefit accruing to the one party, or some forbearance, detriment, loss or responsibility given, suffered or undertaken by the other." Courts "will not ask whether the thing which forms the consideration does in fact benefit the promisee or a third party, or is of any substantial value to anyone. It is enough that something is promised, done, forborne or suffered by the party to whom the promise is made as consideration for the promise made to him." (ANSON'S PRIN. OF CON. 63.)

"In general a waiver of any legal right at the request of another party is a sufficient consideration for a promise." (PARSONS ON CONTRACTS, 444.)

"Any damage, or suspension, or forbearance of a right will be sufficient to sustain a promise." (KENT, VOL. 2, 465, 12TH ED.)

Pollock, in his work on contracts, page 166, after citing the definition given by the Exchequer Chamber already quoted, says: "The second branch of this judicial description is really the most important one.

Consideration means not so much that one party is profiting as that the other abandons some legal right in the present or limits his legal freedom of action in the future as an inducement for the promise of the first."

Now, applying this rule to the facts before us, the promisee used tobacco, occasionally drank liquor, and he had a legal right to do so. That right he abandoned for a period of years upon the strength of the promise of the testator that for such forbearance he would give him $5,000. We need not speculate on the effort which may have been required to give up the use of those stimulants. It is sufficient that he restricted his lawful freedom of action within certain prescribed limits upon the faith of his uncle's agreement, and now having fully performed the conditions imposed, it is of no moment whether such performance actually proved a benefit to the promisor, and the court will not inquire into it, but were it a proper subject of inquiry, we see nothing in this record that would permit a determination that the uncle was not benefited in a legal sense. Few cases have been found which may be said to be precisely in point, but such as have been support the position we have taken.

In *Shadwell v. Shadwell*, an uncle wrote to his nephew as follows:

> My Dear Lancey — I am so glad to hear of your intended marriage with Ellen Nicholl, and as I promised to assist you at starting, I am happy to tell you that I will pay to you 150 pounds yearly during my life and until your annual income derived from your profession of a chancery barrister shall amount to 600 guineas, of which your own admission will be the only evidence that I shall require.
>
> Your affectionate uncle,
> CHARLES SHADWELL

It was held that the promise was binding and made upon good consideration.

In *Lakota v. Newton*, an unreported case in the Superior Court of Worcester, Mass., the complaint averred defendant's promise that "if you (meaning plaintiff) will leave off drinking for a year I will give you $100," plaintiff's assent thereto, performance of the condition by him, and demanded judgment therefore. Defendant demurred on the ground, among others, that the plaintiff's declaration did not allege a valid and sufficient consideration for the agreement of the defendant. The demurrer was overruled.

In *Talbott v. Stemmons* (a Kentucky case not yet reported), the step-grandmother of the plaintiff made with him the following agreement: "I do promise and bind myself to give my grandson, Albert R. Talbott, $500 at my death, if he will never take another chew of tobacco or smoke another cigar during my life from this date up to my death, and if he breaks this pledge he is to refund double the amount to his mother." The executor of Mrs. Stemmons demurred to the complaint on the ground that the agreement was not based on a sufficient consideration. The demurrer was sustained and an appeal taken therefrom to the Court of Appeals, where the decision of the court below was reversed. In the opinion of the court it is said that "the right to use and enjoy the use of tobacco was a right that belonged to the plaintiff and not forbidden by law. The abandonment of its use may have saved him money or contributed to his health, nevertheless, the surrender of that right caused the promise, and having the right to contract with reference to the subject-matter, the abandonment of the use was a sufficient consideration to uphold the promise." Abstinence from the use of intoxicating liquors was held to furnish a good consideration for *a promissory note* in *Lindell v. Rokes* (60 Mo. 249).

The cases cited by the defendant on this question are not in point. In *Mallory v. Gillett* (21 N. Y. 412), *Belknap v. Bender* (75 Id. 446), and *Berry v. Brown* (107 Id. 659), the promise was in contravention of that provision of the Statute of Frauds, which declares void all promises to answer for the debts of third persons unless reduced to writing. In *Beaumont v. Reeve*, and *Porterfield v. Butler* (47 Miss. 165), the question was whether a moral obligation furnishes sufficient consideration to uphold a subsequent express promise. In *Duvoll v. Wilson* (9 Barb. 487), and *In re Wilber v. Warren* (104 N. Y. 192), the proposition involved was whether an executory covenant against encumbrances in a deed given in consideration of natural love and affection could be enforced. In *Vanderbilt v. Schreyer* (91 N. Y. 392), the plaintiff contracted with defendant to build a house, agreeing to accept in part payment therefore a specific bond and mortgage. Afterwards he refused to finish his contract unless the defendant would guarantee its payment, which was done. It was held that the guarantee could not be enforced for want of consideration. For in building the house the plaintiff only did that which he had contracted to do. And in *Robinson v. Jewett* (116 N. Y. 40), the court simply held that "The performance of an act which the party is under a legal obligation to perform cannot constitute a consideration for a new contract." It will be observed that the agreement which we have been considering was within the condemnation of the Statute of Frauds, because not to be performed within a year, and not in writing. But this defense the promisor could waive, and his letter and oral statements subsequent to the date of final performance on the part of the promisee must be held to amount to a waiver. Were it otherwise, the statute could not now be invoked in aid of the defendant. It does not appear on the face of the complaint that the agreement is one prohibited by the Statute of Frauds, and, therefore, such defense could not be made available unless set up in the answer. (*Porter v. Wormser*, 94 N. Y. 431, 450.) This was not done.

In further consideration of the questions presented, then, it must be deemed established for the purposes of this appeal, that on the 31st day of January, 1875, defendant's testator was indebted to William E. Story, 2d, in the sum of $5,000, and if this action were founded on that contract it would be barred by the Statute of Limitations which has been pleaded, but on that date the nephew wrote to his uncle as follows:

> Dear Uncle — I am now 21 years old today, and I am now my own boss, and I believe, according to agreement, that there is due me $5,000. I have lived up to the contract to the

letter in every sense of the word.

A few days later, and on February sixth, the uncle replied, and, so far as it is material to this controversy, the reply is as follows:

> Dear Nephew — Your letter of the 31st ult. came to hand all right saying that you had lived up to the promise made to me several years ago. I have no doubt but you have, for which you shall have $5,000 as I promised you. I had the money in the bank the day you was 21 years old that I intended for you, and you shall have the money certain. Now, Willie, I don't intend to interfere with this money in any way until I think you are capable of taking care of it, and the sooner that time comes the better it will please me. I would hate very much to have you start out in some adventure that you thought all right and lose this money in one year .... This money you have earned much easier than I did, besides acquiring good habits at the same time, and you are quite welcome to the money. Hope you will make good use of it ....
>
> W. E. STORY.
> P. S. — You can consider this money on interest.

The trial court found as a fact that "said letter was received by said William E. Story, 2d, who thereafter consented that said money should remain with the said William E. Story in accordance with the terms and conditions of said letter." And further, "That afterwards, on the first day of March, 1877, with the knowledge and consent of his said uncle, he duly sold, transferred and assigned all his right, title and interest in and to said sum of $5,000 to his wife Libbie H. Story, who thereafter duly sold, transferred and assigned the same to the plaintiff in this action."

We must now consider the effect of the letter, and the nephew's assent thereto. Were the relations of the parties thereafter that of debtor and creditor simply, or that of trustee and *cestui que trust*①? If the former, then this action is not maintainable, because barred by lapse of time. If the latter, the result must be otherwise. No particular expressions are necessary to create a trust. Any language clearly showing the settler's intention is sufficient if the property and disposition of it are definitely stated. (LEWIN ON TRUSTS, 55.)

A person in the legal possession of money or property acknowledging a trust with the assent of the *cestui que trust*, becomes from that time a trustee if the acknowledgment be founded on a valuable consideration. His antecedent relation to the subject, whatever it may have been, no longer controls. (2 STORY'S EQ. § 972.) If before a declaration of trust a party be a mere debtor, a subsequent agreement recognizing the fund as already in his hands and stipulating for its investment on the creditor's account will have the effect to create a trust. (*Day v. Roth*, 18 N. Y. 448.)

It is essential that the letter interpreted in the light of surrounding circumstances must show an intention on the part of the uncle to become a trustee before he will be held to have become such; but in an effort to ascertain the construction which should be given to it, we are also to observe the rule that the language of the promisor is to be interpreted in the sense in which he had reason to suppose it was understood by the promisee. (*White v. Hoyt*, 73 N. Y. 505, 511.) At the time the uncle wrote the letter he was indebted to his nephew in the sum of $5,000, and payment had been requested. The uncle recognizing the indebtedness, wrote the nephew that he would keep the money until he deemed him capable of taking care of it. He did not say "I will pay you at some other time," or use language that would indicate that the relation of debtor and creditor would continue. On the contrary, his language indicated that he had set apart the money the nephew had "earned" for him so that when he should be capable of taking

trustee 信托关系中的受托人
cestui que trust 信托受益人
lapse of time 时光的流逝[指因一段时间过去而不作为(因此产生法律后果)]
settler (settlor) 信托关系中的委托人
disposition 处分,转让,放弃

antecedent 先前的,既有的

stipulate (明确)约定,规定

indebtedness 受惠,蒙恩;感激;负债;债务

set ... apart 把……与其他分开

---

① "*Cestui que trust*" means the "beneficiary" in a trust relationship.

care of it he should receive it with interest. He said: "I had the money in the bank the day you were 21 years old that I intended for you and you shall have the money certain." That he had set apart the money is further evidenced by the next sentence: "Now, Willie, I don't intend to interfere with this money in any way until I think you are capable of taking care of it." Certainly, the uncle must have intended that his nephew should understand that the promise not "to interfere with this money" referred to the money in the bank which he declared was not only there when the nephew became 21 years old, but was intended for him. True, he did not use the word "trust," or state that the money was deposited in the name of William E. Story, 2d, or in his own name in trust for him, but the language used must have been intended to assure the nephew that his money had been set apart for him, to be kept without interference until he should be capable of taking care of it, for the uncle said in substance and in effect: "This money you have earned much easier than I did ... you are quite welcome to. I had it in the bank the day you were 21 years old and don't intend to interfere with it in any way until I think you are capable of taking care of it and the sooner that time comes the better it will please me." In this declaration there is not lacking a single element necessary for the creation of a valid trust, and to that declaration the nephew assented.

The learned judge who wrote the opinion of the General Term, seems to have taken the view that the trust was executed during the life time of defendant's testator by payment to the nephew, but as it does not appear from the order that the judgment was reversed on the facts, we must assume the facts to be as found by the trial court, and those facts support its judgment.

The order appealed from should be reversed and the judgment of the Special Term affirmed, with costs payable out of the estate.

All concur.

Order reversed and judgment of Special Term affirmed.

estate 财产,遗产
concur 同意,赞成

Consideration, and thus, a contract was found in the above case; however, no contract was found in the following case. Read and compare the two cases to see how and why the courts determined the cases differently.

3.3 Case 6: Harris v. Time, Inc.

Harris v. Time, Inc.
191 Cal. App. 3d 465, 236 Cal. Rptr. 471 (1987)

King, J.

It all began one day when Joshua Gnaizda, the three-year-old son of a prominent Bay area public interest attorney, received what he (or his mother) thought was a <u>tantalizing</u> offer in the mail from Time. The front of the envelope contained two see-through windows partially revealing the envelope's contents. One window showed Joshua's name and address. The other revealed the following statement: "JOSHUA A. GNAIZDA, I'LL GIVE YOU THIS VERSATILE NEW CALCULATOR WATCH FREE Just for Opening this Envelope Before Feb. 15, 1985." Beneath the offer was a picture of the calculator watch itself. Joshua's mother opened the envelope and apparently realized she had been <u>deceived</u> by a <u>ploy</u> to get her to open a piece of <u>junk mail</u>. The see-through window had not revealed the full text of Time's offer. Printed below the picture of the calculator watch and not viewable through the <u>see-through window</u>, were the following additional words: "AND MAILING THIS CERTIFICATE TODAY!" The certificate itself clearly required that Joshua purchase a subscription to Fortune magazine in order to receive the free calculator watch.

The action was <u>prosecuted</u> by Joshua, through his father, and by Mark Harris and Richard Baker, who had also received the same mailer. We are not informed of the ages of Harris and Baker.

The complaint <u>sought</u> the following <u>relief</u>: (1) a <u>declaration</u> that all recipients of the mailer were entitled to receive the promised item or to <u>rescind</u> subscriptions

tantalize 逗弄,使干着急

deceive 欺骗,蒙蔽
ploy 策略,活动
junk mail 邮寄宣传品,垃圾邮件

see-through window 窗口 信封中的透明窗口

prosecute 起诉(一般指公诉人对刑事被告的起诉,这里指民事案件的起诉,同"initiate")
seek relief 请求救济
declaration (法庭或法官就法律或权利问题所作的)确权判决
rescind 撤销,解除,废除

injunction 禁制令（系一项衡平法上的救济措施，指法院签发的要求当事人做某事或某行为或者禁止其做某事或某行为的命令）

compensatory 补偿性的

punitive damages 惩罚性的损害赔偿

advocacy 拥护，提倡

commence 开始，着手

litigation 诉讼

demand 向……提出正式合法要求

cause of action 诉因，诉讼理由

equivalence 同等，等值，等价

bombard 轰击，攻击

solicitation 招徕，恳求，诱惑

resort 求助，凭借，诉诸；采取（某种手段等）

ruse 策略，诡计，谋略

trick 诡计，谋略，欺诈

de minimis non curat lex 对琐事法律不以为意，法不干涉琐事原则

class action 集体诉讼，集团诉讼

maxim 法律格言，法律原则，法律准则

de minimis 关于琐事的；次要得可忽略的

they had purchased, (2) an <u>injunction</u> against future similar mailings, (3) <u>compensatory</u> damages in an amount equal to the value of the item, and (4) $15 million <u>punitive damages</u> to be awarded to a consumer fund "to be used for education and <u>advocacy</u> on behalf of consumer protection and enforcement of laws against unfair business practices."

The complaint also alleged that before <u>commencing litigation</u>, Joshua's father <u>demanded</u> that Time give Joshua a calculator watch without requiring a subscription. Time not only refused to give a watch, it did not even give Joshua or his father the time of day. There was no allegation that Harris or Baker made such a demand on Time.

In sustaining [Time's] demurrer as to the <u>cause of action</u> for breach of contract, the court stated no specific grounds for its ruling. Time had argued the complaint did not allege adequate consideration, and did not allege notice of performance by the plaintiffs. Time argues that there was no contract because the mere act of opening the envelope was valueless and therefore did not constitute adequate consideration. Technically, this is incorrect. It is basic modern contract law that any bargained-for act or forbearance will constitute adequate consideration for a unilateral contract. Courts will not require <u>equivalence</u> in the values exchanged or otherwise question the adequacy of the consideration.

Moreover, the act at issue here — the opening of the envelope, with consequent exposure to Time's sales pitch — may have been relatively insignificant to the plaintiffs, but it was of great value to Time. At a time when our homes are <u>bombarded</u> daily by direct mail advertisements and <u>solicitations</u>, the name of the game for the advertiser or solicitor is to get the recipient to open the envelope. Some advertisers, like Time in the present case, will <u>resort</u> to <u>ruse</u> or <u>trick</u> to achieve this goal. From Time's perspective, the opening of the envelope was "valuable consideration" in every sense of that phrase.

As a final argument, Time claims the judgment of dismissal was correct based on the legal maxim "<u>de minimis non curat lex</u>," or "the law disregards trifles." (Civ. Code, § 3533.) In this age of the consumer <u>class action</u> this <u>maxim</u> usually has little value. However, the present action is "<u>de minimus</u>" in the extreme. This lawsuit is an absurd waste of the resources of this court, the superior court, the public interest law firm handling the case and the citizens of California whose taxes fund our judicial system. It is not a use for which our legal system is designed.

As a practical matter, plaintiffs' real complaint is that they were tricked into opening a piece of junk mail, not that they were misled into buying anything or expending more than the effort necessary to open an envelope. For many, an unpleasant aspect of contemporary American life is returning to the sanctity of one's home each day and emptying the mailbox, only to be inundated with advertisements and solicitations. Some days, among all of the junk mail, one is fortunate to be able to locate a bill, let alone a letter from a friend or loved one. Insult is added to injury when one realizes that individual citizens must pay first class postage rates to send their mail, while junk mail for reasons apparent only to Congress and the United States Postal Service, is sent at less than one-half of that rate.

As much as one might decry this intrusion into our lives and our homes and sympathize with Joshua's plight, eliminating it lies with Congress, not the courts. Our courts are too heavily overburdened to be used as a vehicle to punish by one whose only real damage is feeling foolish for having opened what obviously was junk mail. Only in circumstances of actual detriment should a court intrude upon the exercise of what the senders of junk mail might call commercial free speech and the recipients might call intrusive harassment. We therefore affirm the judgment. ①

3.4 Invalid Consideration

In *Harris v. Times, Inc.*, the court found consideration but decided to dismiss the case. In other situations, courts may determine a consideration invalid based on various grounds.

Past Consideration. As indicated above, one of the elements of consideration is legal value, which will be satisfied when one party promises to do something

absurd 不合理的,荒谬的

sanctity 圣洁,崇高,虔诚
inundate 淹没,泛滥

insult 侮辱

decry 对……不赞成,(强烈)反对,(公开)谴责
intrusion (intrude) 侵扰,闯入,侵入
sympathize 同情
plight 困境,苦境
overburden 使装载过多,使负担过重

harassment 骚扰,烦扰

past consideration 过去的对价,以往的对价(指合同订立前已完成的行为、已支持过另外一个合同的对价)

---

① Apparently the court found consideration in this case, but think about why the court granted no relief to the plaintiff?

that he is not legally obligated to do, or forbears from doing something that he is legally entitled to do. Consideration in the form of a benefit conferred in the past — known as past consideration — is not sufficient consideration to support a contract because at the time the promise is made, the promisee is under no obligation to the promisor and suffers no legal detriment in exchange for the promise. At common law, the consideration supporting an existing contract is a past consideration and cannot support the modification of the contract. New consideration is needed in order for the modification to be effective. However, under the UCC, such a modification does not require additional consideration.

Preexisting Obligations. A promise to do something that one is already obligated to do or a promise to refrain from doing something that one is already bound not to do is known as a preexisting obligation. A promise to perform such a preexisting obligation does not constitute consideration. For example, a promise to refrain or to actually refrain from criminal or tortuous activities does not constitute sufficient consideration to support a contract because individuals in society have an existing obligation not to engage in such activities. An officeholder has an existing obligation to perform the acts that the holder of the office is obligated to perform. If he promised to perform such an act in return for benefit, there is no consideration to support such a contract. The existing obligation may also be a past consideration. For example, when one promises to perform an act which he is under a contractual duty to the promisee to perform, which is an existing obligation and a past consideration, in exchange for an additional compensation, it is not enforceable because there was no legal detriment to the promisor who is already obligated to perform.

Discharge of Debts. If one person owes a debt to another person and the parties are in complete agreement as to the amount, such a debt is a liquidated debt. If the debtor promises to discharge such a liquidated debt on payment of part of the debt at the place where the debt is payable and at or after the time the debt is due, such a promise does not constitute legal consideration and a contract based on such a promise will not be

---

be legally obligated to do something 依法律有义务做某事

be legally entitled to do something 依法律有权做某事

confer 给予,赋予

preexisting 事先存在的

criminal activity 犯罪的行为

tortuous activity 侵权行为

officeholder 公务员,官员

discharge of debts 债务免除;债务清偿;债务履行

a liquidated debt 额定债务(指金额已由当事人协议确定或经法律程序确定的债务)

enforceable in the courts. The Restatement (Second) of Contracts § 73 states that "[p]erformance of a legal duty owed to a promisor which is neither doubtful nor the subject of honest dispute is not consideration; but a similar performance is consideration if it differs from what was required by the duty in a way which reflects more than a <u>pretense</u> of bargain." However, a creditor may make a gift of a <u>balance</u> following <u>a partial payment</u> or the debtor may offer some additional consideration in the form of something he was not obligated to do and then the contract will be enforced.

There are exceptions to the above general rule. For example, if the alleged debtor and creditor have an honest dispute as to the existence or amount of a claim, that is, the debt is not liquidated, they may make a <u>compromise</u> to allow the debtor to discharge the debt by making partial payment. Such a compromise, sometimes called "<u>accord and satisfaction</u>," will be held to constitute consideration and will be enforceable. Another example is a <u>composition</u>, which is an agreement between a debtor and two or more of his creditors whereby the debtor agrees to pay each creditor <u>a pro rata share</u> of his claim and each creditor agrees to accept that amount in full satisfaction of his claim. Such agreements are generally enforced, as long as they are free from misrepresentation, fraud, duress, or undue influence, on the grounds that sound business practice requires enforcement.

pretense 假装, 伪称
balance 余额
a partial payment 部分支付, 部分偿付
compromise 和解, 妥协（这里指争议双方或各方互相妥协解决争议的协议, 如债务人以部分偿付换取债权人不再追究其余欠债）
accord and satisfaction 和解和清偿（指解除债务的一种方法, 双方当事人协议由一方为一定给付而另一方接受, 从而解除债务）
composition 和解协议（指债务人不能足额偿还债务时, 债务人同两个或两个以上债权人就只偿还部分债务而免除全部债务责任所达成的协议）
a pro rata share 按比例

3.5 Case 7: Slattery v. Wells Fargo Armored Service Corp.

Court of Appeal of Florida, Third District
Slattery v. Wells Fargo Armored Service Corp.
366 So. 2d 157
January 16, 1979

Opinion by: *Per Curiam* ①
Appellant/plaintiff, a licensed <u>polygraph</u> operator,

per curiam 由法庭全体（同意）
appellant 上诉人
polygraph 测谎仪

---

① Most of the cases we have read so far tell us the author of the opinion in the beginning of it; however, sometimes the author of the opinion is not indicated for various reasons, such as the case is very sensitive or very simple. In that case, "*Per Curiam*" will be found in the beginning of the opinion meaning that this opinion was written by the whole court instead of indicating the judge who actually wrote this opinion.

appeals from an "order granting summary judgment and summary final judgment" rendered in favor of appellee/defendant Wells Fargo Armored Service Corp., in an action wherein appellant claimed and was denied the following reward offered by appellee:

$25,000 REWARD

Wells Fargo Armored Service Corporation of Florida announces a reward of up to $25,000 for information leading to the arrest and conviction of the person or persons participating in the shooting of a Wells Fargo agent, the subsequent robbery which occurred on Saturday, February 22, 1975 at Miami, Florida, and the recovery of valuables lost as a result of this occurrence.

Information should be directed to Wells Fargo Armored Service Corporation of Florida, P. O. Box 011028, Miami, Florida 33101, Telephone Number (305) 324-4900. The person or persons to whom the reward or any part thereof should be paid will be determined by the Board of Directors of Wells Fargo Armored Service Corporation of Florida.

Appellant contends that he was entitled to the reward by virtue of his questioning of the perpetrator of the crime during a polygraph examination on an unrelated matter. Such questioning, which occurred on two separate days, eventually resulted in a statement by the perpetrator that he had shot and killed the Wells Fargo guard, which ultimately led to his conviction and sentence for the crime. Appellant argues that, but for his expertise in interrogation and the operation of a polygraph, the authorities would not have linked the perpetrator to the crime. Thus, appellant contends, he is entitled to the reward offered by appellee.

The trial judge, rejecting appellant's argument, entered summary final judgment in favor of appellee on the ground that the offer of reward was never accepted by appellant in that the performance called for by the terms of the offer had not been completed. In particular, the trial judge referred to a stipulation entered into by the parties whereby it was agreed that the stolen property belonging to appellee had not been returned. In that both requirements of the unilateral offer of contract had not been performed (the arrest and conviction of the perpetrator and the return of the stolen property to Wells Fargo) the trial judge determined that appellant had not accepted the offer and thus, no contract had been established. Therefore, the trial judge entered summary final judgment in favor of appellee.

After carefully reviewing the record on appeal, it is our opinion that summary judgment was proper, but not for the reason relied upon by the trial judge. Initially, it must be kept in mind that a reward is contractual in nature, requiring the acceptance of an offer supported by consideration. *Sumerel v. Pinder*, 83 So. 2d 692 (Fla. 1955). The trial judge based his ruling upon the reason that the terms of the offer amounted to dependent covenants, necessitating the performance of each as a prerequisite to an "acceptance." On the other hand, appellant argues that the covenants are independent of each other and acceptance of the offer of reward was completed upon the satisfaction of one covenant (the arrest and conviction of the culprit). Whether or not the conditions of the offer amounted to independent or dependent covenants is a factual question of intent, the resolution of which *sub judice*①, was improper on motion for summary judgment. *Duncan Properties, Inc. v. Key Largo Ocean View, Inc.*, 360 So. 2d 471; *Mabry Corporation v. Dobry*, 141 So. 2d 335. As such, the entrance of summary final judgment for the above reason was incorrect, as the record revealed an issue of fact as to the intent of appellee in making its offer of reward.

The record, however, additionally reveals the following facts which do support the entrance of summary judgment. Firstly, while appellant was an independent contractor, during the polygraph interrogation he was employed by either the office of the State Attorney or the Dade County Public Safety

ruling 决定,裁决(指法官在庭审过程中对证据的可采性、对申请是否许可等问题所作的决定)

dependent covenant 附条件合同条款,在先履行合同条款

necessitate 使成为必需,需要;迫使

prerequisite 先决条件,必要条件,前提

culprit 刑事被告人,犯罪人

sub judice 在审判中,尚未裁决,未决审理

entrance (enter) 作出(判决)

reveal 披露,透露,显示

an issue of fact 事实上的争点

independent contractor 独立承揽人,独立合同当事人(其虽受雇承担特定工作任务,但却可以自由从事该特定工作并自由选择完成任务的方法)

---

① "*Sub Judice*" means something undetermined; under or before a judge or court; under judicial consideration.

ascertain 查明,弄清,确定	
capacity 身份,地位	
law enforcement 执法	

Department and was paid for his services on an hourly rate. Further, while so employed, appellant was under a duty to provide his employers with any and all information ascertained by him through interrogation which might be of aid to the State Attorney or Public Safety Department in their capacity as law enforcement agencies.

Secondly, the record demonstrates that through the first day of interrogation, appellant was unaware of the offer of reward. Only on the second day of questioning did appellant have the knowledge that a reward had been offered by appellee. On that second day, the perpetrator of the crime confessed prior to the actual interrogation by appellant.

confess 承认,供认,坦白

The law is well settled in this state that before a reward is entitled to be collected, the offeree must have knowledge of the existence of the offer of reward. *Sumerel v. Pinder, supra, see* generally ANNOTATION, 86 A. L. R. 3d 1142, *Knowledge of Reward as Condition of Right Thereto* (1978). *Sub judice*, appellant had no knowledge of the reward until the second day of questioning, at which time the perpetrator confessed prior to any interrogation. On this basis alone, summary judgment would have been proper.

We, however, choose to uphold the summary judgment on the ground that appellant was under a pre-existing duty to furnish his employers with all useful information revealed to him through interrogation of the perpetrator. Thus, when appellant "accepted" the offer of reward by furnishing information to the authorities, he was doing no more than he was already bound to do as part of his employment. The performance of a pre-existing duty does not amount to the consideration necessary to support a contract. *Brinson v. Herlong*, 121 Fla. 505, 164 So. 137 (1935). As such, no contract was formed.

furnish with 供给,提供

corollary 必然结果;推断,推论

public policy 公共政策,公共利益

tantamount to 相当于

undermine 渐渐破坏,暗地里破坏

integrity 正直,诚实,廉洁(用以指官员、受托人等的品性)

Further, as a corollary to the above and as a matter of public policy, it is our opinion that to allow appellant to recover a reward for the furnishing of information to the authorities, when he was under a duty to furnish such information as part of his employment, would be tantamount to undermining the integrity and the efforts of those involved in law enforcement. *See Davis v. Mathews*, 361 F. 2d 899 (4th Cir. 1966); *Chester v. State*, 176 So. 2d 104 (Fla. 1st DCA 1965); American Law Institute, RESTATEMENT OF THE LAW OF CONTRACTS 2D (TENTATIVE DRAFT) § 76A.

Accordingly, as no genuine issues of material fact were left unresolved, and as it affirmatively appears that appellee was entitled to judgment as a matter of law, the summary final judgment entered in favor of appellee is hereby affirmed.

Affirmed. ①

3.6 Promissory Estoppel

A contract may also be validated by a substitute to consideration in order to avoid injustices. The most common doctrine is promissory estoppel, which is also called <u>detrimental reliance</u>. Where a person makes a promise which he reasonably can expect will induce the promisee to rely on the promise and to take some definite and substantial action or forbear from some substantial course of action which is detrimental to the promisor, then the promise will be enforced on the grounds of promissory estoppel. The <u>rational</u> is that since the promise led the promisee to <u>justifiably</u> rely on the promise and to change the position to his or her detriment, the promisor <u>is estopped from</u> setting up the lack of consideration as a defense to enforcement of the promise.

The fundamental difference between consideration and promissory estoppel is the absence of bargained-for-exchange in the detrimental reliance situation. The classic consideration <u>formula</u> is that the promise must induce the detriment and the detriment must induce the promise, at least to some degree. Under the promissory estoppel concept, however, where the promisor should reasonably expect the promisee to suffer a detriment and the promisee does suffer such a detriment, the promise will now be enforceable where the promise induces the detriment but the detriment does not induce the promise. Thus, unlike consideration, promissory

detrimental reliance 不利益的信赖,致人损害的信赖(由于一方当事人对他人的行为或陈述产生信赖,从而导致自己处于不利地位,则该种信赖即属不利益的信赖。不利益的信赖是"允诺不容否定"的另一种说法,可以替代合同的对价,使某一单方的允诺成为可强制执行的合同)

rational 理论,道理,原则

justifiably 合理地,有正当理由地

be estopped from 不容否认,被禁止

formula 公式,规则

---

① The appellate court affirmed the trial court's decision; however, the appellate court did not agree with the trial court's reasoning at all. What is the difference?

estoppel does not require a bargained-for-exchange.

A common example of a situation where promissory estoppel may be applied is the charitable subscription — the promise to make a gift to some religious, educational, or charitable organization. If the organization changes its position in reliance on the promised gift, then the promise to make a gift will be enforced. The following is one of the most famous cases discussing this doctrine.

3.7 Case 8: Ricketts v. Scothorn

Supreme Court of Nebraska
Ricketts v. Scothorn
57 Neb. 51, 77 N.W. 365
Dec. 8, 1898.

Sullivan, J.

In the district court of Lancaster county, the plaintiff, Katie Scothorn, recovered judgment against the defendant, Andrew D. Ricketts, as executor of the last will and testament of John C. Ricketts, deceased. The action was based upon a promissory note, of which the following is a copy: "May the first, 1891. I promise to pay to Katie Scothorn on demand, $2,000, to be at 6 per cent. per annum. J.C. Ricketts."

In the petition the plaintiff alleges that the consideration for the execution of the note was that she should surrender her employment as bookkeeper for Mayer Bros., and cease to work for a living. She also alleges that the note was given to induce her to abandon her occupation, and that, relying on it, and on the annual interest, as a means of support, she gave up the employment in which she was then engaged.

These allegations of the petition are denied by the administrator. The material facts are undisputed. They are as follows:

John C. Ricketts, the maker of the note, was the grandfather of the plaintiff. Early in May — presumably on the day the note bears date — he called on her at the store where she was working. What transpired between them is thus described by Mr.

Flodene, one of the plaintiff's witnesses:

> A. Well, the old gentleman came in there one morning about nine o'clock, probably a little before or a little after, but early in the morning, and he unbuttoned his vest, and took out a piece of paper in the shape of a note; that is the way it looked to me; and he says to Miss Scothorn, "I have fixed out something that you have not got to work any more." He says, "none of my grandchildren work, and you don't have to."
>
> Q. Where was she?
>
> A. She took the piece of paper and kissed him, and kissed the old gentleman, and <u>commenced</u> to cry.

commence 开始

It seems Miss Scothorn immediately notified her employer of her intention to <u>quit</u> work, and that she did soon after abandon her occupation. The mother of the plaintiff was a witness, and testified that she had a conversation with her father, Mr. Ricketts, shortly after the note was executed, in which he informed her that he had given the note to the plaintiff to enable her to quit work; that none of his grandchildren worked, and he did not think she ought to. For something more than a year the plaintiff was without an occupation, but in September, 1892, with the consent of her grandfather, and by his assistance, she <u>secured a position</u> as bookkeeper with Messrs. Funke & Ogden. On June 8, 1894, Mr. Ricketts died. He had paid one year's interest on the note, and a short time before his death expressed regret that he had not been able to pay the balance. In the summer or fall of 1892 he stated to his daughter, Mrs. Scothorn, that if he could sell his farm in Ohio he would pay the note out of the <u>proceeds</u>. He at no time <u>repudiated</u> the obligation.

quit 停止,中断,放弃

secure a position 获得职位

proceeds 收入,收益(指因出售财产或从事其他商业活动所得的收益,如变卖财产所得的价款)

repudiate 拒绝履行(合同或义务等),拒绝接受,抛弃

peremptorily 专横地,不容分说地

We quite agree with counsel for the defendant that upon this evidence there was nothing to submit to the jury, and that a verdict should have been directed <u>peremptorily</u> for one of the parties. The testimony of Flodene and Mrs. Scothorn, taken together, conclusively establishes the fact that the note was not given in consideration of the plaintiff pursuing, or agreeing to pursue, any particular line of conduct. There was no promise on the part of the plaintiff to do, or refrain from doing, anything. Her right to the money promised in the note was not made to depend upon an abandonment of her employment with Mayer Bros., and future abstention from like service. Mr. Ricketts made no condition, requirement, or request. He exacted no quid pro quo①. He gave the note as a gratuity, and looked for nothing in return. So far as the evidence discloses, it was his purpose to place the plaintiff in a position of independence, where she could work or remain idle, as she might choose. The abandonment of Miss Scothorn of her position as bookkeeper was altogether voluntary. It was not an act done in fulfillment of any contract obligation assumed when she accepted the note. The instrument in suit, being given without any valuable consideration, was nothing more than a promise to make a gift in the future of the sum of money therein named.

Ordinarily, such promises are not enforceable, even when put in the form of a promissory note. *Kirkpatrick v. Taylor*, 43 Ill. 207; *Phelps v. Phelps*, 28 Barb. 121; *Johnston v. Griest*, 85 Ind. 503; *Fink v. Cox*, 18 Johns. 145. But it has often been held that an action on a note given to a church, college, or other like institution, upon the faith of which money has been expended or obligations incurred, could not be successfully defended on the ground of a want of consideration. *Barnes v. Perine*, 12 N. Y. 18; *Philomath College v. Hartless*, 6 Or. 158; *Thompson v. Board*, 40 Ill. 379; *Irwin v. Lombard University*, 56 Ohio St. 9, 46 N. E. 63. In this class of cases the note in suit is nearly always spoken of as a gift or donation, but the decision is generally put on the ground that the expenditure of money or assumption of liability by the donee on the faith of the promise constitutes a valuable and sufficient consideration. It seems to us that the true reason is the preclusion of the

---

① Giving one valuable thing for another. It is nothing more than the mutual consideration which passes between the parties to a contract, and which renders it valid and binding.

defendant, under the doctrine of estoppel, to deny the consideration. Such seems to be the view of the matter taken by the supreme court of Iowa in the case of *Simpson Centenary College v. Tuttle*, 71 Iowa, 596, 33 N. W. 74, where Rothrock, J., speaking for the court, said:

> "Where a note, however, is based on a promise to give for the support of the objects referred to, it may still be open to this defense [want of consideration], unless it shall appear that the donee has, prior to any revocation, entered into engagements, or made expenditures based on such promise, so that he must suffer loss or injury if the note is not paid. This is based on the equitable principle that, after allowing the donee to incur obligations on the faith that the note would be paid, the donor would be estopped from pleading want of consideration."

equitable principle 衡平法原则

donor 赠与人，捐赠人

And in the case of *Reimensnyder v. Gans*, 110 Pa. St. 17, 2 Atl. 425, which was an action on a note given as a donation to a charitable object, the court said: "The fact is that, as we may see from the case of *Ryerss v. Trustees*, 33 Pa. St. 114, a contract of the kind here involved is enforceable rather by way of estoppel than on the ground of consideration in the original undertaking." It has been held that a note given in expectation of the payee performing certain services, but without any contract binding him to serve, will not support an action. *Hulse v. Hulse*, 84 E. C. L. 709. But when the payee changes his position to his disadvantage in reliance on the promise, a right of action does arise. *McClure v. Wilson*, 43 Ill. 356; *Trustees v. Garvey*, 53 Ill. 401.

payee 受款人，收款人

Under the circumstances of this case, is there an equitable estoppel which ought to preclude the defendant from alleging that the note in controversy is lacking in one of the essential elements of a valid contract? We think there is. An *estoppel in pais* is defined to be "a right arising from acts, admissions, or conduct which have induced a change of position in accordance with the real or apparent intention of the

estoppel in pais 因既有行为而不容否认（指当事人由于其先前的行为或不当沉默而自受约束，以后不得自相矛盾，作相反的主张）

party against whom they are alleged." Mr. Pomeroy has formulated the following definition:

> Equitable estoppel is the effect of the voluntary conduct of a party whereby he is absolutely precluded, both at law and in equity, from asserting rights which might, perhaps, have otherwise existed, either of property, of contract, or of remedy, as against another person who in good faith relied upon such conduct, and has been led thereby to change his position for the worse, and who on his part acquires some corresponding right, either of property, of contract, or of remedy.

2 POM. EQ. JUR. 804.

According to the undisputed proof, as shown by the record before us, the plaintiff was a working girl, holding a position in which she earned a salary of $10 per week. Her grandfather, desiring to put her in a position of independence, gave her the note, accompanying it with the remark that his other grandchildren did not work, and that she would not be obliged to work any longer. In effect, he suggested that she might abandon her employment, and rely in the future upon the bounty which he promised. He doubtless desired that she should give up her occupation, but, whether he did or not, it is entirely certain that he contemplated such action on her part as a reasonable and probable consequence of his gift. Having intentionally influenced the plaintiff to alter her position for the worse on the faith of the note being paid when due, it would be grossly inequitable to permit the maker, or his executor, to resist payment on the ground that the promise was given without consideration. The petition charges the elements of an equitable estoppel, and the evidence conclusively establishes them. If errors intervened at the trial, they could not have been prejudicial.

A verdict for the defendant would be unwarranted. The judgment is right, and is affirmed.

Review Questions

1. Do you think the *Mirror Image Rule* is essential to the formation of contract? Does the modern trend bring any problems?
2. Explain the possible problems that may be raised by the advertisements, rewards, bids, or auctions, and analyze the solutions to them.
3. Explain the exceptions to the general rule that an offer may be revoked by the offeror at any time before it is accepted.
4. Do you think the mailbox rule is acceptable? Explain.
5. Is it easy to understand the concept of legal detriment and legal benefit? Think of some examples to illustrate.
6. Distinguish the past consideration and pre-existing consideration.
7. Explain the doctrine of promissory estoppel.

CHAPTER 3
DEFENSES

　　如果一方当事人(原告)想起诉另一方(被告)违约,则原告必须首先证明原告与被告之间的合同已然有效成立。然而,即便原告能够证明合同已然有效成立,也并不能当然得出原告必然胜诉的结论,因为被告可能会提出抗辩。只有当被告没有任何合法抗辩理由时,法院才会认定原告与被告之间的合同有效成立,然后接下来才可能讨论被告是否违约的问题。因此,如果用公式来说明:

原告"初步证明"合同有效成立 + 被告没有任何合法抗辩理由 = 合同有效成立

　　前一章介绍了英美合同法中合同初步成立的要件,本章则具体讨论几种常见的针对合同有效成立的抗辩理由,包括虚假陈述、错误理解、胁迫、不当影响、当事人系限制或无民事行为能力人、合同非法、合同形式违反反欺诈法要求以及违反口头证据规则等。只要任何一种抗辩理由得到法院的支持,则原告的违约之诉就必败无疑。因此,在证明合同初步成立之余,原告往往需要排除被告有任何合法抗辩理由的可能性。

CHAPTER 3 DEFENSES

1. Misrepresentation

In order for a contract to be enforceable, it must have been entered into voluntarily, fairly, and honestly. If an offer or acceptance was induced by misrepresentations, it is not binding on the person so induced to make the offer or acceptance. In that case, misrepresentation can be used as an effective defense to <u>negate</u> the plaintiff's allegations.

Misrepresentation is the creation of an impression in the mind of another person which is not <u>in accord with</u> the actual facts of the situation. If the person making the misrepresentation did not know it was false, then this misrepresentation may be called an <u>innocent misrepresentation</u>. If the person made the misrepresentation knowing it was false, it is an <u>intentional misrepresentation</u>, or referred to as <u>fraud</u>. So, fraud is defined as an intentional misrepresentation of <u>a material fact</u> made with the intent to induce another to rely on it and to surrender a legal right or piece of property. Whether or not the person making the misrepresentation knew it was false does not affect the <u>voidability</u> of the contract.

The misrepresentation must be of a material fact, that is, the fact must have been a <u>relevant</u> or <u>contributing factor</u> in the decision to contract, and the circumstances must be such that it can be assumed that the contract would not have been made if the person had known the true facts. In addition, the party seeking the remedy must have been justified in relying on the misrepresentations. He must neither know they were false nor be in a position that in view of his knowledge and experience and in view of facts and circumstances he should have discovered the <u>falsity</u>.

Once innocent misrepresentation is found, the person to whom the misrepresentation is made has the right to rescind the contract — that is, he may return what he has received and recover what he has given, or its value. Where actual fraud is shown, the injured party who justifiably relied on the <u>fraudulent</u>

negate 否定,抵消
in accord with 与……一致
innocent misrepresentation 善意的误述(指当事人并非出于欺骗或欺诈目的,而是因为错误地相信该陈述系真实而作出的误述)
intentional misrepresentation 故意的误述,故意作出的虚假陈述
fraud (fraudulent) 欺诈(欺诈性的)
a material fact 重大事实

voidability 无效,可撤销

relevant 有关的,相关的
contributing factor 起作用的因素

falsity 虚假,虚妄,不真实,不正确

statement has a choice of remedies. He may either rescind the contract or may affirm the contract and bring a tort action for deceit, which would allow him or her to recover damages for the injury sustained. In all circumstances, the aggrieved party must act within a reasonable time after discovery of the misrepresentation or fraud so as to preserve his rights.

2. Mistake

Mistake is a belief that is not in accord with the facts. A contract is not enforceable if it is formed based on a mistake which results from an ambiguity in the negotiation of the contract, or where there was a mistake as to a material fact which induced the making of the contract. Thus mistake is one of the defenses the defendant may use in a breach of contract litigation to relieve his contractual obligations. Here the mistake does not mean ignorance, inability, bad bargain, or bad judgment. For instance, if in negotiating a contract, the parties used language which is susceptible to more than one interpretation, and one party honestly draws one interpretation while the other party draws another, then the courts will usually hold that no contract resulted since there was no meeting of the minds or mutual agreement.

A mistake can occur at the time of formation, integration, or performance. A mistake may be mutual or unilateral. If both parties were under a misunderstanding as to the existence or nonexistence of the material fact, this is known as a mutual mistake and it is grounds for rescission of the contract. Where the mistake is unilateral in that it is made by only one of the parties, the contract may or may not be enforced. If one of the parties realizes that the other person is operating under a mistaken belief and seeks to take advantage of the error, relief will be granted. While negligence on the part of the party making the mistake usually will not justify the granting of relief, it will be granted where the negligence was slight, where enforcement would impose an unwarranted hardship on the person who made the mistake, and where relief would not impose a material loss on the other party. Relief will also be granted to reform a written document which contains a mistake and which does not correctly set out the actual agreement of the parties. A mistake as to one's legal rights under a contract is usually not sufficient grounds for granting relief, as ignorance of the law is not considered to be excusable.

In *Sherwood v. Walker*, 66 Mich. 568, 33 N.W. 919 (1887), Walker, a breeder of cattle, sold a cow to Sherwood, a banker. Because both parties believed that the cow was sterile the purchase price was $80. Walker discovered that the cow Rose was not sterile. He refused to deliver the cow because it was worth $750 or more. Sherwood brought an action to replevy the cow and the court held for Walker: "If there is a difference or misapprehension as to the substance of the thing bargained for; if the thing actually delivered or received is different in substance from the thing bargained for, and intended to be sold, then there is no contract; but if it be only a difference in some quality or accident, even though the mistake may have been the actuating motive to the purchaser or seller, or both of them, yet the contract remains binding."

In *Boise Junior College District v. Mattefs Construction Co.*, 92 Idaho 757, 450 P.2d 604 (1969), the defendant submitted a bid on a construction contract which was irrevocable for 45 days after the bids were opened. After the bids were opened, it was found that only one of ten bids was lower and the lowest bidder withdrew. On the day the bids were opened, defendant learned that it had made a mistake in its bid by failing to include the cost of glass in the construction. When plaintiff demanded compliance with the bid, defendant refused. The court applied the following criteria in determining whether relief should be granted to the contractor because of this clerical error: (1) Was the mistake material? (2) Would enforcement of the contract be unconscionable? (3) Did the mistake resulted from "any positive duty or culpable negligence"? (4) Would the plaintiff suffer severe hardship if the contractor were afforded relief? and (5) Was prompt notice of the mistake given?

reform 修改（合同）

ignorance of the law 对法律的不知
excusable 可原谅的，可辩解的，可免除的

sterile 不育的

replevy 取回被扣押的财物

misapprehension 误会，误解

criteria 标准，规范，准据
clerical error （文书中的）笔误，书写错误
unconscionable 显失公平的，极不公平的
culpable negligence 应受惩罚的过失，有责过失，负有罪责的过失
severe hardship 严重困难
afford 给予
prompt notice 及时通知，迅速通知

3. Duress

Duress is the exercise of some unlawful constraint on a person whereby one is forced to do an act that one would not otherwise have done. In contract law, duress means the use of threats of bodily or other harm which are used to overcome a person's free will and induce the person to enter a contract through fear or force. As presently interpreted, duress includes threats of physical harm, threats to bring a criminal action which are used to gain an advantage to which the maker of the threat is not legally entitled, and the unjustified withholding of a person's goods for the purpose of forcing that person to pay an unreasonable charge. A threat to initiate a civil suit is not considered to be duress unless it amounts to an abuse of civil process or unless it is based on an unfounded claim and the maker of the threat knows that because of the financial position of the other person the suit would likely bring financial ruin to that person. Duress is one of the defenses to the validity of the contract.

4. Undue Influence

Undue influence is the use of a confidential relationship, in which one person owes another a duty to look out for the latter person's interests, and where the duty-bound person uses this position for personal benefit at the expense of the person to whom the duty is owed. By allowing such contracts to be voided, the courts protect against unfair contracts which are shocking to the conscience and are obtained through breach of a confidential position. Thus a contract is void if undue influence is found.

5. Capacity of Parties

Capacity is the ability to perform legally valid acts, i.e., the ability to incur legal liability or to acquire legal rights. To have a legally binding contract there must be two parties to the contract — a promisor and a promisee. Without the capacity, nobody can form a valid contract. Everyone is presumed to have the capacity to contract, so the defendant must affirmatively set out the defense of incapacity in the answer to the complaint.

Minors who are generally defined by statute as persons under 21 years of age in some states and under 18 years of age in others do not own full legal capacity under common law. It often happens that an adult may sign a contract with a minor. In order to protect the minors' interests, the law allows a minor to disaffirm or ratify his contracts. In other words, a minor's contract binds both the minor and the adult unless the minor exercises his right to disaffirm the contract. Thus the minor's contracts are not void but rather only voidable at his option. If the minor chooses to be bound by the contract, *i.e.*, ratify the contract, then the relation between the parties is the same as it is between two parties who both have the same capacity to contract.

Although the minors have the absolute right to disaffirm their executed contract, they are liable for the reasonable value of necessaries furnished to them based on *quasi* contract theory and not on any express promise to pay. The minors' right to disaffirm their contracts is not without limitation. Generally, this right must be exercised at any time from the time the contract is entered into until a reasonable time after the minor reaches majority age. Contracts affecting the title to real estate cannot be disaffirmed during minority but only during a reasonable time after reaching majority age. The minor is bound until he does disaffirm, and failure to do so within a reasonable time after reaching majority amounts to a waiver of the right to disaffirm. The right to disaffirm is not conditioned upon the minor's ability to return any consideration received, but the minor normally must return any consideration still in his or her possession so as to prevent the right of disaffirmance from being used as a device to defraud adults. The minor will be entitled to recover any consideration given the adult after disaffirming a contract. If the minor misrepresented his age to the adult, this does not prevent the minor from disaffirming in most states; however, on disaffirmance of the contract the minor must return the consideration received and

capacity 行为能力,责任能力
full legal capacity 完全民事行为能力
adult 成年人
disaffirm (disaffirmance) 撤销
ratify 追认,认可

necessaries 必需品(在英美合同法中,尽管未成年人或心智不健全者没有缔约能力,但如果其缔约目的是为了获得必需品,则该合同具有法律约束力。这里的必需品并不仅指为维护未成年人或心智不健全者生存所需的东西,而应依其经济能力、身份、地位、职业、其社交圈中的习惯、其本人或其父母的财富等各种情况为标准进行判断,与上述情况相适应的合理所需亦属必需品)
majority age 法定成年年龄

device 工具,诡计
defraud 欺诈

account for its use and depreciation in value.

A minor may not ratify his or her contract until he reaches majority age. Ratification consists of words or acts which signify an intent to be bound by the contract. In the case of an executed contract, failure to act within a reasonable time after reaching majority age amounts to ratification regardless of whether the minor has realized he has the right to disaffirm. Some courts do not hold mere inaction sufficient to ratify an executory contract. Ratification makes the contract valid from its inception and once accomplished, it cannot be undone.

The contract of an insane person is voidable if it was made while he was under that incapacity; however, if the person had been declared insane by a court then most states hold contracts made by the insane person to be void and of no effect. The usual test of insanity is whether or not the contracting person at the time the contract was entered into had sufficient capacity to comprehend the nature of the business being transacted. Like minors, insane persons are liable for the reasonable value of necessaries furnished to them. If the contract is fair and the other person had no reason to know of the insanity, then upon disaffirmance the insane person must return the other party to the status quo. Alternatively, if the other party had reason to know of the insanity, then upon disaffirmance the insane person need only return any consideration or proceeds of the consideration still remaining in his or her possession. An insane person may be ratified by his or her legal guardian. Any person who at the time of contracting is too intoxicated to comprehend the business being transacted is generally treated in the same manner as if he were insane.

Case 9: Bobby Floars Toyota, Inc. v. Smith, Jr.

Court of Appeals of North Carolina
Bobby Floars Toyota, Inc. v. Smith, Jr.
48 N.C. App. 580; 269 S.E.2d 320
September 2, 1980

Morris, J.

The only question posed for review is whether

defendant Charles Smith's voluntary relinquishing the automobile ten months after attaining the age of majority constitutes a timely disaffirmance of his contract with plaintiff.

The rule in North Carolina regarding a minor's contract liability is as follows:

> It is well settled that the conventional contracts of an infant, except those for necessities and those authorized by statute, are voidable at the election of the infant and may be disaffirmed by the infant during minority or within a reasonable time after reaching majority.
>
> "[W]hat is a reasonable time depends upon the circumstances of each case, no hard-and-fast rule regarding precise time limits being capable of definition." *Insurance Co. v. Chantos*, 25 N.C. App. 482, 490, 214 S.E. 2d 438, 444, cert. denied, 287 N.C. 465, 215 S.E. 2d 624 (1975).

This concept of "reasonable time" is more fully explained in *Weeks v. Wilkins*, 134 N.C. 516, 522, 47 S.E. 24, 26 (1904), where the Court quoted from DEVLIN ON DEEDS, VOL. I, sec. 91:

> The most reasonable rule seems to be that the right of disaffirmance should be exercised within a reasonable time after the infant attains his majority, or else his neglect to avail himself of this privilege should be deemed an acquiescence and affirmation on his part of his conveyance. The law considers his contract a voidable one, on account of its tender solicitude for his rights and the fear that he may be imposed upon in his bargain. But he is certainly afforded ample protection by allowing him a reasonable time after he reaches his majority to determine whether he will abide by his conveyance, executed while he was a minor, or will disaffirm it. And it is no more than just and reasonable that if he silently acquiesces in his deed and makes no effort to express his dissatisfaction with his act, he should, after the lapse of a reasonable time, dependent

relinquish 放弃,抛弃,弃权
attain（the age）达到（一定年龄）

conventional 传统的,惯例的,常规的
infant 未成年人（指未满法定成年年龄之人）
at the election of 有权从……中选择其一

hard-and-fast rule 硬性规则

cert.（certiorari）denied 调卷令被拒绝（指针对上诉法院的判决向最高法院提起的上诉请求被驳回）

neglect 懈怠,不作为
avail oneself of 利用
privilege 特权,特惠,特免
deem 理解为,视为
acquiescence（acquiesce）默认,默许
affirmation 确认
conveyance 财产（权）转移

abide by 遵守,信守

deed 不动产交易文书

upon circumstances, be considered as fully ratifying it.

This rule was cited and applied in many early cases, sometimes modified by a special rule applying exclusively to conveyances of land, where the court in some situations deemed three years after majority as a reasonable time within which to disaffirm a deed or mortgage executed before majority. *Faircloth v. Johnson*, 189 N.C. 429, 127 S.E. 346 (1925).

Applying the general rule in an action involving a contract concerning personalty, the Court in *Hight v. Harris*, 188 N.C. 328, 124 S.E. 623 (1924), for example, held that an infant may avoid such a contract on account of his infancy during his minority or on coming of age, "if he acts promptly in the matter." 188 N.C. at 330, 124 S.E. at 624. *See also Insurance Co. v. Chantos*, 293 N.C. 431, 238 S.E. 2d 597 (1977); *Eubanks v. Eubanks*, supra. In *Insurance Co. v. Chantos*, 25 N.C. App. 482, 214 S.E. 2d 438, cert. denied, 287 N.C. 465, 215 S.E. 2d 624 (1975), this Court stated that "the defendant's silence or acquiescence for eight months after reaching majority may work as an implied ratification, that determination depending upon whether his failure to disaffirm within that eight-month period was within a reasonable time . . . ." 25 N.C. App. at 490, 214 S.E. 2d at 444. In the instant case, we believe that ten months is an unreasonable time within which to elect between disaffirmance and ratification, in that this case involves an automobile, an item of personal property which is constantly depreciating in value. Modern commercial transactions require that both buyers and sellers be responsible and prompt.

We are of the further opinion that defendant waived his right to avoid the contract. The privilege of disaffirmance may be lost where the infant affirms or otherwise ratifies the contract after reaching majority. Our Supreme Court has held that, under the particular circumstances, certain affirmations or conduct evidencing ratification were sufficient to bind the infant, regardless of whether a reasonable time for disaffirmance had passed. *E.g.*, *Watson v. Watson*,

204 N. C. 5, 167 S. E. 389 (1933) (acceptance of proceeds from sale of land); *Baggett v. Johnson*, *supra* (inaction); *Weeks v. Wilkins*, *supra* (delay); *Gaylord v. Respass*, 92 N.C. 553 (1885) (inaction); *Caffey v. McMichael*, 64 N. C. 507 (1870) (act of ownership); *McCormic v. Leggett*, 53 N. C. 425 (1862) (acceptance of payment). *See also Chandler v. Jones*, *supra*. *See generally* 43 C. J. S. *Infants* § 168 (1978); SIMPSON ON CONTRACTS § § 106-108 (2d ed. 1965). Application of this rule often leads to an equitable result, particularly where the infant can be fairly said to have recognized and adopted as binding a contract under which the infant accepts the benefits of the contract to the prejudice of the other party.

In the present case, it is clear that defendant Smith recognized as binding the installment note evidencing the debt owed from his purchase of an automobile. It is undisputed that he continued to possess and operate the automobile after his eighteenth birthday, and he continued to make monthly payments as required by the note for ten months after becoming eighteen. In fact, defendant's conduct in returning the automobile and acquiescing in default being entered against him is strong evidence that defendant recognized the security agreement, which provided for repossession after default, as controlling. There is no evidence to indicate that defendant ever made a demand for rescission of the contract because of his infancy or that he ever had any intention of doing so. We hold, therefore, that defendant's acceptance of the benefits and continuance of payments under the contract constituted a ratification of the contract, precluding subsequent disaffirmance.

Reversed and remanded.

6. Illegality

If a statute or other governmental regulation expressly prohibits the enforcement of a contract, the contract is illegal, and courts will not enforce it, notwithstanding the presence of all requirements for an otherwise enforceable agreement.

A contract is illegal if either its formation or its

installment 分期付款

default 未履行债务,违约
security agreement 担保协议,担保合同
repossession 取回,收回(指在赊销或分期付款购物中,如买方未按约定付款,卖方或贷款银行可以取回标的物)

illegality 违法,不合法,非法,非法行为

notwithstanding 尽管

contrary to the public interest	违背公共权益
commission of a crime	犯罪实施
article	物件,商品
usury law	高利贷法(指禁止贷款人以违法高利率收取利息的法律)
Sunday closing law	禁止星期天营业的法规
blue law	严格的法律(旧时禁止星期日营业、饮酒、娱乐等的规定)
penalty	处罚,惩罚
forfeiture	剥夺,没收,充公,丧失
license	许可证,特许证,执照
partnership	合伙,合作关系
corporation	公司,社团,法人
distinction	区分,区别,辨别
regulatory statute	目的为行业监管的制定法
revenue-raising statute	目的为增加财政收入的制定法
unlicensed person	没有执照的人

performance violates law or is contrary to the public interest and to public policy. A contract which provides for the commission of a crime or whose nature tends to induce the commission of a crime is illegal. A contract made for the purpose of aiding the commission of a crime is illegal; however, mere knowledge that the article sold will be used illegally does not make the sale illegal unless the intended use is the commission of a serious crime. Similarly, a contract which cannot be performed without the commission of a tort is illegal; however, the fact that a tort is committed during the performance of a contract does not in itself make the contract illegal. A contract may also be illegal for violating a standard of public policy.

If a statute expressly prohibits or regulates certain types of contract, a contract not in compliance with the statute is illegal. For example, some states have usury laws and Sunday closing or blue laws which may make the relevant contracts void and may subject the parties involved to various penalties and forfeitures. Some states have statutes requiring the obtaining of a license before a person, partnership, or corporation engages in a regulated activity such as the practice of law or medicine or the carrying on of a trade such as barbering or plumbing. If a person contracts to perform such a service or engages in a regulated business without first having obtained the required license, any contracts he makes are illegal. However, a distinction must be made between regulatory statutes which require proof of skill and character before the issuance of a license, and those statutes designed to raise revenue and which permit the issuance of a license to anyone who pays a certain, often substantial, fee. The failure to obtain a license required by a revenue-raising statute does not affect the legality of a contract made by the unlicensed person.

As a general rule, a court will not enforce an illegal contract and will leave the parties in the same position in which it finds them. One party cannot recover damages for breach of an illegal contract, and there is normally no recovery in *quasi* contract for benefits conferred. However, if the interests of the public, as opposed to the interests of one of the parties, are served by allowing a recovery of some sorts, the courts will allow such a recovery. A party who is justifiably ignorant of the facts or special regulation which make the bargain illegal may recover the consideration conferred on the other party. And a person protected by a regulatory statute may recover for breach of contract entered into with a person who has not complied with the statute.

A party may rescind an executory illegal contract before the performance of the illegal act and recover any consideration he has given to the other party. When a contract is only illegal in part, the lawful part may or may not be enforceable. If the illegality is of such a serious kind that a considerable degree of <u>moral turpitude</u> attaches to it, it is probable that the whole bargain will be <u>taint</u>ed and no part of the contract will be enforced. However, if the illegality is not of such a serious character, the result may be different. In this case, if the illegal portion is <u>divisible</u>, then the legal portion may be enforced and the rest disregarded. However, if such a contract cannot be so divided, the entire contract is illegal and void.

Under the UCC, a court may refuse to enforce a contract or a contract clause if it finds the contract or clause to be unconscionable. To be unconscionable, it must be <u>commercially unreasonable</u> and <u>unfair</u> at the time the contract was made. This provision is commonly used to refuse enforcement of contracts where one of the parties used a position of economic or strategic superiority to drive an unreasonable and unfair bargain.

> moral turpitude 违反公德的行为
> taint 污染,败坏

> divisible 可分割的,可分离的

> commercially unreasonable 商业上不合理的
> unfair 不公平的,(商业上)不正当的

Case 10: Strictland v. Gulf Life Ins. Co.

Supreme Court of Georgia
Strickland v. Gulf Life Ins. Co.
240 Ga. 723; 242 S.E. 2d 148
February 14, 1978

Undercofler, Justice.

This is a *certiorari*. *Strickland v. Gulf Life Ins.*

Co., 143 Ga. App. 67 (237 SE2d 530) (1977). It involves a life-accident policy issued in 1946 which, among other things, insures against the loss of a leg. The policy provides coverage if within 90 days of the injury there is "dismemberment by severance." Strickland injured his right lower leg. Medical efforts to save the leg continued for 118 days. They proved unsuccessful and the leg was amputated. Gulf Life denied coverage because severance of the leg was beyond the 90 day limitation. The trial court granted Gulf Life's motion for summary judgment. The Court of Appeals affirmed. We reverse in order that the trial court may consider in the light of this opinion Strickland's pleadings that the condition requiring severance within 90 days is contrary to public policy.

The Court of Appeals, in considering Strickland's appeal from the trial court's grant of summary judgment in favor of the insurance company, relied on our case of *State Farm Mut. Auto. Ins. Co. v. Sewell*, 223 Ga. 31 (153 SE2d 432) (1967), which it had reluctantly followed earlier in *Travelers Ins. Co. v. Pratt*, 130 Ga. App. 331 (203 SE2d 302) (1973) and *Boyes v. Continental Ins. Co.*, 139 Ga. App. 609 (229 SE2d 75) (1976).

In *Sewell* and *Boyes*, the issue was whether the loss incurred was the loss covered by the policy. The plaintiff in *Sewell* had suffered partial loss of his vision; he could make out images and colors and retained some peripheral vision. The Court of Appeals, in *State Farm Mut. Ins. Co. v. Sewell*, 114 Ga. App. 331 (151 SE2d 231) (1966), and in *Ga. Life &c. Ins. Co. v. Sewell*, 113 Ga. App. 443 (148 SE2d 447) (1966), construed the policy language, "the irrecoverable loss of the entire sight" as meaning a loss of sight "for all practical purposes" and affirmed such a charge given in the trial court. This court reversed, holding that the word "entire" had to be construed as meaning entire.

Similarly in *Boyes*, *supra*, the Court of Appeals, following *Sewell*, 223 Ga., *supra*, held that the total loss of use of the plaintiff's left arm was not covered by an insurance policy covering only a loss of a member by severance. This court denied *certiorari*.

A time limitation, as is involved in the case now before us, was presented to the Court of Appeals in *Pratt, supra*. The plaintiff's left foot had been injured in a hunting accident, but was not amputated for eighteen months. During this time he was under constant treatment to avoid the amputation. Although the leg as originally injured was completely useless, there remained the possibility that regeneration might occur. It did not, and amputation was eventually necessary. The policy covered a loss by severance within 90 days of the injury. At that point, the plaintiff's leg was still in a cast. The Court of Appeals, relying on *Sewell*, 223 Ga., *supra*, held that, since the policy required severance within 90 days, rather than merely loss of use during that time, the insurance company was not liable for the loss. *Certiorari* was denied by a divided court.

The plaintiff raised the public policy argument regarding the time limitation now before us in *Pratt*, but the Court of Appeals denied the challenge on the authority of *Randall v. State Mut. Ins. Co.*, 112 Ga. App. 268 (145 SE2d 41) (1965) (death not within 90 days), *Metropolitan Life Ins. Co. v. Jackson*, 79 Ga. App. 263 (53 SE2d 378) (1949) (loss of sight not within 90 days) and *Bennett v. Life & Cas. Ins. Co.*, 60 Ga. App. 228 (3 SE2d 794) (1939) (death not within 30 days). In all of these cases, the Court of Appeals had held that time limitations in an insurance policy were "valid." This court has not directly ruled on this issue. However, "[s]tandardized contracts such as insurance policies, drafted by powerful commercial units and put before individuals on the 'accept this or get nothing' basis, are carefully scrutinized by the courts for the purpose of avoiding enforcement of 'unconscionable' clauses." 6A CORBIN, CONTRACTS § 1376, p. 21.

Where loss of a limb is involved at an arbitrary point in time, here 90 days, the insured under these cases is confronted with the ugly choice whether to continue treatment and retain hope of regaining the use of his leg or to amputate his leg in order to be eligible for insurance benefits which he would forgo if amputation became necessary at a later time. We find

regeneration 恢复,重新生长

a divided court 法官意见有分歧的法院(指上诉审法院对某一具体案件作出判决时,法官不能形成一致意见,尤指多数意见比较微弱的情形)

insurance policy 保单,保险单

standardized contract 格式合同

scrutinize 详细检查,细审

arbitrary 专制的
the insured 被保险人
be confronted with 面临

eligible 合格的
forgo 放弃

gruesome 可怕的,阴森的,令人毛骨悚然的	

an insurance limitation forcing such a gruesome choice may be unreasonable and thus may be void as against public policy.

Finding such a limitation unreasonable is not without precedent. In *Burne v. Franklin Life Ins. Co.*, 451 Pa. 218（301 A2d 799, 801）(1973), a pedestrian had been struck by an automobile and had lain in a vegetative state for 4½ years. The insurance company paid the life policy, but refused to pay the double indemnity accidental death benefits which were "payable only if '... such death occurred ... within ninety days from the date of the accident.'"

pedestrian 行人,步行者
in a vegetative state 处于植物人状态的

double indemnity 双重补偿,双重赔偿

As stated in *Burne*, 301 A2d 799, *supra*, at pp. 801 – 802 (*footnote omitted*), "[t]here are strong public policy reasons which militate against the enforceability of the ninety day limitation. The provision has its origins at a much earlier stage of medicine. Accordingly, the leading [Pennsylvania] case construing the provision predates three decades of progress in the field of curative medicine. Advancements made during that period have enabled the medical profession to become startlingly adept at delaying death for indeterminate periods. Physicians and surgeons now stand at the very citadel of death, possessing the awesome responsibility of sometimes deciding whether and what measure should be used to prolong, even though momentarily, an individual's life. The legal and ethical issues attending such deliberations are gravely complex.

militate 产生作用或影响

predate 在日期上早于
curative 治病的,有治病效力的
advancement 前进,进步
startlingly 惊人地,使人惊奇地
adept at 对……很熟练,很内行,很拿手
indeterminate 不明确的,不确定的
awesome 引起敬畏的
prolong 延长,拉长
momentarily 暂时地
ethical 道德的;合乎职业道德标准的
gravely 严重地
paradox 似非而是的论点;自相矛盾的话
victim 受害人
endure 忍耐,忍受
agony (极度的)痛苦

"The result reached by the trial court presents a gruesome paradox indeed — it would permit double indemnity recovery for the death of an accident victim who dies instantly or within ninety days of an accident, but would deny such recovery for the death of an accident victim who endures the agony of prolonged illness, suffers longer, and necessitates greater expense by his family in hopes of sustaining life even momentarily beyond the ninety day period. To predicate liability under a life insurance policy upon death occurring only on or prior to a specific date, while denying policy recovery if death occurs after that fixed date, offends the basic concepts and fundamental objectives of life insurance and [is]

predicate 断定

contrary to public policy. Hence, the ninety day limitation is unenforceable.

"All must recognize the mental anguish that quite naturally accompanies these tragic occurrences. Surely that anguish ought not to be aggravated in cases of this kind with concerns of whether the moment of death permits or defeats the double indemnity claim. So too, the decisions as to what medical treatment should be accorded an accident victim should be unhampered by considerations which might have a tendency to encourage something less than the maximum medical care on penalty of financial loss if such care succeeds in extending life beyond the 90th day. All such factors should, wherever possible, be removed from the antiseptic halls of the hospital. Rejection of the arbitrary ninety day provision does exactly that."

The New Jersey court has also found this reasoning persuasive. "The rule in almost every jurisdiction which has considered the question is that the time limitations set forth in the policy are controlling and that recovery must be denied in a case such as the present one. See Appleman, INSURANCE LAW AND PRACTICE (2D ED. 1963), §612. However, a recent decision by the Supreme Court of Pennsylvania has held that such time limitations are unenforceable and has allowed recovery where death by accident occurred well after the period stipulated in the policy. [Cit. omitted.] Although it is presently very much a minority rule, I am persuaded that the rule announced in *Burne* is the better rule and should be followed." *Karl v. New York Life Ins. Co.*, 139 N.J. Super. 318 (353 A2d 564, 565) (1976). The court thus allowed the beneficiary of a man who had sustained a skull injury in a criminal assault to recover under the accidental double indemnity provisions in his two policies, which contained 90 and 120 day limitations, even though he died 11 months after the assault.

We note further that in *Karl*, *supra*, the court considered the question whether with the minimal cost of the accidental death benefit, it would be unfair to the insurance company to ignore these time limitations in light of the company's economic risk calculations. It concluded, however, that the real purpose of the time

mental anguish 精神上的痛苦

tragic occurrence 悲惨的事件

aggravate (aggravation) (病情、负担等)加重,加剧,使恶化

defeat the claim 使(索赔等)主张落空

accord 给予

unhampered 不受影响,不受妨碍的

tendency 趋向,倾向

persuasive 有说服力的

a minority rule 少数(州或法院采纳的)规则

a criminal assault 企图伤害罪

causal connection 因果联系,因果关系	
premium 保险费	
causation 因果关系	
burden 负担,责任,这里指举证责任	
claimant 提出请求一方,有时也指原告	
establish 确立,证明	
causative relationship 因果关系	
weighty enough problem 有足够分量的问题,足够重要的问题	
liberty of contract 契约自由	
operative 有效的,运作的	
penalize 惩罚	
extol 颂扬,吹捧,称赞	
boon 恩惠,福利	
principal 首要的,主要的,最重要的	
mandate 命令,指示(尤指上诉法院要求下级法院采取指定措施的命令)	

limitation was to limit disputes concerning the causal connection between the death and the accident rather than because of any economic relationship between the premium and the time limitation. Also, the court observed that the reason the cost of accidental death policies was so low was that relatively few deaths occurred because of accidents.

In *INA Insurance Co. v. Commonwealth Ins. Dept.*, 376 A2d 670 (Pa. Cmwlth. 1977), the insurance company also argued that the causation problem was the main reason for these time limitations. That court rejected the argument, observing that the burden was on the claimant to establish the causative relationship, and held that causation was not a weighty enough problem to deny benefits arbitrarily to those surviving beyond the time limitation set out in the policy, but who had died as a result of the accident. Following *Burne*, the court upheld the insurance commissioner's ruling① that all similar time limitations in accident policies are arbitrary and unreasonable and thus against public policy.

"[I]t may be pointed out that 'liberty of contract' as that term is used by its admirers includes two very different elements. These are the privilege of doing the acts constituting the transaction and the power to make it legally operative. One does not have 'liberty of contract' unless organized society both forbears and enforces, forbears to penalize him for making his bargain and enforces it for him after it is made.

"This is the 'liberty of contract' that has so often been extolled as one of the great boons of modern democratic civilization, as one of the principal causes of prosperity and comfort. And yet the very fact that a chapter on 'legality' of contract must be written shows that we have never had and never shall have unlimited liberty of contract, either in its phase of

---

① We note that in the Georgia Insurance Code (Code Ann. Ch. 56), the legislature mandates that "[t]he Commissioner shall disapprove any such form [contract] ... (5) if it contains provisions which are *unfair or inequitable or contrary to the public policy of this State*, or would, because such provisions are unclear or deceptively worded, encourage misrepresentation." Code Ann. § 56-2411. (Emphasis supplied.)

societal forbearance or in its phase of societal enforcement. There are many contract transactions that are definitely forbidden by the law, forbidden under pains and penalties assessed for crime and tort; and there are many more such transactions that are denied judicial enforcement, even though their makers are not subjected to affirmative pains and penalties." 6A CORBIN, CONTRACTS § 1376, p. 20.

Corbin, in his treatise on contracts, also observes that the declaration of public policy is the proper function of the courts, as well as of the legislature. "Constitutions and statutes are declarations of public policy by bodies of men authorized to legislate. It is the function of the courts to interpret and apply these, so far as they go and so far as they are understandable. Some judges have thought that they must look solely to constitutions and statutes and to earlier decisions interpreting and applying them as the sources from which they may determine what public policy requires. This is far from true, even though these are the sources that are first to be considered and that often may be conclusive.①

"In determining what public policy requires, there is no limit whatever to the 'sources' to which the court is permitted to go; and there is no limit to the 'evidence' that the court may cause to be produced, ..." 6A CORBIN, CONTRACTS, § 1375, pp. 15-19. Then, the validity of the contract in question is one of law for the court.② 17A CJS 1238, CONTRACTS, § 615.

"The court can not postpone decision until all

treatise 专著,论述

legislate 立法,制定或通过法律,履行立法职责

cornerstone 基石,基础

---

① "'Public policy is the cornerstone — the foundation of all Constitutions, statutes, and judicial decisions, and its latitude and longitude, its height and its depth, greater than any or all of them. If this be not true, whence came the first judicial decision on matter of public policy? There was no precedent for it, else it would not have been the first.' *Pittsburgh, C. C. & St. L. R. Co. v. Kinney*, 115 NE 505, 507, 95 Ohio St. 64, 67, quoted and applied in *Snyder v. Ridge Hill Memorial Park*, 22 NE2d 559, 61 Ohio App. 271 (1938)." 6A CORBIN, CONTRACTS, § 1375, p. 15, n. 12. (Footnote in original).

② When the validity of a contract is in issue before a court, the judge is obliged to make decision whatever the degree of his ignorance or wisdom. Before decision there should be some debate and much evidence; afterwards the decision is subject to criticism, by litigant and lawyer, by juryman and jurist, by the learner and the scholar. It is thus that the mores, the considered notions as to what makes for human welfare and survival are formed, to be constantly verified or altered in new cases, forever hammered on the anvil of life experience.

judicial notice 司法认知（指法庭对众所周知的且无争议的事实予以承认和接受，从而免除当事人对该事实的举证责任）

at stake 处于危险中或有利害关系

disinterested 公正的，没有利害关系的

pronouncement 宣言，宣告

rehabilitation 康复

possible evidence is in. Sometimes the judge may properly take 'judicial notice' of what is common knowledge and generally held opinion. But it is never wise to jump to a conclusion or to disregard experience; and it is never necessary to decide an issue as to public policy without expert briefing of former decisions and without listening to the testimony of those whose interests are at stake and of disinterested and experienced observers." 6A CORBIN, CONTRACTS §1375, pp. 10 – 11. (Footnotes omitted).

Although we are impressed by the persuasive reasoning of the above authorities, we do not here reach the question of law whether all such policy limitations are void as against public policy, nor indeed whether the 90 day severance clause before us is unenforceable. The trial court granted summary judgment in favor of the insurance company on the authority of *Sewell*, *Pratt*, and *Boyes*, *supra*, and on the basis of the pleadings, the contract of insurance and a stipulation of fact by counsel. The stipulated facts included only the date Strickland had been injured and the date over 90 days later that his right lower leg had been amputated, naming the doctor and place of the amputation. No evidence was produced on the issue, raised in Strickland's pleadings, that the contract was unreasonable, and thus void as against public policy. We are reluctant to make such an important pronouncement without further evidence. For example, medical evidence reported in *Reliance Ins. Co. v. Kinman*, 483 SW2d 166 (Ark. 1972), that it takes about 18 months for bone and nerve tissue to regenerate would be relevant to the reasonableness of the 90 day clause in this insurance policy. Other information important to the court's decision may include, for example, (1) the present state of medical science on rehabilitation of injured limbs; (2) whether the insured had a choice of other policies with other time limitations; (3) whether the time limitation is related to the economic risk of the insurance company and (4) whether there is a relationship between the time limitation and the difficulty of proving causation.

We reverse the Court of Appeals in order that the

trial court may fully consider the public policy issue.
Judgment reversed.

Bowles, Justice, dissenting.

As I read the opinion of the majority, I find only one conclusion reached — that the opinion of the Court of Appeals is reversed so that the matter may be referred back to the trial court to hear evidence, and "*fully consider*" the public policy issue.

Heretofore in Georgia, where the contract is unambiguous, our courts have been able to decide, without the benefit of evidentiary hearings, whether or not a given contract or clause in a given contract violates the public policy of this state. While I do not contend that it is impermissible for a trial judge to hear evidence to aid him in making such a decision, I conclude that the trial judge in this case made his determination based on his experience, common sense, general knowledge prevailing in his community regarding the habits and customs of his people, and prior decisions of our courts touching the question. He was not required by law to hear evidence.

Now, for the first time, we require the trial judge to receive or hear evidence on whether a given contract clause violates public policy. Having done so, he can again use his experience, common sense, and general knowledge, and can again consider prior case law in making a determination as to whether or not the 90 day contract clause in question violates the public policy of this state. Thus, we are forcing him to do what he did not consider necessary in the first instance, in addition to his customary procedure.

The majority opinion does not specifically overrule *Travelers Ins. Co. v. Pratt*, 130 Ga. App. 331 (203 SE2d 302), which has heretofore decided the exact question contra to this position. But to support their argument the majority quotes approvingly from two decisions in other states representing the minority view in America and which are without precedent. The majority says, "An insurance limitation forcing such a gruesome choice may be unreasonable and thus may be void as against public policy." It also castigates "powerful commercial units" and suggests that the

dissenting opinion 异议意见,反对意见(指在法官评议案件中,少数法官不同意多数法官的意见)
majority opinion 多数意见(指在法官评议案件中多数法官的意见,该意见构成判例)
refer back 重审,再审
heretofore 此前
evidentiary hearing 证据性听证,有关证据的听证会

impermissible 不许可的,不容许的

determination 判决,决定,结论
prevail 盛行,通行,被普遍接受,被广泛采用

the first instance 初审,案件的第一审

contra to this position 与此立场不同
quote 引用,引证
approvingly 赞许地,满意地
minority view 少数(州或法院)的观点
be without precedent 没有先例
castigate 严厉批评,谴责

policy of insurance offered in this case may have been offered to the insured on an "accept this or get nothing basis."

The fundamental right of our citizens to legally contract; the fact that the right to contract is paramount public policy of our state and should not be interfered with lightly; and the fact that our appellate courts have heretofore ruled on the exact question one time, and similar questions many times, are disregarded. Unless there is some compelling reason to do so, we do the citizens of Georgia, the practicing lawyers and the lower courts an injustice when we attempt to overrule precedent without justification. I find no compelling reason, in this case, to deviate from the precedent laid down by this court in earlier cases.

I would affirm the opinion of the Court of Appeals without further ado.

I am authorized to state that Justice Jordan joins in this dissent.

7. Statute of Frauds

Except for formal contracts, i.e., contracts under seal, the common law does not require contracts to be evidenced by a writing. However, many common law jurisdictions enacted statutes requiring that certain types of contracts must be in writing signed by the party to be bound and are not enforceable unless they are evidenced by such a writing. These statutes are referred to as the statute of frauds. These classes of contracts falling within the statute of frauds include collateral contracts, contracts for the sale of an interest in real property, contracts which are not capable of performance within a year after they are made, contracts for the sale of goods of a value above a certain fixed amount, contracts to pay a commission for the sale of real estate, and contracts agreeing to pay a debt barred by the statute of limitations or discharged in bankruptcy.

A collateral contract is also called a suretyship contract, which is a three-party relationship in which a principal debtor or obligor promises to pay a certain indebtedness to a <u>creditor</u> or <u>obligee</u>, and a third party, <u>surety</u>, promises to pay the creditor if the principal debtor does not pay. In other words, it is contract one made with an obligee whereby a third person promised to pay the debt, default, or <u>miscarriage</u> of the obligor in the event the obligor fails to perform as obligated. Whether a contract is a collateral contract or is an original contract depends primarily on the intent of the parties. In an original contract the party in question has promised to perform in all events, whereas in the collateral contract the party's performance is required only upon the default of another promisor. For instance, the promise of a father to <u>make good a debt</u> owed by his son in the event the son fails to <u>satisfy</u> it is a collateral contract. The promise of an executor or administrator to be <u>answerable</u> from her own estate of a duty of the decedent's estate is also a collateral contract. Such a contract must be in writing to be enforceable under the statute of frauds.

Any contract which will affect the ownership rights in real property such as contracts to sell, to mortgage, to remove minerals, or to grant <u>easements</u> must be in writing to be enforceable. While <u>leases</u> fall into this category, they are normally covered separately by statute of frauds and whether or not a writing is required will depend on the length of the lease.

Only those executory bilateral contracts that will not be performed within a year after the making of the contract fall under the statute of frauds and must be evidenced by a writing. However, the contract must be bilateral as opposed to unilateral and it cannot have yet been fully performed. And no writing is required if the contract can be performed within a year of the time the contract is made. The one year period is computed from the time the contract comes into existence and not from the time that performance of it is to begin. When a contract is made extending the time in which to perform an existing contract, the time is computed from the day the contract to extend time is entered into until the time for performance under the extended contract will be completed; if this

creditor 债权人
obligee 权利人,债权人
surety 保证人

miscarriage（债务等的）不履行

make good a debt 还债
satisfy 清偿（债务等），履行（义务等）
answerable 应承担（还款等）责任的;有责任的

easement 地役权（指为实现自己土地的利益而使用他人土地的权利）
lease 租赁,租赁权

time period is more than a year, the contract to extend the time for performance must be in writing. Where the time for performance is stated in indefinite terms such as "for life," and under existing conditions it is possible to perform the contract within a year, then no writing is required even though the contract actually takes more than one year to complete.

Contracts for the sale of goods are subject to the UCC, which has its own statute of frauds provisions differing in some slight respects from the general statutes of frauds. Under the UCC, the statute of frauds does not apply to an oral contract for the sale of goods unless the price of the goods is $500 or more. If the goods are of more than this price, then the contract will not be enforceable unless it is evidenced by a memorandum sufficient to indicate that a contract of sale has been entered into by the parties and has been signed by the party against whom enforcement is sought. It is not insufficient if it omits or incorrectly states a term, but if the quantity of goods is understated the contract is not enforceable beyond the quantity of goods so stated. Under the UCC, if an oral contract is made between two merchants, and within a reasonable time thereafter one of the merchants sends the other a written confirmation which would be sufficient as a writing, then the confirmation binds the other party, even though he does not sign it, if he does not object to it in writing within 10 days after its receipt. Part payment or delivery of goods takes the contract out of the statute of frauds but only with respect to the goods paid for or delivered and accepted. Oral contracts for the sale of specially manufactured goods are enforceable if the goods are not suitable for sale in the ordinary course of the seller's business and if the seller has made a substantial beginning on their manufacture or commitment for their procurement prior to repudiation of the oral contract by the buyer. The statute of frauds in the UCC makes contracts unenforceable, not void or voidable, if the provisions of the statute are not complied with.

Although some states require a written contract, the statute of frauds of most states provides that a "memorandum" is required. The memorandum or contract may be made at any time up until the time when the suit is filed, and in the case of a memorandum may consist of several documents which show that they should be taken together as evidence of a single contract. The memorandum or contract must include the names of the parties to the contract, contain the material terms of the contract, and describe the subject matter of the contract with reasonable certainty. In addition, it must be signed by the party against whom enforcement of the contract is to be sought or by that party's authorized agent. An oral variation of a contract which is not evidenced by a sufficient writing or memorandum is not enforceable, although the original contract would be enforceable.

variation 变更,变化

An oral contract which comes within the statute of frauds is not made void or voidable; rather, it is unenforceable in that a court will not aid in its enforcement. A party who has performed his or her duties under an oral contract cannot recover on the contract; but he may recover in *quasi* contract for the value of the benefits conferred on the other party. Part performance of an oral contract for the sale of land where one party has entered into possession and made extensive improvements to the property takes the contract out of the statute of frauds. And an oral contract, once completed, cannot be rescinded on the grounds that it was not evidenced by a writing.

Case 11: Colorado Carpet Installation, Inc. v. Palermo

Court of Appeals of Colorado, Division One
Colorado Carpet Installation, Inc. v. Palermo
647 P. 2d 686
March 18, 1982

Coyte, J.
Defendants appeal from a judgment entered against them for damages for breach of contract. We reverse.
The evidence revealed that plaintiff and defendants negotiated for plaintiff to furnish and install carpeting and tile in the defendants' home.

Plaintiff submitted several bids to defendants, one of which defendant Zuma Palermo orally accepted. Plaintiff then ordered the carpeting and tile from various companies. When the tile arrived, plaintiff delivered it to defendants' home and left it there until the house was ready for it to be laid. When plaintiff's employee arrived to install the tile, a dispute developed and defendant Zuma refused to let plaintiff proceed with the job. Plaintiff removed the tile. Subsequent negotiations proved <u>futile</u> and plaintiff <u>instituted this action</u>.

Defendants contend that plaintiff's claim is barred by the application of §4-2-201, C.R.S. 1973 (the statute of frauds), in that the contract was for the sale of goods with a value in excess of $500 and was not signed by the party to be charged. We agree.

The trial court found that the contract came under the specially manufactured goods exception to the statute of frauds and was therefore enforceable notwithstanding the lack of a signed writing. However, the specially manufactured goods exception applies only when goods are not a <u>stock item</u> and are <u>unsuitable for sale to others in the ordinary course of business</u>. See §4-2-201(3)(a), C.R.S. 1973; *Saliba v. Reed Electric Co.*, 90 Colo. 287, 8 P. 2d 1095 (1932).

Here, the carpeting was a standard item carried by a number of carpeting distributors. It was not specially cut to fit the particular dimensions of defendants' rooms, but rather, was taken off a full roll of carpeting. The plaintiff was able to resell two of the rugs, which fact further indicates that it was suitable for sale to others in the ordinary course of business. See *Saliba v. Reed Electric Co.*, *supra*.

Thus, the trial court erred when it found the carpeting came within the specially manufactured goods exception to the statute of frauds.

Plaintiff argues that the trial court's judgment may also be upheld under the part performance exception to the statute of frauds. We disagree.

While <u>part performance</u> can be sufficient to remove the bar of the statute of frauds, it will remove only that portion of the contract which relates to goods that have actually been received and accepted. Section 4-2-201, C.R.S. 1973 (Official Comment 2); 3 UCC Serv. (MB) § 2.04[4][c] at 2-92.

Here, the tile was the only item which was delivered to and initially accepted by the defendants. However, plaintiff removed the tile, and payment for the tile forms no part of plaintiff's present claim. As the carpeting was neither received nor accepted by the defendant, the part performance exception cannot apply to validate that portion of the contract.

Plaintiff also argues that the contract was <u>exempt from</u> the operation of the statute of frauds because it was <u>primarily</u> <u>a service</u> rather than a sale of goods <u>contract</u>. We disagree.

A contract which contemplates both the performance of services and the sale of goods must be examined to determine whether its primary purpose is the sale of goods or the <u>rendition of services</u>. *See Bonebrake v. Cox*, 499 F. 2d 951 (8th Cir. 1974). If the primary purpose of the contract is the sale of goods and the performance of services is merely incidental, then the statute of frauds will bar any claim which lacks the <u>requisite writing</u>. *See Bonebrake v. Cox, supra.*

Here, the unsigned contract between the parties reveals that the primary <u>thrust</u> of the contract was the sale of carpeting. The <u>invoices</u> detailed the quantities, types, and prices for each item ordered. The major portion of the contract price was the cost of the carpeting, rather than the labor needed to install it. On most invoices, the labor charge was included in the total price charged for the carpeting. Furthermore, all correspondence between the parties refers to the buyer and seller. This language indicates that the plaintiff considered the contract to be primarily a sale of carpeting with the installation services being merely incidental to that sale. Hence, under these circumstances, it is apparent that the contract was primarily one for the sale of goods. Plaintiff's claim is thus barred by the operation of the statute of frauds, § 4-2-201, C.R.S. 1973.

Judgment reversed.

Judge Pierce and Judge Smith, concur.

---

exempt from 免除，豁免

primarily 主要地
a service contract 服务合同

rendition of service 提供服务

requisite writing 所要求的书面形式

thrust 主要目标，最为关切的事情
invoice 发票,发货票,发货清单（指由商品销售者或劳务提供者向购买人开具的载明所售商品或所提供劳务的种类、数量、金额等事项的书面凭证）

8. The Parol Evidence Rule

When parties to a contract embody the terms of their agreement in a writing, intending that writing to be the final expression of their agreement, the terms of the writing may not be contradicted by evidence of any prior agreement. This is a description of the common law parol evidence rule. Under this rule, oral or extrinsic evidence is not admissible in court to add to, alter, or vary the terms of a written contract. However, parol evidence is admissible to prove that a written contract is illegal or void; that at the time it was executed it was agreed that it would not be operative except on the occurrence of a future, uncertain event; that a subsequent contract was later entered into; or to clear up ambiguities in a written contract. Under contracts for the sale of goods under the UCC, such parol evidence is admissible to supplement or to explain a written contract but not to contradict it unless the writing states that it is the exclusive agreement in which case parol evidence cannot be used to supplement or explain.

In order to avoid the potential problem, people would add a clause in the contract which may read as this: "This agreement contains the whole agreement between the Seller and Buyer and there are no other terms, obligations, covenants, representations, statements, or conditions, oral or otherwise, of any kind whatsoever." Such a clause is called a "merger" or "integration" clause. It is likely to conclude the issue whether the agreement is completely integrated; however, absent evidence that the parties have consciously considered and assented to a printed merger clause, the court may still refuse to accord such a clause conclusive effect.

Review Questions

1. What are the functions of the various defenses to the validity of a contract?
2. What is the difference between duress and undue influence?
3. Does the fact that the person making the misrepresentation knew it was false affect the validity of the contract? Does it affect the remedies granted to the person who received the misrepresentation?
4. Distinguish the mutual mistake and unilateral mistake and their legal

effects.
5. Is it fair to give the minors and insane people the option to void the contract they enter into with other people?
6. What types of contract must be in writing in order to be enforceable?
7. Explain the parol evidence rule.

CHAPTER 4
SELECTED TOPICS ON COMMON LAW OF CONTRACT

　　在原告证明了合同初步成立、且被告没有任何合法抗辩理由时,法院就会认定原告与被告之间的合同有效成立,接下来才会讨论被告是否违约的问题。合同有效成立后,双方应该按照合同约定履行各自的义务。然而,经常有一方甚至双方对合同没有履行或者没有完全履行的情况发生,因此,合同的履行情况可能包括最理想的完全履行、差强人意的部分履行和令人无法容忍的完全不履行。与之相对应,违约行为也可分为重大违约与轻度违约。法律对这些不同的履约或违约情况分别作出了规定。本章将介绍合同的履行以及违约救济等问题。同时,由于合同权利的让与、合同义务的转让以及第三方受益合同等也是英美合同法中的重要内容,本章也对此进行简要介绍。

CHAPTER 4 SELECTED TOPICS ON COMMON LAW OF CONTRACT

1. Performance

After a contract is formed, the parties to the contract are supposed to perform the contract according to the terms and conditions agreed upon. However, the duty to perform is not absolute. For example, the parties may make their duties under a contract <u>contingent</u> on the happening of some future, uncertain events. Such a <u>contingency</u> is known as <u>a condition precedent</u>. Likewise, the parties may provide that upon the occurrence of a future, uncertain event a party will be relieved of the performance of a duty that he otherwise would have to perform. Such a condition is known as a <u>condition subsequent</u>. Some contracts provide that the parties are to perform their duties <u>simultaneously</u>; such a provision is a <u>concurrent condition</u> and more often arises by <u>implication</u> rather than by express provision.

The promisor may or may not perform his or her obligations pursuant to the contract. The courts recognize three stages of performance: <u>complete</u> or <u>satisfactory performance</u>, <u>substantial performance</u>, and <u>material breach</u>. Complete or satisfactory performance is achieved when the obligation is performed to the letter or to such a degree that it is all that could reasonably be expected. Substantial performance implies an honest effort to perform but a performance less than that reasonably expected. In such a case, the promisor is entitled to the contract price less any damage sustained by the promisee as a result of the <u>defective performance</u>. If there is a major defect in performance, there has been a material breach, and the promisor cannot recover on the contract but may be entitled to some recovery in *quasi* contract for benefits conferred. If <u>time is of the essence</u> in the performance of a contract, then failure to perform within the expected time is a material breach of the contract. On the other hand, if time is

contingent 不确定的,附条件的
contingency 未来事件,意外事件,偶发事件
condition precedent 停止条件,延缓条件,先决条件
condition subsequent 解除条件(指合同或约定义务已经生效,但如双方约定的某一事件或行为发生,则该合同或约定义务即告终止,失去效力)
simultaneously 同时地
concurrent condition 相互依存条件
implication 推断,默示
complete performance (full performance) 完全履行
satisfactory performance 完全履行,令人满意的(合同)履行,令人满意的(债务)清偿
substantial performance (合同的)实质履行(指对某一份合同虽非完全履行,但已善意地根据合同履行了其中主要的、必需的内容。该种履行仅与合同规定存在某些细小的或相对次要的不同)
material breach 重大违约,实质性违约(是违约的一种,对方当事人可免于继续履行合同,并有权诉请损害赔偿)
defective performance 瑕疵履行(指一方履行合约的质量或水平低于合约所规定的水平。如无过错的合约人在知情的情况下接受该瑕疵履行,他会被视为已肯定承认合约存在)
time is of the essence 时限是(合约的)重要要素或要件(如果合同中规定时限为其重要要素或要件,没有按照合同规定的时限履行则构成重大违约)

not of the essence, then as long as the promisor performs within a reasonable time the performance must be accepted although the promisee may be able to recover damages for <u>late performance</u>.

Performance of a contract becomes impossible and is excused on the happening of the following events: death or incapacitating illness of the promisor where his performance is personal in nature, intervening illegality of the contract, and destruction of the subject matter of the contract. Death of the promisor will always terminate a contract calling for personal service. Whether illness will terminate a contract depends on the length of the contract, the type of work involved, and the seriousness and probable length of the illness. Intervening illegality occurs when a government statute or regulation makes performance of the contract illegal; it is not enough that such a statute or regulation merely makes performance more difficult or less profitable. If the subject matter of the contract is destroyed prior to performance, then performance is excused; however, the destruction must be of something essential to the contract and not merely something of utility to its performance. Under the UCC, nonperformance is excused if performance was made commercially impracticable by the occurrence of a contingency, the <u>nonoccurrence</u> of which was <u>a basic assumption</u> on which the contract was made.

If the parties to the contract have fully performed the contract, it is said that the contract is <u>discharged</u> and all parties to it are <u>released</u> from their obligations. Parties may be discharged by the occurrence or nonoccurrence of conditions subsequent and precedent as well as by <u>impossibility of performance</u>. If the other party is guilty of a material breach, a party is discharged from any duty to perform his part of the contract.

Since a contract is created by the agreement of the parties, it may also be discharged by agreement unless the rights of third parties will <u>be adversely affected</u>. The discharge of one party from his or her obligations by an agreement of the parties must be supported by consideration; however, mutual promises to rescind are supported by consideration since both parties have surrendered their rights under the contract. A party may specifically or impliedly relinquish a right he has under a contract; such a relinquishment is known as a waiver. To avoid being considered to have waived his rights, the party should give prompt notice whenever he considers the other party's performance under the contract to be defective. So-called "statutes of limitations" commonly provide that a person must bring suit on a contract within a reasonable time after the cause of action arises or be barred from bringing the suit; each state sets a specific time within which suits on contracts must be brought and commonly distinguished between oral and written contracts as far as the time allowed to bring suit.

Case 12: Beckman v. Vassall-Dillworth Lincoln-Mercury, Inc.

Superior Court of Pennsylvania
Beckman v. Vassall-Dillworth Lincoln-Mercury, Inc.
321 Pa. Super. 428; 468 A. 2d 784
November 10, 1983

Montgomery, J.

The instant action was instituted in the lower court by the Plaintiff-Appellant, Howard Beckman, against the Defendant-Appellees Vassall-Dillworth Lincoln-Mercury, Inc. (hereinafter referred to as "Vassall-Dillworth"), an automobile dealership, and Lincoln-Mercury, Division of Ford Motor Company (hereinafter referred to as "Ford"). The Plaintiff, alleging a breach of an agreement for the sale of a new automobile, sought equitable relief in the nature of an order for specific performance, as well as damages. He files the instant appeal to our court from an order of the lower court which granted a motion for summary judgment filed by Ford.

Our scope of review in cases involving the review of summary judgments is very clear. As our Court stated in *Husak v. Berkel, Inc.*, 234 Pa. Super. 452, 458, 341 A. 2d 174, 177 (1975):

dealership 代理,经销商

hereinafter 在下文

equitable relief 衡平法上的救济（指在衡平法院寻求的救济。例如,请求法院发布禁制令或强制实际履行的命令,而非金钱赔偿）

deposition 美国审前调查(discovery)的一种方式(指开庭前诉讼双方为取得对方当事人或证人的证言而组织的口头问答程序,其书面记录可以作为庭审证据)

interrogatory 书面质询书,美国审前调查(discovery)的一种方式(指开庭前诉讼双方为取得对方当事人或证人的证言而组织的书面质询程序,可以作为庭审证据)

admission 当事人承认

disposition (事件的)最终解决;(案件的)裁决

pertinent 适当的;与争议有关的

principal 被代理人,本人

maintain 坚持意见,主张

"Summary judgment is made available by Pa. R. C. P. No. 1035, 12 P. S. Appendix, when the pleadings, depositions, answers to interrogatories, admissions on file and supporting affidavits considered together reveal no genuine issue as to any material fact and the moving party is entitled to a judgment as a matter of law. This severe disposition should only be granted in cases where the right is clear and free from doubt. To determine the absence of genuine issue of fact, the court must take the view of the evidence most favorable to the non-moving party, and any doubts must be resolved against the entry of the judgment." (Citations omitted.)

The pertinent facts of record, read in the light most favorable to the Appellant, shows that on December 14, 1978, the Appellant and the Defendant Vassall-Dillworth entered into a written agreement for the Appellant's purchase of a 1979 Lincoln Continental automobile. The agreement provided for a purchase price of $12,286.00. The agreement contained the following relevant "no agency" provision:

"It is understood that there is no relationship of principal and agent between the dealer and the manufacturer and that the dealer is not authorized to act, or attempt to act, or represent himself, directly or by implication as agent of the manufacturer, or in any manner assume or create, or attempt to assume or create any obligation on behalf of or in the name of the manufacturer."

The Plaintiff maintained that approximately four weeks after the agreement was executed for the purchase of the automobile, when the Plaintiff inquired about the car, he was advised by Vassall-Dillworth that the order agreement could not be found so that no car had then been ordered for him. However, he alleges that the dealer asserted a willingness to order another car, but at a price different from the price originally agreed to between Plaintiff and the dealer.

CHAPTER 4 SELECTED TOPICS ON COMMON LAW OF CONTRACT

After various preliminary procedural problems not relevant to this appeal were resolved in the lower court, Ford filed an Answer and New Matter.① The Appellant filed a Reply to New Matter, and <u>discovery proceedings</u> followed. On May 21, 1981, Appellee Ford filed a Motion for Summary Judgment. The Appellant filed responses to that Motion, and after argument before the lower court, an order was entered granting summary judgment.

The lower court determined that there were no genuine issues of material fact in dispute and that Ford could not be held liable for any breach of contract on Plaintiff-Appellant's theory that Ford was a principal of the dealer Defendant, Vassall-Dillworth. In reaching this conclusion, the lower court determined that the "no agency" provision of the sales agreement, recited above, precluded any finding of a principal-agent relationship between the manufacturer and the dealer. The lower court rejected Appellant's claim that Ford failed to raise the lack of agency defense properly in its pleadings. Further, the court found no <u>merit</u> in the Appellant's contentions that Ford's possible liability could be based upon the Pennsylvania Unfair Trade Practices and Consumer Protection Law, Act of December 17, 1968, P. L. 1224, No. 387, § 1, as amended by the Act of November 24, 1976, P. L. 1166, No. 260, § 1, 73 P. S. § 201 – 3.1, and the regulations issued <u>pursuant to</u> that statute. The lower court also determined, contrary to the Appellant's contentions, that the exclusion of agency clause was not unconscionable, and that the Appellant would not be entitled to equitable relief in the nature of specific performance, as he had failed to demonstrate the absence of an adequate remedy at law.

The Appellant raises several contentions of error on this appeal. He first argues that the lower court should not have addressed the Appellee's defense based upon the no agency provision of the agreement, as it was not pleaded as New Matter, pursuant to Pa. R. C.

discovery proceeding（美国民事诉讼中的）一种审前调查或审前披露程序（当事人可以通过该程序从对方当事人处获得与案件有关的事实与信息,以助于准备庭审）

merit 优点,价值

pursuant to 依据,按照,依照

---

① Vassall-Dillworth ceased business in March, 1979, and a default judgment was entered against it in this litigation in August, 1979. Ford remains as the only active party defendant in the case.

allude to 间接地提到，暗指

averment（诉状中积极或者肯定的）主张，宣称，陈述

intrinsic 内在的，固有的，本质的

affirmative defense 肯定性答辩，积极的答辩（指被告并不否认原告所主张之事实的真实性，而是提出其他理由来说明为什么自己不应承担责任的答辩。因此，它并不反驳原告诉求之真实性，而只是否认原告在法律上有起诉的权利）

including but not limited to 包括但不限于

laches 懈怠，迟延（指当事人在主张或实现其权利方面的疏忽、懈怠或有不合理的拖延）

res judicata 一事不再理（当事人不得就此再提起诉讼的）已决事件

contributory negligence 混合过错，混合过失，与有过失，促成的过失，可归责于己的过失

assumption of risk 自担风险（指依照法律，当事人不得就自己同意遭受的损害获得补偿，即，如果当事人自愿置身于其觉察和了解的危险中，则不得就所受损害获得赔偿）

P. 1030 and 1045(b). ① He maintains that the failure to so plead resulted in the waiver by Appellee of this defense, which was raised for the first time in Ford's Motion for Summary Judgment.

This contention does not appear to have been raised by the Plaintiff in his written Answer to Ford's Motion for Summary Judgment, and the lower court does not allude to it in its Opinion. Even if we assume that the Plaintiff raised it in a timely manner in the lower court, and that it was not thereby waived, we nevertheless find no substantive merit to the claim. Rule 1030 does not specifically require one to raise a "no-agency" defense affirmatively in New Matter. Our Court has explained that an affirmative defense is distinguished from a denial of the facts which make up the plaintiff's cause of action in that an affirmative defense will require an averment of facts *extrinsic* to the plaintiff's claim for relief. Lewis v. Spitler, 266 Pa. Super. 201, 209, 403 A. 2d 994, 998 (1979). See also Watson v. Green, 231 Pa. Super. 115, 331 A. 2d 790 (1974). In this case, the agreement containing the "no-agency" clause was appended to the Appellant's Amended Complaint, and alleged to be a part of that pleading. Ford's Answer to the Amended Complaint specifically denied that Vassall-Dillworth was its agent. Accordingly, Ford properly responded with a denial in its Answer to a fact *intrinsic* in the Amended

---

① Rule 1030 states:
"All affirmative defenses, including but not limited to the defenses of accord and satisfaction, arbitration and award, discharge in bankruptcy, duress, estoppel failure of consideration, fraud, illegality, immunity from suit, impossibility of performance, laches, license, payment, release, *res judicata*, and waiver and, unless previously raised by demurrer and sustained, the defenses of statute of frauds and statute of limitations, shall be pleaded in a responsive pleading under the heading 'New Matter'. A party may set forth as new matter any other material facts which are not merely denials of the averments of the preceding pleading."
Rule 1045(b) states:
"All affirmative defenses, including but not limited to those enumerated in Rule 1030, and the defenses of consent, qualified privilege, fair comment, truth and justification, and, unless previously raised by demurrer and sustained the defenses of statute of limitations and statute of frauds, shall be pleaded under the heading 'New Matter'. A party may set forth as new matter any other material facts which are not merely denials of the averments of the preceding pleading. The defenses of contributory negligence and assumption of risk need not be pleaded. A plaintiff who fails to file a reply to averments of the defendant's new matter shall be deemed to admit all such averments other than averments relating to contributory negligence or assumption of risk."

Complaint. Further pleading of the same response, by stating it as an affirmative defense in New Matter, was not necessary under the particular facts of the instant case.① Accordingly, we find no merit in the Appellant's initial claim of error.

Next, we examine several arguments raised by the Appellant in connection with his contention that the "no agency" provision of the sales agreement was unconscionable. Initially, we address the claim that the lower court was mandated to hold a full evidentiary hearing on the issue of unconscionability. The Act of November 1, 1979, P. L. 255, No. 86, §1, as set forth in 13 Pa. C. S. A. §2302, which applies to this issue, provides:

> (a) Finding and authority of court. — If the court as a matter of law finds the contract or any clause of the contract to have been unconscionable at the time it was made, the court may:
> (1) refuse to enforce the contract;
> (2) enforce the <u>remainder</u> of the contract without the unconscionable clause; or
> (3) so limit the application of any unconscionable clause as to avoid any unconscionable result.
> (b) Evidence by parties. — When it is claimed or appears to the court that the contract or any clause thereof may be unconscionable the parties shall be afforded a reasonable opportunity to present evidence as to its commercial setting, purpose and effect to aid the court in making the determination.

remainder 这里指合同的其他部分

It appears to be <u>an issue of first impression</u> in the appellate courts of our Commonwealth as to whether a claim of unconscionability may be decided during summary judgment proceedings or whether a full hearing is mandated. Section 2302, recited above,

an issue of first impression 全新的、无先例可循之法律问题(案件)(须由法院作出决定)

---

① Our Court has noted that the right of amendment has always been liberally granted in Pennsylvania. See *Pugh v. Bankers Mutual Insurance Co.*, 206 Pa. Super. 136, 211 A. 2d 135 (1965); *Pellegrine v. Home Insurance Co.*, 200 Pa. Super. 48, 186 A. 2d 662 (1962). Thus, in this case, where it does not appear that any prejudice would have resulted to the Appellant from the granting of such permission, Ford would have properly been permitted to amend its response to plead the "no-agency" defense under New Matter.

does not specifically require that an evidentiary hearing be held, but merely that the parties be afforded a reasonable opportunity to present evidence. In the instant case, we note that the lower court had the benefit of affidavits and deposition testimony when it ruled upon the motion for summary judgment.

While we have found no Pennsylvania appellate precedent on this point, support for the lower court's refusal to schedule an evidentiary hearing may be found in the decision of the United States District Court in *Stanley A. Klopp, Inc. v. John Deere Co.*, 510 F. Supp. 807 (E.D. Pa. 1981). In that case, it was held that unconscionability is a question of law for the court and as long as no issue of material fact exists, a court may conclude on a motion for summary judgment that as a matter of law a contract or a contract clause is enforceable despite an allegation of unconscionability. Further support for such a procedural approach is evident in *Earl M. Jorgensen Co. v. Mark Construction, Inc.*, 56 Haw. 466, 540 P.2d 978 (1975) and *Block v. Ford Motor Credit Co.*, 286 A. 2d 228 (D.C. App. 1972). Based upon our reading of the statute and our agreement with the approach taken in the cases cited above, we conclude that the lower court is not mandated in all cases to hold a full evidentiary hearing when an unconscionability claim is raised in the context of a motion for summary judgment. Further, for reasons explained more fully below, we find that the lower court did not err in refusing to hold an evidentiary hearing on the unconscionability claim of Appellant in the particular circumstances of the instant case, as the record before the court provided sufficient evidence to permit the court to render a decision on the issue of unconscionability.

In connection with his contention that a hearing was mandated on the question, the Appellant also maintains that the lower court erred in finding that the "no-agency" clause was unconscionable. The Appellant supports his position by referring us to an affidavit he submitted to the lower court in opposition to the Appellee's request for summary judgment. In that document, he averred that when he was given the contract for signature, he was "never told or made aware" of the clause on the back of the agreement setting forth the "no-agency" language. This, he argues, presented ample evidence to support his unconscionability claim, and to show that the agreement was a <u>contract of adhesion</u>.

We find this position <u>unconvincing</u>. We must initially note that while the Appellant may not have been "told or made aware" of the print on the back side of the agreement, he nevertheless admitted in a deposition that he had read the whole contract before signing it. ① With regard to his claim of unconscionability, we recognize the rule that a contract or a clause in a contract is to be considered unconscionable if there is "an absence of meaningful choice on the part of one of the parties together with contract terms which are unreasonably favorable to the other." See *Witmer v. Exxon Corp.*, 495 Pa. 540, 551, 434 A. 2d 1222, 1228 (1981), citing *Williams v. Walker-Thomas Furniture Company*, 350 F. 2d 445, 449 (D. C. Cir. 1965). We agree with the finding by the lower court that the Appellant submitted no evidence to show either an absence of meaningful choice on his part or any term which was unreasonably favorable to the Appellee. To accept the Appellant's position in this case, in the absence of any proof, we would have to hold that every exclusion of agency clause is <u>*per se*</u> unconscionable. Such a declaration would clearly be improper. Thus, in the absence of any evidence to support his claim, we reject the Appellant's assertion of unconscionability.

We also find a lack of merit in the argument that the lower court erred when it found no genuine issue of fact with regard to the intention of the parties at the time of the signing of the contract. While the Appellant claims he did not want the "no-agency" clause to be a part of the contract, he has not alleged fraud, mistake, or other unusual circumstances to explain the

contract of adhesion 附合合同(指对商品或服务的消费者所提供的合同,以"接受或不接受"为基础。该合同由缔约双方中的强势方单独拟定合同条款,弱势方对合同条款并无谈判或选择的余地,其实质是一种标准化、格式化的合同)

unconvincing 不足以令人相信的,没有说服力的

per se 本身,自身

---

① It has been held that in the absence of proof of fraud, the failure to read a contract one signs is an unavailing excuse or defense, and cannot justify an avoidance, modification or nullification of the contract or any provision thereof. *Estate of Brant*, 463 Pa. 230, 344 A. 2d 806 (1975). *See also*, *Stanley A. Klopp, Inc. v. John Deere Co.*, *supra*.

subtract from 减去,减少,扣掉

merge into 合并入,吸收进……

supersede 代替,接替,取代

presence of that provision in the agreement he read and signed. In the absence of proof of such unusual conditions, courts will enforce contracts as written. *National Cash Register v. Modern Transfer Co., Inc.*, 224 Pa. Super. 138, 302 A. 2d 486 (1973); *see also Mellon Bank N. A. v. Aetna Business Credit, Inc.*, 619 F. 2d 1001 (3rd Cir. 1980). Not only did the Appellant not allege or prove fraud or other excusing conditions, but the record showed that he was an experienced businessman, equipped to understand the meaning of the terms of the agreement he signed. Moreover, it is well-established that the written terms of a contract constitute the agreement between the parties and its terms cannot be added to nor <u>subtracted from</u> by parol evidence. *Kattelman v. Sabol*, 425 Pa. 197, 228 A. 2d 379 (1967). All preliminary negotiations, conversations and verbal agreements must be considered to be <u>merged into</u> and <u>superseded</u> by the subsequent written contract. Thus, it is evident, in the absence of allegations or proof of fraud, mistake, or the like, that the lower court was justified in finding no genuine issue of fact as to the intention of the parties when the contract was signed.

The Appellant next argues that the lower court erred in finding no genuine issue existed for trial on his contention that Ford violated the Unfair Trade Practices and Consumer Protection Law and the Rules and Regulations promulgated pursuant to that Act. The Law, Act of December 17, 1968, P. L. 1224, No. 387, as amended by the Act of November 24, 1976, P. L. 1166, No. 260, in Section 3. 1 (73 P. S. § 201-3.1) provides that the Attorney General may adopt rules and regulations necessary for the enforcement and administration of the Act, and that such rules and regulations shall have the force and effect of law. Pursuant to that authority, the following Rules and Regulations were adopted, applicable to manufacturers in the automotive industry:

With respect to any manufacturer, the following shall be considered unfair methods of competition and unfair or deceptive acts or practices:

...

(3) To increase prices of motor vehicles which the dealer had ordered for private retail consumers prior to the dealer's receipt of the written official price increase notification. A sales contract signed by a private retail consumer shall constitute evidence of each such order.

After reviewing the record, we find that the Appellant failed to present any evidence which, if true, would establish a violation of this Rule or a cause of action under it. The only evidence that Ford had increased prices was the <u>hearsay</u> statement, in the Appellant's affidavit and in his deposition testimony, that a representative of the dealer told him that there was no record of his original order, but that the dealer would readily place an order for the vehicle he wanted, however, at an increased price because of price increases pronounced by Ford after the Appellant had placed his original order. As discussed above, the lower court was justified in finding that the dealer, based upon the contract, could not be considered an agent of Ford. Thus, his hearsay statements could not constitute an admission or other evidence against Ford. Despite an opportunity to do so, the Appellant never employed discovery to determine the date of receipt by the dealer of any "written official price increase <u>notification</u>." Moreover, while the Appellant did possess a copy of a sales contract, which, under the Rule, constitutes "evidence" of an "order," he testified in his deposition that the car had *already* been ordered by the dealer from Ford for the dealer's *own stock*, and further, that he believed that the dealer had never submitted his order to Ford. Thus, it is clear that though the order constituted "evidence" under the Rule, the record before the lower court demonstrated facts <u>obviating</u> any finding of a violation of the Rule. More specifically, the record demonstrated that the car was not ordered by the dealer for the customer, but rather had already been on order from Ford for the dealer's own stock. Additionally, the Appellant's own testimony negated the other "evidence" that Ford had ever received the order. Finally, we cannot

hearsay 传闻（证据）

notification 通知，告知

obviate 排除，消除，避免

ignore the absence of any evidence as to any written notification of price increases which may have been made by Ford or received by the dealer. It is apparent that the lower court did not err in rejecting the claims of the Appellant based upon the Unfair Trade Practices and Consumer Protection Law, and the Rules and Regulations promulgated pursuant to that statute.

The Appellant next contends that the lower court acted incorrectly in holding that the Appellant was not entitled to specific performance because he failed to show that he had no adequate remedy at law. Although the lower court acted <u>sua sponte</u> in this matter, it has been held that a court may act upon its own motion to dismiss such a request for equitable relief when specific performance would not be appropriate. *Easton Theatres Inc. v. Wells Fargo Land and Mortgage Co.*, 265 Pa. Super. 334, 401 A. 2d 1333 (1979). It is also clear that an order for specific performance is inappropriate where the moving party has an adequate remedy at law. *Roth v. Hartl*, 365 Pa. 428, 75 A. 2d 583 (1950). Our Court has held that specific performance is a proper remedy when the subject matter of an agreement is an asset that is unique or one such that its equivalent cannot be purchased on the open market. *Tomb v. Lavalle*, 298 Pa. Super. 75, 444 A. 2d 666 (1981); *see also* the Act of November 1, 1979, P. L. 255, No. 86, §1, 13 Pa. C. S. A. §2716. In this case, the record shows that the Appellant was given an opportunity by the dealer to purchase the automobile he wanted, but at a higher price. It may not be ignored that the Appellant could also have sought to purchase the same vehicle from another source. His remedy in such circumstances was to seek damages for any difference between the original order price and the actual purchase price he paid. *See* the Act of November 1, 1979, P. L. 255, No. 86, §1, 13 Pa. C. S. A. §2713. Because the subject matter of the contract was not unique, and because it is obvious that an adequate remedy at law was available, we agree with the lower court's rejection of the Appellant's demand for specific performance.

We next examine the contention that the "no-agency" clause was ambiguous and must be construed

---

sua sponte 出于自愿，自愿地，主动地，未受提示或建议地

against the Appellee. We reject this claim summarily. The clause, as quoted earlier in this Opinion, is clear and susceptible to only one interpretation. That is, that the dealer was not an agent of the manufacturer, and had no authority to act as its agent. We find no merit to the Appellant's arguments to the contrary, and no basis for construing any aspect of the clause against the Appellee.

We also find without merit the contention by the Appellant that the lower court erred in not finding an oral or implied contract with the dealer which did not contain a "no-agency" provision as to Ford. The lower court correctly found that such a contract, covering the sale of goods valued in excess of $500.00, had to be in writing to be enforceable. *See* the Act of November 1, 1979, P.L. 255, No. 86, §1, 13 Pa.C.S.A. §2201.

The final contention of the Appellant is that the lower court acted incorrectly in failing to consider factual matters which he claims established the existence of a principal and agent relationship between Ford and the dealer. In this regard, the Appellant cites evidence indicating that Ford made substantial capital contributions to the dealer and owned a two-thirds of the stock of the dealership. In the instant case, there is a complete absence of proof of express, implied or apparent authority from Ford to have the dealer act as its agent. To the contrary, the evidence of the unambiguous no-agency clause in the Sales Agreement mitigates against such a finding. Further, the Appellant after reading the whole contract, including that clause, signed it. The same document has been offered as the very foundation for his suit. Having already rejected the unconscionability and other challenges to the "no-agency" clause in the contract, we cannot ignore its validity and the Appellant's agreement to be bound to it. He cannot avoid his clear acquiescence that there was no principal-agent relationship by his suggestion of ownership or control, while at the same time basing his claims on the remaining aspects of the same

susceptible 易受……影响的

capital contribution 资本出资(主要指设立公司时股东对公司的出资)

express authority 明示授权,明示委托

implied authority 默示授权

apparent authority 表见授权

mitigate 减轻

challenge 异议,质疑

contract.① We therefore reject his final claim of error.

The order of the lower court is hereby affirmed.

2. Remedies

Contract law protects three interests:

First, the plaintiff has in reliance on the promise of the defendant conferred some value on the defendant. The defendant fails to perform his promise. The Court may force the defendant to disgorge the value he received from the plaintiff. The object here may be termed the prevention of gain by the defaulting promisor at the expense of the promisee; more briefly, the prevention of unjust enrichment. The interest protected may be called the restitution interest.

Secondly, the plaintiff has in reliance on the promise of the defendant changed his position. For example, the buyer under a contract for the sale of land has incurred expense in the investigation of the seller's title, or has neglected the opportunity to enter other contracts. We may award damages to the plaintiff for the purpose of undoing the harm which his reliance on the defendant's promise has caused him. Our object is to put him in as good a position as he was in before the promise was made. The interest protected in this case may be called the reliance interest.

Thirdly, without insisting on reliance by the promisee or enrichment of the promisor, we may seek to give the promisee the value of the expectancy which the promise created. We may in a suit for specific performance actually compel the defendant to render the promised performance to the plaintiff, or, in a suit for damages, we may

---

① The Restatement of Agency, Second, provides, in § 150:
"If an integrated contract by its specific terms excludes the principal as a party, extrinsic evidence is inadmissible to show that he is a party; if the integrated contract by its specific terms makes the principal a party, extrinsic evidence is not admissible to show that it was agreed that he should not become a party."

make the defendant pay the money value of this performance. Here our object is to put the plaintiff in as good a position as he would have occupied had the defendant performed his promise. The interest protected in this case we may call the <u>expectation interest</u>.

Fuller & Perdue, *The Reliance Interest in Contract Damages*, 46 YALE L.J. 52, 373 (1936)

In general, the economic theory supports the protection of the expectation interest through <u>substitutional relief</u> in the form of money damages. When one of the parties to the contract fails to perform his obligations under the contract and the other party thereby sustains some injury, the injured party is entitled to be put, as nearly as possible, in the same position as if the contract had been performed. This may mean that he is given some measure of money damages such as the value of the thing he expected to receive or the profit that would have been made if the contract had been fully performed. If money damages would be insufficient to put the injured party in the same position he would have been in had the contract been fully performed, then the party may be granted the equitable remedy of specific performance, or allowed to rescind the contract, or granted some form of <u>injunctive relief</u>. You may want to read the case *Hawkins v. McGee* reprinted in Chapter 1, and think what kind of interest was protected in that case.

In the interests of fairness to the defaulting promisor, it is a universally accepted rule that the promisee cannot recover damages that could have been avoided through the exercise of reasonable <u>diligence</u> and without incurring <u>undue risk</u>, expense, or <u>humiliation</u>. If the promisee does not choose to avoid the <u>enhancement</u> of damages, the only consequence will be that he will not be compensated for damages which could have reasonably been avoided.

To enforce a judgment for money damages, the creditor may have the <u>sheriff</u> <u>execute the judgment</u> on property owned by the debtor, or the creditor may proceed to <u>garnish</u> the debtor's wages pursuant to the

expectation interest 预期利益

substitutional relief 替代救济

injunctive relief 强制令救济,禁制令救济

diligence 谨慎,注意,勤勉
undue risk 不合理的风险
humiliation 屈辱,耻辱,丢脸,蒙耻(指使人有丢脸、显得懦弱、卑微、愚蠢或蔑视的感觉。这是侵权诉讼中要求赔偿的一个因素,但是无法用准确的损害赔偿标准进行衡量)
enhancement 提高,增加
sheriff (县)行政司法官
execute the judgment 执行判决
garnish (garnishee) 扣押(手中有属于被告的财产或债权的第三债务人)

garnishment 对案外债务人的扣押程序	
seize 扣押,用强力占有	
attachment 扣押（指扣押某人的财产以担保将来判决能得到履行或者将扣押的财产变卖以执行判决）	

state garnishment statute. Under some circumstances, the creditor may have the sheriff seize property of the defendant to a suit for breach of contract at the time the suit is initiated; this is known as "attachment" and insures that property will be available to satisfy any judgment obtained against the defendant. The remedies available to aggrieved parties to contracts for the sale of goods are similar to those at common law and have the same objective; that is putting the aggrieved party in the same position as if the contract had been performed.

compensatory damages 补偿性损害赔偿金
consequential damages 间接（附带产生的）损害
liquidated damages 约定违约金,预定违约赔偿金
nominal damages 名义上的损害赔偿金,象征性损害赔偿金

A number of different types of damages may be awarded for breach of a contract: compensatory, consequential, liquidated, and nominal damages.

Compensatory damages are those damages which would usually flow directly from the breach of contract and which are designed to make good or compensate for the wrong or injury sustained. Consequential damages are those damages which do not flow directly from the breach of contract but are due to the special circumstances of the contract. For example, a farmer sustains consequential damages when he is unable to harvest his crops because the combine he ordered did not arrive within the promised time for delivery. In order to recover damages, the aggrieved party must prove to a reasonable degree of certainty the amount of loss and that the loss was the direct result of the breach. Lost profits are recoverable only if they can be proved to a reasonable certainty and if they were within the contemplation of the parties at the time the contract was entered into. They are not recoverable if they are speculative in nature or if the person who breached the contract could not reasonably have been expected to realize that such damages would flow from his or her breach of the contract. The injured party owes a duty to make a reasonable effort to mitigate damages, *i.e.*, to minimize the damage he sustains.

penalty clause 惩罚条款,约定违约赔偿的条款

Liquidated damages refer to a specific amount designated by the parties at the time of contracting which is to be recovered by the injured party in the event of a breach of contract. It is important to distinguish a penalty clause from a provision for liquidated damages. A contractual provision for a penalty is one the prime purpose of which is to prevent a breach of the contract by holding over the head of a contracting party the threat of punishment for a breach. A provision for liquidated damages, on the other hand, is one the real purpose of which is to fix fair compensation to the injured party for a breach of the contract. In order for the liquidated damages to be effective, three conditions must be satisfied. First, the damage which was to be expected as a result of a breach of the contract must be uncertain in amount or difficult to prove. Second, there must be an intent on the part of the parties to liquidate damages in advance. Third, the amount stipulated must be reasonable in the sense that it was not greatly disproportionate to the amount of the damage which, as the parties looked forward, seemed to be the presumable loss which would be sustained by the contractee in the event of a breach of the contract.

in advance 事先

disproportionate 不成比例的,不相称的
presumable 可推测的;可能有的
contractee 合同当事人

Nominal damages are awarded where there has been a technical breach of the contract but no damages or loss have been sustained as a result of the breach.

Courts may decree specific performance of a contract when a damage remedy would be inadequate. Specific performance is most likely to be decreed where the sale of unique items such as pieces of land, antiques, or art objects are involved and where it would be difficult to place a value on the item or to acquire a satisfactory substitute for it. Specific performance is not granted where a contract for personal services is involved or where such a decree would require prolonged and detailed supervision by the court, such as where the contract called for the construction of a building. The remedy of an injunction may be available to prevent or protect against hardship, and is commonly used as a court directive to a person threatening to breach a contract to restrain from his threatened course of action.

decree 判决,裁定

directive 指令

3. Assignment of Contract Rights and Delegation of Duties

assignment 合同权利的转让,让与
delegation 合同义务的转让,让与,债务人的变更

Assignment of a contractual right is a present

transfer of a right in the assignor which creates a similar right in the assignee and extinguishes the right in the assignor. Since the promisee on a contract cannot demand performance of the contract in a manner which differs in any material respect from that promised, the promisee may not assign the promisee's interest in a contract if the duties of the promisor would be changed in any material respect by the assignment. Only those contracts the performance of which can be rendered by the promisor to the assignee without materially altering or increasing the burdens of performance may be assigned. Contracts which are personal in nature may not be assigned; thus, for example, any contract calling for personal skill, judgment, or character, or a contract to support another for life, cannot be assigned. On the other hand, a contract calling for the payment of money is a common example of a contract which is assignable.

The assignee of a contract can obtain no greater rights in the contract than the assignor had, since an assignment is essentially a sale of the assignor's contract rights. The assignee takes the contract subject to all defenses that the promisor has against the assignor on the contract. An assignee who wishes to protect the rights he acquired by assignment should give notice of the assignment to the promisor on the contract. When such notice is given to the promisor, he then becomes liable to render performance to the assignee.

Where the promisee wrongfully makes two assignments of the same right without the second assignee realizing that a prior assignment of that right had already been made, the courts may follow one of two different rules: under the so-called "American rule," the first assignee has the better right; whereas under the so-called "English rule," the assignee who first gives notice of the assignment has the better right. If an assignor should make two assignments of the same claim, he is liable for any damages sustained by any of the assignees because of such fraud. In most states there are statutes regulating efforts to assign future wages.

When an assignor assigns a claim for value to an

assignee, he makes certain <u>implied warranties</u>: (1) that the claim is valid, (2) that the parties have capacity to contract, (3) that the claim is not void for illegality, (4) that the claim has not been discharged, and (5) that he has, and is passing, good title to the claim to the assignee. The assignor also warrants that any written instrument involved is valid and that he will do nothing to <u>impair</u> the value of the assignment; at the same time the assignor does not warrant the <u>solvency</u> of the promisor.

The duties owed under a contract may not be assigned but may be delegated if they are <u>impersonal</u> in nature. A party may perform his duty through <u>a delegate</u> unless otherwise agreed or unless the other party has a substantial interest in having his original promisor perform or control the acts required by the contract. No <u>delegation</u> of performance relieves the party delegating of any duty to perform or any liability for breach. Even though a promisor has delegated his or her duties to someone else, he remains liable for their performance in the event the delegatee fails to perform.

4. Third Party Beneficiaries

A contract may expressly provide that performance of the contract is to be rendered to a third person who is not a party to the contract, or a third person may benefit by the performance of a contract even though the third person is not named in it. A person so benefited is known as a third-party beneficiary. Three different categories of third-party beneficiaries are recognized by the law: (1) <u>donee beneficiaries</u>, (2) <u>creditor beneficiaries</u>, and (3) <u>incidental beneficiaries</u>.

If the primary purpose of the promisee, in requesting that performance of a contract be made to a third person, is to make a gift to that third person, then the third person is a donee beneficiary. For example, A makes a promise to B, for a consideration furnished by B, to render a performance to C as a gift to C, or which, at any rate, will not operate to discharge any legal obligation then owing by B to C. As such, C is the donee beneficiary, and the donee —

implied warranty 默示担保

impair (impairment) 损害,损伤,削弱,减少
solvency 具备偿债能力（指债务人有能力在一般商业过程中偿付全部到期债务）
impersonal 客观的,非个人的,和个人无关的
a delegate （得到委托授权的）代表,代理人
delegation 委托,授权

third party beneficiary 受益第三人,第三方受益人（指虽非合同当事人但可从合同履行中获益的人）
donee beneficiary 受赠获益第三人（被指定的从合同的任一方当事人按约履行义务中受益的第三人,其所获之利益纯属受赠性质）
creditor beneficiary 债权受益人（指经另一方同意后,由合同一方指定的接受合同履行利益的第三人。因合同债权人对其负有债务,故债权受益人有权请求合同的任一方当事人履行义务）
incidental beneficiary 附带受益人（指那些可能受益、但却并非出于契约各方当事人的本意使其受益的人,因此他们不能请求契约的执行）

C, as well as the promisee — B, may bring suit to enforce the promise in the event the promisor — A defaults on his or her promise. Another example of a donee beneficiary is the beneficiary of a life insurance policy.

If the performance of a promise made to a promisee will satisfy an actual or supposed legal duty owed by the promisee to the beneficiary, then the beneficiary is a creditor beneficiary. For example, if B owes C a legal obligation, and A makes a promise to B, for a consideration furnished by B, to render a performance to C, which is intended to operate, and which will operate to, discharge a legal obligation then owing from B to C. C is a third-party creditor beneficiary of the agreement between A and B. A creditor beneficiary may also sue in his or her own name to enforce performance of the promise by the promisor.

A person is an incidental beneficiary if he benefits from the performance of a contract to which he is not a party. An incidental beneficiary has no rights in the contract and cannot sue to enforce it or to recover damages for nonperformance.

nonperformance 未履行，未履约（指当事人未能履行义务，尤指当事人未按约定的条件履行合同义务）

The third party beneficiary contract is the product of the intention of the promisee and promisor who, at the moment of formation, created rights in the third party. An assignment, however, is the unilateral act of a party who has rights under an existing contract and chooses to make a present transfer of those rights to an assignee without the consent and usually without the knowledge of the other party to the contract, the obligor. It is important to distinguish these two concepts.

Review Questions

1. What are the legal effects of the assignment of contract and delegation of duties?
2. How to distinguish the assignment of contract from the third-party beneficiaries?
3. How many kinds of third-party beneficiaries are there? Do they have the same rights?
4. What interests does the contract law protect?
5. Explain the remedies the aggrieved party to a contract may get from the breaching party.
6. What is equitable relief? Comparing it with the legal remedies.

PART II
COMMON LAW OF TORTS

CHAPTER 5
INTRODUCTION TO TORT LAW

　　合同法规范合同当事人之间的权利义务,而侵权法是用来解决没有合同关系的民事活动当事人之间发生的纠纷的一种民事法律。侵权法的内容虽主要包括人身伤害与财产损失责任,但其范围却几乎囊括了所有的人类活动。本章首先将侵权与犯罪、侵权与合同等进行区分,然后介绍英美侵权法的类型化特点及其法律救济。

1. Torts vs. Crimes

Torts as private wrongs are different from crimes, although the same act may be both a tort and a crime.

A crime is an offense against society as a whole. The state acts as society's representative in criminal proceedings and prosecutes criminals. The purpose of criminal proceedings is to protect the public and satisfy its sense of justice by punishing wrongdoers, such as <u>imprisoning</u> defendants, and sometimes by <u>imposing fines</u> which <u>inure to</u> the <u>coffers</u> of the state. The state must prove that a defendant committed a crime "<u>beyond a reasonable doubt</u>" in order to convict him or her.

In contrast, a tort is a civil action initiated by an individual — the injured party seeking to obtain personal relief, such as money damages or perhaps an injunction. Its primary purpose is to protect an individual's interests by compensating him at the wrongdoer's expense. The standard of proof is a more-likely-than-not "<u>preponderance of the evidence.</u>"

2. Torts vs. Breach of Contracts

A tort is also different from a breach of contract, although the same act may constitute both a breach of contract and a tort.

People who have chosen to deal with one another create duties voluntarily assumed by them through making a contract. Breach of contract cases involve these essentially self-imposed duties. The law of contract will put the aggrieved party to the position where he or she would have been in should the contract be duly performed in order to protect the expectation interests of the aggrieved party.

In contrast, a tort is an omission or a wrongful act against a person or his property, *i.e.*, a violation of one person's legal duty to another. Torts obligations are involuntarily imposed by operation of law. They do not depend upon the consent of the parties. The law of torts will put the aggrieved party back to the

---

imprison 监禁,囚禁,限制自由
impose fines 罚款
inure to 对……有利
coffer 金库（这里指政府的财政）
beyond a reasonable doubt 排除合理怀疑（指刑事诉讼中陪审团认定被告人有罪时使用的证明标准）
preponderance of the evidence 证据优势

position where he or she was originally in should the tortuous act not have been done.

3. Classifications of Torts

Torts may be classified according to the gravity of the fault of the wrongdoer. By this way of classification, there are three types of torts: intentional torts, torts of negligence, and strict liability torts.

Intentional torts are those wrongs in which the persons charged must have acted in such a manner that they either wanted to harm someone or knew that what they did would result in harm. In the former case, the tortfeasor acted with a purpose, *i.e.*, a personal desire to produce a particular result; while in the latter case, the tortfeasor acted with the knowledge, *i.e.*, a substantial certainty that a particular result will occur, even if it is not desired. Intent to cause a result that the law forbids is a sufficient predicate for intentional tort liability, even if one does not "intend to cause harm."

Negligence is the unintentional causing of harm that could have been prevented if the defendant had acted as a reasonable and prudent person. It is a conduct that creates an unreasonable risk of harm. If a risk is reasonably to be perceived, the defendant must exercise due care to prevent the risk from coming to fruition. Thus, the concept of foreseeability plays a central role in the law of negligence. Every tort of negligence shares three elements: a legal duty owed by the defendant to the plaintiff, a breach of that duty, and damage caused to the plaintiff as a result.

Strict liability tort is a new area of tort law, and it is liability without fault. Any fault-based liability normally has two prerequisites: foreseeability of injury and blameworthy conduct. If liability is imposed even though one or both of those features have been dispensed with, the liability is strict. It assigns liability regardless of fault as a matter of social policy.

4. Remedies

The purpose of tort litigation is to require a

gravity 严重性
fault 过错

intentional tort 故意侵权 (指某人以一般意图或专门目的而实施的侵权行为)
negligence 过失, 过失侵权行为
strict liability 严格责任

tortfeasor 侵权人

perceive 察觉, 意识到, 感知
fruition 实现, 成就
foreseeability 可预见性 (指有能力预先知道, 例如对作为或不作为可能造成的损害或伤害的合理预测)

wrongdoer or the party at fault to compensate a victim for the injury incurred, which is called compensatory damages. Compensatory damages in a typical tort case usually include medical expenses, lost income from earnings, property damages, pain and suffering, and loss of life or limb. These losses include those actually sustained in the past and those estimated in the future.

There is also another kind of damages called punitive damages, or exemplary damages, which are awarded to punish defendants for committing intentional torts and for negligent behavior considered "gross" or "willful and wanton."

For an award of punitive damages, the defendant's motive must be malicious, fraudulent, or evil. Increasingly, punitive damages are also awarded for dangerously negligent conduct that shows a conscious disregard for the interests of others. These damages are used to deter future wrongdoing.

exemplary damages 惩罚性损害赔偿金（指由于被告的暴力、强制、诈欺、恶意行为加重了原告的损害，从而判决给予原告以超过实际或通常程度的损害赔偿金，以示对被告的惩罚）

gross 严重的，极端的，恶劣的

willful and wanton 蓄意而放任的

malicious 恶意的，蓄意的

evil 邪恶的，有害的

conscious disregard 有意忽视，不考虑，不注意

deter 威慑，吓住，阻止，防止

Review Questions

1. What are the differences among crime, tort, and breach of contract?
2. Explain the categories of torts.
3. What is the purpose of the law of torts?
4. What kind of remedies a plaintiff in a tort litigation may be granted?

CHAPTER 6
INTENTIONAL TORTS

　　故意侵权是指侵权人有意侵犯他人利益的行为。如果已经发生的损害是行为人行为时所期待发生的,或者行为人明知其行为几乎肯定会造成该损害,那么,该行为可以认定为故意行为。这意味着故意侵权责任并不要求行为人对受害人有敌意或恶意。由于行为人的行为在多数场合都是有过错的,因此侵权法允许受害人得到最大限度的损害赔偿。原告不仅能得到对其所受损害的补偿性赔偿,还可能得到惩罚性赔偿。英美侵权法中认定的故意侵权类型包括对人身的故意侵权、对财产的故意侵权,以及对经济和精神利益的故意侵权。本章将逐一介绍美国侵权法中这三种故意侵权类型、每种故意侵权的初步证明所要求的要素以及各种抗辩理由。

1. The General Elements of Intentional Torts

Although each intentional tort varies, they share some common elements. First, there must be a volitional act by the defendant. A volitional act is a movement dictated by a person's mind. For example, A tripped and was falling. To break the fall, he stretched out his hand, which struck B. A's movement was reflexive, but it was dictated by his mind, and hence it will be characterized as volitional.

Second, the plaintiff must prove that the defendant had intent to do the volitional act. If the goal of the defendant was to bring about the consequences, then specific intent is found. If the defendant knew with substantial certainty that these consequences would result, then general intent is found. For example, A, a five-year-old boy pulls a chair out from under B as B is sitting down. Even if A did not desire that B hit the ground (*i.e.*, without specific intent), if A knew with substantial certainty that B was trying to sit and would hit the ground, A had the general intent necessary for intentional tort. The intent will be found even if the actor did not intend to injure the plaintiff.

Where A intends to commit a tort against one person but instead commits a different tort against that person, or commits the same tort as intended but against a different person, or commits a different tort against a different person, the intent to commit a tort against one person is transferred to the other tort or to the injured person for purposes of establishing a *prima facie* case of intentional tort. However, the transferred intent doctrine only applies to assault, battery, false imprisonment, trespass to land, and trespass to chattels.

The third element the plaintiff must prove is the causation, *i.e.*, the result giving rise to liability must have been legally caused by the defendant's act or something set in motion thereby. The causation requirement will be satisfied where the conduct of the defendant is a substantial factor in bringing about the injury.

Several of the most common torts are discussed

below.

2. Intentional Torts to the Person

2.1 Battery and Assault

Battery is the intentional, unprivileged, and either harmful or offensive contact with the person of another. People may be held liable for battery if they intend to bring about such a contact, or if such a contact directly or indirectly results from their actions. The elements which the plaintiff must prove to make out a *prima facie* case of battery are: an act by the defendant which brings about harmful or offensive contact to the plaintiff's person or effects, the defendant's intent to make such a contact, and the causation between the defendant's act and the offensive or harmful touching of the plaintiff's person or effects.

Assume that A is walking along the sidewalk and sees B, whom A dislikes intensely, approaching from the opposite direction. A punches B on the jaw, knocking out three of B's teeth and rendering B unconscious. On these facts A has committed a harmful battery upon B for which A may be held liable in tort. All of the elements of harmful battery are present: A intentionally contacted B's person in a harmful manner under circumstances that did not give rise to a privilege on A's part. It should be noted that the fact that A dislikes B explains A's conduct, but is not a necessary element of the tort. Even if B were a stranger to A, A's conduct would be tortuous if the above-described elements are present.

Assault is an act by the defendant creating a reasonable apprehension in the plaintiff of immediate harmful or offensive contact to the plaintiff's person. The threat can be used to show intent, but there must be some act short of actually striking the other person. Mere words are not enough, although words may make otherwise inoffensive movements appear to be hostile. The basic elements the plaintiff must prove include intent to cause apprehension of contact, present apparent ability of the defendant to cause contact, a threatening gesture by the defendant, and well-grounded apprehension of imminent, unconsented

unprivileged 无特权的,享受不到特权的
harmful contact （对身体)有害的接触
offensive contact 令人精神上感到冒犯的身体接触

prima facie case 初步证据确实的案件

effects 财物,动产

apprehension 恐惧

hostile 怀有敌意的
gesture 手势,姿态
well-grounded 有充分根据的
imminent (imminency) 即将来临的,逼近的(紧迫性)
unconsented 未经同意的

contact. Apprehension here does not necessarily require the plaintiff actually be frightened, but rather, it refers to an expectation of the contact. The general test is whether a reasonable person <u>in like circumstances</u> would normally feel apprehensive. To arouse apprehension, a display of force must be directed specifically towards the plaintiff. Furthermore, the victim must be aware of the threatening conduct and must actually feel threatened.

In *Bouton v. Allstate Insurance Co.*, 491 So. 2d 56 (La. App. 1986), the plaintiff claimed that a thirteen-year-old boy committed an assault upon him by going to the front door of plaintiff's house on Halloween night dressed <u>in military fatigues</u> and carrying a plastic model <u>submachine gun</u>. The plaintiff shot and killed the boy, believing him to be <u>an armed assailant</u>. After plaintiff's <u>acquittal</u> on <u>second degree murder</u> charges, plaintiff brought this action against the boy's insurers, alleging that the boy's assault caused plaintiff to be tried criminally, incur legal expenses, lose his job, and suffer a damaged reputation. The court rejected this claim as a matter of law, stating that a reasonable person under these circumstances would not have been apprehensive of imminent harmful bodily contact.

Assault and battery often go hand in hand, but they are legally distinct torts. Battery does not necessarily involve assault. Likewise, assault can take place without battery. Following are some leading cases discussing battery and assault. The first case is also famous for the so-called "<u>Eggshell Skull Rule</u>," *i.e.*, an intentional tortfeasor is ordinarily liable for all consequences, whether foreseeable or not, which are actual cause of his conduct.

2.1.1 Case 13: Vosburg v. Putney

Supreme Court of Wisconsin
Vosburg v. Putney
80 Wis. 523, 50 N.W. 403
Nov. 17, 1891

The action was brought to recover damages for an

---

in like circumstances 在类似或同样情况下

in military fatigues 身着军装

submachine gun 小型轻机枪、冲锋枪

an armed assailant 携带武器的攻击者、袭击者

acquittal 宣告无罪（指通过法庭判决、陪审团裁断或其他法律程序，正式确认被指控犯罪的人在法律上无罪）

second degree murder 二级谋杀

Eggshell Skull Rule 脆弱原则，"易碎蛋壳脑袋原则"

assault and battery, alleged to have been committed by the defendant upon the plaintiff on February 20, 1889. The answer is a general denial. At the date of the alleged assault the plaintiff was a little more than 14 years of age, and the defendant a little less than 12 years of age. The injury complained of was caused by a kick inflicted by defendant upon the leg of the plaintiff, a little below the knee. The transaction occurred in a school-room in Waukesha, during school hours, both parties being pupils in the school. A former trial of the cause resulted in a verdict and judgment for the plaintiff for $2,800. The defendant appealed from such judgment to this court, and the same was reversed for error, and a new trial awarded. 78 Wis. 84, 47 N. W. Rep. 99.

 The case has been again tried in the circuit court, and the trial resulted in a verdict for plaintiff for $2,500. The facts of the case, as they appeared on both trials, are sufficiently stated in the opinion by Mr. Justice Orton on the former appeal ...

 [The facts of this case as stated in the first supreme court opinion referred to are briefly as follows: The plaintiff was about 14 years of age, and the defendant about 11 years of age. On the 20th day of February, 1889, they were sitting opposite to each other across an aisle in the high school of the village of Waukesha. The defendant reached across the aisle with his foot, and hit with his toe the shin of the right leg of the plaintiff. The touch was slight. The plaintiff did not feel it, either on account of its being so slight or of loss of sensation produced by the shock. In a few moments he felt a violent pain in that place, which caused him to cry out loudly. The next day he was sick, and had to be helped to school. On the fourth day he was vomiting, and Dr. Bacon was sent for, but could not come, and he sent medicine to stop the vomiting, and came to see him the next day, on the 25th. There was a slight discoloration of the skin entirely over the inner surface of the tibia an inch below the bend of the knee. The doctor applied fomentations, and gave him anodynes to quiet the pain. This treatment was continued, and the swelling so increased by the 5th day of March that counsel was

inflict 予以（打击）；使遭受（损伤、苦痛等）；使承受（负担等）

circuit court 巡回法院（此处指下级法院）

shin 胫部，胫骨

vomit 呕吐
discoloration 变色
inner surface 内表面
tibia 胫骨
bend of the knee 膝盖的弯曲部位
fomentation 热敷
anodynes 止痛剂，镇痛剂，缓和物
swell 肿胀

limb 肢
incision 切成开口,切割
pus 脓,脓汁
drainage tube 引流管
insert 插入

exfoliate 使片状脱落,使鳞片脱落

heal up 愈合

microbe 微生物,细菌
wound 伤,伤口
revivify 使还原,使再生
exciting cause 诱因
remote cause 远因

called, and on the 8th of March an operation was performed on the limb by making an incision, and a moderate amount of pus escaped. A drainage tube was inserted, and an iodoform dressing put on. On the sixth day after this, another incision was made to the bone, and it was found that destruction was going on in the bone, and so it has continued exfoliating pieces of bone. He will never recover the use of his limb. There were black and blue spots on the shin bone, indicating that there had been a blow. On the 1st day of January before, the plaintiff received an injury just above the knee of the same leg by coasting, which appeared to be healing up and drying down at the time of the last injury. The theory of at least one of the medical witnesses was that the limb was in a diseased condition when this touch or kick was given, caused by microbes entering in through the wound above the knee, and which were revivified by the touch, and that the touch was the exciting or remote cause of the destruction of the bone, or of the plaintiff's injury. It does not appear that there was any visible mark made or left by this touch or kick of the defendant's foot, or any appearance of injury until the black and blue spots were discovered by the physician several days afterwards, and then there were more spots than one. There was no proof of any other hurt, and the medical testimony seems to have been agreed that this touch or kick was the exciting cause of the injury to the plaintiff. The jury rendered a verdict for the plaintiff of \$2,800. The learned circuit judge said to the jury: "It is a peculiar case, an unfortunate case, a case, I think I am at liberty to say that ought not to have come into court. The parents of these children ought, in some way, if possible, to have adjusted it between themselves." We have much of the same feeling about the case. It is a very strange and extraordinary case. The cause would seem to be very slight for so great and serious a consequence. And yet the plaintiff's limb might have been in just that condition when such a slight blow would excite and cause such a result, according to the medical testimony. That there is great uncertainty about the case cannot be denied. But perfect certainty is not required. It is sufficient that it is the opinion of the medical witnesses that such a cause even might produce such a result under the peculiar circumstances, and that the jury had the right to find, from the evidence and reasonable inferences therefrom, that it did. We will refrain from further comment on the case, as another trial will have to be had in it.]

On the last trial the jury found a special verdict, as follows:"(1) Had the plaintiff during the month of January, 1889, received an injury just above the knee, which became inflamed, and produced pus? Answer. Yes. (2) Had such injury on the 20th day of February, 1889, nearly healed at the point of the injury? A. Yes. (3) Was the plaintiff, before said 20th of February, lame, as the result of such injury? A. No. (4) Had the tibia in the plaintiff's right leg become inflamed or diseased to some extent before he received the blow or kick from the defendant? A. No. (5) What was the exciting cause of the injury to the plaintiff's leg? A. Kick. (6) Did the defendant, in touching the plaintiff with his foot, intend to do him any harm? A. No. (7) At what sum do you assess the damages of the plaintiff? A. Twenty-five hundred dollars." The defendant moved for judgment in his favor on the verdict, and also for a new trial. The plaintiff moved for judgment on the verdict in his favor. The motions of defendant were overruled, and that of the plaintiff granted. Thereupon judgment for plaintiff, for $2,500 damages and costs of suit, was duly entered. The defendant appeals from the judgment.

Lyon, J. (after stating the facts).

Several errors are assigned, only three of which will be considered.

I. The jury having found that the defendant, in touching the plaintiff with his foot, did not intend to do him any harm, counsel for defendant maintain that the plaintiff has no cause of action, and that defendant's motion for judgment on the special verdict should have been granted. In support of this proposition counsel quote from 2 GREENL. EV. §83, the rule that "the intention to do harm is of the

a special verdict 特别裁断(指陪审团就其认定的案件事实作出裁断,但不确定案件的哪一方胜诉,而是将此问题留给法官通过对所认定的事实适用法律来作出判决)

inflame 发炎

lame 变跛

essence of an assault." Such is the rule, no doubt, in actions or prosecutions for mere assaults. But this is an action to recover damages for an alleged assault and battery. In such case the rule is correctly stated, in many of the authorities cited by counsel, that plaintiff must show either that the intention was unlawful, or that the defendant is in fault. If the intended act is unlawful, the intention to commit it must necessarily be unlawful. Hence, as applied to this case, if the kicking of the plaintiff by the defendant was an unlawful act, the intention of defendant to kick him was also unlawful. Had the parties been upon the play-grounds of the school, engaged in the usual boyish sports, the defendant being free from malice, wantonness, or negligence, and intending no harm to plaintiff in what he did, we should hesitate to hold the act of the defendant unlawful, or that he could be held liable in this action. Some consideration is due to the implied license of the play-grounds. But it appears that the injury was inflicted in the school, after it had been called to order by the teacher, and after the regular exercises of the school had commenced. Under these circumstances, no implied license to do the act complained of existed, and such act was a violation of the order and <u>decorum</u> of the school, and necessarily unlawful. Hence we are of the opinion that, under the evidence and verdict, the action may be sustained.

　　II. The plaintiff testified, as a witness in his own behalf, as to the circumstances of the alleged injury inflicted upon him by the defendant, and also in regard to the wound he received in January, near the same knee, mentioned in the special verdict. The defendant claimed that such wound was the <u>proximate cause</u> of the injury to plaintiff's leg, in that it produced a diseased condition of the bone, which disease was in active progress when he received the kick, and that such kick did nothing more than to change the location, and perhaps somewhat <u>hasten</u> the progress, of the disease. The testimony of Dr. Bacon, a witness for plaintiff, (who was plaintiff's <u>attending physician</u>), <u>elicit</u>ed on cross-examination, tends to some extent to establish such claim. Dr. Bacon first saw the injured leg on February 25th, and Dr. Philler, also one of plaintiff's witnesses, first saw it March 8th. Dr. Philler was called as a witness after the examination of the plaintiff and Dr. Bacon. On his <u>direct examination</u> he testified as follows: "I heard the testimony of Andrew Vosburg in regard to how he received the kick, February 20th, from his playmate. I heard read [sic] the testimony of Miss More, and heard where he said he received this kick on that day." (Miss More had already testified that she was the teacher of the school, and saw defendant standing in the aisle by his seat, and kicking across the aisle, hitting the plaintiff.) The following question was then <u>propounded</u> to Dr. Philler: "After hearing that testimony, and what you know of the case of the boy, seeing it on the 8th day of March, what, in your opinion, was the exciting cause that produced the <u>inflammation</u> that you saw in that boy's leg on that day?" An objection to this question was <u>overruled</u>, and the witness answered: "The exciting cause was the injury received at that day by the kick on the shin-bone." It will be observed that the above question to Dr. Philler calls for his opinion as a medical expert, based in part upon the testimony of the plaintiff, as to what was the proximate cause of the injury to plaintiff's leg. The plaintiff testified to two wounds upon his leg, either of which might have been such proximate cause. Without taking both of these wounds into consideration, the expert could give no intelligent or reliable opinion as to which of them caused the injury complained of; yet, in the <u>hypothetical</u> question propounded to him, one of these <u>probable causes</u> was excluded from the consideration of the witness, and he was required to give his opinion upon an imperfect and insufficient hypothesis — one which excluded from his consideration a material fact essential to an intelligent opinion. A consideration by the witness of the wound received by the plaintiff in January being thus prevented, the witness had but one fact upon which to base his opinion, <u>towit</u>, the fact that defendant kicked plaintiff on the shin-bone. Based, as it necessarily was, on that fact alone, the opinion of Dr. Philler that the kick caused the injury was <u>inevitable</u>, when, had the proper hypothesis been submitted to him, his

direct examination 直接询问,主询问

propound 提出

inflammation 发炎,炎症
overrule (an objection) (指在审判过程中,法官)驳回(律师提出的反对意见)

hypothetical 假定的,基于假定的
probable cause 合理根据,可成立的理由(指极有可能是确实的根据,其可信程度大于怀疑但小于确切无误)

towit 即,就是

inevitable 不可避免的,无法规避的,必然(发生)的

vital 重要的

fatal 重大的,致命的

ex contractu 来自契约,源于契约

ex delicto 由于侵权,源自侵权

opinion might have been different. The answer of Dr. Philler to the hypothetical question put to him may have had, probably did have, a controlling influence with the jury, for they found by their verdict that his opinion was correct. Surely there can be no rule of evidence which will tolerate a hypothetical question to an expert, calling for his opinion in a matter vital to the case, which excludes from his consideration facts already proved by a witness upon whose testimony such hypothetical question is based, when a consideration of such facts by the expert is absolutely essential to enable him to form an intelligent opinion concerning such matter. The objection to the question put to Dr. Philler should have been sustained. The error in permitting the witness to answer the question is material, and necessarily fatal to the judgment.

III. Certain questions were proposed on behalf of defendant to be submitted to the jury, founded upon the theory that only such damages could be recovered as the defendant might reasonably be supposed to have contemplated as likely to result from his kicking the plaintiff. The court refused to submit such questions to the jury. The ruling was correct. The rule of damages in actions for torts was held in *Brown v. Railway Co.*, 54 Wis. 342, 11 N. W. Rep. 356, 911, to be that the wrongdoer is liable for all injuries resulting directly from the wrongful act, whether they could or could not have been foreseen by him. The chief justice and the writer of this opinion dissented from the judgment in that case, chiefly because we were of the opinion that the complaint stated a cause of action *ex contractu*, and not *ex delicto*, and hence that a different rule of damages — the rule here contended for — was applicable. We did not question that the rule in actions for tort was correctly stated. That case rules this on the question of damages. The remaining errors assigned are upon the rulings of the court on objections to testimony. These rulings are not very likely to be repeated on another trial, and are not of sufficient importance to require a review of them on this appeal. The judgment of the circuit court must be reversed, and the cause will be remanded for a new trial.

2.1.2 Case 14: Hackbart v. Cincinnati Bengals, Inc.

United States Court of Appeals, Tenth Circuit
Dale Hackbart v. Cincinnati Bengals, Inc.
601 F. 2d 516
June 11, 1979

Williame E. Doyle, Circuit Judge.

The question in this case is whether in a regular season professional football game an injury which is inflicted by one professional football player on an opposing player can give rise to liability in tort where the injury was inflicted by the intentional striking of a blow during the game.

The injury occurred in the course of a game between the Denver Broncos and the Cincinnati Bengals, which game was being played in Denver in 1973. The Broncos' defensive back, Dale Hackbart, was the recipient of the injury and the Bengals' offensive back, Charles "Booby" Clark, inflicted the blow which produced it.

By agreement the liability question was determined by the United States District Court for the District of Colorado without a jury. The judge resolved the liability issue in favor of the Cincinnati team and Charles Clark. Consistent with this result, final judgment was entered for Cincinnati and the appeal challenges this judgment. In essence the trial court's reasons for rejecting plaintiff's claim were that professional football is a species of warfare and that so much physical force is tolerated and the magnitude of the force exerted is so great that it renders injuries not actionable in court; that even intentional batteries are beyond the scope of the judicial process.

Clark was an offensive back and just before the injury he had run a pass pattern to the right side of the Denver Broncos' end zone. The injury flowed indirectly from this play. The pass was <u>intercepted</u> by Billy Thompson, a Denver <u>free safety</u>, who returned it to mid-field. The subject injury occurred as an <u>aftermath</u> of the pass play.

As a consequence of the interception, the roles of Hackbart and Clark suddenly changed. Hackbart,

intercept 拦截,截断

free safety （橄榄球）
（殿后）自由后卫

aftermath 结果,后果

who had been defending, instantaneously became an offensive player. Clark, on the other hand, became a defensive player. Acting as an offensive player, Hackbart attempted to block Clark by throwing his body in front of him. He thereafter remained on the ground. He turned, and with one knee on the ground, watched the play following the interception.

The trial court's finding was that Charles Clark, "acting out of anger and frustration, but without a specific intent to injure ... stepped forward and struck a blow with his right forearm to the back of the kneeling plaintiff's head and neck with sufficient force to cause both players to fall forward to the ground." Both players, without complaining to the officials or to one another, returned to their respective sidelines since the ball had changed hands and the offensive and defensive teams of each had been substituted. Clark testified at trial that his frustration was brought about by the fact that his team was losing the game.

Due to the failure of the officials to view the incident, a foul was not called. However, the game film showed very clearly what had occurred. Plaintiff did not at the time report the happening to his coaches or to anyone else during the game. However, because of the pain which he experienced he was unable to play golf the next day. He did not seek medical attention, but the continued pain caused him to report this fact and the incident to the Bronco trainer who gave him treatment. Apparently he played on the specialty teams for two successive Sundays, but after that the Broncos released him on waivers. (He was in his thirteenth year as a player.) He sought medical help and it was then that it was discovered by the physician that he had a serious neck fracture injury.

Despite the fact that the defendant Charles Clark admitted that the blow which had been struck was not accidental, that it was intentionally administered, the trial court ruled as a matter of law that the game of professional football is basically a business which is violent in nature, and that the available sanctions are imposition of penalties and expulsion from the game. Notice was taken of the fact that many fouls are overlooked; that the game is played in an emotional and noisy environment; and that incidents such as that here complained of are not unusual.

The trial court spoke as well of the unreasonableness of applying the laws and rules which are a part of injury law to the game of professional football, noting the unreasonableness of holding that one player has a <u>duty of care</u> for the safety of others. He also talked about the concept of assumption of risk and contributory fault as applying and concluded that Hackbart had to recognize that he accepted the risk that he would be injured by such an act.

duty of care 注意义务

I. The Issues and Contentions

1. Whether the trial court erred in ruling that as a matter of policy the principles of law governing the infliction of injuries should be entirely refused where the injury took place in the course of the game.

2. Did the trial court err in concluding that the employee was not <u>vicariously liable</u> for an activity for which he had not received express authorization?

vicariously liable 承担替代(间接)责任(一个人即使没有过错,因其特殊地位,也可能为他人的行为承担责任,通常适用于雇主对雇员的行为承担责任)

3. Whether it was error to receive in evidence numerous episodes of violence which were unrelated to the case at bar, that is, incidents of intentional infliction of injury which occurred in other games.

4. Whether it was error for the trial court to receive in evidence unrelated acts on the part of the plaintiff.

5. The final issue is whether the evidence justifies consideration by the court of the issue of reckless conduct as it is defined in A. L. I. RESTATEMENT OF THE LAW OF TORTS SECOND, § 500, because (admittedly) the assault and battery theory is not available because that tort is governed by a one-year statute of limitations.

II. Whether the Evidence Supported the Judgment

The evidence at the trial <u>uniformly</u> supported the proposition that the intentional striking of a player in the head from the <u>rear</u> is not an accepted part of either the playing rules or the general customs of the game of professional football. The trial court, however, believed that the unusual nature of the case called for the consideration of underlying policy which it defined

uniformly 一致地

rear 后部,后面

as common law principles which have evolved as a result of the case to case process and which necessarily affect behavior in various contexts. From these considerations the belief was expressed that even intentional injuries incurred in football games should be outside the framework of the law. The court recognized that the potential threat of legal liability has a significant deterrent effect, and further said that private civil actions constitute an important mechanism for societal control of human conduct. Due to the increase in severity of human conflicts, a need existed to expand the body of governing law more rapidly and with more certainty, but that this had to be accomplished by legislation and administrative regulation. The judge compared football to coal mining and railroading insofar as all are inherently hazardous. Judge Matsch said that in the case of football it was questionable whether social values would be improved by limiting the violence.

Thus the district court's assumption was that Clark had inflicted an intentional blow which would ordinarily generate civil liability and which might bring about a criminal sanction as well, but that since it had occurred in the course of a football game, it should not be subject to the restraints of the law; that if it were it would place unreasonable impediments and restraints on the activity. The judge also pointed out that courts are ill-suited to decide the different social questions and to administer conflicts on what is much like a battlefield where the restraints of civilization have been left on the sidelines.

We are forced to conclude that the result reached is not supported by evidence.

III. Whether Intentional Injury is Allowed by Either Written Rule or Custom

Plaintiff, of course, maintains that tort law applicable to the injury in this case applies on the football field as well as in other places. On the other hand, plaintiff does not rely on the theory of negligence being applicable. This is in recognition of the fact that subjecting another to unreasonable risk of harm, the essence of negligence, is inherent in the game of football, for admittedly it is violent. Plaintiff maintains that in the area of contributory fault, a vacuum exists in relationship to intentional infliction of injury. Since negligence does not apply, contributory negligence is inapplicable. Intentional or reckless contributory fault could theoretically at least apply to infliction of injuries in <u>reckless disregard</u> of the rights of others. This has some similarity to contributory negligence and undoubtedly it would apply if the evidence would justify it. But it is highly questionable whether a professional football player consents or submits to injuries caused by conduct not within the rules, and we have seen no evidence which shows this. However, the trial court did not consider this question and we are not deciding it.

 Contrary to the position of the court then, there are no principles of law which allow a court to rule out certain tortious conduct by reason of general roughness of the game or difficulty of administering it.

 Indeed, the evidence shows that there are rules of the game which prohibit the intentional striking of blows. Thus, Article 1, Item 1, Subsection C, provides that:

 All players are prohibited from striking on the head, face or neck with the heel, back or side of the hand, wrist, forearm, elbow or clasped hands.

 Thus the very conduct which was present here is expressly prohibited by the rule which is quoted above.

 The general customs of football do not approve the intentional punching or striking of others. That this is prohibited was supported by the testimony of all of the witnesses. They testified that the intentional striking of a player in the face or from the rear is prohibited by the playing rules as well as the general customs of the game. Punching or hitting with the arms is prohibited. Undoubtedly these restraints are intended to establish reasonable boundaries so that one football player cannot intentionally inflict a serious injury on another. Therefore, the <u>notion</u> is not correct that all reason has been abandoned, whereby the only possible remedy for the person who has been the victim of an unlawful blow is <u>retaliation</u>.

reckless disregard 放任, 极其漠视

notion 概念, 想法, 观念

retaliation 报复, 同态复仇

IV. Was It Legally Justifiable for the Trial Court to Hold, as a Matter of Policy, that Jurisdiction Should Not Be Assumed Over the Case in View of the Fact that It Arose Out of a Professional Football Game?

A. Whether the theory of judicial restraint applies.

It is a well-settled principle of federal jurisdiction that where a federal court does not have a discretion to accept or reject jurisdiction, if it does not have jurisdiction, it will not take it; but it is ruled, on the other hand, that if it has jurisdiction it must take it. This principle has been expressed many times with perhaps one of the best expressions being found in an early opinion, that of Mr. Chief Justice Marshall in *Cohens v. Virginia*, 19 U.S. (6 Wheat.) 264, 404, 5 L. Ed. 257 (1821):

> It is most true, that this court will not take jurisdiction if it should not; but it is equally true, that it must take jurisdiction, if it should. The judiciary cannot, as the legislature may, avoid a measure, because it approaches the confines of the constitution. We cannot pass it by, because it is doubtful. With whatever doubts, with whatever difficulties, a case may be attended, we must decide it, if it be brought before us. We have no more right to decline the exercise of jurisdiction which is given, than to usurp that which is not given. The one or the other would be treason to the constitution. Questions may occur, which we would gladly avoid; but we cannot avoid them. All we can do is, to exercise our best judgment, and conscientiously to perform our duty. In doing this, on the present occasion, we find this tribunal invested with appellate jurisdiction in all cases arising under the constitution and laws of the United States. We find no exception to this grant, and we cannot insert one.

Much more recently the Supreme Court in the case of *Willcox v. Consolidated Gas Co.*, 212 U.S. 19, 40 (1909), speaking through Mr. Justice Peckham, stated that where a federal court is appealed to in the case over which it has by law jurisdiction, it is its duty to take such jurisdiction.

They assume to criticize that court (United States District Court for the Southern District of New York) for taking jurisdiction of this case, as <u>precipitate</u>, as if it were a question of discretion or <u>comity</u>, whet her or not that court should have heard the case. On the contrary, there was no discretion or comity about it. When a Federal court is properly appealed to in a case over which it has by law jurisdiction, it is its duty to take such jurisdiction (*Cohens v. Virginia*, 19 U.S. 264), and, in taking it, that court cannot be truthfully spoken of as precipitate in its conduct. That the case may be one of local interest only is entirely immaterial, so long as the parties are citizens of different States or a question is involved which by law brings the case within the jurisdiction of a Federal court. The right of a party plaintiff to choose a Federal court where there is a choice cannot be properly denied.

Mr. Justice Peckham expressed the view that the rule is based on the right of a party plaintiff to choose a federal court where there is a choice.

There are some recognized limitations on federal courts assuming jurisdiction, but none of these permit a court to exercise its own discretion on the subject. One example of limitation is the political question. Another is the <u>doctrine of abstention</u>, which is exercised where a state court is involved and <u>deference</u> is exercised in favor of the state court. *See*, for example, *Colorado River Water Conservation District v. United States*, 424 U.S. 800 (1976). These, however, are the exceptions and not the rule as was pointed out in the cited case. Abstention itself is limited. It does not contemplate that federal courts <u>abdicate</u> their jurisdiction. See *American Trial Lawyers Association v. New Jersey Supreme Court*, 409 U.S. 467 (1973).

The Supreme Court has been known to refuse to exercise its <u>original jurisdiction</u>. *Ohio v. Wyandotte Chemicals Corporation*, 401 U.S. 493 (1971). At the same time, it <u>reiterated</u> the traditional rule that where a federal court has jurisdiction it must exercise it. It is

 precipitate 轻率的,贸然的

 comity 司法礼让,法院间的礼让承认

 doctrine of abstention 避让原则(美国对涉及州法律或政策的案件,为避免与各州对本州事务的管理发生不必要的冲突,联邦法院可自主决定放弃对该案行使管辖权,而由州法院或其他州机构首先予以处理)

 deference 顺从,尊重

 abdicate 完全放弃(权利、责任、要求等)

 original jurisdiction 初审管辖权

 reiterate 重申

not at liberty to refuse to do so unless it is in accordance with one of the principles mentioned above. Original jurisdiction in the Supreme Court allows much more <u>leeway</u> to refusing acceptance of jurisdiction than does an <u>inferior</u> federal court.

It is clear that none of the grounds for refusing access to the courts are present in the instant case. One writer, Professor Keeton, has said that courts properly participate in the evolution and development of common law. We <u>submit</u> that this approach is <u>at odds with</u> refusing to accept the case. See Keeton, *Creative Continuity of Tort Law*, 75 HARV. L. REV. 463 (1962). *See also* Widener, *Some Random Thoughts on Judicial Restraint*, 31 WASH. AND LEE L. REV. 505 (1974).①

The spirit and the letter of the decisions are that if jurisdiction to hear or determine cases exists, as it does in the case at bar, the cause is to be tried on its merits.

The position which was adopted by the trial court in this case was then directly contrary to all of the law dealing with the exercise of jurisdiction by federal courts.

B. Whether <u>diversity jurisdiction</u> provides any discretion.

It is of high importance to note the fact that in <u>a diversity of citizenship case</u> the federal district court sits as a state trial court and applies the law of <u>the forum state</u>. See *Erie Railroad Co. v. Tompkins*, 304 U. S. 64 (1938). In this highly important decision the Supreme Court, through the late Justice Brandeis, overruled the early case of *Swift v. Tyson*, 41 U. S. (16 Pet.) 1 (1842), which had allowed federal trial courts to apply their own common law. The rule was established in *Erie* that the law of the state in which the court sat had to be applied to the diversity case. In rejecting the principle that the federal court could apply its own common law rule, the Court rejected the idea that a <u>transcendental</u> body of law existed for

---

leeway 余地
inferior 下级的

submit 认为
at odds with 与……不和,与……争吵,与……不一致

diversity jurisdiction 美国联邦法院对不同州(国)籍当事人之间诉讼的管辖权
a diversity of citizenship case (诉讼当事人的)州(国)籍不同,公民身份不同的案子
the forum state 法院所在国

transcendental 超凡的,卓越的

---

① Judge Widener of the U. S. Court of Appeals for the Fourth Circuit concluded that if a problem exists it "is not to say that the federal courts must avoid all the hard, or unpleasant, or distasteful questions," but rather the limitations should be on the basis that jurisdiction prohibits the acceptance of the case. Since Congress prescribed jurisdiction, the boundaries set by it should be followed.

federal courts. It was said that there was no backup federal authority in the federal government to provide this power for federal courts; that the authoritative governing force was in the state courts.

Justice Holmes was quoted by Justice Brandeis (the author of *Erie*) for the proposition that the authority in this diversity area must come from the state. A second basis for disapproval of federal authority or ability to innovate in diversity cases also originated with Justice Holmes, who said that the *Swift v. Tyson* rule was an unconstitutional assumption of power by the courts of the United States. The Supreme Court in *Erie* thus declared that in applying the theory of *Swift v. Tyson*, the Supreme Court and lower federal courts had invaded rights protected by the Constitution of the United States and the several states.

So, applying the *Erie* doctrine, the conclusion is that there does not exist an independent basis which allows a federal court to, in effect, outlaw a particular activity absent legal evidence that either state policy or state law dictates or allows such action. Absent any such evidence, the trial court cannot turn to public policy in order to support a conclusion that the courts cannot entertain a particular case.

Second, it is also fundamental that for every injury wrongfully inflicted, some redress under the state common law must be afforded since it is essential that citizens be able to look to their government for redress. As was said in *Marbury v. Madison*, 5 U.S. (1 Cranch) 137 (1803), "The very essence of civil liberty certainly consists in the right of every individual to claim the protection of the law, whenever he received an injury. One of the first duties of government is to afford that protection."

The right of citizens to get relief in federal courts is similar to the same right in state court, bearing in mind that the federal courts in diversity cases are applying state law. We must also be cognizant that federal courts are limited to deciding cases or controversies. This was pointed out in *Flast v. Cohen*, 392 U.S. 83, 94-95 (1968). The Court there said:

those words limit the business of federal courts to questions presented in an adversary context and in a form historically viewed as capable of resolution through the judicial process. And in part those words define the role assigned to the judiciary in a tripartite allocation of power to assure that the federal courts will not intrude into areas committed to the other branches of government.

392 U. S. at 95.

The Court in *Flast* was recognizing the right of a federal taxpayer to enjoin the spending of federal funds for the buying of books for use in religious schools. 392 U. S. at 105 – 06.

The concurrence of Justice Douglas is worth noting, for he spoke on the right of access to the courts as follows:

> The judiciary is an indispensable part of the operation of our federal system. With the growing complexities of government it is often the one and only place where effective relief can be obtained. If the judiciary were to become a super-legislative group sitting in judgment on the affairs of people, the situation would be intolerable. But where wrongs to individuals are done by violation of specific guarantees, it is abdication for the courts to close their doors.

392 U. S. at 111.

C. Does Colorado law provide or allow any restraint?

The next question is whether there are applicable restrictions in the Colorado law. On the contrary, the Colorado Constitution, Art. II, s 6, provides: "Court of justice shall be open to every person, and a speedy remedy afforded for every injury to person, property or character; and right and justice should be administered without sale, denial or delay." The district courts are said to be courts of unlimited jurisdiction unlike the federal courts. However, in a diversity case the federal court inherits the jurisdictional scope that is enjoyed by the state court within the district. Art. VI, s 9, subsection (1), provides:

> The district courts shall be trial courts of record with general jurisdiction, and shall have original jurisdiction in all civil, probate, and criminal cases, except as otherwise provided herein, and shall have such appellate jurisdiction as may be prescribed by law.

general jurisdiction 普通管辖权（指法院依据法律的规定对所有刑事和民事案件都具有管辖权）
original jurisdiction 初审管辖权
probate 遗嘱检验的
appellate jurisdiction 上诉管辖权,复审和改正下级法院的裁决的权力
prescribe 规定

The Colorado courts have liberally construed these provisions. See Patterson v. People, 23 Colo. App. 479, 130 P. 618 (1913); People ex rel. Cruz v. Morley, 77 Colo. 25, 234 P. 178 (1924). In the Morley case it was said: "[t]he constitutional jurisdiction of the district court is unlimited. It should not be limited without circumspection and no statute should be held to limit it unless it says so plainly ..." 234 P. at 179.

circumspection 慎重,谨慎

The Colorado Supreme Court has held that under Art. II, s 6 of the Colorado Constitution, where there exists a right under the law, the courts of the state will assure the protection of that right. O'Quinn v. Walt Disney Productions, Inc., 177 Colo. 190, 493 P. 2d 344 (1972).

The common law, of course, obtains in Colorado. The legislature may modify it, but in the absence of evidence that the common law has been modified by legislation, the courts, that is, the district court and the federal district court in a diversity case, must apply it.

We are constrained to hold that the trial court's ruling that this case had to be dismissed because the injury was inflicted during a professional football game was error.

V. Is the Standard of Reckless Disregard of the Rights of Others Applicable to the Present Situation?

The Restatement of Torts Second, s 500, distinguishes between reckless and negligent misconduct. Reckless misconduct differs from negligence, according to the

negligent misconduct 过失行为
reckless misconduct 不顾后果的胡作非为（指行为人在知道或者应当知道可能对他人造成重大危险的情况下,有意作为或不作为）

authors, in that negligence consists of mere inadvertence, lack of skillfulness or failure to take precautions; reckless misconduct, on the other hand, involves a choice or adoption of a course of action either with knowledge of the danger or with knowledge of facts which would disclose this danger to a reasonable man. Recklessness also differs in that it consists of intentionally doing an act with knowledge not only that it contains a risk of harm to others as does negligence, but that it actually involves a risk substantially greater in magnitude than is necessary in the case of negligence. The authors explain the difference, therefore, in the degree of risk by saying that the difference is so significant as to amount to a difference in kind.

Subsection (f) also distinguishes between reckless misconduct and intentional wrongdoing. To be reckless the Act must have been intended by the actor. At the same time, the actor does not intend to cause the harm which results from it. It is enough that he realized, or from the facts should have realized, that there was a strong probability that harm would result even though he may hope or expect that this conduct will prove harmless. Nevertheless, existence of probability is different from substantial certainty which is an ingredient of intent to cause the harm which results from the act.

Therefore, recklessness exists where a person knows that the act is harmful but fails to realize that it will produce the extreme harm which it did produce. It is in this respect that recklessness and intentional conduct differ in degree.

In the case at bar the defendant Clark admittedly acted impulsively and in the heat of anger, and even though it could be said from the admitted facts that he intended the act, it could also be said that he did not intend to inflict serious injury which resulted from the blow which he struck.

In ruling that recklessness is the appropriate standard and that assault and battery is not the exclusive one, we are saying that these two liability concepts are not necessarily opposed one to the other. Rather, recklessness under s 500 of the Restatement might be regarded, for the purpose of analysis at least, a lesser included act.

Assault and battery, having originated in a common law writ, is narrower than recklessness in its scope. In essence, two definitions enter into it. The assault is an attempt coupled with the present ability to commit a violent harm against another. Battery is the unprivileged or unlawful touching of another. Assault and battery then call for an intent, as does recklessness. But in recklessness the intent is to do the act, but without an intent to cause the particular harm. It is enough if the actor knows that there is a strong probability that harm will result. Thus, the definition fits perfectly the fact situation here. Surely, then, no reason exists to compel appellant to employ the assault and battery standard which does not comfortably apply fully in preference to the standard which meets this fact situation.

a lesser included act 被包含（在较重违法行为中）的较轻违法行为（根据一事不再审理原则，这一较轻违法行为与较重违法行为被视为同一违法行为，不得重复审判）

writ 书面命令,令状

VI. Which of the Statutes of Limitations Applies?

The appellees contend that Clark was guilty of an assault and battery, if he was guilty of anything; that this is barred by the applicable statute of limitations for a one-year period. Appellant, however, contends that the injury was the result of reckless disregard of the rights of the plaintiff and that the six-year statute provided in Colo. Rev. Stat. Ann. § 13 - 80 - 110, is applicable.

guilty 有罪的

Our court in the recent decision in *Zuniga v. Amfac Foods, Inc.*, 580 F. 2d 380 (10th Cir. 1978), adopted the position that actions in tort are governed by the six-year provision in the cited statute. It is also to be noted that Colorado fully recognizes the action of reckless disregard for the rights of others. See *Pettingell v. Moede*, 129 Colo. 484, 271 P. 2d 1038 (1954); *Fanstiel v. Wright*, 122 Colo. 451, 222 P. 2d 1001 (1950); *Shoemaker v. Mountain States Tel. & Tel. Co.*, 559 P. 2d 721 (Colo. App. 1976). The definitions contained in s 500 are fully applicable here, and the Colorado Supreme Court in *Fanstiel v. Wright*, supra, has adopted the definition contained in s 500. A Comment to the section discusses the distinctions which we have previously mentioned.

adopt 采纳

We conclude that if the evidence establishes that the injuries were the result of acts of Clark which were in reckless disregard of Hackbart's safety, it can be said that he established a claim which is subject to the six-year statute. The cause has not been tried on its merits, but there is substantial evidence before us that supports the notion that Clark did act in accordance with the tests and standards which are set forth in s 500, *supra*. We are not prejudging this issue of fact, but are merely saying that considered in a light favorable to the plaintiff, at this stage of the proceedings the hypothesis exists that Clark's conduct would constitute a violation of s 500 and the appellant should be given an opportunity to offer his proofs in court on this subject.

VII. Did the Court Err in Receiving in Evidence Films of Violence that Took Place in Other Football Games Regardless of the Identity of the Players and Teams?

There was a film of the actual injury suffered by plaintiff. It showed the sequence of events and also depicted the manner of infliction. Obviously we need not consider the relevancy of this.

There were incidents that were designed to show that the plaintiff Hackbart was a dirty player.

Finally, films were shown which depicted acts of violence between other players and other teams.

The Federal Rules of Evidence, Rule 401, define relevant evidence as follows:

> "Relevant evidence" means evidence having any tendency to make the existence of any fact that is of consequence to the determination of the action more probable or less probable than it would be without the evidence.

Rule 404 deals with character evidence and other crimes. That which deals with character states as follows:

> (a) Character evidence generally. Evidence of a person's character or a trait of his character is

not admissible for the purpose of proving that he acted in conformity therewith on a particular occasion, except:

(1) Character of accused. Evidence of a pertinent trait of his character offered by an accused, or by the prosecution to rebut the same;

(2) Character of victim. Evidence of a pertinent trait of character of the victim of the crime offered by an accused, or by the prosecution to rebut the same, or evidence of a character trait of peacefulness of the victim offered by the prosecution in a homicide case to rebut evidence that the victim was the first aggressor;

(3) Character of witness. Evidence of the character of a witness, as provided in Rules 607, 608, and 609.

pertinent 适当的;(与争议)有关的
trait 品质
rebut 否定,反驳,推翻

homicide 杀人
aggressor 侵犯者,挑衅者(即首先使用暴力或胁迫者,这使得对侵犯行为的还击成为合法)

Subsection (b) of Rule 404 deals with other wrongs or acts and states the traditional rule that:

(b) Other crimes, wrongs, or acts. Evidence of other crimes, wrongs, or acts is not admissible to prove the character of a person in order to show that he acted in conformity therewith. It may, however, be admissible for other purposes, such as proof of motive, opportunity, intent, preparation, plan, knowledge, identity, or absence of mistake or accident.

Unless the game of football is on trial, and it appeared to be in the case at bar, the acts of violence which occurred in other games and between other teams and players were without relevance. The view we take is that the game of football is not on trial, but, rather, the trial involves a particular act in one game.

Although we recognize that the trial court has a broad discretion in receiving or rejecting evidence along this line, we fail to see the relevancy of other acts which are unconnected with the incident being tried.

admissibility（证据的）可采性(指具有在听审、庭审或其他程序中被允许作为证据提出的品质或状况。证据的可采性部分取决于有关法律规则或诉讼规则的规定，部分取决于证据本身与待证事实是否具有相关性。同一证据可能为此目的具有可采性，而为另一目的则不具有可采性。错误地采信或排除证据可构成上诉的理由)

The other aspect, namely the proof of the character of the plaintiff by production of prior acts, would be admissible only if his character was an issue in the case. Unless the plaintiff was shown to have been an unlawful aggressor in the immediate incident, his prior acts could not be relevant. The indications from the picture of the action here are that he threw a body block and after the lapse of some time, a short period of time, the blow was struck while Hackbart was down on his knee watching the action. Therefore, this evidence would appear to be questionable if not irrelevant.

On retrial the admissibility of prior unrelated acts should be very carefully considered and should not be received merely for the purpose of showing that the defendant himself had violated rules in times past since this is not *per se* relevant. Indeed it would be necessary for an issue to exist as to whether Hackbart was the aggressor in order for such evidence to be relevant.

In sum, having concluded that the trial court did not limit the case to a trial of the evidence bearing on defendant's liability but rather determined that as a matter of social policy the game was so violent and unlawful that valid lines could not be drawn, we take the view that this was not a proper issue for determination and that plaintiff was entitled to have the case tried on an assessment of his rights and whether they had been violated.

The trial court has heard the evidence and has made findings. The findings of fact based on the evidence presented are not an issue on this appeal. Thus, it would not seem that the court would have to repeat the areas of evidence that have already been fully considered. The need is for a reconsideration of that evidence in the light of that which is taken up by this court in its opinion. We are not to be understood as limiting the trial court's consideration of supplemental evidence if it deems it necessary.

The cause is reversed and remanded for a new trial in accordance with the foregoing views.

supplemental evidence
补充证据

2.1.3 Case 15: Fisher v. Carrousel Motor Hotel, Inc.

Supreme Court of Texas
Emmit E. Fisher v. Carrousel Motor Hotel, Inc., *et al.*
424 S.W.2d 627
Dec. 27, 1967

Greenhill, Justice.

This is a suit for actual and exemplary damages growing out of an alleged assault and battery. The plaintiff Fisher was a mathematician with the Data Processing Division of the Manned Spacecraft Center, an agency of the National Aeronautics and Space Agency, commonly called NASA, near Houston. The defendants were the Carrousel Motor Hotel, Inc., located in Houston, the Brass Ring Club, which is located in the Carrousel, and Robert W. Flynn, who as an employee of the Carrousel was the manager of the Brass Ring Club. Flynn died before the trial, and the suit proceeded as to the Carrousel and the Brass Ring. Trial was to a jury which found for the plaintiff Fisher. The trial court rendered judgment for the defendants notwithstanding the verdict. The Court of Civil Appeals affirmed. 414 S.W.2d 774. The questions before this Court are whether there was evidence that an actionable battery was committed, and, if so, whether the two corporate defendants must respond in exemplary as well as actual damages for the malicious conduct of Flynn.

The plaintiff Fisher had been invited by Ampex Corporation and Defense Electronics to a one day's meeting regarding telemetry equipment at the Carrousel. The invitation included a luncheon. The guests were asked to reply by telephone whether they could attend the luncheon, and Fisher called in his acceptance. After the morning session, the group of 25 or 30 guests adjourned to the Brass Ring Club for lunch. The luncheon was buffet style, and Fisher stood in line with others and just ahead of a graduate student of Rice University who testified at the trial. As Fisher was about to be served, he was approached by Flynn, who snatched the plate from Fisher's hand and shouted that he, a Negro, could not be served in

---

exemplary damages 惩罚性损害赔偿金（指由于被告的暴力、强制、诈欺、恶意行为加重了原告的损害,从而判决给予原告以超过实际或通常程度的损害赔偿金,以示对被告的惩罚）

judgment notwithstanding the verdict (JNOV) 与陪审团裁断相反的判决（指法庭在陪审团已作出一方当事人胜诉的裁断后作出的对方当事人胜诉的判决）
corporate defendant 公司被告

adjourn 休会,中止活动
buffet 自助餐

snatch 夺取,攫取

embarrass 骚扰，阻碍，使困窘，使局促不安

associate 同事，伙伴

forceably 用力地，强迫地

dispossess 剥夺占有

indignity 侮辱（指以各种方式对他人的情感、自尊和荣誉而不是身体进行损害，造成他人难堪、亲朋疏离等）

the club. Fisher testified that he was not actually touched, and did not testify that he suffered fear or apprehension of physical injury; but he did testify that he was highly embarrassed and hurt by Flynn's conduct in the presence of his associates.

The jury found that Flynn "forceably dispossessed plaintiff of his dinner plate" and "shouted in a loud and offensive manner" that Fisher could not be served there, thus subjecting Fisher to humiliation and indignity. It was stipulated that Flynn was an employee of the Carrousel Hotel and, as such, managed the Brass Ring Club. The jury also found that Flynn acted maliciously and awarded Fisher $400 actual damages for his humiliation and indignity and $500 exemplary damages for Flynn's malicious conduct.

The Court of Civil Appeals held that there was no assault because there was no physical contact and no evidence of fear or apprehension of physical contact. However, it has long been settled that there can be a battery without an assault, and that actual physical contact is not necessary to constitute a battery, so long as there is contact with clothing or an object closely identified with the body. 1 Harper & James, THE LAW OF TORTS 216 (1956); RESTATEMENT OF TORTS 2d, §§ 18 and 19. In Prosser, Law of Torts 32 (3d Ed. 1964), it is said:

> The interest in freedom from intentional and unpermitted contacts with the plaintiff's person is protected by an action for the tort commonly called battery. The protection extends to any part of the body, or to anything which is attached to it and practically identified with it. Thus contact with the plaintiff's clothing, or with a cane, a paper, or any other object held in his hand will be sufficient; ... The plaintiff's interest in the integrity of his person includes all those things which are in contact or connected with it.

Under the facts of this case, we have no difficulty in holding that the intentional grabbing of plaintiff's plate constituted a battery. The intentional snatching of an object from one's hand is as clearly an offensive invasion of his person as would be an actual contact with the body. "To constitute an assault and battery, it is not necessary to touch the plaintiff's body or even his clothing; knocking or snatching anything from plaintiff's hand or touching anything connected with his person, when, done in an offensive manner, is sufficient." *Morgan v. Loyacomo*, 190 Miss. 656, 1 So. 2d 510 (1941).

Such holding is not unique to the jurisprudence of this State. In *S. H. Kress & Co. v. Brashier*, 50 S. W. 2d 922 (Tex. Civ. App. 1932), the defendant was held to have committed "an assault or trespass upon the person" by snatching a book from the plaintiff's hand. The jury findings in that case were that the defendant "dispossessed plaintiff of the book" and caused her to suffer "humiliation and indignity."

The rationale for holding an offensive contact with such an object to be a battery is explained in 1 RESTATEMENT OF TORTS 2d § 18 (Comment p. 31) as follows:

> Since the essence of the plaintiff's grievance consists in the offense to the dignity involved in the unpermitted and intentional invasion of the inviolability of his person and not in any physical harm done to his body, it is not necessary that the plaintiff's actual body be disturbed. Unpermitted and intentional contacts with anything so connected with the body as to be customarily regarded as part of the other's person and therefore as partaking of its inviolability is actionable as an offensive contact with his person. There are some things such as clothing or a cane or, indeed, anything directly grasped by the hand which are so intimately connected with one's body as to be universally regarded as part of the person.

We hold, therefore, that the forceful dispossession of plaintiff Fisher's plate in an offensive manner was sufficient to constitute a battery, and the trial court erred in granting judgment notwithstanding the verdict on the issue of actual damages.

In *Harned v. E-Z Finance Co.*, 151 Tex. 641,

holding 裁决
jurisprudence 法理, 法律体系

trespass 侵害, 侵犯, 侵入

rationale 原理的阐述, 理由的说明, 解释

grievance 申诉

inviolability 不可侵犯性, 不可违背性, 免受侵犯, 免受袭击

partake 参加, 参与

mental suffering 精神痛苦

advocate 为……辩护；提倡；拥护，主张

insulting 侮辱的，无礼的

in this regard 在这点上，关于此事

in question 讨论中的，考虑中的

254 S. W. 2d 81 (1953), this Court refused to adopt the "new tort" of intentional interference with peace of mind which permits recovery for mental suffering in the absence of resulting physical injury or an assault and battery. This cause of action has long been advocated by respectable writers and legal scholars. See, for example, Prosser, *Insult and Outrage*, 44 CAL. L. REV. 40 (1956); Wade, *Tort Liability for Abusive and Insulting Language*, 4 VAND. L. REV. 63 (1950); Prosser, *Intentional Infliction of Mental Suffering: A New York*, 37 MICH. L. REV. 874 (1939); 1 RESTATEMENT OF TORTS 2d § 46 (1). However, it is not necessary to adopt such a cause of action in order to sustain the verdict of the jury in this case. The *Harned* case recognized the well established rule that mental suffering is compensable in suits for willful torts "which are recognized as torts and actionable independently and separately from mental suffering or other injury." 254 S. W. 2d at 85. Damages for mental suffering are recoverable without the necessity for showing actual physical injury in a case of willful battery because the basis of that action is the unpermitted and intentional invasion of the plaintiff's person and not the actual harm done to the plaintiff's body. RESTATEMENT OF TORTS 2d § 18. Personal indignity is the essence of an action for battery; and consequently the defendant is liable not only for contacts which do actual physical harm, but also for those which are offensive and insulting. Prosser, supra; *Wilson v. Orr*, 210 Ala. 93, 97 So. 123 (1923). We hold, therefore, that plaintiff was entitled to actual damages for mental suffering due to the willful battery, even in the absence of any physical injury.

We now turn to the question of the liability of the corporations for exemplary damages. In this regard, the jury found that Flynn was acting within the course and scope of his employment on the occasion in question; that Flynn acted maliciously and with a wanton disregard of the rights and feelings of the plaintiff on the occasion in question. There is no attack upon these jury findings. The jury further found that the defendant Carrousel did not authorize or approve the conduct of Flynn. It is argued that there is no evidence to support this finding. The jury verdict concluded with a finding that $500 would "reasonably compensate the plaintiff for the malicious act and wanton disregard of the plaintiff's feelings and rights ..."

The rule in Texas is that a <u>principal or master</u> is liable for exemplary or punitive damages because of the acts of his agent, but only if:

    (a) the principal authorized the doing and the manner of the act, or
    (b) the agent was unfit and the principal was reckless in employing him, or
    (c) the agent was employed in a <u>managerial capacity</u> and was <u>acting in the scope of employment</u>, or
    (d) the employer or a manager of the employer ratified or approved the act.

The above test is set out in the RESTATEMENT OF TORTS § 909 and was adopted in *King v. McGuff*, 149 Tex. 434, 234 S.W. 2d 403 (1950). At the trial of this case, the following stipulation was made in open court:

It is further stipulated and agreed to by all parties that as an employee of the Carrousel Motor Hotel the said Robert W. Flynn was manager of the Brass Ring Club.

We think this stipulation brings the case squarely within part (c) of the rule announced in the *King* case as to Flynn's managerial capacity. It is undisputed that Flynn was acting in the scope of employment at the time of the incident; he was attempting to enforce the Club rules by depriving Fisher of service.

The rule of the Restatement of Torts adopted in the *King* case set out above has four separate and <u>disjunctive categories</u> as a basis of liability. They are separated by the word "or." As applicable here, there is liability if (a) the act is authorized, or (d) the act is ratified or approved, or (c) the agent was employed in a managerial capacity and was acting in the scope of his employment. Since it was established that the

principal or master 委托人，主人

managerial capacity 管理者的身份
act in the scope of employment 在工作范围内行为

disjunctive categories 可分的类型

agent was employed in a managerial capacity and was in the scope of his employment, the finding of the jury that the Carrousel did not authorize or approve Flynn's conduct became immaterial.

The *King* case also cited and relied upon *Ft. Worth Elevator Co. v. Russell*, 123 Tex. 128, 70 S. W. 2d 397 (1934). In that case, it was held not to be material that the employer did not authorize or ratify the particular conduct of the employee; and the right to exemplary damages was supported under what is section (b) of the Restatement of *King* rule: The agent was unfit, and the principal was reckless in employing (or retaining) him.

After the jury verdict in this case, counsel for the plaintiff moved that the trial court disregard the answer to issue number eight (no authorization or approval of Flynn's conduct on the occasion in question) and for judgment upon the verdict. The trial court erred in overruling that motion and in entering judgment for the defendants notwithstanding the verdict; and the Court of Civil Appeals erred in affirming that judgment.

The judgments of the courts below are reversed, and judgment is here rendered for the plaintiff for $900 with interest from the date of the trial court's judgment, and for costs of this suit.

2.2 False Imprisonment

False imprisonment is an act or omission to act of the defendant that confines or restrains the plaintiff to a bounded area. It consists of the intentional detention of a person without his consent. It is not limited to the concept of an unlawful arrest without a warrant. This tort protects a person from loss of liberty and freedom of movement. The essential elements that the plaintiff must prove include: intent to confine the plaintiff; unlawful and unconsented detention of the plaintiff within boundaries fixed by the defendant, apparent lack of a reasonable exit, use of unreasonable force, threat of force, or assertion of legal authority by the defendant, and harm to the plaintiff or knowledge by the plaintiff of the confinement. Read the following case.

Case 16: Marius S. Coblyn v. Kennedy's Inc. et al.

Supreme Judicial Court of Massachusetts, Suffolk
Marius S. Coblyn v. Kennedy's Inc. et al.
359 Mass. 319, 268 N.E. 2d 860
April 15, 1971

Spiegel, Justice.

This is an action of tort for false imprisonment. At the close of the evidence the defendants filed a motion for directed verdicts which was denied. The jury returned verdicts for the plaintiff in the sum of $12,500. The case is here on the defendants' exceptions to the denial of their motion and to the refusal of the trial judge to give certain requested instructions to the jury.

We state the pertinent evidence most favorable to the plaintiff. On March 5, 1965, the plaintiff went to Kennedy's, Inc. (Kennedy's), a store in Boston. He was seventy years of age and about five feet four inches in height. He was wearing a woolen shirt, which was "open at the neck," a topcoat and a hat. "[A]round his neck" he wore an ascot which he had "purchased ... previously at Filenes." He proceeded to the second floor of Kennedy's to purchase a sport coat. He removed his hat, topcoat and ascot, putting the ascot in his pocket. After purchasing a sport coat and leaving it for alterations, he put on his hat and coat and walked downstairs. Just prior to exiting through the outside door of the store, he stopped, took the ascot out of his pocket, put it around his neck, and knotted it. The knot was visible "above the lapels of his shirt." The only stop that the plaintiff made on the first floor was immediately in front of the exit in order to put on his ascot.

Just as the plaintiff stepped out of the door, the defendant Goss, an employee, "loomed up" in front of him with his hand up and said: "Stop. Where did you get that scarf?" The plaintiff responded, "[W]hy?" Goss firmly grasped the plaintiff's arm and said: "[Y]ou better go back and see the manager." Another employee was standing next to him. Eight or ten other people were standing around and were staring at the

---

a motion for directed verdict 请求法院指示裁断（指直接依案件承审法官的命令而对案件作出判决）的动议

exception（对法庭命令或裁决的）反对，异议

loom up 突然出现

plaintiff. The plaintiff then said, "Yes, I'll go back in the store" and proceeded to do so. As he and Goss went upstairs to the second floor, the plaintiff paused twice because of chest and back pains. After reaching the second floor, the salesman from whom he had purchased the coat recognized him and asked what the trouble was. The plaintiff then asked: "[W]hy these two gentlemen stop me?" The salesman confirmed that the plaintiff had purchased a sport coat and that the ascot belonged to him.

The salesman became alarmed by the plaintiff's appearance and the store nurse was called. She brought the plaintiff into the nurse's room and gave him a soda mint tablet. As a direct result of the emotional upset caused by the incident, the plaintiff was hospitalized and treated for a "myocardial infarct."

hospitalize 就医
myocardial infarct 心肌梗死

Initially, the defendants contend that as a matter of law the plaintiff was not falsely imprisoned. They argue that no unlawful restraint was imposed by either force or threat upon the plaintiff's freedom of movement. *Wax v. McGrath*, 255 Mass. 340, 342, 151 N.E. 317. However, "[t]he law is well settled that '[a]ny genuine restraint is sufficient to constitute an imprisonment ... ' and '(a)ny demonstration of physical power which, to all appearances, can be avoided only by submission, operates as effectually to constitute an imprisonment, if submitted to, as if any amount of force had been exercised.' 'If a man is restrained of his personal liberty by fear of a personal difficulty, that amounts to a false imprisonment' within the legal meaning of such term." *Jacques v. Childs Dining Hall Co.*, 244 Mass. 438, 438–439, 138 N.E. 843.

We think it is clear that there was sufficient evidence of unlawful restraint to submit this question to the jury. Just as the plaintiff had stepped out of the door of the store, the defendant Goss stopped him, firmly grasped his arm and told him that he had "better go back and see the manager." There was another employee at his side. The plaintiff was an elderly man and there were other people standing around staring at him. Considering the plaintiff's age and his heart condition, it is hardly to be expected that with one employee in front of him firmly grasping his arm and another at his side the plaintiff could do other than comply with Goss's "request" that he go back and see the manager. The physical restraint imposed upon the plaintiff when Goss grasped the plaintiff's arm readily distinguishes this case from *Sweeney v. F. W. Woolworth Co.*, 247 Mass. 277, 142 N.E. 50, relied upon by the defendants.

In addition, as this court observed in the *Jacques* case, *supra*, at p.441, 138 N.E. at p.844, the "honesty and veracity (of the plaintiff) had been openly ... challenged. If she had gone out before ... (exonerating herself), her departure well might have been interpreted by the lookers-on as an admission of guilt, or of circumstances from which guilt might be inferred. The situation was in the control of the defendant. The restraint or duress imposed by the mode of investigation the jury could say was for the accomplishment of the defendant's purpose, even if no threats of public exposure or of arrest were made, and no physical restraint of ... (the plaintiff) was attempted." For cases in other jurisdictions, where the evidence tended to support the tort of false imprisonment, see *Clark v. Kroger Co.*, 382 F. 2d 562, 563 (7th Cir.); *Patrick v. Esso Standard Oil Co., D.C.N.J.*, 156 F. Supp. 336, 340; *Daniel v. Phillips Petroleum Co.*, 229 Mo. App. 150, 155, 73 . S. W. 2d 355; *Lukas v. J.C. Penney Co.*, 233 Or. 345, 354, 378 P. 2d 717.

The defendants next contend that the detention of the plaintiff was sanctioned by G. L. c. 231, s 94B, inserted by St. 1958, c. 337. This statute provides as follows: "In an action for false arrest or false imprisonment brought by any person by reason of having been detained for questioning on or in the immediate vicinity of the premises of a merchant, if such person was detained in a reasonable manner and for not more than a reasonable length of time by a person authorized to make arrests or by the merchant or his agent or servant authorized for such purpose and if there were reasonable grounds to believe that the person so detained was committing or attempting to commit larceny of goods for sale on such premises, it

veracity 真实性
exonerate 使免罪,免除……的罪责
lookers-on 旁观者,观看者
guilt 罪,过失

vicinity 邻近,接近,附近

larceny 偷盗罪

shall be a defense to such action. If such goods had not been purchased and were concealed on or amongst the belongings of a person so detained it shall be presumed that there were reasonable grounds for such belief."

The defendants argue in accordance with the conditions imposed in the statute that the plaintiff was detained in a reasonable manner for a reasonable length of time and that Goss had reasonable grounds for believing that the plaintiff was attempting to commit larceny of goods held for sale.

It is conceded that the detention was for a reasonable length of time. See *Proulx v. Pinkerton's Natl. Detective Agency, Inc.*, 343 Mass. 390, 392-93, 178 N.E. 2d 575. We need not decide whether the detention was effected in a reasonable manner, for we are of opinion that there were no reasonable grounds for believing that the plaintiff was committing larceny and, therefore, he should not have been detained at all. However, we observe that Goss's failure to identify himself as an employee of Kennedy's and to disclose the reasons for his inquiry and actions, coupled with the physical restraint in a public place imposed upon the plaintiff, an elderly man, who had exhibited no aggressive intention to depart, could be said to constitute an unreasonable method by which to effect detention. See *Lukas v. J. C. Penney Co.*, 233 Or. 345, 352, 360, 378 P. 2d 717.

The pivotal question before us as in most cases of this character is whether the evidence shows that there were reasonable grounds for the detention. At common law in an action for false imprisonment, the defense of probable cause, as measured by the prudent and cautious man standard, was available to a merchant. *Standish v. Narragansett S. S. Co.*, 111 Mass. 512, 517. *Jacques v. Childs Dining Hall Co.*, 244 Mass. 438, 439, 138 N. E. 843. *Muniz v. Mehlman*, 327 Mass. 353, 358, 99 N. E. 2d 37. In enacting G. L. c. 231, s 94B, the Legislature inserted the words, "reasonable grounds." Historically, the words "reasonable grounds" and "probable cause" have been given the same meaning by the courts. In the case of *United States v. Walker*, 7 Cir., 246 F. 2d 519, 526, it was said: "'probable cause' and 'reasonable grounds' are concepts having virtually the same meaning." The following cases have expressly stated that the words may be used interchangeably and without distinction. *Draper v. United States*, 358 U.S. 307, 310. *United States v. Vasquez*, D.C.N.Y., 183 F. Supp. 190, 193. *Smallwood v. Commonwealth*, 305 Ky. 520, 524, 204 S.W. 2d 945. *McKeon v. National Cas. Co.*, 216 Mo. App. 507, 524, 270 S.W. 707. In the case of *Lukas v. J.C. Penney Co.*, *supra*, at p. 361, 378 P. 2d 717, the Oregon Supreme Court construed the meaning of the words "reasonable grounds" in its "shoplifting statute" as having the same meaning as they have in a statute authorizing arrest without a warrant and applied the probable cause standard to the facts before it.

The defendants assert that the judge improperly instructed the jury in stating that "grounds are reasonable when there is a basis which would appear to the reasonably prudent, cautious, intelligent person." In their brief, they argue that the "prudent and cautious man rule" is an objective standard and requires a more rigorous and restrictive standard of conduct than is contemplated by G.L. c. 231, s 94B. The defendants' requests for instructions, in effect, state that the proper test is a subjective one, *viz.*, whether the defendant Goss had an honest and strong suspicion that the plaintiff was committing or attempting to commit larceny.①

The defendants' brief refers only to request No. 1 although their argument appears to touch on the periphery of the remaining two requests.

We do not agree. As we have attempted to show, the words "reasonable grounds" and "probable cause"

interchangeably 可交换地,可替换地

shoplift 冒充顾客入店行窃

brief 上诉状或上诉程序中的应诉状
an objective standard 客观标准
rigorous 严格的,苛刻的,严厉的
a subjective test 主观标准
viz 即,那就是
suspicion 怀疑,猜疑,嫌疑(没有证据或证据不足的情况下,对某事存在与否的断定)

periphery 外围

---

① The bill of exceptions recites that "[t]he defendants duly excepted to the failure of the Court to give their requested instructions 1, 2 and 3." These requests are as follows:

1. If the defendant Goss had a belief to the extent of an honest and strong suspicion that the plaintiff had committed larceny or was attempting to commit larceny of goods for sale on Kennedy's premises, the jury should find that he acted reasonably.

2. If the jury find the ascot ... was concealed on or amongst the belongings of the plaintiff, they must find that the defendants had reasonable grounds to believe that larceny had been attempted or committed.

3. If the jury find that the defendant Goss reasonably suspected the plaintiff of theft or failing to pay for goods belonging to Kennedy's, they must return verdicts for the defendants on all counts.

have traditionally been accorded the same meaning. In the case of *Terry v. Ohio*, 392 U.S. 1, involving the question whether a police officer must have probable cause within the Fourth Amendment to "stop-and-frisk" a suspected individual, the Supreme Court of the United States held that the "probable cause" requirement of the Fourth Amendment applies to a "stop-and-frisk" and that a "stop-and-frisk" must "be judged against an objective standard: would the facts available to the officer at the moment … 'warrant a man of reasonable caution in the belief' that the action taken was appropriate? … Anything less would invite intrusions upon constitutionally guaranteed rights based on nothing more substantial than inarticulate hunches, a result this Court has consistently refused to sanction." pp. 21 - 22.

If we adopt the subjective test as suggested by the defendants, the individual's right to liberty and freedom of movement would become subject to the "honest … suspicion" of a shopkeeper based on his own "inarticulate hunches" without regard to any discernible facts. In effect, the result would be to afford the merchant even greater authority than that given to a police officer. In view of the well established meaning of the words "reasonable grounds" we believe that the Legislature intended to give these words their traditional meaning. This seems to us a valid conclusion since the Legislature has permitted an individual to be detained for a "reasonable length of time." This would be at least analogous to a "stop" within the meaning of the *Terry* case. ①

We also note that the *Terry* case allows "a reasonable search for weapons for the protection of the police officer, where he has reason to believe that he is dealing with an armed and dangerous individual, regardless of whether he has probable cause to arrest the individual for a crime." Even in such circumstances,

---

① See *Terry v. Ohio*, supra, at p. 19, where the Supreme Court rejects "the notions that the Fourth Amendment does not come into play at all as a limitation upon police conduct if the officers stop short of something called a 'technical arrest.'" At p. 19, fn. 16, the court states that "[o]nly when the officer, by means of physical force or show of authority, has in some way restrained the liberty of a citizen may we conclude that a 'seizure' has occurred."

however, the court said that "in determining whether the officer acted reasonably in such circumstances, due weight must be given, not to his inchoate and unparticularized suspicion or 'hunch,' but to the specific reasonable inferences which he is entitled to draw from the facts in light of his experience." p. 27.

We also note that an objective standard is the criterion for determining probable cause or reasonable grounds in malicious prosecution and false arrest cases. *Bacon v. Towne*, 4 Cush. 217, 238 – 239. *Wax v. McGrath*, 255 Mass. 340, 343, 151 N. E. 317. We see no valid reason to depart from this precedent in regard to cases involving false imprisonment.

Applying the standard of reasonable grounds as measured by the reasonably prudent man test① to the evidence in the instant case, we are of opinion that the evidence warranted the conclusion that Goss was not reasonably justified in believing that the plaintiff was engaged in shoplifting. There was no error in denying the motion for directed verdicts and in the refusal to give the requested instructions.

We also note here that the defendants incorrectly rely on certain language in the case of *Pihl v. Morris*, 319 Mass. 577, 580, 66 N. E. 2d 804, 806, to support their argument that only "an honest and strong suspicion" is needed rather than "reasonable grounds." That case states that "'an honest and strong suspicion' is a necessary part of probable cause" (emphasis supplied).

Exceptions overruled.

2.3 Intentional Infliction of Emotional Distress

The tort of intentional infliction of emotional distress, also called the tort of outrage, recognizes the right to be free from serious, intentional and unprivileged invasions of mental and emotional tranquility. It covers acts causing severe emotional distress of any kind, including fright, grief, shame,

---

① The test for determining probable cause or reasonable grounds was established long ago in *Bacon v. Towne*, supra, at pp. 238 – 39, where Chief Justice Shaw wrote: "Probable cause is such a state of facts ... as would lead a man of ordinary caution and prudence to believe, or entertain an honest and strong suspicion, that the person arrested is guilty."

humiliation, embarrassment and anger.

The elements of a *prima facie* case for intentional infliction of emotional distress are: an act by the defendant amounting to extreme and outrageous conduct, intent of the defendant to cause the plaintiff to suffer severe emotional distress, or recklessness as to the effect of the defendant's conduct, the severe emotional distress suffered by the plaintiff as a result, and the causation between the defendant's act and the plaintiff's damage. For conduct to be "extreme and outrageous," it must be "beyond all possible bounds of decency." The emotional distress must be so substantial or persistent that no reasonable person in a civilized society should be expected to endure it. Damage does not need to be proved for other intentional torts we discussed so far, but it needs to be proved in order to establish the intentional infliction of emotional distress, although it is not necessary to prove physical injuries in order for the plaintiff to recover. The case below demonstrates how the court dealt with a case involving intentional infliction of emotional distress.

Case 17: Robert Logan v. Sears, Roebuck & Co.

Supreme Court of Alabama
Robert Logan v. Sears, Roebuck & Co.
466 So. 2d 121
Feb. 22, 1985

Maddox, Justice.

Robert Logan operates a beauty salon in Birmingham. On May 11, 1982, an employee of Sears, Roebuck and Company phoned Logan at his place of business to inquire whether he had made his monthly charge account payment. While looking for his checkbook, Logan heard the Sears employee tell someone on her end of the line, "This guy is as queer as a three-dollar bill. He owns a beauty salon, and he just told me that if you'll hold the line I will check my checkbook." No one on Logan's end of the conversation, other than Logan, heard the statement.

Logan brought suit against Sears, seeking damages

based on the torts of outrage and invasion of privacy. Sears moved for summary judgment as to both causes of action. The trial court granted Sear's motion, holding that although the statement of the Sears employee was insulting, it was not sufficient to support a claim of outrage or invasion of privacy. Logan appeals here.

It is undisputed that the Sears employee indeed made the statement complained of by Logan. It is further undisputed that Logan is, in fact, a homosexual. Thus, the only issue presented is whether the trial court erred in granting summary judgment. We find that it did not.

The tort of outrage, as proposed in Restatement (Second) of Torts §46 (1948), and adopted by this Court in *American Road Service Co. v. Inmon*, 394 So. 2d 361 (Ala. 1980), provides that:

> One who by extreme and outrageous conduct intentionally or recklessly causes severe emotional distress to another is subject to liability for such emotional distress, and if bodily harm to the other results from it, for such bodily harm.

While *Inmon*, *supra*, did recognize a cause of action in Alabama based solely upon insulting language, it did not create a cause of action which arises from every insult. As this Court stated therein, the tort of outrage "does not recognize recovery for 'mere insults, indignities, threats, annoyances, petty oppressions, or other trivialities.' The principle applies only to unprivileged, intentional or reckless conduct of an extreme and outrageous nature, and only that which causes severe emotional distress … The emotional distress thereunder must be so severe that no reasonable person could be expected to endure it. Any recovery must be reasonable and justified under the circumstances, liability ensuing only when the conduct is extreme … By extreme we refer to conduct so outrageous in character and so extreme in degree as to go beyond all possible bounds of decency, and to be regarded as atrocious and utterly intolerable in a civilized society." (Citations omitted.) 394 So. 2d at 365.

Similarly, although *Phillips v. Smalley Maintenance Services, Inc.*, 435 So. 2d 705 (Ala. 1983) recognized an action for <u>intrusion upon one's solitude</u> (which is the basis for Logan's claim), that case does not <u>stand for</u> the proposition that there can be recovery based upon every intrusion. This Court in *Phillips*, adopted Restatement (Second) of Torts, § 652 (1977), which states, in pertinent part:

> One who intentionally intrudes, physically or otherwise, upon the solitude or <u>seclusion</u> of another or his private affairs or concerns, is subject to liability to the other for invasion of his <u>privacy</u>, if the intrusion would be highly offensive to a reasonable person.

But in adopting that section, this Court also necessarily adopted that section's limitation on such actions. In other words, while holding that an intrusion on solitude may be actionable, this Court recognized that in order to be actionable, the intrusion must be such as would outrage a person of ordinary sensibilities or cause such a person mental suffering, shame, or humiliation. *Phillips*, *supra*, at 705.

Consequently, the <u>dispositive questions</u> are whether the statement of the Sears employee was such as would outrage, or cause mental suffering to, a reasonable person and whether it was within the trial court's authority to make such a determination.

This Court recognized in *Inmon* that a determination as to whether a statement is sufficiently objectionable to support a cause of action for outrageous conduct may be made by the trial court as a matter of law. 394 So. 2d at 368. We are of the opinion that the same may be said for a suit based on intrusion upon the solitude or seclusion of another; therefore, it was within the trial court's authority to determine if the employee's statement gave rise to a cause of action in either outrage or invasion of privacy.

In this case, the trial court concluded that the statement was not so outrageous as to support an action based on either tort. Even though the statement was an intrusion upon Logan's solitude or seclusion, we do not believe that it was so extreme or outrageous as to offend the sensibilities of an ordinary person similarly situated.

It is evident from Logan's complaint and his testimony that he does not claim that the statements made about him were defamatory or slanderous. He admits that the characterization of him as homosexual is a true characterization; he simply dislikes the use of the adjective "queer" and he was especially annoyed because the term was used on his private telephone line. In his deposition, Logan testified as follows:

Q. Are you gay?
A. Yes…
Q. Well, are you at a point in life where you can accept without any embarrassment being gay?
A. It doesn't bother me.
Q. You just don't want someone else to make any comments about your personal life?
A. I have had clients to come into my salon and say, "Robert" — after general conversation they will say, "Robert, are you gay?" and I will say, "Yes." But they don't come in and say, you know, "I have got this queer hairdresser" or call me up over the phone and make accusations about this — just the word "queer" just bothers me, because I am not "queer."

We are unwilling to say that the use of the word "queer" to describe a homosexual is atrocious and intolerable in civilized society. We recognize that there are other words favored by the homosexual community in describing themselves, but the word "queer" has been used for a long time by those outside that community. It has been in use longer than the term "gay," which has recently become the most frequently used term to describe homosexuals.

Since Logan is admittedly a homosexual, can it be said realistically that being described as "queer" should cause him shame or humiliation? We think not. In order to create a cause of action, the conduct must be

---

solitude 单独

an ordinary person similarly situated 一个处于同样情形下的普通人

evident 明白的,明显的,显然的

defamatory 诬蔑的,诽谤的,中伤的,败坏(他人)声誉的

slanderous 中伤性的,诽谤的

gay 男同性恋者

accusation 控告,指控

such that would cause mental suffering, shame, or humiliation to a person of ordinary sensibilities, not conduct which would be considered unacceptable merely by homosexuals. *Cf. Norris v. Moskin Stores, Inc.*, 272 Ala. 174, 177, 132 So.2d 321, 323 (1961).

Professor Prosser summarized the law on this issue in the following language:

> Our manners, and with them our law, have not yet progressed to the point where we are able to afford a remedy in the form of tort damages for all intended mental disturbance. Liability of course cannot be extended to every trivial indignity. There is no occasion for the law to intervene with balm for wounded feelings in every case where a flood of Billingsgate is loosed in an argument over a back fence. The plaintiff must necessarily be expected and required to be hardened to a certain amount of rough language, and to acts that are definitely inconsiderate and unkind. There is still, in this country at least, such a thing as liberty to express an unflattering opinion of another, however wounding it may be to his feeling; and in the interest not only of freedom of speech but also of avoidance of other more dangerous conduct, it is still very desirable that some safety valve be left through which irascible tempers may blow off relatively harmless steam. There is the further, and still more significant, evident and serious danger of fictitious claims and vexatious suits in such cases. Petty insult or indignity lacks, from its very nature, any convincing assurance that the asserted mental distress is genuine, or that if genuine it is serious, and reasonable. When a citizen who has been called a son of a bitch testifies that the epithet has destroyed his slumber, ruined his digestion, wrecked his nervous system, and permanently impaired his health, other citizens who on occasion have been called the same thing without catastrophic harm may have legitimate doubts that he was really so upset, or that if he were his sufferings could possibly be so reasonable

---

billingsgate 骂人话,粗俗话
loose 释放

harden 使冷酷,使坚强
inconsiderate 不顾别人的

unflattering 不奉承的,不讨好的

irascible temper 易怒的脾气,暴躁的脾气

fictitious claim 虚假索赔
vexatious suit 缠讼(旨在困扰对方的诉讼),无理或无根据的缠讼

epithet 诨名,称号,绰号
slumber 睡眠
digestion 消化力
wreck (使)遭受严重损失或损害,毁坏
catastrophic 灾难的,悲惨的
legitimate 合法的,法律认可的

and justified under the circumstances as to be entitled to compensation.

Accordingly, it is generally held that there can be no recovery for mere profanity, obscenity, or abuse, without circumstances of aggravation, or for insults, indignities or threats which are considered to amount to nothing more than mere annoyances. The plaintiff cannot recover merely because he has had his feelings hurt. Even the dire affront of inviting an unwilling woman to illicit intercourse has been held by most courts to be no such outrage as to lead to liability — "the view being, apparently," in Judge Magruder's well-known words, "that there is no harm in asking."

W. Prosser, LAW OF TORTS, 54 - 55 (4th ed. 1971) (citations omitted).

Based on the above, we hold that the statement was one of those relatively trivial insults for which the law grants no relief; therefore, the trial court did not err in granting summary judgment.

Affirmed.

3. Intentional Torts to Property

3.1 Trespass and Nuisance

At common law, trespass was the most common tort used to define actions that infringe upon both real and personal property interests. The first type is called trespass to land, and the second type is trespass to chattels.

Trespass to land infringes a possessor's interest in exclusive possession of land. In order to establish a *prima facie* case of trespass on land, the plaintiff must prove the act of physical invasion of the plaintiff's real property by the defendant, the intent of the defendant to bring about a physical invasion of the plaintiff's real property, and the causation between the act and the result. The state of mind that is necessary to support liability for trespass to land is merely intent to be present at the place in question, not intent to go upon the land of another, nor intent to violate another's rights. So a reasonable and honest mistake by the defendant as to ownership or permission to enter is irrelevant unless the mistake is induced by the plaintiff. The plaintiff must also prove that the defendant was actually present on, under, or above his land. This requirement is satisfied if the defendant, instead of entering, intentionally casts an object upon the land or causes another to enter. There is no requirement of damage. For example, if A pushes B onto C's property, A is liable for trespass on land, but B is not liable, unless B fails to leave with reasonable dispatch. The person who ventures onto the land of another without permission is a trespasser.

Trespass to chattels infringes a possessor's interest in freedom from minor intentional interference with personal property. In order to establish trespass to chattels, the plaintiff must prove an act of the defendant that interferes with the plaintiff's right of possession in the chattel, the intent of the defendant to affect the chattel, the minor interference with the plaintiff's possessory interest by dispossession, use, or intermeddling by the defendant, and the causation between the act and the damage. One of the differences between trespass to land and trespass to chattels is that actual damage is not required in the former case, but is required in the latter case. Dispossession itself is deemed to be an actual harm in trespass to chattels. In the absence of dispossession, the plaintiff must prove damage in the form of substantial loss of use, or impairment of condition, quality, or value.

The traditional view regarding trespass is that there must be an actual tangible invasion. Consequently, the projection of light, noise, vibrations are not deemed by the majority of courts to constitute a trespass. Such invasions may amount to an unreasonable interference constituting the tort of nuisance.

3.2 Conversion

Conversion occurs when a person intentionally exercises exclusive control over the personal property of another without permission so that the actor may justly be required to pay the other the full value of the chattel. The basic elements of conversion include an act by the defendant interfering with the plaintiff's right of possession in the chattel that is serious enough in nature or consequence to warrant that the defendant pay the full value of the chattel, the intent of the defendant to so interfere with the plaintiff's right of possession in the chattel, and the causation between the act and the result. Conversion is a more serious version of the type of interference which gives rise to trespass to chattels. The difference between trespass to chattels and conversion is a matter of degree. In determining the seriousness of the interference and the justice of requiring the actor to pay the full value, the courts may consider various factors including the duration of time the defendant has exercised control over the property, the defendant's motive and the harm done.

Conversion may be committed in a number of ways, including <u>acquisition</u> of property without justification, wrongful transfer of the chattel, wrongful detention of the chattel, substantially changing of the chattel, severely damaging or destroying the chattel, or misusing the chattel. The subject matter of conversion includes tangible personal property and <u>intangibles</u> that have been reduced to physical form, such as a promissory note, and documents in which title to a chattel is merged, like a <u>bill of lading</u> or a <u>warehouse receipt</u>. The proper remedy in the event of a conversion is either the <u>fair market value</u> of the chattel as of the time and place of conversion, or, at the plaintiff's <u>election</u>, the return of the property to the plaintiff, which is called <u>replevin</u>.

acquisition 取得，获得（指成为某项财产所有人的行为，尤指用任何方法取得的实际占有）

intangibles 无形的东西，无形资产

bill of lading 提单
warehouse receipt 仓单，提货单，仓库收据
fair market value 公平市场价格，公允市价
election 选择权
replevin 返还原物之诉（指要求返还被非法扣押或取走的财物的诉讼，也指一种临时性措施，即在诉讼进行阶段，原告可在判决前自被告处取走并保留争议的财物）

Case 18: Russell-Vaughn Ford, Inc. v. E. W. Rouse

Supreme Court of Alabama
Russell-Vaughn Ford, Inc. , et al. v. E. W. Rouse
281 Ala. 567, 206 So. 2d 371
Jan. 11, 1968

Simpson, Justice.
The plaintiff in this case filed suit against Russell-

Vaughn Ford, Inc. and several individuals. All individual defendants were stricken by plaintiff before trial except the appellant James Parker, and one Virgil Harris who has not participated in this appeal.

The complaint was amended several times but ultimately issue was joined and the case went to the jury on a common count for conversion of plaintiff's 1960 Falcon automobile and a second count charging the defendants with conspiracy to convert the automobile.

Essentially the facts are as follows:

On April 24, 1962, the appellee went to the place of business of Russell-Vaughn Ford, Inc., to discuss trading his Falcon automobile in on a new Ford. He talked with one of the salesmen for a while who offered to trade a new Ford for the Falcon, plus $1,900. The trade was not consummated on this basis, but Mr. Rouse went to his house and picked up his wife and children and returned to the dealer. With his wife and children there Mr. Rouse discussed further the trade but no deal was made that night.

The following night he returned with a friend where further discussions on the trade were had. At the time of this visit one of the salesmen, Virgil Harris, asked Mr. Rouse for the keys to his Falcon. The keys were given to him and Mr. Rouse, his friend, and appellant Parker looked at the new cars for a time and then proceeded with the negotiations with regard to the trade. The testimony indicates that in this conversation the salesman offered to trade a new Ford for the Falcon, plus $2,400. The plaintiff declined to trade on this basis.

At this stage of the negotiations, Mr. Rouse asked for the return of the keys to the Falcon. The evidence is to the effect that both salesmen to whom Rouse had talked said that they did not know where the keys were. Mr. Rouse then asked several people who appeared to be employees of Russell-Vaughn for the keys. He further asked several people in the building if they knew where his keys were. The testimony indicates that there were a number of people around who were aware of the fact that the appellee was seeking to have the keys to his car returned. Several mechanics and salesmen were, according to plaintiff's testimony, sitting around on cars looking at him and laughing at him.

After a period of time the plaintiff called the police department of the City of Birmingham. In response to his call Officer Montgomery came to the showroom of Russell-Vaughn Ford and was informed by the plaintiff that he was unable to get his keys back. Shortly after the arrival of the policeman, according to the policeman's testimony, the salesman Parker threw the keys to Mr. Rouse with the statement that he was a cry baby and that "they just wanted to see him cry a while."

The evidence is <u>abundant</u> to the effect that Mr. Rouse made a number of efforts to have his keys returned to him. He talked to the salesmen, to the manager, to mechanics, *etc.* and was met in many instances with laughter as if the entire matter was a "big joke."

As noted, the case was tried to a jury, and submitted on a conversion count in code form and on a second count charging conspiracy to convert. The jury returned a <u>general verdict</u> in favor of the plaintiff in the amount of $5,000. This appeal followed, after the trial court denied a motion for new trial.

The appellants have made several assignments of error. Initially it is argued that the facts of this case do not make out a case of conversion. It is argued that the conversion if at all, is a conversion of the keys to the automobile, not of the automobile itself. It is further contended that there was not under the case here presented a conversion at all. We are not persuaded that the law of Alabama supports this proposition. As noted in *Long-Lewis Hardware Co. v. Abston*, 235 Ala. 599, 180 So. 261,

> It has been held by this court that "the fact of conversion does not necessarily <u>import</u> an acquisition of property in the defendant." *Howton v. Mathias*, 197 Ala. 457, 73 So. 92, 95. The conversion may consist, not only in an <u>appropriation</u> of the property to one's own use, but in its destruction, or in exercising <u>dominion</u> over it in exclusion or <u>defiance</u> of plaintiff's right. *McGill v. Hollman*,

abundant 充分的,充足的

general verdict 总括裁断(指陪审团作出的概括地宣布原告胜诉或被告胜诉或者刑事被告人有罪或无罪的裁断)

import 含……的意思

appropriation 占用,挪用,盗用

dominion 控制,支配,占有

defiance 挑衅,挑战,对抗

208 Ala. 9, 93 So. 848.

It is not contended that the plaintiff here had no right to demand the return of the keys to his automobile. Rather, the appellants seem to be arguing that there was no conversion which the law will recognize under the facts of this case because the defendants did not commit sufficient acts to amount to a conversion. We cannot agree. A remarkable admission in this regard was elicited by the plaintiff in examining one of the witnesses for the defense. It seems that according to salesman for Russell-Vaughn Ford, Inc. it is a rather usual practice in the automobile business to "lose keys" to cars belonging to potential customers. We see nothing in our cases which requires in a conversion case that the plaintiff prove that the defendant appropriated the property to his own use; rather, as noted in the cases referred to above, it is enough that he show that the defendant exercised dominion over it in exclusion or defiance of the right of the plaintiff. We think that has been done here. The jury so found and we cannot concur that a case for conversion has not been made on these facts.

Further, appellants argue that there was no conversion since the plaintiff could have called his wife at home, who had another set of keys and thereby gained the ability to move his automobile. We find nothing in our cases which would require the plaintiff to exhaust all possible means of gaining possession of a chattel which is withheld from him by the defendant, after demanding its return. On the contrary, it is the refusal, without legal excuse, to deliver a chattel, which constitutes a conversion. *Compton v. Sims*, 209 Ala. 287, 96 So. 185.

We find unconvincing the appellants contention that if there were a conversion at all, it was the conversion of the automobile keys, and not of the automobile. In *Compton v. Sims, supra*, this court sustained a finding that there had been a conversion of cotton where the defendant refused to deliver to the plaintiff "warehouse tickets" which would have enabled him to gain possession of the cotton. The court spoke of the warehouse tickets as a symbol of the

exhaust 用尽

cotton and found that the retention of them amounted to a conversion of the cotton. So here, we think that the withholding from the plaintiff after demand of the keys to his automobile, without which he could not move it, amounted to a conversion of the automobile.

It is next argued by appellants that the amount of the verdict is excessive. It is not denied that punitive damages are recoverable here in the discretion of the jury. In *Roan v. McCaleb*, 264 Ala. 31, 84 So. 2d 358, this court held:

> If the conversion was committed in known violation of the law and of plaintiff's rights with circumstances of insult, or contumely, or malice, punitive damages were recoverable in the discretion of the jury.

contumely 无礼,傲慢,侮辱

We think that the evidence justifies the jury's conclusion that these circumstances existed in this case.

We have carefully considered each assignment of error made and argued by appellants. We are clear to the conclusion that the evidence supports the verdict of the jury and find no error in the court's refusal to grant a new trial. In our opinion no assignment justifies a reversal.

Affirmed.

4. Defenses to Intentional Torts

The law provides specific lines of defense for each kind of intentional tort. The widely used defenses to the intentional torts to the person and to property are consent and privilege.

Even though a tort has been committed, the law does not compensate the injured party if, in fact, that person consented to the tort. Put it in another way, consent by the plaintiff negates the wrongful element of the defendant's conduct and prevents the existence of an intentional tort. Consent may be expressed as well as implied. The law will not infer consent unless it is reasonable under the circumstances. Consent is not a defense when a wrongdoer deliberately

deliberately 蓄意地,故意地,有目的地,有预谋地

take advantage of one's ignorance 乘其不意	takes advantage of another person's ignorance. Furthermore, consent must also be voluntary. It is not valid if given under duress.

Privilege is a special exemption from liability for allegedly tortuous behavior. <u>Self-defense</u>, <u>defense of others</u>, <u>defense of property</u>, <u>reentry onto land</u>, <u>recapture of chattels</u>, <u>public and private necessity</u>, and <u>discipline</u> all fall within the general category of privileges.

self-defense 自身防卫
defense of others 防卫他人
defense of property 防卫财产
reentry onto land 重新进入土地，恢复占有土地
recapture of chattels 重新占有动产，合法取回动产
public necessity 公共(利益)必需(为公共利益而紧急避险)
private necessity 私人(利益)必需(为私人利益而紧急避险)
discipline 惩戒，教导
deadly force 致死力量，致命力量，可能致人死亡或造成人身重伤的力量

A person may have the privilege to defense himself if he can prove that he reasonably believes that force is necessary to protect himself from bodily harm, and the force that is used be reasonably necessary to prevent the harm under the circumstances. This privilege may be invoked by anyone other than an aggressor who wrongfully initiated the confrontation. However, <u>deadly force</u> may be used only to defend against deadly force. The self-defense privilege does not permit retaliation either. Therefore, once there is no longer a threat of continued harm, the privilege terminates.

The privilege of defense of others may be invoked by anyone who reasonably believes that force is necessary to protect another from physical harm. The force that is used by an <u>intervenor</u> must be reasonable under the circumstances. But some courts would hold that if the other person did not have the privilege to defend himself, the intervenor did not have the privilege of defense for others no matter what the intervenor believes.

intervenor 参加诉讼人，加入诉讼人（指自愿并经法庭许可而加入某一诉讼中，并成为该诉讼的一方当事人，以维护自己的权利或利益的人）

desist 停止，控制

A possessor may also have the privilege to defend his property, but a request to <u>desist</u> is usually required, and this defense is limited to preventing commission of torts. Moreover, the possessor can only use reasonable force and deadly force may never be used to <u>repel</u> a threat against land or chattels, unless there is also a threat to the safety of the defendant and others. The cases reprinted later illustrate this doctrine.

repel 击退，拒绝，排斥，抵抗

Necessity is a privilege for the defendant to interfere with the real or personal property of another where the interference is reasonably and apparently necessary to avoid threatened injury from a natural or other force and where the threatened injury is substantially more serious that the invasion that is undertaken to avert it. The defendant must prove that there was an apparent necessary for him to do so under the circumstance. If the class to be protected by the action is the public as a whole, or a substantial number of persons, the privilege is public necessity, which is an absolute privilege and the defendant bears no liability for the damage suffered by the plaintiff. If the public interest is not involved and the defendant acts merely to protect personal interests or those of a few other persons, the privilege is private necessity, which is only a qualified privilege, and the defendant is liable for harm actually incurred, except if the act is for the benefit of the plaintiff.

A parent or teacher may use reasonable force in disciplining children, taking into account the age and sex of the child and the seriousness of the behavior.

Shopkeepers have a privilege to detain suspected thief for investigation under common law, which may negate one of the elements of false imprisonment. The defendant must prove that he reasonably believed that the plaintiff was a suspected thief, the detention was only for a reasonable time, only reasonable force was used, and the only purpose of the detention was for reasonable investigation.

avert 避免,防止

absolute privilege 绝对特权,使行为人免予受到起诉的一种特权。

qualified privilege 授予性特权(指行为人在履行其法律或道德义务时正确地行使其特权的情况下,可免予被提起诉讼)

4.1 Case 19: Katko v. Briney

Supreme Court of Iowa
Katko v. Briney
183 N. W. 2d 657
Feb. 9, 1971

Moore, Chief Justice.

The primary issue presented here is whether an owner may protect personal property in an unoccupied boarded-up farm house against trespassers and thieves by a spring gun capable of inflicting death or serious injury.

We are not here concerned with a man's right to protect his home and members of his family. Defendants' home was several miles from the scene of the incident to which we refer *infra*.

Plaintiff's action is for damages resulting from serious injury caused by a shot from a 20-gauge spring

spring gun 触发枪(扳机上系有金属丝,由侵入的人或动物自身触发)

infra 在下,以下,下文

shotgun set by defendants in a bedroom of an old farm house which had been uninhabited for several years. Plaintiff and his companion, Marvin McDonough, had broken and entered the house to find and steal old bottles and dated fruit jars which they considered antiques.

At defendants' request plaintiff's action was tried to a jury consisting of residents of the community where defendants' property was located. The jury returned a verdict for plaintiff and against defendants for $20,000 actual and $10,000 punitive damages.

After careful consideration of defendants' motions for judgment notwithstanding the verdict and for new trial, the experienced and capable trial judge overruled them and entered judgment on the verdict. Thus we have this appeal by defendants.

I. In this action our review of the record as made by the parties in the lower court is for the correction of errors at law. We do not review actions at law *de novo*. Rule 334, Rules of Civil Procedure. Findings of fact by the jury are binding upon this court if supported by substantial evidence. Rule 344(f), par. 1, R.C.P.

II. Most of the facts are not disputed. In 1957 defendant Bertha L. Briney inherited her parents' farm land in Mahaska and Monroe Counties. Included was an 80 - acre tract in southwest Mahaska County where her grandparents and parents had lived. No one occupied the house thereafter. Her husband, Edward, attempted to care for the land. He kept no farm machinery thereon. The outbuildings became dilapidated.

For about 10 years, 1957 to 1967, there occurred a series of trespassing and housebreaking events with loss of some household items, the breaking of windows and "messing up of the property in general." The latest occurred June 8, 1967, prior to the event on July 16, 1967 herein involved.

Defendants through the years boarded up the windows and doors in an attempt to stop the intrusions. They had posted "no trespass" signs on the land several years before 1967. The nearest one was 35 feet from the house. On June 11, 1967 defendants set "a shotgun trap" in the north bedroom. After Mr.

Briney cleaned and oiled his 20‑gauge shotgun, the power of which he was well aware, defendants took it to the old house where they secured it to an iron bed with the barrel pointed at the bedroom door. It was rigged with wire from the doorknob to the gun's <u>trigger</u> so it would fire when the door was opened. Briney first pointed the gun so an intruder would be hit in the stomach but at Mrs. Briney's suggestion it was lowered to hit the legs. He admitted he did so "because I was mad and tired of being <u>tormented</u>" but "he did not intend to injure anyone." He gave to [sic] explanation of why he used a loaded shell and set it to hit a person already in the house. Tin was nailed over the bedroom window. The spring gun could not be seen from the outside. No <u>warning</u> of its presence was posted.

 Plaintiff lived with his wife and worked regularly as a gasoline station <u>attendant</u> in Eddyville, seven miles from the old house. He had observed it for several years while hunting in the area and considered it as being abandoned. He knew it had long been uninhabited. In 1967 the area around the house was covered with high weeds. Prior to July 16, 1967 plaintiff and McDonough had been to the premises and found several old bottles and fruit jars which they took and added to their collection of antiques. On the latter date about 9:30 p.m. they made a second trip to the Briney property. They entered the old house by removing a board from a porch window which was without glass. While McDonough was looking around the kitchen area plaintiff went to another part of the house. As he started to open the north bedroom door the shotgun <u>went off</u> striking him in the right leg above the ankle bone. Much of his leg, including part of the tibia, was blown away. Only by McDonough's assistance was plaintiff able to get out of the house and after crawling some distance was put in his vehicle and rushed to a doctor and then to a hospital. He remained in the hospital 40 days.

 Plaintiff's doctor testified he seriously considered amputation but eventually the healing process was successful. Some weeks after his release from the hospital plaintiff returned to work <u>on crutches</u>. He was required to keep the injured leg in a cast for approximately a year and wear a special brace for another year. He continued to suffer pain during this period.

There was undenied medical testimony plaintiff had a permanent deformity, a loss of tissue, and a shortening of the leg.

The record discloses plaintiff to trial time had incurred $710 medical expense, $2056.85 for hospital service, $61.80 for orthopedic service and $750 as loss of earnings. In addition thereto the trial court submitted to the jury the question of damages for pain and suffering and for future disability.

III. Plaintiff testified he knew he had no right to break and enter the house with intent to steal bottles and fruit jars therefrom. He further testified he had entered a plea of guilty to larceny in the nighttime of property of less than $20 value from a private building. He stated he had been fined $50 and costs and paroled during good behavior from a 60-day jail sentence. Other than minor traffic charges this was plaintiff's first brush with the law. On this civil case appeal it is not our prerogative to review the disposition made of the criminal charge against him.

IV. The main thrust of defendants' defense in the trial court and on this appeal is that "the law permits use of a spring gun in a dwelling or warehouse for the purpose of preventing the unlawful entry of a burglar or thief." They repeated this contention in their exceptions to the trial court's instructions 2, 5 and 6. They took no exception to the trial court's statement of the issues or to other instructions.

In the statement of issues the trial court stated plaintiff and his companion committed a felony when they broke and entered defendants' house. In instruction 2 the court referred to the early case history of the use of spring guns and stated under the law their use was prohibited except to prevent the commission of felonies of violence and where human life is in danger. The instruction included a statement breaking and entering is not a felony of violence.

Instruction 5 stated: "You are hereby instructed that one may use reasonable force in the protection of his property, but such right is subject to the qualification that one may not use such means of force as will take human life or inflict great bodily injury. Such is the rule even though the injured party is a trespasser and is in violation of the law himself."

Instruction 6 state: "An owner of premises is prohibited from willfully or intentionally injuring a trespasser by means of force that either takes life or inflicts great bodily injury; and therefore a person owning a premise is prohibited from setting out 'spring guns' and like dangerous devices which will likely take life or inflict great bodily injury, for the purpose of harming trespassers. The fact that the trespasser may be acting in violation of the law does not change the rule. The only time when such conduct of setting a 'spring gun' or a like dangerous device is justified would be when the trespasser was committing a felony of violence or a felony punishable by death, or where the trespasser was endangering human life by his act."

Instruction 7, to which defendants made no objection or exception, stated: "To entitle the plaintiff to recover for compensatory damages, the burden of proof is upon him to establish by a preponderance of the evidence each and all of the following propositions:

 1. That defendants erected a shotgun trap in a vacant house on land owned by defendant, Bertha L. Briney, on or about June 11, 1967, which fact was known only by them, to protect household goods from trespassers and thieves.
 2. That the force used by defendants was in excess of that force reasonably necessary and which persons are entitled to use in the protection of their property.
 3. That plaintiff was injured and damaged and the amount thereof.
 4. That plaintiff's injuries and damages resulted directly from the discharge of the shotgun trap which was set and used by defendants."

The overwhelming weight of authority, both textbook and case law, supports the trial court's statement of the applicable principles of law.

Prosser on Torts, Third Edition, pages 116–118, states:

> ... the law has always placed a higher value upon human safety than upon mere rights in property, it is the accepted rule that there is no privilege to use any force calculated to cause death or serious bodily injury to repel the threat to land or chattels, unless there is also such a threat to the defendant's personal safety as to justify a self-defense ... spring guns and other mankilling devices are not justifiable against a mere trespasser, or even a petty thief. They are privileged only against those upon whom the landowner, if he were present in person would be free to inflict injury of the same kind.

Restatement of Torts, section 85, page 180, states:

> The value of human life and limb, not only to the individual concerned but also to society, so outweighs the interest of a possessor of land in excluding from it those whom he is not willing to admit thereto that a possessor of land has, as is stated in s 79, no privilege to use force intended or likely to cause death or serious harm against another whom the possessor sees about to enter his premises or meddle with his chattel, unless the intrusion threatens death or serious bodily harm to the occupiers or users of the premises ... A possessor of land cannot do indirectly and by a mechanical device that which, were he present, he could not do immediately and in person. Therefore, he cannot gain a privilege to install, for the purpose of protecting his land from intrusions harmless to the lives and limbs of the occupiers or users of it, a mechanical device whose only purpose is to inflict death or serious harm upon such as may intrude, by giving notice of his intention to inflict, by mechanical means and indirectly, harm which he could not, even

mankilling 致命的

after request, inflict directly were he present.

In Volume 2, Harper and James, The Law of Torts, section 27.3, pages 1440, 1441, this is found:

> The possessor of land may not arrange his premises intentionally so as to cause death or serious bodily harm to a trespasser. The possessor may of course take some steps to repel a trespass. If he is present he may use force to do so, but only that amount which is reasonably necessary to effect the repulse. Moreover if the trespass threatens harm to property only — even a theft of property — the possessor would not be privileged to use deadly force, he may not arrange his premises so that such force will be inflicted by mechanical means. If he does, he will be liable even to a thief who is injured by such device.

repulse 击退,拒绝,败退

Similar statements are found in 38 Am. Jur., Negligence, section 114, pages 776, 777, and 65 C.J.S. Negligence s 62(23), pages 678, 679; Anno. 44 A.L.R.2d 383, entitled "Trap to protect property."

In *Hooker v. Miller*, 37 Iowa 613, we held defendant vineyard owner liable for damages resulting from a spring gun shot although plaintiff was a trespasser and there to steal grapes. At pages 614, 615, this statement is made: "This court has held that a mere trespass against property other than a dwelling is not a sufficient justification to authorize the use of a deadly weapon by the owner in its defense; and that if death results in such a case it will be murder, though the killing be actually necessary to prevent the trespass. *The State v. Vance*, 17 Iowa 138." At page 617 this court said: "[T]respassers and other inconsiderable violators of the law are not to be visited by barbarous punishments or prevented by inhuman inflictions of bodily injuries."

barbarous 野蛮的,粗野的,残暴的

inhuman 残忍的,无人性的

The facts in *Allison v. Fiscus*, 156 Ohio 120, 110 N.E.2d 237, 44 A.L.R.2d 369, decided in 1951, are very similar to the case at bar. There plaintiff's right to damages was recognized for injuries received when he feloniously broke a door latch and started to enter

feloniously 有犯罪意图的,邪恶地

defendant's warehouse with intent to steal. As he entered a trap of two sticks of dynamite buried under the doorway by defendant owner was set off and plaintiff seriously injured. The court held the question whether a particular trap was justified as a use of reasonable and necessary force against a trespasser engaged in the commission of a felony should have been submitted to the jury. The Ohio Supreme Court recognized plaintiff's right to recover punitive or exemplary damages in addition to compensatory damages.

In *Starkey v. Dameron*, 96 Colo. 459, 45 P. 2d 172, plaintiff was allowed to recover compensatory and punitive damages for injuries received from a spring gun which defendant filling station operator had concealed in an automatic gasoline pump as protection against thieves.

In *Wilder v. Gardner*, 39 Ga. App. 608, 147 S. E. 911, judgment for plaintiff for injuries received from a spring gun which defendant had set, the court said: "A person in control of premises may be responsible even to a trespasser for injuries caused by pitfalls, mantraps, or other like contrivances so dangerous in character as to imply a disregard of consequences or a willingness to inflict injury."

In *Phelps v. Hamlett*, Tex. Civ. App., 207 S. W. 425, defendant rigged a bomb inside his outdoor theater so that if anyone came through the door the bomb would explode. The court reversed plaintiff's recovery because of an incorrect instruction but at page 426 said: "While the law authorizes an owner to protect his property by such reasonable means as he may find to be necessary, yet considerations of humanity preclude him from setting out, even on his own property, traps and devices dangerous to the life and limb of those whose appearance and presence may be reasonably anticipated, even though they may be trespassers."

In *United Zinc & Chemical Co. v. Britt*, 258 U. S. 268, 275, the court states: "The liability for spring guns and mantraps arises from the fact that the defendant has ... expected the trespasser and prepared an injury that is no more justified than if he had held the gun and fired it."

In addition to civil liability many jurisdictions hold a land owner criminally liable for serious injuries or homicide caused by spring guns or other set devices. See *State v. Childers*, 133 Ohio 508, 14 N. E. 2d 767 (melon thief shot by spring gun); *Pierce v. Commonwealth*, 135 Va. 635, 115 S. E. 686 (policeman killed by spring gun when he opened unlocked front door of defendant's shoe repair shop); *State v. Marfaudille*, 48 Wash. 117, 92 P. 939 (murder conviction for death from spring gun set in a trunk); *State v. Beckham*, 306 Mo. 566, 267 S. W. 817 (boy killed by spring gun attached to window of defendant's chili stand); *State v. Green*, 118 S. C. 279, 110 S. E. 145 (intruder shot by spring gun when he broke and entered vacant house. Manslaughter conviction of owner — affirmed); *State v. Barr*, 11 Wash. 481, 39 P. 1080 (murder conviction affirmed for death of an intruder into a boarded up cabin in which owner had set a spring gun).

manslaughter 过失杀人

In Wisconsin, Oregon, and England the use of spring guns and similar devices is specifically made unlawful by statute. 44 A. L. R., section 3, pages 386, 388.

The legal principles stated by the trial court in instructions 2, 5 and 6 are well established and supported by the authorities cited and quoted *supra*. There is no merit in defendants' objections and exceptions thereto. Defendants' various motions based on the same reasons stated in exceptions to instructions were properly overruled.

V. Plaintiff's claim and the jury's allowance of punitive damages, under the trial court's instructions relating thereto, were not at any time or in any manner challenged by defendants in the trial court as not allowable. We therefore are not presented with the problem of whether the $10,000 award should be allowed to stand.

We express no opinion as to whether punitive damages are allowable in this type of case. If defendants' attorneys wanted that issue decided it was their duty to raise it in the trial court.

The rule is well established that we will not consider a contention not raised in the trial court. In other words we are a court of review and will not consider a contention raised for the first time in this court. *Ke-Wash Company v. Stauffer Chemical Company*, Iowa, 177 N.W.2d 5, 9; *In re Adoption of Moriarty*, 260 Iowa 1279, 1288, 152 N.W.2d 218, 223; *Verschoor v. Miller*, 259 Iowa 170, 176, 143 N.W.2d 385, 389; *Mundy v. Olds*, 254 Iowa 1095, 1100, 120 N.W.2d 469, 472; *Bryan v. Iowa State Highway Commission*, 251 Iowa 1093, 1096, 104 N.W.2d 562, 563, and citations.

In our most recent reference to the rule we say in *Cole v. City of Osceola*, Iowa, 179 N.W.2d 524, 527: "Of course, questions not presented to and not passed upon by the trial court cannot be raised or reviewed on appeal."

Under our law punitive damages are not allowed as a matter of right. *Sebastian v. Wood*, 246 Iowa 94, 100, 101, 66 N.W.2d 841, 844. When malice is shown or when a defendant acted with wanton and reckless disregard of the rights of others, punitive damages may be allowed as punishment to the defendant and as a deterrent to others. Although not meant to compensate a plaintiff, the result is to increase his recovery. He is the <u>fortuitous</u> beneficiary of such an award simply because there is no one else to receive it.

The jury's findings of fact including a finding defendants acted with malice and with wanton and reckless disregard, as required for an allowance of punitive or exemplary damages, are supported by substantial evidence. We are bound thereby.

This opinion is not to be taken or construed as authority that the allowance of punitive damages is or is not proper under circumstances such as exist here. We hold only that question of law not having been properly raised cannot in this case be resolved.

Study and careful consideration of defendants' contentions on appeal reveal no <u>reversible error</u>.

Affirmed.

All Justices concur except Larson, J., who dissents.

Larson, Justice.

I respectfully dissent, first, because the majority

wrongfully assumes that by installing a spring gun in the bedroom of their unoccupied house the defendants intended to shoot any intruder who attempted to enter the room. Under the record presented here, that was a fact question. Unless it is held that the property owners are liable for any injury to a intruder from such a device regardless of the intent with which it is installed, liability under these pleadings must rest upon two definite issues of fact, *i.e.*, did the defendants intend to shoot the invader, and if so, did they employ unnecessary and unreasonable force against him?

It is my feeling that the majority oversimplifies the impact of this case on the law, not only in this but other jurisdictions, and that it has not thought through all the ramifications of this holding.

There being no statutory provisions governing the right of an owner to defend his property by the use of a spring gun or other like device, or of a criminal invader to recover punitive damages when injured by such an instrumentality while breaking into the building of another, our interest and attention are directed to what should be the court determination of public policy in these matters. On both issues we are faced with a case of first impression. We should accept the task and clearly establish the law in this jurisdiction hereafter. I would hold there is no absolute liability for injury to a criminal intruder by setting up such a device on his property, and unless done with an intent to kill or seriously injure the intruder, I would absolve the owner from liability other than for negligence. I would also hold the court had no jurisdiction to allow punitive damages when the intruder was engaged in a serious criminal offense such as breaking and entering with intent to steal.

It appears to me that the learned trial court was and the majority is now confused as to the basis of liability under the circumstances revealed. Certainly, the trial court's instructions did nothing to clarify the law in this jurisdiction for the jury. Timely objections to Instructions Nos. 2, 5, and 6 were made by the defendants, and thereafter the court should have been aware of the questions of liability left unresolved, *i.e.*, whether in this jurisdiction we by judicial

oversimplify 使过分简单化

impact 影响,冲击力,作用

ramification 分歧

break into 破门而入

absolve 解除……的义务(债务、责任等)

clarify 澄清,阐明,消除混乱

declaration bar the use in an unoccupied building of spring guns or other devices capable of inflicting serious injury or death on an intruder regardless of the intent with which they are installed, or whether such an intent is a vital element which must be proven in order to establish liability for an injury inflicted upon a criminal invader.

Although the court told the jury the plaintiff had the burden to prove "that the force used by defendants was in excess of that force reasonably necessary and which persons are entitled to use in the protection of their property," it utterly failed to tell the jury it could find the installation was not made with the intent or purpose of striking or injuring the plaintiff. There was considerable evidence to that effect. As I shall point out, both defendants stated the installation was made for the purpose of scaring or frightening away any intruder, not to seriously injure him. It may be that the evidence would support a finding of an intent to injure the intruder, but obviously that important issue was never adequately or clearly submitted to the jury.

Unless, then, we hold for the first time that liability for death or injury in such cases is absolute, the matter should be remanded for a jury determination of defendant's intent in installing the device under instructions usually given to a jury on the issue of intent.

I personally have no objection to this court's determination of the public policy of this state in such a case to ban the use of such devices in All instances where there is no intruder threat to human life or safety, but I do say we have never done so except in the case of a mere trespasser in a vineyard. *Hooker v. Miller*, 37 Iowa 613 (1873). To that extent, then, this is a case of first impression, and in any opinion we should make the law in this jurisdiction crystal clear. Although the legislature could pronounce this policy, as it has in some states, since we have entered this area of the law by the *Hooker* decision, I believe it proper for us to declare the applicable law in cases such as this for the guidance of the bench and bar hereafter. The majority opinion utterly fails in this regard. It fails to recognize the problem where such a device is installed in a building housing valuable property to ward off criminal intruders, and to clearly place and burden necessary to establish liability.

My second reason for this dissent is the allowance of an award of punitive damages herein. Plaintiff claimed a remedy which our law does not allow, and the trial court should not have submitted that issue to the jury. Like the law establishing liability for installing a spring gun or other similar device, the law recognizing and allowing punitive or exemplary damages is court-made law, not statutory law. As to the property owner's liability for exemplary damages where one is engaged in a serious criminal offense at the time of his injury, we also have a case of first impression. We have never extended this right to such a claimant, and I would not do so now. Unless we do, or there is a compelling reason or authority for such a right, which I fail to find, the trial court erred in submitting that issue to the jury. Like the case where a judgment is entered without jurisdiction of the subject matter, I would hold the award of $10,000 to plaintiff is void.

I do not wish to criticize, but believe the factual statement of the majority fails to give a true perspective of the relative facts and issues to be considered.

Plaintiff's petition at law asking damages alleged willful and malicious setting of a trap or device for the purpose of killing or inflicting great bodily harm upon any trespasser on defendants' property. We are, therefore, factually concerned with how such force may be properly applied by the property owner and whether his intent is relevant to liability. Negligent installation of a dangerous device to frighten and ward off an intruder or thief is not alleged, so unless the proof submitted was sufficient to establish a willful setting of the trap with a purpose of killing or seriously injuring the intruder, no recovery could be had. If the evidence submitted was such that a jury could find defendants had willfully set the spring gun with a purpose to seriously injure the plaintiff intruder, unless they were privileged under the law to set the gun under these circumstances, liability for the injury

ward off 避开,挡住

court-made law 判例法
(法院通过审判确立的法律,
又叫 judge-made law)
statutory law 制定法
(由立法机关制定的法律)

claimant 主张权利者
(这里指原告)

petition at law 起诉状
(相当于 complaint)

would follow.

From the record we learn that plaintiff and a companion made a second trip to a furnished but uninhabited house on defendants' farmland in Mahaska County on the night of July 16, 1967. They tore a plank from a porch window, entered the house with an intent to steal articles therein, and in search of desired articles plaintiff came to a closed bedroom door where he removed a chair braced under the door knob and pulled the door toward him. This action triggered a single shot 20 - gauge shotgun which defendants had wired to the bottom of a bed. The blast went through the door and struck plaintiff two or three inches above the right ankle.

The Mahaska County Grand Jury issued a true bill charging plaintiff with breaking and entering in the nighttime, but the county attorney accepted a plea of guilty to the lesser offense of larceny in the nighttime of property of a value of less than $20 and did not press the greater charge.

At the trial of this case Mr. Briney, one of the defendants, testified that the house where plaintiff was injured had been the home of Mrs. Briney's parents. He said the furniture and other possessions left there were of considerable value and they had tried to preserve them and enjoy them for frequent visits by Mrs. Briney. It appeared this unoccupied house had been broken into repeatedly during the past ten-years and, as a result, Mr. Briney said "things were pretty well torn up, a lot of things taken." To prevent these intrusions the Brineys nailed the doors and some windows shut and boarded up others. Prior to this time Mr. Briney testified he had locked the doors, posted seven no trespassing signs on the premises, and complained to the sheriffs of two counties on numerous occasions. Mr. Briney further testified that when all these efforts were futile and the vandalism continued, he placed a 20 - guage shotgun in a bedroom and wired it so that it would shoot downward and toward the door if anyone opened it. He said he first aimed it straight at the door but later, at his wife's suggestion, reconsidered the aim and pointed the gun down in a way he thought would only

---

grand jury 大陪审团（在刑事法庭审案期间由行政司法官选定并召集。其职责为受理刑事指控，听取控方提出的证据，决定是否将犯罪嫌疑人交付审判，而不是认定其是否有罪）

a true bill（大陪审团）正式认可的起诉书

lesser offense 较轻的罪

vandalism 破坏公私财产的行为

scare someone if it were discharged. On cross-examination he admitted that he did not want anyone to know it was there in order to preserve the element of surprise.

Plaintiff testified he knew the house was unoccupied and admitted breaking into it in the nighttime without lawful reason or excuse. He claimed he and his companion were seeking old bottles and dated fruit jars. He also admitted breaking in on one prior occasion and stated the reason for the return visit was that "we decided we would go out to this place again and see if there was something we missed while we was out there the first time." An old organ fascinated plaintiff. Arriving this second time, they found that the window by which they had entered before was now a "solid mass of boards" and walked around the house until they found the porch window which offered less resistance. Plaintiff said they crawled through this window. While searching the house he came to the bedroom door and pulled it open, thus triggering the gun that delivered a charge which struck him in the leg.

Plaintiff's doctor testified that he treated the shotgun wound on the night it was sustained and for some period thereafter. The healing process was successful and plaintiff was released after 40 days in the hospital. There was medical testimony that plaintiff had a permanent deformity, a loss of tissue, and a shortening of the leg.

That plaintiff suffered a grievous wound is not denied, and that it constituted a serious bodily injury cannot be contradicted.

As previously indicated, this appeal presents two vital questions which are as novel as they are difficult. They are, (1) is the owner of a building in which are [sic] kept household furniture, appliances, and valuables, but not occupied by a person or persons, liable in damages to an intruder who in the nighttime broke into and entered the building with the intent to steal and was shot and seriously injured by a spring gun allegedly set by the owner to frighten intruders from his property, and (2) if he is liable for compensatory damages, is this a proper case for the allowance of exemplary or punitive damages?

The trial court overruled all objections to the instructions and denied defendants' motion for a new trial. Thus, the first question to be resolved is the status of the law in this jurisdiction as to the means of force a property owner is privileged to use to repel (1) a mere trespasser, (2) a criminal invader, thief or burglar, where he presents no threat to human life or safety, and (3) an intruder or criminal breaking and entering a dwelling which poses a threat to human life and safety. Overlooked by the majority is the vital problem relating to the relevancy and importance of the owner's intent in placing the device.

I have been unable to find a case exactly like the case at bar, although there have been many cases which consider liability to a mere trespasser for injuries incurred by a spring gun or other dangerous instruments set to protect against intrusion and theft. True, some of these cases seem to turn on the negligence of the party setting the trap and an absence of adequate warning thereof, but most of them involve an alleged intentional tort. It is also true some hold as a matter of public policy there is liability for any injury following the setting of a device which is intended to kill or inflict great bodily injury on one coming on the owner's property without permission, unless the invader poses a threat to human life, and this is so even though there is no statutory prohibition against the setting of spring guns in the jurisdiction.

Since our decision in *Hooker v. Miller*, *supra*, we have recognized in this state the doctrine that the owner of a premise is liable in damages to a mere trespasser coming upon his property for any injury occasioned by the unsafe condition of the property which the owner has intentionally permitted to exist, such as installed spring guns, unless adequate warning is given thereof. In *Hooker*, which involved stealing grapes from a vineyard, we held a property owner had no right to resist such a trespass by means which may kill or inflict great bodily injury to the trespasser. But it does appear therein that we recognized some distinction between a mere trespass against property and a trespass involving a serious crime or involving a dwelling. Except when the trespass involves a serious crime, a crime posing a threat to human life, it may be argued that the law in this jurisdiction should limit the right of one to protect his property, that he does not have a privilege to resist a mere trespass by using a spring gun or other device which poses a threat to life.

However, left unsettled by this and other court pronouncements is the means which may be used to repel, prevent, or apprehend a trespasser engaged in a more serious criminal offense. True, there is a line of cases which seem to apply the same rule to all criminal trespasses except those involving arson, rape, assault, or other acts of violence against persons residing on the property invaded. *State v. Vance*, 17 Iowa 138 (1864); *State v. Plumlee*, 177 La. 687, 149 So. 425 (1933); *Pierce v. Commonwealth*, 135 Va. 635, 115 S. E. 686 (1923); *Simpson v. State*, 59 Ala. 1 (1877); *State v. Barr*, 11 Wash. 481, 39 P. 1080 (1895); *Starkey v. Dameron*, 96 Colo. 459, 21 P. 2d 1112 (1933); *State v. Beckham*, 306 Mo. 566, 267 S. W. 817 (1924); *Bird v. Holbrook*, 4 Bingham's Reports 628 (England, 1828). *Also see* annotation, 44 A. L. R. 2d 391, § 5, and citations. There are others which at least infer that any serious law violation by the trespasser might permit the reasonable use of dangerous instrumentalities to repel the intruder and prevent loss or damage to one's valuable property. *Scheuermann v. Scharfenberg*, 163 Ala. 337, 50 So. 335; *Marquis v. Benfer*, Tex. Civ. App., 298 S. W. 2d 601 (Texas 1956); *Grant v. Hass*, 31 Tex. Civ. App. 688, 75 S. W. 342 (1903); *Gray v. Combs*, 7 J. J. Marshall 478 (Ky., 1832), 23 Am. Dec. 431; *Ilott v. Wilkes*, 3 B. & A. 304 (1820 K. B.).

Also see the following articles on this subject: 68 YALE LAW JOURNAL 633, *Duties to Trespassers: A Comparative Survey and Revaluation*; 35 YALE LAW JOURNAL 525, *The Privilege to Protect Property by Dangerous Barriers and Mechanical Devices*; annotation, 44 A. L. R. 2d 383, *Use of Set Gun, Trap, or Similar Device on Defendant's Own Property*.

Most of these discussions center around what should be public policy regarding a property owner's right to use a dangerous weapon or instrumentality to

resist 抵抗,对抗

unsettled 未处理的,未决定的

arson（普通法）放火罪,纵火罪
rape 普通法强奸罪

protect his premises from intruders or trespassers, and his duty to protect the trespasser from serious injury while upon his premises.

Some states, including Wisconsin, have statutes which announce the jurisdiction's public policy. Often they prohibit the use of spring guns or such devices to protect real and personal property, and of course in those instances a property owner, regardless of his intent or purpose, has no right to make use of them and is liable to anyone injured thereby. Since there has been no such statutory prohibition or direct judicial pronouncement to that effect prior to this time in this state, it could not be said as a matter of law that the mere placing of a spring gun in a building on one's premises is unlawful. Much depends upon its placement and purpose. Whether an owner exceeds his privilege to reasonably defend his property by such an installation, and whether liability is incurred in a given case, should therefore depend upon the circumstances revealed, the intent of the property owner, and his care in setting the device. In any event, I question whether it should be determined solely by the results of his act or its effect upon the intruder.

It appears there are cases and some authority which would relieve one setting a spring gun on his premises of any liability if adequate warning had been given an intruder and he ignores the warning. In all of these cases there is a question as to the Intent of the property owner in setting the device. Intent, of course, may be determined from both <u>direct</u> and <u>indirect evidence</u>, and it is true the physical facts may be and often are sufficient to present a jury issue. I think they were here, but no clear instruction was given in this regard.

direct evidence 直接证据
indirect evidence 间接证据

intent 故意

If, after proper instructions, the finder of fact determines that the gun was set with an <u>intent</u> and purpose to kill or inflict great bodily injury on an intruder, then and only then may it be said liability is established unless the property so protected is shown to be an occupied dwelling house. Of course, under this concept, if the finder of fact determines the gun set in an unoccupied house was intended to do no more than to frighten the intruder or sting him a bit, no liability would be incurred under such pleadings as are now presented. If such a concept of the law were adopted in Iowa, we would have here a question for the fact-finder or jury as to whether the gun was willfully and intentionally set so as to seriously injure the thief or merely scare him away.

I feel the better rule is that an owner of buildings housing valuable property may employ the use of spring guns or other devices intended to repel but not seriously injure an intruder who enters his secured premises with or without a criminal intent, but I do not advocate its general use, for there may also be liability for negligent installation of such a device. What I mean to say is that under such circumstances as we have here the issue as to whether the set was with an intent to seriously injure or kill an intruder is a question of fact that should be left to the jury under proper instructions, and that the mere setting of such a device with a <u>resultant</u> serious injury should not as a matter of law establish liability.

resultant 作为结果的

In the case of a mere trespass able authorities have reasoned that absolute liability may rightfully be fixed on the landowner for injuries to the trespasser because very little damage could be inflicted upon the property owner and the danger is great that a child or other innocent trespasser might be seriously injured by the device. In such matters they say no privilege to set up the device should be recognized by the courts regardless of the owner's intent. I agree.

On the other hand, where the intruder may pose a danger to the inhabitants of a dwelling, the privilege of using such a device to repel has been recognized by most authorities, and the mere setting thereof in the dwelling has not been held to create liability for an injury as a matter of law. In such cases intent and the reasonableness of the force would seem relevant to liability.

Although I am aware of the often-repeated statement that personal rights are more important than property rights, where the owner has stored his valuables representing his life's accumulations, his livelihood business, his tools and implements, and his

ward off 防御

treasured antiques as appears in the case at bar, and where the evidence is sufficient to sustain a finding that the installation was intended only as a warning to ward off thieves and criminals, I can see no compelling reason why the use of such a device alone would create liability as a matter of law.

For cases considering the devices a property owner is or is not privileged to use to repel a mere trespasser, see Hooker v. Miller, supra, 37 Iowa 613 (trap gun set in orchard to repel); State v. Vance, supra, 17 Iowa 138 (1864); Phelps v. Hamlett, Tex. Civ. App., 207 S. W. 425 (1918) (bomb set in open air theater); State v. Plumlee, supra, 177 La. 687, 149 So. 425 (1933) (trap gun set in open barn); Starkey v. Dameron, supra, 96 Colo. 459, 21 P. 2d 1112 (1933) (spring gun in outdoor automatic gas pump); State v. Childers, 133 Ohio St. 508, 14 N. E. 2d 767 (1938) (trap gun in melon patch); Weis v. Allen, 147 Or. 670, 35 P. 2d 478 (1934) (trap gun in junkyard); Johnson v. Patterson, 14 Conn. 1 (1840) (straying poultry poisoned); Bird v. Holbrook, supra, 4 Bingham's Reports 628 (England, 1828) (spring gun in garden enclosed by wall of undisclosed height).

For cases apparently holding dangerous devices may be used to ward off and prevent a trespasser from breaking and entering into an inhabited dwelling, see State v. Vance, supra; Grant v. Hass, supra; Scheuermann v. Scharfenberg, supra; Simpson v. State, supra; United States v. Gilliam, 1 Hayw. & H. 109, 25 Fed. Cas. 1319, 1320 (D. C. 1882); State v. Childers, supra; Gramlich v. Wurst, 86 Pa. 74, 80 (1878).

Also, for cases considering the devices a property owner is privileged to use to repel an invader where there is no threat to human life or safety, see Allison v. Fiscus, 156 Ohio St. 120, 100 N. E. 2d 237; State v. Barr, 11 Wash. 481, 39 P. 1080 (1895); State v. Childers, supra; Weis v. Allen, supra; Pierce v. Commonwealth, supra; Johnson v. Patterson, supra; Marquis v. Benfer, supra.

In Allison v. Fiscus, supra, at page 241 of 100 N. E. 2d, it is said: "Assuredly, ... the court had no right to hold as a matter of law that defendant was liable to plaintiff, as the defendant's good faith in using the force which he did to protect his building and the good faith of his belief as to the nature of the force he was using were questions for the jury to determine under proper instructions." (Emphasis supplied.)

In *State v. Barr*, *supra*, at page 1081 of 39 P., the court said: "... whether or not what was done in a particular case was justified under the law must be a question of fact, or mixed law and fact, and not a pure question of law."

In *State v. Childers*, *supra*, it is said at page 768 of 14 N.E.2d: "Of course the act in question must be done maliciously ... and That fact must be proved and found by the jury to exist." (Emphasis supplied.)

Also see *State v. Metcalfe*, 203 Iowa 155, 212 N.W. 382, where this court discussed the force that a property owner may use to oppose an unlawful effort to carry away his goods, and held the essential issue in such matters which must be explained to the jury is not the nature of the weapon employed but whether the defendant employed only that degree of force to accomplish such purpose which a reasonable person would deem reasonably necessary under the circumstances as they appeared in good faith to the defendant.

Like the Ohio Supreme Court in *Allison v. Fiscus*, *supra*, I believe that the basis of liability, if any, in such a case should be either the intentional, reckless, or grossly negligent conduct of the owner in setting the device.

If this is not a desirable expression of policy in this jurisdiction, I suggest the body selected and best fitted to establish a different public policy would be the State Legislature.

The next question presented is, which view of the law set out above did the trial court take, the view that the mere setting of a spring gun or like device in defendants' building created liability for the resulting injury, or the view that there must be a setting of the device with an intent to shoot, kill, or seriously injure one engaged in breaking and entering this house? Appellants argue this was not made clear in the court's instructions to the jury and, being material, is error. I agree.

They contend Instructions Nos. 2, 5, and 6, to which proper and timely exceptions were taken, are improper, that they were so inadequate and confusing as to constitute reversible error and required the trial court to grant their motion for a new trial.

Instruction No. 5 provides:

"You are hereby instructed that one may use reasonable force in the protection of his property, but such right is subject to the qualification that one may not use such means of force as will take human life or inflict great bodily injury. Such is the rule even though the injured party is a trespasser and is in violation of the law himself." (Emphasis supplied.)

Instruction No. 6 provides:

"An owner of premises is prohibited from willfully or intentionally injuring a trespasser by means of force that either takes life or inflicts great bodily injury; and therefore a person owning a premise is prohibited from setting out 'spring guns' and like dangerous devices which will likely take life or inflict great bodily injury, For the purpose of harming trespassers. The fact that the trespasser may be acting in violation of the law does not change in the rule. The only time when such conduct of setting a 'spring gun' or a like dangerous device is justified would be when the trespasser was committing a <u>felony</u> of violence or a felony punishable by death, or where the trespasser was endangering human life by his act." (Emphasis supplied.)

Specific objections were made to Instruction No. 2, <u>inter alia</u>, to the statement that in this jurisdiction the use of force which may take life or inflict serious bodily injury might be used was restricted to occupied dwellings or where specific statutes permitted its use; to the reference to an Iowa case wherein the subject related to a Simple trespass in a vineyard where no breaking and entry of a building was involved, without pointing out the difference as to permissible force permitted to repel one entering the owner's buildings with intent to <u>ravish</u> and steal valuable personal property; and to the error resulting when the court

---

felony 重罪

inter alia 除了别的因素以外,就中(同 among other things)

ravish 强夺,抢走

wrongfully directed the jury to find defendants' acts were illegal by stating "that in so doing he violated the law and became liable for injuries sustained by the plaintiff."

In other words, defendants contended that this instruction failed to tell the jury the extent of defendants' rights to defend against burglary in buildings other than their dwelling, inferring they have no right to employ a device which is dangerous to life and limb, regardless of its intended purpose only to ward off or scare the intruder.

burglary 夜盗罪（指怀着犯重罪意图在夜里打开并且进入他人住宅的行为）

Defendants also specifically objected to Instruction No. 5 because it also limited the right or privilege of one to use dangerous devices in any way to protect his property, and made it applicable to cases where the invader was in violation of the law, without classifying his offense.

Instruction No. 6 was specifically objected to as not being a proper statement of the law, as being inadequate, confusing, and misleading to the jury in regard to the vital issues in this case, because it would not be possible for a jury to understand the court when it told the jurors an owner of premises is prohibited from willfully or intentionally injuring a trespasser by means of force that either takes life or inflicts great bodily injury, and then told them a person owning premises is prohibited from setting out spring guns and like dangerous devices which will "likely" take life or inflict great bodily injury, For the purpose of harming trespassers.

misleading 误导性的

likely 可能性很大地

Appellants argue from these instructions the jury could conclude it must find any setting of a spring gun or such other device to protect his property from a burglar or other criminal invader made the owner Absolutely liable for injuries suffered by the intruder, unless the building being so protected was a dwelling, regardless of the owner's intent and purpose in setting the device in his building. On the other hand, in Instruction No. 6 the court refers to such a Setting with the intent and purpose of killing or seriously injuring the intruder in order to make the owner liable for damages.

I too find these instructions are confusing. If the

court was telling the jury, as appellants contend, that an owner of a premise may not set a spring gun to protect his property unless the trespasser's act amounts to a felony of violence and endangers human life, the phrase used, "for the purpose of harming trespassers," introduces the element of intent and would tend to confuse the jury as to the law on that issue. If the issue here was that such an intent was necessary to establish liability, the instruction was erroneous and confusing; otherwise the error was without prejudice.

I would, therefore, conclude there is merit in appellants' contention that the law was not made clear to the jury as to whether the act of placing a spring gun on this premise was prohibited by law, or whether the act of placing such a device requires a finding of intention to shoot the intruder or cause him great bodily injury to establish liability. I cannot tell whether the jury found liability on the mere act of placing the gun as Mr. Briney did in this house or on the fact that he did so with the intent to seriously harm a trespasser.

In the case at bar, as I have pointed out, there is a sharp conflict in the evidence. The physical facts and certain admissions as to how the gun was aimed would tend to support a finding of intent to injure, while the direct testimony of both defendants was that the gun was placed so it would "hit the floor eventually" and that it was set "low so it couldn't kill anybody." Mr. Briney testified, "My purpose in setting up the gun was not to injure somebody. I thought more or less that the gun would be at a distance of where anyone would grab the door, it would scare them," and in setting the angle of the gun to hit the lower part of the door, he said, "I didn't think it would go through quite that hard."

If the law in this jurisdiction permits, which I think it does, an explanation of the setting of a spring gun to repel invaders of certain private property, then the intent with which the set is made is a vital element in the liability issue.

In view of the failure to distinguish and clearly give the jury the basis upon which it should determine that liability issue, I would reverse and remand the entire case for a new trial.

As indicated, under these circumstances the trial court should not have submitted the punitive damages issue to the jury in this case. By Instruction No. 14 the learned trial judge wrongfully instructed the jury that the law of Iowa allows a jury in such a case to award exemplary damages if it is found that the act complained of is wanton and reckless or where the defendants are guilty of malice. True, this instruction was in accordance with certain past pronouncements of this court and no objection was taken to the substance of the instruction, but defendants have always contended under these circumstances the court should not have submitted the question of exemplary damages to the jury. We have never extended the exemplary damages law to cover such cases and I maintain we should not do so now, directly or indirectly. Without such a pronouncement to that extent, or some legislation extending that right to a person engaged in a serious criminal offense at the time of his injury, I believe the trial court possessed no jurisdiction to permit the jury to pass on such a claim, even though no objections thereto were made by the defendants.

Although this subject has been considered and discussed in several Iowa cases, including *Sebastian v. Wood*, 246 Iowa 94, 66 N. W. 2d 841, and citations, granting exemplary damages for injury due to alleged reckless driving, and *Amos v. Prom*, 115 F. Supp. 127, relating to alleged mental suffering and humiliation when denied admission to a public dance hall, none seem to consider whether punitive damages are permitted where the injured party was, as here, engaged in a criminal act such as breaking and entering, burglary, or other serious offense. Also see *Morgan v. Muench*, 181 Iowa 719, 156 N. W. 819, and *Stricklen v. Pearson Construction Co.*, 185 Iowa 95, 169 N. W. 628, and citations in each.

Although I have found no authority to assist me in my view, I am convinced it is correct in principle and should be adopted in this jurisdiction. In so doing, I adhere to the rule recognized in *Amos v. Prom*, *supra*, at 137, *et seq.*, where it is stated: "... the principle that intentional wrongful action in disregard for the rights of others amounts to conduct to which the law will attach a penalty and deterrent by way of exemplary damages." However, I would not extend this privilege to a case where the injured party's conduct itself was criminal and extremely violative of good public behavior.

From a general review of the subject of exemplary or punitive damages beginning with *Wilkes v. Wood* (1763), Lofft 1, 98 English Rep. 489, 498, which stated such "Damages are designed not only as a satisfaction to the injured person, but likewise as a punishment to the guilty, to deter from any such proceeding for the future, ..." I find that both in England and the United States the purpose of this law was to restrain arbitrary and outrageous use of power. *See* 70 HARVARD L. REV. 517, 519 (1957), *Exemplary Damages in the Law of Torts*.

In *Hawk v. Ridgway*, 33 Ill, 473, 475 (1864), the Illinois court said, "Where the wrong is wanton, or it is willful, the jury are authorized to give an amount of damages beyond the actual injury sustained, as a punishment, and to preserve the public tranquility."

Some courts rationalize punitive damages on the basis that they provide an outlet for the injured party's desire for revenge and thereby help keep the peace. Some others rationalize it as a punishment to defendant and to deter him and others from further antisocial conduct. It has also been said punitive damages are ordinarily a means of increasing the severity of the admonition inherent in the compensatory award. *See* 44 Harvard L. Rev. 1173 (1931).

A further study of this law indicates punitive damages have a direct relation to the criminal law. Historically, it was undoubtedly one of the functions of tort law To deter wrongful behavior. However, in modern times its priority has become that of compensating the victim of the injury. The business of punishing wrongdoers has increasingly become the exclusive purview of the criminal law. *See* Pollock and Maitland, HISTORY OF ENGLISH LAW, VOL. II, 2d Ed. (1898), § 1, pp. 449 - 462.

The award of punitive damages in modern tort law

gives rise to considerable anomalies. Such damages, of course, go to the private purse of the individual plaintiff and may be classified a windfall as to him in excess of his actual losses due entirely to a social judgment about defendant's conduct.

In properly applying this law, Professor McCormick, in his treatise on damages found on pages 276 and 277 in McCormick on Damages (1935), said, "Perhaps the principal advantage is that it does tend to bring to punishment a type of cases of oppressive conduct, such as slanders, assaults, minor oppressions, and cruelties, which are theoretically criminally punishable, but which in actual practice go unnoticed by prosecutors occupied with more serious crimes .... The self-interest of the plaintiff leads to the actual prosecution of the claim for punitive damages, where the same motive would often lead him to refrain from the trouble incident to appearing against the wrongdoer in criminal proceedings."

So understood, punitive damages are an adjunct to the criminal law, yet one over which the criminal law has no control, and in the United Kingdom, the land of its birth, punitive damages are close to extinct. In *Rookes v. Barnard*, Appeal Cases (House of Lords, 1964) 1129, at 1221 *et seq.*, the English court of last resort confined the award of punitive damages to a very narrow range of situations. It ruled in an intentional tort case that exemplary damages could be awarded only in cases (1) for oppressive, arbitrary, or unconstitutional acts by government servants, (2) for defendant's conduct which had been calculated by him to make a profit for himself which might well exceed the compensation payable to the injured party, and (3) where expressly authorized by statute.

In the case at bar the plaintiff was guilty of serious criminal conduct, which event gave rise to his claim against defendants. Even so, he may be eligible for an award of compensatory damages which so far as the law is concerned redresses him and places him in the position he was prior to sustaining the injury. The windfall he would receive in the form of punitive damages is bothersome to the principle of damages, because it is a response to the conduct of the defendants rather than any reaction to the loss suffered by plaintiff or any measurement of his worthiness for the award.

When such a windfall comes to a criminal as a result of his <u>indulgence</u> in serious criminal conduct, the result is intolerable and indeed shocks the conscience. If we find the law upholds such a result, the criminal would be permitted <u>by operation of law</u> to profit from his own crime.

Furthermore, if our civil courts are to sustain such a result, it would in principle interfere with the purposes and policies of the criminal law. This would certainly be ironic since punitive damages have been thought to assist and promote those purposes, at least so far as the conduct of the defendant is concerned.

We cannot in good conscience ignore the conduct of the plaintiff. He does not come into court with clean hands, and attempts to make a claim to punitive damages in part on his own criminal conduct. In such circumstances, to enrich him would be unjust, and compensatory damages in such a case itself would be a sufficient deterrent to the defendant or others who might intend to set such a device.

The criminal law can take whatever action is appropriate in such cases, but the civil law should not compound the breach of proper social conduct by rewarding the plaintiff for his crime. I conclude one engaged in a criminal activity is an unworthy object of <u>largesse</u> <u>bestowed</u> by punitive damages and hold the law does not support such a claim to enrichment in this case.

The <u>admonitory</u> function of the tort law is adequately served where the compensatory damages claimed are high and the granted award itself may act as a severe punishment and a deterrence. In such a case as we have here there is no need to hold out the prospect of punitive damages as an incentive to sue and <u>rectify</u> a minor physical damage such as a redress for lost dignity. Certainly this is not a case where defendants might profit in excess of the amount of <u>reparation</u> they may have to pay.

In a case of this kind there is no overwhelming social purpose to be achieved by punishing defendants beyond the compensatory sum claimed for damages.

Being convinced that there was reversible error in the court's instructions, that the issue of intent in placing the spring gun was not clearly presented to the jury, and that the issue as to punitive damages should not have been presented to the jury, I would reverse and remand the matter for a new trial.

The majority seem to ignore the evident issue of punitive policy involved herein and uphold the punitive damages award on a mere technical rule of civil procedure.

convince 说服,使相信
reversible 应当推翻原判的

4.2 Case 20: Courvoisier v. Raymond

Supreme Court of Colorado
Courvoisier v. Raymond
23 Colo. 113, 47 P.284
Sept. 21, 1896

Edwin S. Raymond, appellee, as plaintiff below, complains of Auguste Courvoisier, appellant, and alleges that on the 12th day of June, A. D. 1892, plaintiff was a regularly appointed and duly qualified acting special policeman in and for the city of Denver; that, while engaged in the discharge of his duties as such special policeman, the defendant shot him in the abdomen, thereby causing a serious and painful wound; that in so doing the defendant acted willfully, knowingly, and maliciously, and without any reasonable cause. It is further alleged that, by reason of the wound so received, plaintiff was confined to his bed for a period of 10 days, during which time he was obliged to employ, and did employ, a physician and nurse, the reasonable value of such services being $100, which sum the plaintiff had obligated himself to pay; that the wound rendered him incapable of performing his duties as special policeman for a period of three weeks. It is further alleged that the injury caused the plaintiff great physical pain, and permanently impaired his health. Plaintiff alleges special and general damages to the amount of $30,150, and asks judgment for that sum, with costs. The defendant, answering the complaint, denies each allegation thereof, and in addition to such denials pleads five separate defenses. These defenses are all, in effect, a justification by reason of unavoidable necessity. A trial resulted in a verdict and judgment for plaintiff for the sum of $3,143. To reverse this judgment, the cause is brought here by appeal.

Hayt, C. J. (after stating the facts).

It is admitted, or proven beyond controversy, that appellee received a gunshot wound at the hands of the appellant at the time and place designated in the complaint, and that, as the result of such wound, the appellee was seriously injured. It is further shown that the shooting occurred under the following circumstances: That Mr. Courvoisier, on the night in question, was asleep in his bed, in the second story of a brick building, situated at the corner of South Broadway and Dakota streets, in South Denver; that he occupied a portion of the lower floor of this building as a jewelry store. He was aroused from his bed, shortly after midnight, by parties shaking or trying to open the door of the jewelry store. These parties, when asked by him as to what they wanted, insisted upon being admitted, and, upon his refusal to comply with this request, they used profane and abusive epithets towards him. Being unable to gain admission, they broke some signs upon the front of the building, and then entered the building by another entrance, and, passing upstairs, commenced knocking upon the door of a room where defendant's sister was sleeping. Courvoisier partly dressed himself, and, taking his revolver, went upstairs, and expelled the intruders from the building. In doing this he passed downstairs, and out on the sidewalk, as far as the entrance to his store, which was at the corner of the building. The parties expelled from the building, upon reaching the rear of the store, were joined by two or three others. In order to frighten these parties away, the defendant fired a shot in the air; but, instead of retreating, they passed around to the street in front, throwing stones and brickbats at the defendant, whereupon he fired a second, and perhaps a third, shot. The first shot fired attracted the attention of plaintiff, Raymond, and two deputy sheriffs, who were at the tramway depot across the street. These officers started towards Mr. Courvoisier, who still continued to shoot; but two of them stopped, when they reached the men in the street, for the purpose of arresting them, Mr. Raymond alone proceeding towards the defendant, calling out to him that he was an officer, and to stop shooting. Although the night was dark, the street was well lighted by electricity, and, when the officer approached him, defendant shaded his eyes, and, taking deliberate aim, fired, causing the injury complained of. The plaintiff's theory of the case is that he was a duly-authorized police officer, and in the discharge of his duties at the time; that the defendant was committing a breach of the peace; and that the defendant, knowing him to be a police officer, recklessly fired the shot in question. The defendant claims that the plaintiff was approaching him at the time in a threatening attitude, and that the surrounding circumstances were such as to cause a reasonable man to believe that his life was in danger, and that it was necessary to shoot in self-defense, and that defendant did so believe at the time of firing the shot.

The first error argued brings up for review the action of the district court in overruling a challenge interposed by the defendant to the juror Gibbons. The ground of this challenge will appear from the following:

Q. Have you served as a juror within the year last past?

A. I was called a few weeks ago on one case in the county court.

Q. As a talesman?

A. Yes, sir.

The Court: When did you serve, Mr. Gibbons?

A. A few weeks ago.

The Court: Since the 1st of January?

A. Yes, sir.

The statute relied upon to support the challenge reads as follows:

The fact that any juror in any district or county court shall have served as a juror of the regular panel, or as talesman, in either of said courts at any time within the year next preceding shall be a sufficient excuse for such juror from service in the same court and may also be ground for <u>challenge for cause</u> to such individual juror.

Sess. Laws 1889, p. 220, §1.

The statute limits the exception to service a second time within the year in the same court, and we think it was likewise intended to thus restrict this ground of challenge for cause. This has been the uniform practice under the statute, and we think it must be upheld as the obvious meaning of the act.

The second error assigned is upon the overruling of defendant's objections to certain hypothetical questions propounded by plaintiff to medical experts. These questions called for the opinion of the witnesses as to the natural result of the wound received by plaintiff. It is claimed that the questions do not describe the wound with sufficient certainty, and that the evidence of the extent of the injury is not sufficient to form a basis for any hypothetical questions, or for <u>expert opinions</u> upon the probable effects of the wound. We think the objections to these questions were properly overruled. The questions contain such a description of the wound as is easily understood by the <u>lay mind</u>, and the answers show that it was fully understood by the experts. The questions are framed upon the <u>assumption</u> that the evidence tended to prove certain facts. This assumption, being within the probable or possible range of the evidence, is permissible. *Jackson v. Burnham*, 20 Colo. 532, 39 Pac. 577.

The third assignment of error challenges the refusal of the court to permit witnesses for the defendant to testify as to whether or not, as a result of a criminal prosecution, one of the participants was convicted of "throwing a stone and hitting Mr. Courvoisier that night." The objection to this question was properly sustained. If proof of such conviction was admissible, the record is the best evidence thereof, except in the instances specified by statute (Mills' Ann. St. §4822); but, as this action is between other parties, even the record is not admissible in this case. It was attempted to prove, by the witness Reed, who was at the time marshal of the town of South Denver, that the neighborhood in the immediate vicinity of defendant's house had been the scene of frequent robberies and disturbances shortly prior to this shooting. This evidence was offered for the purpose of justifying the defendant's action. It is claimed that conduct which would cause no apprehension in a quiet and peaceful neighborhood would naturally and reasonably excite alarm if disturbances and breaches of the peace were frequent. We think, however, the court was justified in refusing this evidence. Its tendency is to raise collateral issues, and thereby divert the attention of the jury.

marshal 执法官,职责与行政司法官〔sheriff〕类似

vicinity 邻近,附近,近处
robbery 抢劫
disturbance 干扰,骚乱

divert 转移

Under the fourth assignment of error it is claimed that evidence of the financial standing of the defendant was not admissible. If the jury believed, from the evidence, that the shooting was done with malice, or that the injury was the result of a wanton and reckless disregard of plaintiff's rights, and not in necessary self-defense, exemplary damages might have been awarded; and, wherever such damages are permissible, the financial condition of the defendant may be shown. In a number of cases, commencing with *Murphy v. Hobbs*, 7 Colo. 541, 5 Pac. 119, it has been held that, in civil actions for injuries resulting from torts, exemplary damages, as a punishment, were not permissible, if the offense is punishable under the criminal laws. These decisions were based upon the common law. In 1889 the legislature provided, by statute, that exemplary damages may be given in certain cases. Before the passage of this act the question was one upon which the courts disagreed, but the statute has now settled the practice in this state.

The next error assigned relates to the instructions given by the court to the jury, and to those requested by the defendant and refused by the court. The second instruction given by the court was clearly erroneous. The instruction is as follows: "The court instructs you that if you believe, from the evidence, that, at the time the defendant shot the plaintiff, the plaintiff was not assaulting the defendant, then your verdict should be for the plaintiff." The vice of this instruction is that it excluded from the jury a full consideration of the justification claimed by the defendant. The evidence for the plaintiff tends to show that the shooting, if not malicious, was wanton and reckless; but the evidence for the defendant tends to show that the circumstances surrounding him at the time of the shooting were such as to lead a reasonable man to believe that his life was in danger, or that he was in danger of receiving great bodily harm at the hands of the plaintiff, and the defendant testified that he did so believe. He swears that his house was invaded, shortly after midnight, by two men, whom he supposed to be burglars; that, when ejected, they were joined on the outside by three or four others; that the crowd so formed assaulted him with stones and other missiles, when, to frighten them away, he shot into the air; that, instead of going away, someone approached him from the direction of the crowd; that he supposed this person to be one of the rioters, and did not ascertain that it was the plaintiff until after the shooting. He says that he had had no previous acquaintance with plaintiff; that he did not know that he was a police officer, or that there were any police officers in the town of South Denver; that he heard nothing said at the time, by the plaintiff or any one else, that caused him to think the plaintiff was an officer; that his eyesight was greatly impaired, so that he was obliged to use glasses; and that he was without glasses at the time of the shooting, and for this reason could not see distinctly. He then adds: "I saw a man come away from the bunch of men, and come up towards me, and as I looked around I saw this man put his hand to his hip pocket. I didn't think I had time to jump aside, and therefore turned around and fired at him. I had no doubts but it was somebody that had come to rob me, because, some weeks before, Mr. Wilson's store was robbed. It is next door to mine."

By this evidence two phases of the transaction are presented for consideration: First. Was the plaintiff assaulting the defendant at the time plaintiff was shot? Second, If not, was there sufficient evidence of justification for the consideration of the jury? The first question was properly submitted, but the second was excluded by the instruction under review. The defendant's justification did not rest entirely upon the proof of assault by the plaintiff. A riot was in progress, and the defendant swears that he was attacked with missiles, hit with stones, brickbats, *etc.*; that he shot plaintiff, supposing him to be one of the rioters. We must assume these facts as established in reviewing the instruction, as we cannot say that the jury might have found had this evidence been submitted to them under a proper charge. By the second instruction, the conduct of those who started the fracas was eliminated from the consideration of the jury. If the jury believed, from the evidence, that the defendant would have been justified in shooting one of the rioters, had such person advanced towards him, as did the plaintiff, then it became important to determine whether the defendant mistook plaintiff for one of the rioters; and, if such a mistake was in fact made, was it excusable, in the light of all the circumstances leading up to and surrounding the commission of the act? If these issues had been resolved by the jury in favor of the defendant, he would have been entitled to a judgment. *Morris v. Platt*, 32 Conn. 75; *Patten v. People*, 18 Mich. 318; *Kent v. Cole*, 84 Mich. 579, 48 N. W. 168; *Higgins v. Minaghan*, 76 Wis. 298, 45 N. W. 127. The opinion of the first of the cases above cited contains an exhaustive review of the authorities, and is very instructive. The action was for damages resulting from a pistol-shot wound. The defendant justified under the plea of self-defense. The proof for the plaintiff tended to show that he was a mere bystander at a riot, when he received a shot aimed at another; and the court held that, if the defendant was justified in firing the shot at his antagonist, he was not liable to the plaintiff, for the reason that the act of shooting was lawful under the circumstances. Where a defendant, in a civil action like the one before us, attempts to

---

fracas 吵闹,喧噪
eliminate 消除,排除

advance toward somebody
走向某人

antagonist 敌手,敌人

justify on a plea of necessary self-defense, he must satisfy the jury, not only that he acted honestly in using force, but that his fears were reasonable under the circumstances, and also as to the reasonableness of the means made use of. In this case, perhaps, the verdict would not have been different, had the jury been properly instructed; but it might have been, and therefore the judgment must be reversed.

Reversed.

5. Intentional Torts to Economic and Dignitary Interests

5.1 Defamation

Defamation is the false communications made with the intention of harming the reputation of an individual or a corporation. The defamation laws are intended to protect the right to a reputation unsullied by the publication of false claims or statements.

There are two forms of defamation: slander and libel. Generally, libel consists of the publication of defamatory matter by recording in writing or some other permanent form, or by any other form of communication which has the similar potentially harmful qualities and characteristics. Slander, in contrast, consists of spoken words, transitory gestures, and other less permanent and less-harmful forms of communication.

The main difference between libel and slander is that, at common law, libel was actionable *per se*, i.e., a plaintiff in a libel case could recover damages without proof of any injury. In that case, general damage is presumed by law. In slander cases, by contrast, the plaintiff had to prove special damage, i.e., he must specifically prove that he suffered pecuniary loss as a result of the defamatory statement's effect on his reputation. Special damage may include the loss of a job, a prospective gift or inheritance, an advantageous business relationship, or customers, unless the slander is slander *per se*. Slander *per se* may be identified if the slanderous statement accused the plaintiff of any of four particularly odious types of

---

defamation 诬蔑,诽谤,中伤,损害(他人)名誉

false communication 错误的传播

right to a reputation 名誉权

unsullied 无污点的,清白的

slander 口头诽谤
libel 书面诽谤

transitory 短暂的,可变换的,变动的

actionable *per se* 可起诉的当然诽谤

general damage 一般损害
special damage 特定损害

pecuniary loss 金钱上的损失

slander *per se* 以行为本身构成的口头诽谤
slanderous 诽谤的,中伤的

odious 讨厌的,可憎的

conduct: committing a serious crime involving moral turpitude, having a loathsome disease, being incompetent to practice a business, trade, or profession, or being an unchaste woman. The courts have expanded the scope of the last type to cover serious sexual misconduct by a plaintiff of either sex.

In order to establish a *prima facie* case of defamation, the plaintiff must prove the following elements. First, there must be a defamatory language on the part of defendant, which tends to adversely affect the plaintiff's reputation, such as impeaching his honesty, integrity, virtue, sanity, or the like. Second, the defamatory language must be "of or concerning" the plaintiff, *i.e.*, it must identify the plaintiff to a reasonable reader, listener, or viewer. Third, there must be a publication of the defamatory language by the defendant to a third person who understands it. Fourth, the plaintiff's reputation must be harmed by the defamatory statement. In addition to these elements, the plaintiff must also prove special damage if slander is involved unless it falls within the slander *per se*.

If the defamation refers to a public figure or involves a matter of public concern, two additional elements must be proved as part of the *prima facie* case. First, the defamatory language must be fault. Second, there must be fault on the part of the defendant as to the statement's falsity.

A defamation litigation may be initiated by any living person, as well as on behalf of corporations, partnerships, unincorporated associations, and non-profit institutions. Suit may not be brought to vindicate the reputation of a deceased person, although defamation of the dead may reflect on the living, in which case any action may lie. For example, Mary died with her three kids survived her. A said in her funeral: "Poor Mary, she never married!" The implication is that Mary's three kids are illegitimate. So Mary's kids were defamed by such a statement.

a crime involving moral turpitude 有伤风化的犯罪
a loathsome disease 恶心的疾病,肮脏的疾病
incompetent 无能力的,不合格的
unchaste 不贞洁的

impeach 指摘,弹劾
integrity 正直
virtue 美德,德行
sanity 明智,通情达理

a public figure 公众人物
a matter of public concern 公众关心的事务

falsity 虚伪,谎言,错误

unincorporated association 非法人团体,非注册社团,不具备法人资格的社团
non-profit institution 非营利机构
vindicate 维护,证明
deceased person 死去的人

implication 暗示,含义
illegitimate 私生的

5.1.1 Case 21: Hedgpeth v. Coleman

Supreme Court of North Carolina.
Hedgpeth v. Coleman
183 N.C. 309, 111 S.E. 517
April 12, 1922

In an action for libel contained in a typewritten letter to plaintiff of unavowed authorship, the court did not err in refusing an instruction that, owing to the large number of typewriters of different kinds and makes and the similarity in styles of typewriting in the various schools, the jury should scan with care the evidence of an expert witness that the letter was written by the same person as one the authenticity of which defendant did not dispute.

The defendant was a merchant, depot and express agent, and postmaster at Lyon. In February, 1918, his storehouse and safe were broken into; and soon thereafter the plaintiff, a boy then between 14 and 15 years of age, found in his individual mail box the following paper writing, sealed in an envelope addressed to him:

"Washington, D. C.
Read All This.

We saw you next day after it happened. You showed guilt, but we wanted more evidence. We have plenty of it now, and would come right on and get you, but on account of your age, and for the sake of your relatives, we will give you one chance to make good by taking everything you got, tie it up and throw it into cat hole of shed room door. If he finds it before next Sunday, he will let us know, but unless it is found by Sunday, we will come and get you and there will be no more chance to stop it this side of Atlanta Pen.

If it is found, no one will know that you put it there, and you may not be suspected by everybody, but if we come back, then it matters not who knows it, for we will push it clear

CHAPTER 6　INTENTIONAL TORTS

through and do it quickly.

　　Two men, who saw you on Wednesday."

The plaintiff showed this paper to W. T. Hedgpeth, his brother, and to T. M. Parrott, and his brother showed it to the plaintiff's father. The communication received by the plaintiff was typewritten. An expert witness compared it with a typewritten letter received from the defendant, and testified that in his opinion each paper was written on an Oliver typewriter No. 4 or 5. He said:

"The type is the same, and the general appearance is the same. The body of each letter is written in <u>single space</u>. It is <u>double spaced</u> between paragraphs. The <u>marginal indentation</u> starts immediately after the <u>salutation</u> in each letter, and the paragraphs down through the letter follow that beginning point; the spacing after the comma and before the next letter is the same. The letters E, A, C, D, and B, and the small letter s and the capital S and the period on each letter are out of <u>alignment</u>. The letter E is <u>clogged</u> at the top — not plain; also the letter T and W and the letter U are clogged and not plain; periods after the letter C and after the letter E in each letter. In each of these letters, the letter C is struck out of place — the same impression and the same clearness. The margins on the right-hand side are similar. The periods and the <u>dash</u> are struck with such force as to leave an <u>indentation</u> on the back of each letter, and the comma is distinct; that is, the period and the <u>tail</u> are distinct in each letter. The spacing after the comma is the same. These are some of the main characteristics in these two letters. That the style of the type is the same, and the space between each written line, that is, from the bottom of the first line to the top of the second line, is the same. From these similarities pointed out he formed his opinion that they were written by the same person and on the same machine."

single space 单倍行距
double space 双倍行距
marginal indentation 边际缩进
salutation 称呼语

alignment 排成直线
clog 阻塞,障碍

dash 破折号
indentation 压痕,印记

tail 尾部、后部

After reading the paper received by plaintiff, W. T. Hedgpeth showed it to the defendant, who denied writing it, but said that "he was knowing to it; that efforts were being made to locate the person who had broken into the store, and that the matter was in the hands of a detective." Defendant told plaintiff's father that he would be wonderfully surprised when he found out who had broken into the store; that if the person who did so would bring back all he had and put it in the cat hole of the shedroom his name would not be exposed.

The defendant introduced no evidence. At the close of the evidence the defendant moved to dismiss as in case of nonsuit. Motion allowed as to the alleged slander and blackmail, and denied as to the alleged libel. Defendant excepted and appealed.

Adams, J.

In *O'Brien v. Clement*, 15 M. & W. 435, Parke, B., said:

"Everything, printed or written, which reflects on the character of another, and is published without lawful justification or excuse, is a libel, whatever the intention may have been."

Many charges which if merely spoken of another would not be actionable without proof of special damage may be libelous *per se* when written or printed and published, although such charges may not impute the commission of a crime. *Simmons v. Morse*, 51 N. C. 6; *Brown v. Lumber Co.*, 167 N.C. 11, 82 S. E. 961; *Hall v. Hall*, 179 N. C. 571, 103 S. E. 136; *Paul v. Auction Co.*, 181 N. C. 1, 105 S. E. 881. In the case before us, however, the anonymous communication appears to charge the plaintiff with an offense punishable by confinement in a federal prison; and while the defendant does not deny that it is libelous *per se*, he controverts, chiefly on two grounds, the plaintiff's right to recover damages. These grounds are: (1) that the defendant did not write the paper referred to; and (2) that, even if he did, there has been no publication of it in contemplation of law.

As to the first, the defendant admitted that, while he did not write the communication, "he was knowing to it"; and there was expert evidence tending to show that this paper and a letter, the authenticity of which the defendant did not dispute, were written by the same person on an Oliver typewriter. This was not mere vague, uncertain, and irrelevant matter, but it was evidence of a character sufficiently substantial to warrant the jury in finding as a fact that the defendant was responsible for this typewritten paper of unavowed authorship.

As to the second ground of defense, the general rule unquestionably requires that the defamatory words be communicated to some one other than the person defamed. FOLKARD'S STARKIE ON SLAN. & LIB. 37.

> "The publication of a slander involves only one act by the defendant; he must speak the words, so that some third person hears and understands them. But the publication of a libel is a more composite act. First, the defendant must compose and write the libel; next, he must hand what he has written, or cause it to be delivered, to some third person; then that third person must read and understand its contents; or, it may be that, after composing and writing it, the defendant reads it aloud to some third person, who listens to the words and understands them: in this case the same act may be both the uttering of a slander and the publication of a libel."

ODGERS ON LIB. AND SLAN. 157.

But it is not necessary that the defamatory words be communicated to the public generally, or even to a considerable number. It is sufficient if they be communicated only to a single person other than the person defamed. *Jozsa v. Moroney*, 125 La. 813, 51 South. 908. For example, it has been held that the publication was sufficient where the defendant had communicated the defamatory matter to the plaintiff's agent, or attorney; or had read it to a friend before posting it to the plaintiff; or had procured it to be copied, or sealed in the form of a letter addressed to the plaintiff and left in the house of a neighbor by whom it was read; or had caused it to be delivered to and read by a member of the plaintiff's family. The fact, therefore, that the paper under consideration may have been seen only by the plaintiff's brother and Parrott cannot exonerate the defendant on the ground that there was no communication to the public. *Tuson v. Evans*, 12 A. & E. 733; *Snyder v. Andrews*, 6 Barb. (N. Y.) 43; *Kiene v Ruff*, 1 Iowa, 482.

But the defendant argued that, even if this be granted, still there was no publication by him, because the paper was communicated directly to the plaintiff, and the plaintiff alone divulged its contents. We have stated the general rule to be that the communication of libelous matter to the person defamed does not of itself constitute a publication. The defendant's argument involves the question whether the rule is inflexible or whether it is subject to exception or qualification. The suggestion that as a principle it is immutable cannot be adopted. The ultimate concern is the relation that existed between the writing of the paper and the disclosure of its contents by the plaintiff. For running through the entire law of tort is the principle that a causal relation must exist between the damage complained of and the act which occasions the damage. Unless such relation exists, the damage is held to be remote, and cannot be recovered; but, if such relation does exist, the wrongful act is held to be the cause of the damage. So in this case we cannot disregard the relation of cause and effect.

"There is no publication such as to give rise to a civil action where libelous matter is sent to the person libeled, unless the sender intends or has reason to suppose that the matter will reach third persons (which in fact happens) or such result naturally flows from the sending." STREET'S FOUND. LEG. LIAB. VOL. 1, 296.

Under this principle the mailing of a libelous letter to a person whose clerk, in pursuance of a custom known to the sender, opens and first reads the

CHAPTER 6 INTENTIONAL TORTS **227**

letter constitutes a publication. *Delacroix v. Theyenot*, 2 Starkie, 63; *Pullman v. Hill*, 1 Q. B., 524; *Rumney v. Worthley*, 186 Mass. 144, 71 N. E. 316, 1 Ann. Cas. 189. Whether the principle extends to a disclosure by the person libeled is to be determined by the causal relation existing between the libel and the publication. The sending of libelous matter to a person known by the sender to be blind, or having sight, to be unable to read, and therefore obliged to have it read by another, is, when read, a publication by the sender, because such exposure of the subject-matter is the proximate result of the writing and sending of the communication. *Allen v. Wortham*, 89 Ky. 485, 13 S. W. 73; *Wilcox v. Moon*, 64 Vt. 450, 24 Atl. 244. These exceptions are based upon the principle that the act of disclosure arises from necessity. But necessity is not predicated exclusively on conditions which are physical. Necessity may be superinduced by a fear which is akin to duress. A threat may operate so powerfully upon the mind of an immature boy as to amount to coercion; and, when an act is done through coercion, it is not voluntary.

In the letter referred to there is a threat of prosecution and imprisonment. When it was received the plaintiff was between 14 and 15 years of age, and his youth was known to the defendant. With knowledge of the plaintiff's immaturity, of the character of the accusation and menace contained in the letter, of the probable emotion of fear, and the impelling desire for advice on the part of the plaintiff, the defendant must have foreseen the plaintiff's necessary exposure of the letter as the natural and probable result of the libel. Indeed, under the charge of his honor the jury found from the evidence that the defendant had reasonable ground to know that the letter would necessarily be seen by third persons. Obviously, then, the act of the defendant was the proximate cause of the publication. *Fonville v. McNease*, Dudley Law (S. C.) 303, 31 Am. Dec. 556; *Miller v. Butler*, 6 Cush. (Mass.) 71, 52 Am. Dec. 768; *Rollard v. Batchelder*, 84 Va. 664, 5 S. E. 695. This conclusion disallows all the exceptions relating to the motion for nonsuit, and to the

exposure 暴露,曝光,揭露
proximate result 直接结果

superinduce 增添
akin 相近似的

coercion 胁迫

immaturity 未成年,未成熟(指因年轻而缺乏辨别力或判断力,尚未完全成熟)
menace 胁迫,威胁,恐吓
impelling desire 强烈的欲望

disallow 驳回,否决,拒绝

defendant's prayer for peremptory instructions.

The defendant excepted to his honor's refusal to give the jury this instruction:

> "That owing to the large number of typewriters of different kinds and makes now in use, and the similarity in styles of typewriting in the various schools, the jury should scan with care the evidence of the expert before arriving at a conclusion that defendant wrote the letter complained of."

The defendant relies on *Buxly v. Buxton*, 92 N.C. 479. There the issue was whether the bond sued on had been executed by the defendant's intestate. The plaintiff introduced evidence of the intestate's admission that he had signed the note, and each party introduced expert evidence relating to the alleged signature. The trial judge instructed the jury that evidence of the intestate's admission, if accepted as true, was entitled to greater weight than the expression of opinion by expert witnesses, and that an opinion as to handwriting should be received with caution. On appeal it was held that an exception to this instruction was untenable; but it may be remarked that the learned justice who wrote the opinion was contrasting the relative value of positive with opinion evidence and pertinently said that there "could be no harm in making the observation in regard to these classes of evidence and their relation to the controversy." But he did not say that refusal to give the instruction would have constituted reversible error. We should hesitate to hold that there may not be cases in which it would be proper for the court to tell the jury that expert testimony should be received with caution; and we should be equally reluctant to pronounce such instruction an inflexible necessity. As the testimony of an expert ought neither to be blindly accepted nor arbitrarily rejected, so the question whether it is to be considered like other evidence or received with caution may depend upon the circumstances developed in the trial. But, generally speaking, expert testimony should be subject to the tests that are ordinarily applied to the evidence of other witnesses, and to the court's instruction that the jury must find the facts upon their own sound judgment. *Railroad v. Thurl*, 32 Kan. 255, 4 Pac. 352. We find nothing in the record which removes the evidence referred to from the operation of the general principle, and for this reason exception 7 is overruled.

The exceptions disposed of are those which were chiefly relied on in the argument. We have not overlooked the others, but have given them due consideration; and, having regard to the evidence and the charge, we have concluded that they cannot be sustained. Upon a careful review of the entire record, we find no sufficient cause for disturbing the result of the trial.

No error.

5.1.2 Case 22: Fisher v. Detroit Free Press, Inc.

Court of Appeals of Michigan
Fisher v. Detroit Free Press, Inc.
158 Mich. App. 409, 404 N.W. 2d 765
March 3, 1987

Hood, Presiding Judge.

Plaintiff, William L. Fisher, an attorney acting in *propria persona*, appeals as of right from a circuit court bench opinion and order granting summary disposition in favor of defendant pursuant to MCR 2.116(C)(8) and (10) on plaintiff's suit for defamation. Plaintiff's complaint was filed on January 9, 1984, and alleged in relevant part that:

> 4. On or about January 12, 1983, defendant falsely and maliciously published of plaintiff in a prominent place in said newspaper for said persons to read a matter addressed to the eye which was calculated to bring plaintiff into contempt, ridicule or obliquy [sic] or to cause him to be shunned or avoided.
>
> 5. Defendant published said matter in its report of a court decision concerning a suit to recover damages for injury to a tree and therein made it appear that said decision used reasoning while the plaintiff, Fisher, did not and that

propria persona 亲自,本人

bench opinion 法院(或法官)判决意见书(指在没有陪审团参加的庭审中法官作出的判决意见)

contempt 轻蔑,蔑视
ridicule 嘲笑,笑柄,愚弄
shun 避开,避免

| loss of companionship 失去陪伴 |
| deficient 有缺陷的,不足的,缺乏的,有缺点的 |
| indignation 愤怒,义愤,愤慨 |
| shame 羞耻 |
| mental anxiety 精神焦虑 |
| insulted honor 受损害的名誉 |
| pride 自尊 |

rhyme 韵,押韵,韵脚

Fisher sought "loss of companionship of the sick tree" meaning that Fisher keeps, for companion, a tree, so deficient is he.

6. Plaintiff has been damaged in person, property and reputation and has suffered injury to his feelings including indignation, shame, mental anxiety, insulted honor, and wounds to his pride and manly feelings consequent upon defendant's wrong.

The prior court decision referred to is an opinion written in rhyme by Judge J. H. Gillis of this Court, *Fisher v. Lowe*, 122 Mich. App. 418, 333 N. W. 2d 67 (1983), and sometimes referred to as the "trees" opinion.

Although plaintiff does not clearly allege in his complaint that a false statement of fact was made in the newspaper article, he compares the defendant's article with one concerning the same subject matter which appeared in the *Kalamazoo Gazette* which plaintiff found unobjectionable. Defendant's article set forth the text of the opinion and included additional remarks made by Judge Gillis to defendant's reporter. Comparing the defendant's article with the *Kalamazoo Gazette* article and considering plaintiff's complaint and appellate briefs, it is clear that the statement in defendant's article that plaintiff considered defamatory is the following:

> The car's insurer offered to pay the tree surgeon's bill — $550 — but Fisher sought $15,000 for the equivalent of "loss of companionship of the sick tree," Gillis said.

off the record 没有记录的(这里指在正式记录之外的)

frivolous litigation 无意义的诉讼

levy 征收(罚款或税款),处以(罚款),征税

The trial court, in granting summary disposition, held that:"there is nothing in the story, quoting Judge Gillis off the record, which is slanderous in any way or nature." In response to defendant's motion for sanctions for frivolous litigation under MCR 2.114(D) and (E) the judge ruled:

> [P]ossibly they should be levied here, and to my mind this case appears entirely frivolous. It is

not, certainly in the mind of Mr. Fisher, so I am going to rule against you on sanctions.

However, subsequently, the trial court did conditionally grant defendant's motion to assess actual costs for plaintiff's rejection of a mediation evaluation pursuant to MCR 2.403(O) if this Court ultimately affirms the circuit court. Plaintiff now contends that the circuit court erred in granting summary disposition to the defendant. Defendant has cross-appealed from the trial court's refusal to levy sanctions against the plaintiff under MCR 2.114.

Libel may be defined as a statement of and concerning the plaintiff which is false in some material respect and is communicated to a third person by written or printed words and has a tendency to harm the plaintiff's reputation. A libel may consist of a statement of fact or a statement in the form of an opinion, but a statement of opinion is actionable only if it implies the allegation of undisclosed defamatory facts as the basis for the opinion. The meaning of a statement is that meaning which, under the circumstances, a reasonable person who sees the statement reasonably understands to be the meaning intended. It is, of course, plaintiff's burden to prove the elements of an alleged libel. *See* generally SJI2d 118.01, 118.03, 118.04, 118.05; *see also* PROSSER AND KEETON ON TORTS (5th ed), §§ 111 – 113A; 3 RESTATEMENT TORTS, 2d, §§ 558 – 568.

The question of whether or not the meaning of a particular communication is defamatory is one for the court. *Rouch v. Enquirer & News*, 137 Mich. App. 39, 43, n. 2, 357 N.W.2d 794 (1984); PROSSER AND KEETON ON TORTS, *supra* at 774. The trial court in this case is correct that, as a matter of law, there was nothing defamatory in nature in defendant's newspaper article. While plaintiff seems to attempt to allege falsity in defendant's newspaper report in two aspects, he quite simply fails to sufficiently plead a material falsehood in his complaint. First, plaintiff argues that he did not sue in the underlying action for $15,000 as Judge Gillis allegedly told defendant's reporter, but rather for "whatever legal damages in

assess 评估,估价
rejection 拒绝
mediation 调解

cross-appeal 反上诉(指在败诉方当事人已对判决提出上诉的情况下,胜诉方当事人也对该判决提出的上诉,即被上诉人对上诉人提出的上诉,其目的通常为寻求驳回败诉方的上诉。对反上诉通常和原上诉一起辩论、审理)

falsehood 说谎,假话,不真实

excess of $10,000 the court deems just." Second, plaintiff contends that the article falsifies in implying by the "loss of companionship of the sick tree" remark that plaintiff keeps, for a companion, a tree.

As to the amount of damages pled, assuming for purposes of challenging defendant's summary disposition motion that plaintiff did not specifically seek $15,000, but merely alleged the required jurisdictional amount, the trial court was nonetheless correct. In *Rouch v. Enquirer & News*, supra, p. 43, n. 2, 357 N. W. 2d 794, this Court, citing *McCracken v. Evening News Assn.*, 3 Mich. App. 32, 141 N. W. 2d 694 (1966), stated that, "[i]f the gist, the sting, of the article is substantially true, the defendant is not liable." In *McCracken*, this Court held that a newspaper report that plaintiff was charged with a $100,000 fraud when the warrant specified a fraud amounting to approximately $50,000 is an inaccuracy that does not alter the complexion of the charge and would have no different effect on the reader than that which the literal truth would produce absent proof that such variance caused plaintiff damage. This rule should apply equally to the instant situation, particularly in view of the fact that in any event the amount of damages sought by plaintiff in his complaint was greater than $10,000.

As to defendant's quote from Judge Gillis that plaintiff's suit was for the equivalent of "loss of companionship of the sick tree," the trial court was correct in holding that the remark was not reasonably capable of defamatory meaning. Instead, the analogy represented the appellate judge's effort to characterize and explain plaintiff's novel legal theory to the public. Further, the statement was no more than the opinion of Judge Gillis. In First Amendment defamation cases involving a media defendant, an opinion is constitutionally protected whether made by newspaper itself or the speaker quoted.

For example, in *Orr v. Argus-Press Co.*, 586 F. 2d 1108 (CA 6, 1978), cert. den., 440 U. S. 960 (1979), the federal court applying both Michigan common law and federal constitutional law, held that characterizations of a legal theory are constitutionally protected opinions when based upon disclosed facts of the case. Citing *Gertz v. Robert Welch, Inc.*, 418 U.S. 323, 339 – 340 (1974), the *Orr* court held that a newspaper's "opinion" about the meaning of an indictment cannot be made the basis of a libel suit against the newspaper:

"Under the First Amendment there is no such thing as a false idea. However pernicious an opinion may seem, we depend for its correction not on the conscience of judges and juries but on the competition of other ideas." *Orr*, *supra* at 1114.

In the instant case, we do not doubt that plaintiff honestly believes that his reputation was harmed by defendant's article. Nonetheless, plaintiff's honest belief that he has been defamed is not determinative. The article complained of may not reasonably be understood to be defamatory. Because the statements concerning the plaintiff contain no material falsehood, the trial court was correct in concluding as a matter of law that there was nothing of a defamatory nature in defendant's newspaper article.①

Plaintiff's "honest belief" in his pleadings is at the crux of the second issue, defendant's cross-appeal from the trial court's refusal to impose sanctions under MCR 2.114. Plaintiff's complaint was filed on January 9, 1984, well prior to the March 1, 1985, effective date of MCR 2.114. Defendant did not file a notice of its intention to seek sanctions under the new court rule until June 17, 1985.② Prior to the defendant's filing of its July 22, 1985, summary disposition motion, on July 16, 1985, the case was submitted to mediation and was unanimously evaluated by the panel as a zero-award case in favor of defendant, which defendant accepted and plaintiff rejected. Although the trial court, in

indictment 刑事案件中的公诉书,起诉状,控告

pernicious 有害的

defame 诽谤,破坏名誉,中伤

at the crux of 在……的关键

unanimously 无异议地,全体一致地
zero-award case 零赔偿案件(在该案件的判决中,法院认为被告不需要向原告赔偿任何损失)

---

① To the extent that plaintiff's appellate brief seeks to allege a cause of action based on what he calls "invasion of privacy, unwarantable [sic] intrusion, false light publicity, public disclosure of private facts or wrongful appropriation of plaintiff's name," it suffices to note that plaintiff was also acting in *propria persona* in *Fisher v. Lowe*, *supra*. This Court has previously held that a trial attorney is a public figure for purposes of comment on his conduct at trial. *Hayes v. Booth Newspapers, Inc.*, 97 Mich. App. 758, 295 N. W. 2d 858 (1980). The manner in which plaintiff pleaded the case and conducted himself in a public judicial proceeding invited the media attention and comment about which he now complains.

② This statement should not be interpreted to mean that the court rules require the filing of such a notice.

granting summary disposition, declined to sanction plaintiff under MCR 2.114(D) and (E), the court subsequently, on December 13, 1985, granted defendant's motion to assess actual costs against plaintiff for plaintiff's rejection of mediation pursuant to MCR 2.403(O).

While plaintiff attempts to challenge the lower court's mediation sanctions in his appellate brief, his claim of appeal in this case was filed on October 18, 1985, from the summary disposition order and could not have included an appeal from this December 13, 1985, order. No appeal was ever taken from the December 13, 1985, order. Thus, based upon the <u>unchallenged</u> application of mediation sanctions by the lower court and our <u>affirmance</u> of the trial court's grant of summary disposition, plaintiff, pursuant to MCR 2.403(O)(3), is required to pay "those costs <u>taxable</u> in any civil action and a reasonable <u>attorney fee</u> as determined by the trial judge for services necessitated by the rejection of the mediation evaluation."

Because the lower court will be assessing costs under MCR 2.403(O), we decline to consider whether the assessment of costs under MCR 2.114 would be appropriate. While the court rules do not specifically indicate how we are to treat a request for <u>double recovery</u> of sanctions, we decline to permit a party <u>double compensation</u> for the same expenses. See Martin, Dean & Webster, MICHIGAN COURT RULES PRACTICE, Rule 2.313, *Author's Comment*, p. 371. We further note that the instant suit was commenced under the old court rules. Because the sanctions provisions in MCR 2.114 are derived in substantial measure from the 1983 amendment to F.R.Civ.P. 11, they provide much tougher sanctions for abuses of the pleading process than the former GCR 1963 114 and 111.6. The fact that this suit was brought more than a year before the March 1, 1985, effective date of the new rules and that most of the expenses incurred by defendant in defending it presumably occurred prior to that effective date also persuades us that, as to the lower court proceedings, application of MCR 2.114 sanctions to the instant cause of action "would not be <u>feasible</u> or would work injustice." MCR 1.102.

That leaves only defendant's demand for actual and punitive damages for vexatious proceedings under MCR 7.216(C). MCR 7.216(C)(1)(a) provides:

> The Court of Appeals may, on its own initiative or the motion of any party, assess actual and punitive damages, or take other disciplinary action when it determines that an appeal or any of the proceedings in an appeal was vexatious because
> (a) the appeal was taken for purposes of hindrance or delay or without any reasonable basis for belief that there was a meritorious issue to be determined on appeal; ...

While we decline for the reasons previously stated to consider defendant's arguments for costs in the trial court under MCR 2.114, we nonetheless find those same arguments relevant to its demand for appellate costs.

Defendant asserts that when the trial court has found a suit to be frivolous, as it did in the instant case ("... to my mind this case appears entirely frivolous"), the trial court is required to impose sanctions. Defendant contends that under the "reasonable inquiry" language in MCR 2.114 it is clear that plaintiff utterly failed to investigate the merits of his suit prior to filing and pursuing it. Defendant submits that the trial court erred in considering plaintiff's personal feelings or "honest belief" regarding the merits of his case since it is clear that the complained-of statements are not capable of a defamatory meaning. Because the "reasonable basis for belief that there was a meritorious issue to be determined on appeal" language of MCR 7.216(C)(1)(a) is similar to the language of MCR 2.114, we find that sanctions for taking a vexatious appeal are appropriate.

United States District Court Judge Joiner, analyzing the "reasonable inquiry" language of F.R. Civ. P. 11 in *Mohammed v. Union Carbide Corp.*, 606 F. Supp. 252, 261 (E.D. Mich. 1985), in the context of a frivolous claim of defamation, held that defendant should recover reasonable attorney fees and opined that:

vexatious 无理缠讼的，(诉讼)无根据的
on the court's own initiative 法庭主动

on the motion of any party 一方请求
disciplinary action 惩戒行动
on its own initiative（法院）自主提起

hindrance 妨害，障碍
meritorious 有法律价值的，值得称赞的

opine 想，认为，以为

Unlike the subjective good faith of an attorney, "reasonable inquiry" is an empirically verifiable fact or event, inasmuch as the court can examine the efforts undertaken by the attorney to investigate her claim prior to filing suit.

In this case, a licensed attorney, acting in *propria persona*, filed a lawsuit considered by the trial court to be entirely frivolous without making a reasonable inquiry into its legal merit. Then, in the face of a mediation evaluation of zero and the trial court's summary disposition order, he persisted in taking an appeal to this Court even though he could have had no "reasonable basis to believe that there was a meritorious issue to be determined on appeal." Plaintiff's personal feelings and "honest belief" regarding the merit of his case are not enough — as an attorney licensed to practice in this state he should know better. Accordingly, summary disposition in defendant's favor is affirmed and the case is remanded to the trial court for a determination of mediation sanction costs under MCR 2.403(O) and for a determination of appellate costs under MCR 7.216(C)(2).

5.1.3 Defenses to Defamation

The defendant in a defamation case may use consent, truth, or privileges to defend himself. Consent is a complete defense to defamation. If the plaintiff consents to the publication of the false statement by the defendant, then no defamation will be found. In cases of purely private concern where the plaintiff is not required to prove falsity, the defendant may establish the truth of the statement as a complete defense, and now truth is the best defense.

There are two kinds of privileges a defendant may use in a defamation action: absolute privileges and qualified privileges. Absolute privileges may be applied in cases involving judicial proceedings, legislative proceedings, actions of the executive branch, communications between spouses, and compelled broadcasts or publications required by law. For example, a radio station that gave time to one candidate for public office has an obligation to extend similar treatment to other candidates for the same office. The station had no right to censor these later speeches. Thus, no liability attaches for defamation they might contain.

 Qualified privileges may be applied when the circumstances warrant. The court may consider several factors in determining whether qualified privileges are applicable. These factors may include the relationship between the publisher and the recipient, the risk posed to the interests of the publisher, the recipient, or others, whether the information was solicited or volunteered, the likelihood that the information will enable the recipient to take effective action to avoid the risk of harm from coming to fruition, whether the plaintiff previously engaged in conduct wrongful to the publisher, the recipient, or the public in general. For example, the author of the reports of public proceedings may have such a qualified privilege. A statement by a debtor explaining to a collection agency his reason for not paying a bill is qualifiedly privileged even if defamatory statements are contained therein. Qualified privileges should not be abused.

 In addition to the defenses and privileges discussed above, there are also some mitigating factors that the defendant may use to defend himself. For example, the defendant published the statement without actual malice, he retracted his statement immediately after publication so as to negate the defamatory effect of the statement, or he made the statement out of anger, if provoked by the plaintiff.

5.2 Invasion of Privacy

 Under common law, there was no tort of invasion of privacy before 1890. But thereafter, courts have begun to recognize that unwarranted invasions of privacy are actionable. Most courts follow the "four tort" approach and liability has been found for intrusion, the public disclosure of private matters, false light, and appropriation.

 Intrusion is also called "intrusion upon seclusion," it occurs when a person's privacy is physically invaded. In order to establish a *prima facie* case of intrusion, the plaintiff must prove physical intrusions into such

---

censor 审查,检查;修改;删去

collection agency 代理收款者,代理收款的机构,讨债机构

mitigating factor 减轻因素

retract 撤回
negate 否定,使无效,取消
provoke 挑衅,激起,激怒,刺激,煽动,挑拨,导致

invasion of privacy 侵犯隐私(权)
unwarranted 无根据的
public disclosure of private matters 对私人事务的公共披露
false light (in the public's eyes) 错误暴露(他人)隐私,导致其形象在公众中被扭曲
appropriation 占用,挪用,盗用(这里指未经许可使用他人的姓名或照片为己谋利)
intrusion upon seclusion 侵扰个人生活安宁

pry 窥探,刺探,打听,窥视

objectionable 会引起反对的,讨厌的,有异议的

a reasonable person 理性人(指法律所拟制的、具有正常精神状态、普通知识与经验及审慎处事能力的想象中的人)

places as the plaintiff's home or hotel room. There must be something in the nature of prying or intrusion. The intrusion must be something which would be offensive or objectionable to a reasonable person. In addition, the thing into which there is prying or intrusion must be, and be entitled to be, private. The interest protected by the tort of invasion of privacy is primarily a mental one. Professor William Posser believed that "it had been useful chiefly to fill in the gaps left by trespass, nuisance, the intentional infliction of mental distress, and whatever remedies there might be for the invasion of constitutional rights."

gaze 注视,凝视

Public disclosure of private matters arises when information, private in character, is exposed to the public gaze. The plaintiff must prove that the defendant disclosed a private matter, which is not of legitimate concern to the public, regarding the plaintiff to the public, which would be highly offensive to a reasonable person, and has resulted in damage. The publication element here is different from the publication required in a defamation case. If the defendant disclosed the defamatory statement to any third person who understands its content, the publication element for a defamation is satisfied. However, the publication element for public disclosure requires a disclosure of the plaintiff's private matter to

the public at large 广大公众

the public at large, or to so many persons that the matter must be regarded as substantially certain to become one of public knowledge.

unauthorized use 未授权使用

False light in the public's eyes arises when one publishes false material designed to make a person look bad. For example, the defendant used the plaintiff's picture to illustrate a book or an article with which the plaintiff had no reasonable connection. Other examples include the unauthorized use of the plaintiff's name as a candidate for office, or to advertise for witnesses of an accident. The false light need not necessarily be a defamatory one, although it very often is, and a defamation action will also lie. The plaintiff must

publicity 在公众场合或向公众宣传、宣扬

prove that the defendant gave publicity to false information with actual malice, which placed the plaintiff in a false light that would be highly offensive to a reasonable person, and which resulted in damage. The false light cases are different from those of intrusion or disclosure of private matters. Disclosure involves truth and the false light case sometimes involves a lie. Disclosure involves one's private or secret matters and the false light invented the matter disclosed. The interest protected under the tort of false light is that of reputation, which is similar to the mental distress as in defamation.

Appropriation occurs when a person's name, picture, or other likeness is used for commercial advantage without the person's consent. The plaintiff must prove that there is an appropriation of his or her identity through use of his or her name, likeness, or otherwise. The plaintiff must also prove that the defendant used his or her identity for the benefit of the defendant. Mere incidental mention of the plaintiff's name in a book or a motion picture or even in a commentary upon news which is part of an advertisement, is not an invasion of his privacy; nor is the publication of a photograph or a newsreel in which he incidentally appears. The interests protected here is not so much a mental as a proprietary one, in the exclusive use of the plaintiff's name and likeness as an aspect of his identity.

The same conduct may result in more than one form of invasion of privacy, as well as in other torts. If the defendant breaks into the plaintiff's house, reads the plaintiff's diary, and steals a photo of the plaintiff, which is then used by the defendant to illustrate the cover of a book about an escaped mass murderer of whom the plaintiff had never heard, it is possible that three of the privacy actions will lie (intrusion, appropriation, and false light), as well as trespass on land, and perhaps other torts also.

The defenses to invasions of privacy include consent and the absolute and qualified privileges discussed in the tort of defamation. Truth is not a good defense to most invasions of privacy actions. Inadvertence, good faith, and lack of malice generally are not good defenses either.

likeness 肖像,画像,照片
commercial advantage 商业利益

incidental mention 偶然提到
commentary 评注,评论

newsreel 新闻影片

proprietary 财产性的

inadvertence 疏漏,疏忽
good faith 善意
lack of malice 没有恶意

5.2.1 Case 23: Carl H. Hamberger v. Clifford C. Eastman

Supreme Court of New Hampshire
Carl H. Hamberger *et. al.* v. Clifford C. Eastman
106 N. H. 107, 206 A. 2d 239
Dec. 30, 1964

> companion suit 姐妹案（这里指同时提起的基于同一个诉因但当事人不同的两个以上诉讼）

The plaintiffs, husband and wife, brought companion suits for invasion of their privacy against the defendant who owned and rented a dwelling house to the plaintiffs. The plaintiffs allege that the defendant installed and concealed "a listening and recording device" in their bedroom, which was in the dwelling house rented to them by the defendant and that this device was connected to the defendant's

> adjacent 相邻的，相近的

adjacent residence by wires "capable of transmitting and recording any sounds and voices originating in said bedroom."

The declaration in the suit by the husband reads as follows:

> plea（诉讼中提出的）事实主张，诉状

In a plea of the case, for that the defendant is the owner of a certain dwelling house located at Gilford, County of Belknap, and State of New Hampshire, which was, and still is, occupied by the plaintiff and his family as a dwelling house on a weekly rental basis; that said dwelling house is

> abut 邻接，毗连，紧靠

located adjacent to and abutting other land of the defendant whereon the defendant maintains his place of residence, together with his place of business.

That, sometime during the period from October, 1961, to October 15, 1962, the defendant, wholly without the knowledge and consent of the plaintiff, did willfully and maliciously invade the privacy and sanctity of the plaintiff's bedroom, which he shared with his wife in their dwelling house, by installing and concealing a listening and recording device in said bedroom; that this listening and recording device, which was concealed in an area adjacent to the bed occupied by the plaintiff and his wife was attached and connected to the defendant's place of residence by means of wires capable of transmitting and recording any sounds and voices originating in said bedroom.

That, on or about October 15, 1962, plaintiff discovered the listening and recording device which defendant had willfully and maliciously concealed in his bedroom, and the plaintiff, ever since that time and as a direct result of the actions of the defendant, has been greatly distressed, humiliated, and embarrassed and has sustained and is now sustaining, intense and severe mental suffering and distress, and has been rendered extremely nervous and upset, seriously impairing both his mental and physical condition, and that the plaintiff has sought, and still is under, the care of a physician; that large sums have been, and will be in the future, expended for medical care and attention; that because of his impaired mental and physical condition, the plaintiff has been and still is unable to properly perform his normal and ordinary duties as a father and as a husband, and has been unable to properly perform his duties at his place of employment, and has been otherwise greatly injured.

The declaration in the suit by the wife is identical, with appropriate substitutes of the personal pronoun, and omission of the allegation of inability to perform duties at her place of employment.

In both actions the defendant moved to dismiss on the ground that on the facts alleged, no cause of action is stated. The Court (Morris, J.) reserved and transferred the cases to the Supreme Court without ruling.

Kenison, Chief Justice.

The question presented is whether the right of privacy is recognized in this state. There is no controlling statute and no previous decision in this jurisdiction which decides the question. Inasmuch as invasion of the right of privacy is not a single tort but consists of four distinct torts, it is probably more concrete and accurate to state the issue in the present case to be whether this state recognizes that intrusion

---

identical 同一的,完全相同的,完全相似的

personal pronoun 人称代词

reserve 推迟(判决),延迟

transfer 移送(案件)给上级或下级法院

inasmuch as 因为,鉴于,由于

concrete 具体的,实在的

upon one's physical and mental solitude or seclusion is a tort. The most recent, as well as the most comprehensive, analysis of the problem is found in Prosser, TORTS, § 112 (3d ed. 1964).

 In <u>capsule summary</u> the invasion of the right of privacy developed as an independent and distinct tort from the classic and famous article by Warren and Brandeis, *The Right to Privacy*, 4 HARV. L. REV. 193 (1890), although Judge Cooley had discussed "the right to be let alone" some years previously. Cooley, Torts 29 (1st ed. 1879). In 1902 the New York Court of Appeals decided that the right of privacy did not have "an <u>abiding</u> place in our jurisprudence." *Robertson v. Rochester Folding Box Co.*, 171 N.Y. 538, 556, 64 N.E. 442. The following year the New York Legislature acted promptly to remedy this deficiency. Laws of N.Y. 1903 ch. 132; N.Y. Civil Rights Law, McKinney's Consol. Laws, c. 6, §§ 50 and 51. Shortly thereafter in 1905, *Pavesich v. New England Life Ins. Co.*, 122 Ga. 190, 50 S.E. 68 upheld the right of privacy and became the <u>leading case</u> on the subject. Since that time the right of privacy has been given protection in a majority of the jurisdictions in this country, generally without benefit of statute, and only a small minority have rejected the concept and some of these minority decisions are not recent. See *Henry v. Cherry & Webb*, 30 R.I. 13, 73 A. 97 (1909). See also 1 Harper and James, TORTS §§ 9.5-9.7 (1956). "Today, with something over three hundred cases in the books, some rather definite conclusions are possible. What has <u>emerged</u> is no very simple matter. It is not one tort, but a complex of four. The law of privacy comprises four distinct kinds of invasion of four different interests of the plaintiff which are tied together by the common name, but otherwise have almost nothing in common except that each presents an interference with the right of the plaintiff 'to be let alone.'" Prosser, TORTS, § 112, p.832 (3d ed. 1964).

 The four kinds of invasion comprising the law of privacy include: (1) intrusion upon the plaintiff's physical and mental solitude or seclusion; (2) public disclosure of private facts; (3) publicity which places the plaintiff in a false light in the public eye;

capsule summary 简要的总结

abiding 持续的,持久的,不变的

leading case 重要的判例,主要判例

emerge 浮现,形成

(4) appropriation, for the defendant's benefit or advantage, of the plaintiff's name or likeness. In the present case, we are concerned only with the tort of intrusion upon the plaintiffs' solitude or seclusion. *See Ezer*, *Intrusion on Solitude: Herein of Civil Rights and Civil Wrongs*, 21 LAW IN TRANSITION 63 (1961).

> "It is evident that these four forms of invasion of privacy are distinct, and based on different elements. It is the failure to recognize this which has been responsible for much of the apparent confusion in the decisions. Taking them in order — intrusion, disclosure, false light, and appropriation — the first and second require the invasion of something secret, secluded or private pertaining to the plaintiff; the third and fourth do not. The second and third depend upon publicity, while the first does not, nor does the fourth, although it usually involves it. The third requires falsity or fiction; the other three do not. The fourth involves a use for the defendant's advantage, which is not true of the rest." Prosser, TORTS § 112 p. 842 - 843 (3d ed. 1964).

The tort of intrusion upon the plaintiff's solitude or seclusion is not limited to a physical invasion of his home or his room or his quarters. As Prosser points out, the principle has been carried beyond such physical intrusion "and extended to <u>eavesdropping</u> upon private conversations by means of <u>wire tapping</u> and microphones." Prosser, *supra*, p. 833.

We have not searched for cases where the bedroom of husband and wife has been "<u>bugged</u>" but it should not be necessary — by way of <u>understatement</u>— to observe that this is the type of intrusion that would be offensive to any person of ordinary sensibilities. What married "people do in the privacy of their bedroom is their own business so long as they are not hurting anyone else." Ernst and Loth, FOR BETTER OR WORSE, 79 (1952). The Restatement, Torts § 867 provides that "a person who unreasonably and seriously interferes with another's interest in not having his affairs known to others ... is liable to the

  eavesdropping 偷听，窃听
  wire tapping 搭线，偷听，窃听
  bug 在……装窃听器，通过窃听器窃听
  understatement 低调陈述

other." As is pointed out in comment d "liability exists only if the defendant's conduct was such that he should have realized that it would be offensive to persons of ordinary sensibilities. It is only where the intrusion has gone beyond the limits of decency that liability accrues. These limits are exceeded where intimate details of the life of one who has never manifested a desire to have publicity are exposed to the public..."

The defendant contends that the right of privacy should not be recognized on the facts of the present case as they appear in the pleadings because there are no allegations that anyone listened or overheard any sounds or voices originating from the plaintiffs' bedroom. The tort of intrusion on the plaintiffs' solitude or seclusion does not require publicity and communication to third persons although this would affect the amount of damages, as Prosser makes clear. Prosser, *supra*, 843. The defendant also contends that the right of privacy is not violated unless something has been published, written or printed and that oral publicity is not sufficient. Recent cases make it clear that this is not a requirement. Carr v. Watkins, 227 Md. 578, 177 A. 2d 841; Bennett v. Norba, 396 Pa. 94, 151 A. 2d 476; Norris v. Moskin Stores, Inc., 272 Ala. 174, 132 So. 2d 321.

If the peeping Tom, the big ear, and the electronic eavesdropper (whether ingenious or ingenuous) have a place in the hierarchy of social values, it ought not to be at the expense of a married couple minding their own business in the seclusion of their bedroom who have never asked for or by their conduct deserved a potential projection of their private conversations and actions to their landlord or to others. Whether actual or potential such "publicity with respect to private matters of purely personal concern is an injury to personality. It impairs the mental peace and comfort of the individual and may produce suffering more acute than that produced by a mere bodily injury." III Pound, JURISPRUDENCE 58 (1959). The use of parabolic microphones and sonic wave devices designed to pick up conversations in a room without entering it and at a considerable distance away makes the problem far from fanciful. Dash, Schwartz & Knowlton, THE

EAVESDROPPERS 346-358 (1959).

It is unnecessary to determine the extent to which the right of privacy is protected as a constitutional matter without the benefit of statute. *See* Beaney, *The Constitutional Right to Privacy in the Supreme Court in 1962*, THE SUPREME COURT REVIEW 212 (Kurland ed. 1962); *Olmstead v. United States*, 277 U. S. 438, 478 (1928) (dissenting opinion of Brandeis, J.); Dykstra, *The Right Most Valued by Civilized Man*, 6 UTAH L. REV. 305 (1959); Pound, *The Fourteenth Amendment and the Right of Privacy*, 13 W. RES. L. REV. 34 (1961). For the purposes of the present case it is sufficient to hold that the invasion of the plaintiffs' solitude or seclusion, as alleged in the pleadings, was a violation of their right of privacy and constituted a tort for which the plaintiffs may recover damages to the extent that they can prove them. "Certainly, no right deserves greater protection, for, as Emerson has well said, 'solitude, the safeguard of mediocrity, is to genius the stern friend.'" Ezer, *Intrusion on Solitude: Herein of Civil Rights and Civil Wrongs*, 21 LAW IN TRANSITION 63, 75 (1961).

mediocrity 平常人
genius 天才,天才人物,天赋
stern 坚定的

The motion to dismiss should be denied.

Remanded.

All concurred.

5.2.2　Case 24: Toniann Diaz v. Oakland Tribune, Inc.

Court of Appeal, First District, Division 3, California
Toniann Diaz v. Oakland Tribune, Inc., *et. al.*
139 Cal. App. 3d 118, 188 Cal. Rptr. 762
Jan 18, 1983

Barry-Deal, J.

Plaintiff Toni Ann Diaz (Diaz) sued the Oakland Tribune, Inc., owners and publishers of the Oakland Tribune (the Tribune), and Sidney Jones (Jones), one of its columnists, for invasion of privacy. Diaz claimed that the publication of highly embarrassing private facts in Jones' March 26, 1978, newspaper column was unwarranted and malicious and caused her to suffer severe emotional distress. The jury awarded Diaz $250,000 in compensatory damages and

$525,000 in punitive damages ($25,000 against Jones and $500,000 against the Tribune). Judgment was entered on February 14, 1980. Defendants' motion for a new trial based on insufficiency of the evidence, errors of law, and excessive damages was denied. This timely appeal followed. As discussed below, we reverse the judgment because of instructional errors.

The facts are for the most part undisputed. Diaz is a transsexual. She was born in Puerto Rico in 1942 as Antonio Diaz, a male. She moved to California from New York in 1964. Suffice it to say that for most of her life Diaz suffered from a gender identification problem and the anxiety and depression that accompanied it. She testified that since she was young she had had the feeling of being a woman. In 1968 Diaz began receiving psychological counseling and hormone therapy. In 1970 or 1971 Diaz embarked on the lengthy process of evaluation as a candidate for gender corrective surgery at the Stanford University Gender Dysphoria Clinic. She was ultimately considered to be a good candidate for surgery. In 1975 gender corrective surgery was performed by the Stanford staff.

According to Diaz the surgery was a success. By all outward appearances she looked and behaved as a woman and was accepted by the public as a woman. According to her therapist, Dr. Sable, her physical and psychological identities were now in harmony.

Diaz scrupulously kept the surgery a secret from all but her immediate family and closest friends. She never sought to publicize the surgery. She changed her name to Toni Ann Diaz and made the necessary changes in her high school records, her social security records, and on her driver's license. She tried unsuccessfully to change her Puerto Rican birth certificate. She did not change the gender designation on her draft card, however, asserting that it would be a useless gesture, since she had previously been turned down for induction.

Following the surgery she no longer suffered from the psychological difficulties that had plagued her previously. In 1975 she enrolled in the College of Alameda (the College), a two-year college. The College was one of five colleges of the Peralta

Community College District.

In spring 1977, she was elected student body president for the 1977-1978 academic year, the first woman to hold that office. Her election and an unsuccessful attempt to unseat her were reported in the College newspaper, the Reporter, in the May 17, June 1, and June 14, 1977, editions. At no time during the election did Diaz reveal any information about her sex-change operation.

In 1977 Diaz was also selected to be the student body representative to the Peralta Community College Board of Trustees (the Board). Diaz's selection as student body representative, together with her photograph, appeared in the June 1977 issue of the Peralta Colleges Bulletin.

Near the middle of her term as student body president, Diaz became embroiled in a controversy in which she charged the College administrators with misuse of student funds. The March 15, 1978, issue of the Tribune quoted Diaz's charge that her signature had improperly been "rubber stamped" on checks drawn from the associated students' account.

On March 24, 1978, an article in the Alameda Times-Star, a daily newspaper, mentioned Diaz in connection with the charge of misuse of student body funds.

Shortly after the controversy arose, Jones was informed by several confidential sources that Diaz was a man. Jones considered the matter newsworthy if he could verify the information. Jones testified that he inspected the Tribune's own files and spoke with an unidentified number of persons at the College to confirm this information. It was not until Richard Paoli, the city editor of the Tribune, checked Oakland city police records that the information that Diaz was born a man was verified. The evidence reveals that in 1970 or 1971, prior to the surgery, Diaz was arrested in Oakland for soliciting an undercover police officer, a misdemeanor.①

On March 26, 1978, the following item appeared

---

① The record reveals that pursuant to a plea bargain, Diaz entered a guilty plea to the charge. However, Diaz was later allowed to withdraw her guilty plea. Following a trial she was acquitted of the charge.

in Jones' newspaper column: "More Education Stuff: The students at the College of Alameda will be surprised to learn that their student body president, Toni Diaz, is no lady, but is in fact a man whose real name is Antonio."

"Now I realize, that in these times, such a matter is no big deal, but I suspect his female classmates in P.E. 97 may wish to make other showering arrangements."

Upon reading the article, Diaz became very depressed and was forced to reveal her status, which she had worked hard to conceal. Diaz testified that as a result of the article she suffered from insomnia, nightmares, and memory lapses. She also delayed her enrollment in Mills College, scheduled for that fall.

In her complaint Diaz did not charge that any of the information was untrue, only that defendants invaded her privacy by the unwarranted publicity of intimate facts. Defendants defended on the ground that the matter was newsworthy and hence was constitutionally protected.

At trial the jury returned a special verdict and found that (1) defendants did publicly disclose a fact concerning Diaz; (2) the fact was private and not public; (3) the fact was not newsworthy; (4) the fact was highly offensive to a reasonable person of ordinary sensibilities; (5) defendants disclosed the fact with knowledge that it was highly offensive or with reckless disregard of whether it was highly offensive; and (6) the disclosure proximately caused injury or damage to Diaz.

In this appeal defendants challenge the jury's finding on issues Nos. (2) and (3) above. Defendants also urge instructional error and attack the awards of compensatory and punitive damages. Before we address these issues, it is useful briefly to discuss the competing rights involved herein: the right to privacy and the right to free speech and press.

Background

The concept of a common law right to privacy was first developed in a landmark article by Warren and Brandeis, *The Right to Privacy* (1890) 4 HARV. L. REV. 193, and has been adopted in virtually every state. The specific privacy right with which we are concerned is the right to be free from public disclosure of private embarrassing facts, in short, "the right to be let alone." *Melvin v. Reid*, 297 P. 91 (1931).

The development of the public disclosure tort in California is well documented. The public disclosure tort is one of four distinct torts which are actionable under the general rubric of invasion of privacy. The other three are: (1) intrusion upon plaintiff's solitude or into his or her private affairs; (2) "false light" publicity; and (3) appropriation of plaintiff's name or likeness to the defendant's advantage. *Kapellas v. Kofman*, supra., 1 Cal.3d at p.35, fn. 16; *Virgil v. Time, Inc.* (9th Cir. 1975) 527 F.2d 1122, 1125.

document 用文件证明

rubric 规则

The public disclosure cause of action is distinct from a suit for libel or "false light," since the plaintiff herein does not challenge the accuracy of the information published, but asserts that the publicity is so intimate and unwarranted as to outrage the community's notion of decency. *Briscoe v. Reader's Digest Association, Inc.*, supra., 4 Cal.3d at p.542; *Sidis v. F-R Pub. Corporation* (2d Cir. 1940) 113 F.2d 806, 809. "The gravamen of a defamation action is engendering a false opinion about a person, whether in the mind of one other person or many people. The gravamen in the public disclosure [privacy] cases is degrading a person by laying his life open to public view." *The Right to Speak*, supra., at pp.958–959.

gravamen 请求;抱怨;指控等的要点
engender 引起,产生

degrade 使丢脸

Of course, the right to privacy is not absolute and must be balanced against the often competing constitutional right of the press to publish newsworthy matters. See *Cox Broadcasting Corp. v. Cohn* (1975) 420 U.S. 469, 489. The First Amendment protection from tort liability is necessary if the press is to carry out its constitutional obligation to keep the public informed so that they may make intelligent decisions on matters important to a self-governing people. See *Cox Broadcasting Corp. v. Cohn*, supra., 420 U.S. at pp.491–493.

press 媒体

However, the newsworthy privilege is not without limitation. Where the publicity is so offensive as to constitute a "morbid and sensational prying into private lives for its own sake, …" it serves no

morbid 不健全的,病态的
sensational 耸人听闻的

legitimate public interest and is not deserving of protection. See Virgil v. Time, Inc., supra., 527 F. 2d at p.1129; Rest.2d Torts, §652D, com. h.

As discerned from the decisions of our courts, the public disclosure tort contains the following elements: (1) public disclosure (2) of a private fact (3) which would be offensive and objectionable to the reasonable person and (4) which is not of legitimate public concern. See Forsher v. Bugliosi, supra., 26 Cal.3d at pp.808-809.

Instructional Error

At the outset defendants urge that the trial court misinstructed the jury (1) on the right to privacy and (2) that defendants had the burden of proving newsworthiness. We agree and find that either of these errors was prejudicial and requires reversal.

1. The Right to Privacy

Plaintiff Diaz proffered a jury instruction properly defining the right to privacy.① However, the trial court, sua sponte, added the following language: "It prevents business or government interests from misusing information gathered for one purpose in order to serve other purposes, or to embarrass us. This right should be abridged only when there is a compelling public need."

The language contained in the last sentence was taken from White v. Davis (1975) 13 Cal.3d 757. The trial court misplacedits reliance on that case. In White, supra., plaintiff challenged covert police surveillance of University of California at Los Angeles students in their classrooms. There, the court required the government to demonstrate a "compelling public need" for the intrusion. Id., at p.775. That case did not attempt to balance the competing rights of free speech and press against the right to privacy. Rather, it recognized the heavy burden on the government to justify interference with First Amendment freedoms.

---

① The complete instruction reads as follows: "The California Constitution provides that all persons have an inalienable right of privacy. It is the right to live one's life in seclusion, without being subjected to unwarranted or undesirable publicity. In short, it's the right to be left alone."

Id., at pp. 767 - 773.

Unlike the government's activity in *White*, defendants' publication of the article is a preferred right which is not encumbered by the presumption of illegality. Defendants enjoy the right to publish information in which the public has a legitimate interest. *See Briscoe v. Reader's Digest Association, Inc., supra.*, 4 Cal. 3d at p. 541; *Virgil v. Time, Inc., supra.*, 527 F. 2d at pp. 1128 - 1129; REST. 2D TORTS, *supra.*, § 652D, com. d. To require that the article meet the higher "compelling public need" standard would severely abridge this constitutionally recognized right of free speech and press.

After examining the entire record, we cannot say that this error was harmless. The instruction misstated the law concerning defendants' right to publish newsworthy matters and necessarily lessened plaintiff's burden of proof. Since plaintiff's verdict may have rested on this erroneous theory, the judgment must be reversed. *See Cervantez v. J. C. Penny Co.* (1979) 24 Cal. 3d 579, 589 - 591, 595 P. 2d 975.

encumber 妨碍,阻碍

2. The Burden of Proving Newsworthiness

Next, defendants argue that the trial court improperly instructed the jury that the burden of proving newsworthiness was for the defendants. We agree.

The trial court instructed the jury on plaintiff's burden of proof as follows:

> In this action, the plaintiff has the burden of establishing by a preponderance of the evidence all of the facts necessary to prove the following issues:
> One, that the defendants publicly disclosed a fact concerning plaintiff;
> Two, that before defendants' publication appeared, the fact was private and not public;
> Three, that the fact was one which would be highly offensive to a reasonable person of ordinary sensibilities;
> Four, that the defendants disclosed the fact with knowledge that it was highly offensive or

with reckless disregard of whether it was highly offensive or not;

Five, that the disclosure was a proximate cause of injury or damage to her; and

Six, the nature and extent of the injuries claimed to have been so suffered, the elements of her damage, and the amounts thereof.

As originally proffered by defendants, this instruction also required plaintiff to prove that the article was not newsworthy. The trial court struck this element from the instruction and, instead, directed the jury that defendants had the burden of proving newsworthiness in order to prevail in this action.

Our research has discovered no published decision expressly allocating to one of the parties the burden of proving newsworthiness. While a publisher may defend itself against a public disclosure cause of action by proving that the matter was newsworthy, it is misleading to assert that said defendant has the burden of proving newsworthiness to be free from tort liability. As discussed below, the plaintiff has the burden of proving that the publication was not privileged, i.e., that it was not newsworthy. Of course, defendants may rebut plaintiff's showing with evidence that the matter was newsworthy. However, to assert, as plaintiff does, that defendants have the burden of proving newsworthiness is error.

Recognizing the critical position the right to freedom of speech and press occupies in our society, courts are understandably sensitive to any infringement of these rights. See Miller v. California (1973) 413 U.S. 15, 22-23; New York Times Co. v. Sullivan (1964) 376 U.S. 254, 269-270; Briscoe v. Reader's Digest Association, Inc., supra., 4 Cal.3d at pp. 534-535. Given this awareness, our courts uphold an abridgement of the freedom of expression only in narrowly drawn instances where the benefit of expression is clearly outweighed by the injury to personal or societal interests. See Cox Broadcasting Corp. v. Cohn, supra., 420 U.S. at p. 495.

Mindful of the important role performed by the press, it is therefore proper for the plaintiff, in order to state a cause of action, to prove that the publication is not constitutionally protected. This is the rule in the related area of obscenity law.

In *Blount v. Rizzi* (1971) 400 U.S. 410, the Supreme Court ruled unconstitutional a federal statute which permitted the Postmaster General to refuse delivery of all letters deemed to be obscene and to refuse payment of postal money orders used to purchase obscene matter. The court prescribed certain standards for ensuring the constitutionality of administrative censorship. Among these standards was the requirement that the government bear the burden of initiating judicial review and "of proving that the material is unprotected expression..." *Id.*, at p. 417; see also *Mckinney v. Alabama* (1976) 424 U.S. 669, 683 – 685 (conc. opn. of Brennan, J.).

A similar result was reached in the field of defamation law. In *New York Times Co. v. Sullivan*, *supra.*, 376 U.S. 254, the Supreme Court held that in order for a public official to recover damages against a newspaper in a defamation action, that official must prove that the defamatory statement was made with actual malice, *i.e.*, knowledge of its falsity or a reckless disregard for its truth. *Id.*, at pp. 279 – 280. The effect of this rule was to remove from the defendant newspaper the burden of proving that the article was true in order to defend against the action. Thus, in order to establish a cause of action, the tort plaintiff had to show that the article was not constitutionally protected, *i.e.*, that it was false or made with reckless disregard for the truth. This allowed the press the "breathing space" it needs to pursue its First Amendment obligations. *Id.*, at pp. 271 – 272.

A contrary rule would lead to self-censorship. Even though the matter is believed to be true and is in fact true, the defendant newspaper may be deterred from criticizing official conduct because of doubt whether the truthfulness can be proved at trial or out of fear at the expense of having to do so. *Id.*, at p. 279.

These same concerns are present here. The proof that defendants have published an article containing highly offensive private matters does not itself establish a claim for relief. It certainly must be

obscene（obscenity）淫秽的,下流的,猥亵的（淫秽；下流；可憎）

judicial review 司法审查

recognized that an otherwise embarrassing article may be newsworthy, depending on the circumstances. Only when the embarrassing publicity is not newsworthy can plaintiff recover damages, consistent with defendants' rights of free speech and press. To hold otherwise would permit a plaintiff to obtain a default judgment against a media defendant without any showing that the defendant had exceeded its constitutional prerogative. The effect would be to read the rights of free speech and press out of the Constitution.

Of course, once plaintiff has established a *prima facie* case that the publicity is not constitutionally protected, *i.e.*, not newsworthy, defendants can meet it with a showing that the information was newsworthy. However, to place the burden of proving newsworthiness on the defendants in order to defend against the action would have a chilling effect on their freedom of expression.

That the correct approach is to place the burden of proving non-newsworthiness on the plaintiff is confirmed by the Restatement Second of Torts, *supra.*, section 652D, which limits the cause of action to matters which are not of "legitimate concern to the public." See Virgil v. Time, Inc., *supra.*, 527 F.2d at p.1129, fn. 10.

By parity of reasoning, defendants' constitutional rights of free speech and press should be afforded the same procedural safeguards whether the tort alleged is for defamation or for invasion of privacy. We therefore hold that Diaz had the additional burden of proving that the article was not newsworthy. See also Briscoe v. Reader's Digest Association, Inc., *supra.*, 4 Cal.3d at p.543.

The failure to so instruct was reversible error. See McGee v. Cessna Aircraft Co., *supra.*, 82 Cal. App. 3d at pp.1019-1020.

As a subsidiary contention defendants also argue that the jury was improperly instructed to perform an "*ad hoc* balancing" of the competing rights.① We

---

① The jury was instructed as follows:"In general, determining whether plaintiff, Toni Ann Diaz's right of privacy is subject to the so-called public interest, must be based upon a balancing of the public interest in obtaining such information against her desire for privacy."

disagree. The challenged instruction, when viewed in the context of other instructions, conforms to the standards set forth in the cases. See *Briscoe v. Reader's Digest Association, Inc., supra.*, 4 Cal. 3d at p. 540, fn. 15; *Virgil v. Time, Inc., supra.*, 527 F. 2d at pp. 1129 – 1130.

Although the judgment is reversed, it is in the interests of judicial administration to address the merits of defendants' remaining contentions.

The Public Disclosure Tort

1. Private Facts
Defendants next argue that the evidence establishes as a matter of law that the fact of Diaz's original gender was a matter of public record, and therefore its publicity was not actionable. In support of their contention defendants rely on *Cox Broadcasting Corp. v. Cohn, supra.*, 420 U.S. 469. That reliance is misplaced.

Generally speaking, matter which is already in the public domain is not private, and its publication is protected. See *Kapellas v. Kofman, supra.*, 1 Cal. 3d at p. 38; but see *Briscoe v. Reader's Digest Association, Inc., supra.*, 4 Cal. 3d at pp. 538 – 539; *Melvin v. Reid, supra.*, 112 Cal. App. at pp. 290 –291.

public domain 公有领域

In *Cox Broadcasting Corp.*, the Supreme Court ruled that Cohn, the father of a deceased rape victim, could not maintain a disclosure action against media defendants who identified Cohn's daughter as the victim during the television coverage of the murder trial. *Cox Broadcasting Corp. v. Cohn, supra.*, 420 U.S. at pp. 496 – 497. Central to the court's conclusion was the fact that the reporter obtained the victim's name from the indictment, which had been shown to him in open court. *Id.*, at p. 496.

In a very narrow holding, the court ruled that a state may not impose sanctions on the accurate publication of the name of a rape victim obtained from judicial records which are maintained in connection with a public prosecution and which themselves are open to public inspection. *Id.*, at p. 491. Importantly, the court expressly refused to address the broader question of whether the truthful publication of facts obtained from public records can ever be subjected to civil or criminal liability. *Id*.

Because of its narrow holding, *Cox Broadcasting Corp*. gives us little guidance.

Here there is no evidence to suggest that the fact of Diaz's gender-corrective surgery was part of the public record. To the contrary, the evidence reveals that Diaz took affirmative steps to conceal this fact by changing her driver's license, social security, and high school records, and by lawfully changing her name. The police records, upon which Jones relied, contained information concerning one Antonio Diaz. No mention was made of Diaz's new name or gender. In order to draw the connection, Jones relied upon unidentified confidential sources. Under these circumstances, we conclude that Diaz's sexual identity was a private matter.

We also do not consider Diaz's Puerto Rican birth certificate to be a public record in this instance. In any event, defendants did not rely on that document and cannot be heard to argue that the information contained therein is public.

Moreover, matter which was once of public record may be protected as private facts where disclosure of that information would not be newsworthy. See *Briscoe v. Reader's Digest Association, Inc., supra.*, 4 Cal. 3d at pp. 537 – 538 [publication of identity of ex-offender for past crime was held to be improper]; *Melvin v. Reid, supra.*, 112 Cal. App. at pp. 290 – 291 [disclosure of plaintiff's past life as a prostitute, seven years after she <u>reformed</u>, was actionable].

reform 从良,改良

2. Newsworthiness

As discussed above, whether the fact of Diaz's sexual identity was newsworthy is measured along <u>a sliding scale of competing interests</u>: the individual's right to keep private facts from the public's gaze versus the public's right to know. See *Kapellas v. Kofman, supra.*, 1 Cal. 3d at p. 36. In an effort to <u>reconcile</u> these competing interests, our courts have settled on a three-part test for determining whether matter published is newsworthy: "[1] the social value

a sliding scale of competing interests 相矛盾利益的博弈

reconcile 调和

of the facts published, [2] the depth of the article's intrusion into ostensibly private affairs, and [3] the extent to which the party voluntarily acceded to a position of public notoriety." *Briscoe v. Reader's Digest Association, Inc., supra.*, 4 Cal. 3d at p. 541.

ostensibly 表面上,明显地
accede to 就职,即位
notoriety 众所周知的人物,著名人物;声名狼藉

Defendants argue that in light of Diaz's position as the first female student body president of the College, her "questionable gender" was a newsworthy item. As a subsidiary contention, they assert that the issue of newsworthiness should not have been submitted to the jury. We address the latter contention first.

a. Newsworthiness as a Jury Question

Whether a publication is or is not newsworthy depends upon contemporary community mores and standards of decency. *See Briscoe v. Reader's Digest Association, Inc., supra.*, at p. 541; *Virgil v. Time, Inc., supra.*, 527 F. 2d at p. 1129; REST. 2D TORTS, *supra.*, § 652D, *com. h*. This is largely a question of fact, which a jury is uniquely well-suited to decide. (*Virgil v. Time, Inc., supra.*, 527 F. 2d at p. 1129, fn. 12.)

mores and standards of decency 道德和礼仪标准

"It is the shared understandings of the community that establish the conventions by which it is understood just when others are invited into our lives and when they are not." Gerstein, *California's Constitutional Right to Privacy: The Development of the Protection of Private Life, supra.*, 9 HASTINGS CONST. L. Q. at p. 397, *fn. omitted.*

Defendants argue that the right to publish would suffer at the hands of a jury which, unlike the trial judge, would be more likely to use a general verdict in order to punish unpopular speech and persons. In *Virgil v. Time, Inc., supra.*, 527 F. 2d 1122, the Court of Appeals for the Ninth Circuit in a California case recognized this danger. However, that court concluded that any risk of prejudice may be checked by close judicial scrutiny at the stages of litigation such as summary judgment, directed verdict, and judgment notwithstanding the verdict. *Id.*, at p. 1130. Our trial court judges are entirely capable of correcting such jury overreaching.

unpopular speech 不得人心的演讲

judicial scrutiny 由司法部门进行详细地审查

overreaching 过分,过头

These same concerns are present in the related

field of obscenity law, where community standards define what speech is constitutionally protected. (*See Miller v. California*, *supra*., 413 U. S. 15, 24.) In an obscenity prosecution the jury is required to make an equally important constitutional decision and has been found to be up to the task. *See Id*., at p. 25. Accordingly, where reasonable minds could differ, we see no constitutional infirmity in allowing the jury to decide the issue of newsworthiness. *See Briscoe v. Reader's Digest Association, Inc.*, *supra*., 4 Cal. 3d at p. 543.

 b. Newsworthiness as a Matter of Law

 Next, defendants urge that, as the first female student body president of the College, Diaz was a public figure, and the fact of her sexual identity was a newsworthy item as a matter of law. We disagree.

 It is well settled that persons who voluntarily seek public office or willingly become involved in public affairs waive their right to privacy of matters connected with their public conduct. *Kapellas v. Kofman*, *supra*., 1 Cal. 3d at pp. 36 – 38. The reason behind this rule is that the public should be afforded every opportunity of learning about any facet which may affect that person's fitness for office. *See Briscoe v. Reader's Digest Association, Inc.*, *supra*., 4 Cal. 3d at p. 535, fn. 5; REST. 2D TORTS, *supra*., § 652D, com. e.

 However, the extent to which Diaz voluntarily acceded to a position of public notoriety and the degree to which she opened her private life are questions of fact. *Briscoe v. Reader's Digest Association, Inc.*, *supra*., 4 Cal. 3d at p. 541. As student body president, Diaz was a public figure for some purposes. However, applying the three-part test enunciated in *Briscoe*, we cannot state that the fact of her gender was newsworthy *per se*.

 Contrary to defendants' claim, we find little if any connection between the information disclosed and Diaz's fitness for office. The fact that she is a transsexual does not adversely reflect on her honesty or judgment. Cf. *Kapellas v. Kofman*, *supra*., 1 Cal. 3d 20 [plaintiff, a mother and candidate for Alameda City Council, who repeatedly left her minor children unsupervised, could not maintain an action against a newspaper for publishing information taken from police records of her children's criminal behavior]; *Beruan v. French* (1976) 56 Cal. App. 3d 825 [candidate for secretary-treasurer of union local could not maintain action based on publication of a letter disclosing his six prior criminal convictions].

Nor does the fact that she was the first woman student body president, in itself, warrant that her entire private life be open to public inspection. The public arena entered by Diaz is concededly small. Public figures more celebrated than she are entitled to keep some information of their domestic activities and sexual relations private. See REST. 2D TORTS, *supra.*, § 652D, *com. h.*

Nor is there merit to defendants' claim that the changing roles of women in society make this story newsworthy. This assertion rings hollow. The tenor of the article was by no means an attempt to enlighten the public on a contemporary social issue. Rather, as Jones himself admitted, the article was directed to the students at the College about their newly elected president. Moreover, Jones' attempt at humor at Diaz's expense removes all pretense that the article was meant to educate the reading public. The social utility of the information must be viewed in context, and not based upon some arguably meritorious and unintended purpose.

Therefore, we conclude that the jury was the proper body to answer the question whether the article was newsworthy or whether it extended beyond the bounds of decency.

Insufficient Evidence of Malice

Defendants next urge that the award of punitive damages was improper, since there was insufficient evidence to support a finding of malice on the part of either defendant. The evidence demonstrated that Jones published the article without first contacting Diaz, although he knew that the information contained therein would have a "devastating" impact on her. He testified that he attempted to obtain Diaz's telephone number from his unidentified sources but was unsuccessful. He admitted that he never telephoned the

public arena 公共场合
celebrated 著名的

hollow 空的,虚伪的
tenor（文件等的）大意,要领
enlighten 启发,指导,教育

pretense 借口,伪称

devastating impact 毁灭性的影响

College in order to contact Diaz. Jones also stated that his comment about Diaz's classmates in "P. E. 97" making other shower arrangements was a joke, an attempt to be "flip."

In order to justify the imposition of punitive damages, the defendant "... must act with the intent to vex, injure, or annoy, or with a conscious disregard of the plaintiff's rights." *Taylor v. Superior Court* (1979) 24 Cal. 3d 890, 895, 598 P. 2d 854; see also *Maheu v. Hughes Tool Co.* (9th Cir. 1977) 569 F. 2d 459, 480; cf. *Emerson v. J. F. Shea Co.* (1978) 76 Cal. App. 3d 579, 594-595.

Viewing the article as a whole, as well as Jones' conduct in preparing the article, we cannot say as a matter of law that there was insufficient evidence to support a finding of malice.

Here Jones knew that Diaz would certainly suffer severe emotional distress from the publicity alone. Nevertheless, he added to the indignity by making Diaz the brunt of a joke. The defendants' knowledge of the extent and severity of plaintiff's injuries is relevant to a finding of malice. See *Neal v. Farmer's Ins. Exchange* (1978) 21 Cal. 3d 910, 925, 582 P. 2d 980. The jury could reasonably have inferred from these facts that Jones acted with the intent to outrage or humiliate Diaz or that he published the article with a conscious disregard of her rights.①

The fact that Jones verified the story with unidentified sources does not negate the finding of malice. The jury could well have concluded that Jones' effort to discuss the article with Diaz was *de minimis* when compared to the magnitude of the expected harm. This is especially true since Jones was under no deadline to publish this article. Under these circumstances, the jury could have reasonably concluded that Jones' conduct evidenced a callous and conscious

---

① Respondent also suggests that Jones received the information from Dezzi Woods, director of student affairs at the College. Woods denied this. There is testimony that Jones and Woods had known each other for several years. Also, as part of the College administration, Woods would have been a target of Diaz's accusations of misuse of student funds. Respondent asserts that the reasonable inference could be drawn that Jones agreed to publish this information in order to embarrass Diaz. Based on the evidence before us, such an inference is sheer speculation and is not based on sufficient evidence.

disregard for Diaz's privacy interests. *See*, *generally*, *Cantrell v. Forest Publishing Co.* (1974) 419 U.S. 245, 252. Accordingly, the jury acted well within its discretion in awarding punitive damages.

The Oakland Tribune, Inc., was also liable for punitive damages since the newspaper publishing company reviewed and approved Jones' article for publication. *See Egan v. Mutual of Omaha Ins. Co.* (1979) 24 Cal. 3d 809, 822, 620 P. 2d 141.

We are mindful of the dangerous, inhibiting effect on speech and press a large punitive damage award can have. *See Gertz v. Robert Welch, Inc.* (1974) 418 U.S. 323, 349. If upon retrial the plaintiff recovers a judgment, we caution the trial court to scrutinize strictly any award of punitive damages to ensure that it is not used to silence unpopular persons or speech and that it does not exceed the proper level necessary to punish and deter similar behavior. *See Neal v. Farmer's Ins. Exchange*, *supra*., 21 Cal. 3d at p. 928, fn. 13; *Virgil v. Time, Inc.*, *supra*., 527 F. 2d at p. 1130, fn. 13.

inhibiting effect 抑制效应

silence 使沉默

Excessive Compensatory Damage Award

Finally, defendants urge that the compensatory damage award was excessive. The jury awarded Diaz $250,000, largely for emotional and psychological injury caused by the article. Diaz's special damage for psychotherapy approximated $800.

The evidence adduced at trial established that following the publication of the article Diaz became very depressed and withdrawn. She suffered from insomnia and experienced nightmares. She had frequent memory lapses and experienced difficulty in her social relationships. As a result, in September 1978 she began psychotherapy treatments with Allen Sable, Ph. D.

adduce 提供,提出,举出,出示,通常指提出证据

The actual injury involved herein is not limited to out-of-pocket loss. It generally includes "impairment of reputation and standing in the community, personal humiliation, and mental anguish and suffering." *See Gertz v. Robert Welch, Inc.*, *supra*., 418 U.S. at p. 350. The harm Diaz alleged to have suffered is not easily quantifiable, and the amount of damages must necessarily be left to the sound discretion of the jury.

out-of-pocket loss 用现金支付的损失,实付费用

quantifiable 可以计量的

See *Bertero v. National General Corp.* (1974) 13 Cal. 3d 43, 64, P. 2d 608.

As a rule all presumptions are in favor of the judgment. *Id.*, at p. 61. A reviewing court must not interfere with the verdict unless it can be said that it was the result of "passion or prejudice" on the part of the jury. *Id.*, at p. 64; *Seffert v. Los Angeles Transit Lines* (1961) 56 Cal. 2d 498, 508 – 509, 364 P. 2d 337.

Here the jury fixed the damages after hearing the evidence and being properly instructed. The evidence of Diaz's emotional distress and suffering was uncontradicted. That Diaz was able to earn high marks in her classes after the incident does not necessarily minimize or negate the emotional trauma she suffered and will continue to suffer.

Also, the trial judge denied a motion for a new trial based on this same issue. While that determination is not binding upon this court, it is entitled to great weight. *Bertero v. National General Corp.*, *supra.*, 13 Cal. 3d at p. 64; *Seffert v. Los Angeles Transit Lines*, *supra.*, 56 Cal. 2d at p. 506.

The jury and the trial judge were in the best position to evaluate the scope and severity of Diaz's injuries. They heard the testimony and observed the witnesses. Although the amount of the award is high, it cannot be said that it is so grossly disproportionate, considering the past and future pain and humiliation, as to be excessive as a matter of law.

The judgment is reversed. Appellants and respondent shall each bear their own costs on appeal.

Scott, Acting P. J., concurred.

5.2.3 Case 25: Godbehere v. Phoenix Newspapers, Inc.

Supreme Court of Arizona
Godbehere v. Phoenix Newspapers, Inc.
162 Ariz. 335, 783 P. 2d 781
Oct. 26, 1989

Feldman, Vice Chief Justice.

Richard G. Godbehere, a former Maricopa County Sheriff, and several deputies and civilian employees of the sheriff's office (plaintiffs) brought this action against Phoenix Newspapers, Inc., the publisher of The Arizona Republic and Phoenix Gazette, and fourteen editors and reporters of the two newspapers (publishers), for libel and false light invasion of privacy. The trial court granted publishers' motion to dismiss for failure to state a claim as to the invasion of privacy claims, but refused to dismiss the other counts of the complaint. Plaintiffs appealed and the court of appeals affirmed. We granted review to determine whether Arizona should recognize a cause of action for false light invasion of privacy, and if so, what the proper standard should be. *See* Rule 23, Ariz. R. Civ. App. P., 17B A. R. S. We have jurisdiction pursuant to Ariz. Const. art. 6, § 5(3) and A. R. S. § 12-120.24.

Facts

In the spring and summer of 1985, publishers printed over fifty articles, editorials, and columns (the publications) about plaintiffs' various law enforcement activities. The publications stated that the plaintiffs engaged in illegal activities, <u>staged</u> <u>narcotics</u> arrests to generate publicity, illegally arrested citizens, misused public funds and resources, committed police <u>brutality</u>, and generally were incompetent at law enforcement. Plaintiffs alleged in their eighteen-count complaint that the publications were false, damaged their reputations, harmed them in their profession, and caused them emotional distress.

Publishers moved to dismiss all eighteen counts of the complaint for failure to state a claim, and the court dismissed the false light invasion of privacy claims. In so doing, the trial court relied on *Rutledge v. Phoenix Newspapers, Inc.*, 148 Ariz. 555, 715 P. 2d 1243 (Ct. App. 1986), which held that a plaintiff must prove the elements of intentional infliction of emotional distress to claim false light invasion of privacy. The trial court found the acts in question were not so extreme or outrageous as to constitute the tort of intentional infliction of emotional distress. MINUTE ENTRY (filed June 18, 1986).

On appeal, plaintiffs argued that Arizona should follow the Restatement (Second) of Torts § 652E

stage 筹划
narcotics 麻醉剂,毒品

brutality 暴虐行为,蛮横行为

(1977) (hereafter Restatement), which provides in part:

> One who gives publicity to a matter concerning another that places the other before the public in a false light is subject to liability to the other for invasion of his privacy, if
> (a) the false light in which the other was placed would be highly offensive to a reasonable person, and
> (b) the actor had knowledge of or acted in reckless disregard as to the falsity of the publicized matter and the false light in which the other would be placed.

The court of appeals rejected the Restatement position as inconsistent with its own prior authority. *Godbehere v. Phoenix Newspapers, Inc.*, 155 Ariz. 389, 391, 746 P.2d 1319, 1321 (Ct. App. 1987).

We accepted plaintiffs' petition for review to decide whether Arizona should follow Restatement § 652E, recognizing the tort of false light invasion of privacy without requiring plaintiffs to prove all the elements of the tort of intentional infliction of emotional distress.

Discussion

A. Development of the Right of Privacy

In 1890, Samuel Warren and Louis Brandeis published an article advocating the recognition of a right to privacy as an independent legal concept. Warren & Brandeis, *The Right to Privacy*, 4 HARV. L. REV. 193 (1890). Explaining how courts traditionally recognized claims involving injury to a person's private thoughts or feelings, they also described how courts used contract and property law to protect thoughts, ideas, or expressions from wrongful appropriation. *Id.* Warren and Brandeis contended these were nothing more than "instances and applications of a general right to privacy." *Id.* at 198. Hence, they supported recognition of the right "to be let alone." *Id.* at 203.

In 1905 the Georgia Supreme Court recognized the privacy right in a case involving wrongful appropriation of the plaintiff's name and likeness. *Pavesich v. New England Life Insurance Co.*, 50 S.E. 68 (Ga. 1905). Controversy over recognition of a right to privacy continued, although the Restatement of Torts recognized an independent cause of action for interference with privacy in 1939. RESTATEMENT (FIRST) OF TORTS § 867 (1939). A majority of jurisdictions eventually recognized the right in some form. PROSSER AND KEETON ON THE LAW OF TORTS § 117, at 850 – 51 (5th ed. 1984) (hereafter PROSSER & KEETON).

In 1960, Dean Prosser concluded that four separate torts had developed under the right of privacy rubric: (1) intrusion on the plaintiff's seclusion or private affairs; (2) public disclosure of embarrassing private facts; (3) publicity placing the plaintiff in a false light in the public eye; and (4) appropriation of the plaintiff's name or likeness for the defendant's advantage. Prosser, *Privacy*, 48 CALIF. L. REV. 383 (1960). In 1977, the Restatement adopted Prosser's classification. *See* RESTATEMENT § 652A-I (1977). Although each tort is classified under invasion of privacy, they "otherwise have almost nothing in common except that each represents an interference with the right of the plaintiff 'to be let alone.'" PROSSER & KEETON § 117, at 851.

B. Privacy in Arizona

Arizona first recognized an action for invasion of privacy in *Reed v. Real Detective Publishing Co.*, 63 Ariz. 294, 162 P.2d 133 (1945). Reed involved the unauthorized publication of the plaintiff's photograph. Subsequently, our court of appeals recognized the Restatement's four-part classification of the tort. *See Rutledge*, 148 Ariz. at 556, 715 P.2d at 1244; *Cluff*, 10 Ariz. App. at 563, 460 P.2d at 669.

Although most jurisdictions that recognize a cause of action for invasion of privacy have adopted the Restatement standard of "highly offensive to a reasonable person" or a similar standard, *see* Note, *Is Invasion of Privacy a Viable Cause of Action in Arizona?: Rethinking the Standard*, 30 ARIZ. L. REV.

319, 331 n. 96 (1988), Arizona courts of appeals' decisions have imposed a stricter standard. Rather than following the Restatement, these decisions have held that where the damage alleged is emotional, the plaintiff must prove the elements of the tort of intentional infliction of emotional distress in addition to proving invasion of privacy. To recover for invasion of privacy, a plaintiff must show that the defendant's conduct was "extreme and outrageous." No other state requires a plaintiff to prove that the defendant committed "outrage" in a false light action. *See* Annotation, *False Light Invasion of Privacy-Cognizability and Elements*, 57 A. L. R. 4th 22 (1987); Note, *supra*, 30 ARIZ. L. REV. at 338.

Publishers urge this court to adopt the court of appeals' view. They argue that there is no need for an independent tort of false light invasion of privacy because the action overlaps two other recognized torts: defamation and intentional infliction of emotional distress. These, publishers contend, cover the field and permit recovery in meritorious cases, thus making the false light action an unnecessary burden on the media's first amendment rights. To consider this argument, we must examine the distinctions between the false light action and the torts of intentional infliction of emotional distress and defamation.

C. False Light Invasion of Privacy and Intentional Infliction of Emotional Distress

Arizona has turned to Restatement § 46 to define intentional infliction of emotional distress, also known as the tort of outrage. *Ford v. Revlon, Inc.*, 153 Ariz. 38, 43, 734 P. 2d 580, 585 (1987). This section provides:

[O]ne who by extreme and outrageous conduct intentionally or recklessly causes severe emotional distress to another is subject to liability for such emotional distress, and if bodily harm to the other results from it, for such bodily harm.

The element of "extreme and outrageous conduct" requires that plaintiff prove defendant's conduct exceeded "all bounds usually tolerated by decent society ... and [caused] mental distress of a very serious kind." PROSSER & KEETON § 12, at 60. This standard distinguishes "true claims from false ones, and ... the trifling insult or annoyance from the serious wrong." Prosser, Mental Suffering, 37 MICH. L. REV. 874, 877 (1939); *see also* RESTATEMENT § 46 *comments b, d, and f.*

The court of appeals has advanced two main reasons to justify imposing the intentional infliction standard on privacy actions. First, because the basis of the wrong in both outrage and invasion of privacy is infliction of mental suffering, the two torts are substantively similar and the same standard should apply to both. *Cluff*, 10 Ariz. App. at 564, 460 P.2d at 670; *see also Davis v. First National Bank of Arizona*, 124 Ariz. 458, 462-63, 605 P.2d 37, 41-42 (Ct. App. 1979). Second, the court suggested that the rule was necessary to prevent plaintiffs from circumventing the "stringent standards necessary to otherwise establish a claim for the intentional infliction of emotional distress." *Rutledge*, 148 Ariz. at 557, 715 P.2d at 1245. This stricter standard was necessary "to protect defendants from unwarranted lawsuits." *Duhammel*, 133 Ariz. at 561, 653 P.2d at 18.

Here, as in the above cases, the trial court dismissed plaintiffs' privacy claims for failure to state a cause of action, relying on *Rutledge* and holding that the acts of which plaintiffs complained were not outrageous. MINUTE ENTRY (filed June 18, 1986). Assuming the court was correct on the evidence, we must determine whether it correctly required plaintiffs to prove the tort of outrage in a privacy action.

Publishers emphasize that actions for both intentional infliction of emotional distress and invasion of privacy provide compensation for emotional distress or damage to sensibility. *Cf.* RESTATEMENT §§ 46 and 652E. Thus, the injury from both torts is similar. Although this may be true, the fact that two different actions address the same injury is no reason to refuse to recognize torts that protect against different wrongful conduct. For example, three victims may suffer broken legs in the following ways: (1) a defendant negligently drives a car into the first

stringent 严厉的

victim's car; (2) a defendant's defective product injures the second victim; and (3) a defendant, without justification, attacks the third. Each victim would have a different tort claim: negligence, strict liability, and battery. The fact that each victim suffers the same type of injury does not preclude recognizing separate tort actions. Each tort theory developed separately to deter and provide redress against a different type of wrongful conduct.

Thus, the fact that outrage and invasion of privacy both provide redress for emotional injury does not persuade us that the actions are "merged" or that plaintiffs should be required to prove the former in an action for the latter. The outrage tort protects against conduct so extreme that it would induce "an average member of the community ... to exclaim, 'outrageous!'" RESTATEMENT § 46 comment d. False light invasion of privacy, however, protects against the conduct of knowingly or recklessly publishing false information or innuendo that a "reasonable person" would find "highly offensive." Although false publication may constitute outrageous conduct and *vice versa*, it is also true that the same wrongful conduct will not always satisfy the elements of both tort actions. See Note, *supra*, 30 Ariz. L. Rev. at 342. Because each action protects against a different type of tortious conduct, each has its place, and the common injury should not abrogate the action. See Id.

Nor do we believe that recognizing the false light action without requiring plaintiffs to prove outrage will circumvent the "stringent standards" of the emotional distress tort. See *Rutledge*, 148 Ariz. at 557, 715 P.2d at 1245. The standards for proving false light invasion of privacy are quite "stringent" by themselves. For example, the plaintiff in a false light case must prove that the defendant published with knowledge of the falsity or reckless disregard for the truth. See RESTATEMENT § 652E. This standard is as stringent as the intentional infliction of emotional distress requirement that the plaintiff prove the defendant "intentionally or recklessly caused" the emotional distress. See RESTATEMENT § 46.

We also do not share the court of appeals' concern

with creating unwarranted lawsuits. Freeing a plaintiff from the need to prove outrageous conduct in a privacy suit does not require us to provide a remedy for "every trivial indignity." *See* Prosser, *supra*, 37 MICH. L. REV. at 877. A defendant is not liable in a false light case unless the publication places the plaintiff in a false light highly offensive to a reasonable person. *Time, Inc. v. Hill*, 385 U. S. 374 (1967); RESTATEMENT § 652E. Thus, the plaintiff's subjective threshold of sensibility is not the measure, and "trivial indignities" are not actionable.

We conclude, therefore, that the two torts exist to redress different types of wrongful conduct. Situations exist where a jury could find the defendant's publication of false information or innuendo was not outrageous but did satisfy the false light elements. *See* Zimmerman, *False Light Invasion of Privacy: The Light That Failed*, 64 N. Y. U. L. REV. 364 (1989). Thus, we believe the tort action for false light invasion of privacy provides protection against a narrow class of wrongful conduct that falls short of "outrage," but nevertheless should be deterred.

D. Invasion of Privacy and Defamation

A second argument advanced by publishers is that little distinction exists between a tort action for false light invasion of privacy and one for defamation. Thus, because defamation actions are available, they argue, Arizona need not recognize false light invasion of privacy. Again, we disagree.

Although both defamation and false light invasion of privacy involve publication, the nature of the interests protected by each action differs substantially. *See* PROSSER & KEETON § 117, at 864. A defamation action compensates damage to reputation or good name caused by the publication of false information. *Hill*, 385 U. S. at 384 n. 9. To be defamatory, a publication must be false and must bring the defamed person into <u>disrepute</u>, contempt, or ridicule, or must impeach plaintiff's honesty, integrity, virtue, or reputation. *See Phoenix Newspapers, Inc. v. Choisser*, 82 Ariz. 271, 312 P. 2d 150 (1957).

Privacy, on the other hand, does not protect

disrepute 喪失名譽,不名譽

reputation but protects mental and emotional interests. Indeed, "[t]he gravamen of [a privacy] action ... is the injury to the feelings of the plaintiff, the mental anguish and distress caused by the publication." Reed, 63 Ariz. at 305, 162 P.2d at 139. The remedy is available "to protect a person's interest in being let alone and is available when there has been publicity of a kind that is highly offensive." PROSSER & KEETON § 117, at 864. Under this theory, a plaintiff may recover even in the absence of reputational damage, as long as the publicity is unreasonably offensive and attributes false characteristics. However, to qualify as a false light invasion of privacy, the publication must involve "a major misrepresentation of [the plaintiff's] character, history, activities or beliefs," not merely minor or unimportant inaccuracies. RESTATEMENT § 652E comment c.

Another distinction between defamation and false light invasion of privacy is the role played by truth. To be defamatory, a publication must be false, and truth is a defense. PROSSER & KEETON § 116, at 839. A false light cause of action may arise when something untrue has been published about an individual, see PROSSER & KEETON § 117, at 863 – 66, or when the publication of true information creates a false implication about the individual. In the latter type of case, the false innuendo created by the highly offensive presentation of a true fact constitutes the injury.① See RESTATEMENT § 652E.

nude 裸照
employ 雇佣关系, 工作
nonconsensual use 未经同意而使用

---

① A good example of a false light cause of action based on implication is Douglass v. Hustler Magazine, Inc., 769 F.2d 1128 (7th Cir. 1985), cert. denied, 475 U.S. 1094 (1986). In Douglass, the plaintiff posed nude, consenting to the publication of her photographs in Playboy magazine. Her photographer subsequently left the employ of Playboy for Hustler magazine, a publication of much lower standing in the journalistic community. He sold her photographs to Hustler, which published them. The plaintiff sued for the nonconsensual use of the photographs. Plaintiff had no cause of action for defamation, because essentially, there was nothing untrue about the photographs. She posed for them and, as published, they did not misrepresent her. She also had no claim for outrage. She voluntarily posed for the photographs and consented to their publication in Playboy. Publication was not "outrageous," as it may have been if she were photographed without her knowledge and the photos published without her initial consent. However, the court upheld her recovery for false light invasion of privacy. The jury may have focused on the differences between Playboy and Hustler and concluded that to be published in Hustler, as if she had posed for that publication, falsely placed her in a different light than the Playboy publication. 769 F.2d at 1138.

Thus, although defamation and false light often overlap, they serve very different objectives. The two tort actions deter different conduct and redress different wrongs. A plaintiff may bring a false light invasion of privacy action even though the publication is not defamatory, and even though the actual facts stated are true. Several examples in comment b to Restatement § 652E also illustrate the practical differences between a false light action and defamation and demonstrate how, in a certain class of cases, the false light action is the only redress available.① It is these considerations, we believe, that lead the vast majority of other jurisdictions, including the United States Supreme Court, to recognize the distinction between defamation and false light.

E. Arizona and the False Light Tort

Momentarily leaving aside the free speech considerations, we are persuaded to recognize the distinct tort of false light invasion of privacy as articulated by RESTATEMENT § 652E. The argument that recognition of this action invites much new litigation is of questionable merit. To date, only four cases of false light privacy have been presented in Arizona, including the instant case. States recognizing the false light action have not been deluged with substantially more litigation than afflicts this state. In most cases, the false light theory will add little if anything beyond the relief a defamation or emotional

deluge 淹没,压倒
afflict 使苦恼,折磨
spurious 欺骗性的,假的,伪造的
inferior 差的,低劣的,低下的
democrat 民主党人
narrative 故事,叙述,讲述
fictitious 虚构的,非真实的,假的

---

① Restatement § 652E comment b gives the following illustrations:

   3. A is a renowned poet. B publishes in his magazine a spurious inferior poem, signed with A's name. Regardless of whether the poem is so bad as to subject B to liability for libel, B is subject to liability to A for invasion of privacy. [This example is presumably based on the case from which the false light concept arose-*Lord Byron v. Johnston*, 2 Mer. 29, 35 Eng. Rep. 851 (1816).]

   4. A is a Democrat. B induces him to sign a petition nominating C for office. A discovers that C is a Republican and demands that B remove his name from the petition. B refuses to do so and continues public circulation of the petition, bearing A's name. B is subject to liability to A for invasion of privacy.

   5. A is a war hero, distinguished for bravery in a famous battle. B makes and exhibits a motion picture concerning A's life, in which he inserts a detailed narrative of a fictitious private life attributed to A, including a non-existent romance with a girl. B knows this matter to be false. Although A is not defamed by the motion picture, B is subject to liability to him for invasion of privacy.

   Illustrations 3, 4, and 5.

distress claim will provide. Some cases exist, however, where the theory will protect a small area otherwise lacking protection against invasion of privacy. That interest, we believe, demands protection.

Arizona is one of the first states whose founders thought it necessary to adopt explicit protection for the privacy of its citizens. See ARIZ. CONST. art. 2, § 8. Unless the interest in protecting privacy rights is outweighed by the interest in protecting speech, see *Mountain States Telephone & Telegraph Co. v. Arizona Corporation Commission*, 160 Ariz. 350, 773 P. 2d 455 (1989), we see no reason not to recognize an action for false light invasion of privacy.

F. Free Speech Considerations

As in defamation, a public official in a false light action must always show that the defendant published with knowledge of the false innuendo or with reckless disregard of the truth. See RESTATEMENT § 652E comment b. Any doubt about the application of the actual malice element of the false light tort to public figures has been eliminated. In *Hustler Magazine, Inc. v. Falwell*, 485 U. S. 46 (1988), the Supreme Court held that a public figure plaintiff must prove *Times v. Sullivan* actual malice in order to recover for intentional infliction of emotional distress. Although *Hustler* was an intentional infliction case, the language used by the Court is so broad that it applies to any tort action relating to free speech, particularly "in the area of public debate about public figures." See *Hustler*, 485 U. S. at 53, 108 S. Ct. at 881.① Additional protection for free speech comes from the principle that protection for privacy interests generally applies only to private matters. See RESTATEMENT § 652A comment b; *Reed*, 63 Ariz. at 304, 162 P. 2d at 138.

caveat（为防止误解而作的)解释

---

① To this point, we have spoken of false light as requiring that the plaintiff show actual malice. RESTATEMENT § 652E seems to state that requirement, but the Caveat to section 652E states that the Institute "takes no position" on whether, under some circumstances, a non-public figure may recover for false light invasion of privacy where he does not show actual malice but does show negligent publication. See also RESTATEMENT § 652E comment on Clause (b). Because this case does not present the issue, we also take no position on the validity of a false light action for negligent publication. Suffice it to say that in this case, where we deal with publications concerning public officers performing public duties, the first amendment controls.

G. Is False Light Available in This Case?

Finally, publishers contended that even if we recognize false light actions, the action does not lie in this case. They argue that not only do the publications discuss matters of public interest, but plaintiffs have no right of privacy with respect to the manner in which they perform their official duties. We agree.

We have specifically held that the right of privacy does not exist "where the plaintiff has become a public character..." *Reed*, 63 Ariz. at 304, 162 P. 2d at 138. In addition, privacy rights are absent or limited "in connection with the life of a person in whom the public has a rightful interest, [or] where the information would be of public benefit." *Reed*, 63 Ariz. at 304, 162 P. 2d at 138.

A number of jurisdictions take the position that because false light is a form of invasion of privacy, it must relate only to the private affairs of the plaintiff and cannot involve matters of public interest. *See* Annot., *supra*, 57 A. L. R. 4th 22, § 10. It is difficult to conceive of an area of greater public interest than law enforcement. Certainly the public has a legitimate interest in the manner in which law enforcement officers perform their duties. Therefore, we hold that there can be no false light invasion of privacy action for matters involving official acts or duties of public officers.

conceive 认为，以为

Consequently, we adopt the following legal standard: a plaintiff cannot sue for false light invasion of privacy if he or she is a public official and the publication relates to performance of his or her public life or duties. We do not go so far as to say, however, that a public official has no privacy rights at all and may never bring an action for invasion of privacy. Certainly, if the publication presents the public official's private life in a false light, he or she can sue under the false light tort, although actual malice must be shown.

The Supreme Court has held that "the public official designation applies at the very least to those among the hierarchy of government employees who have, or appear to the public to have, substantial responsibility for or control over the conduct of governmental affairs." *Rosenblatt v. Baer*, 383 U.S. 75 (1966). Police and other law enforcement personnel are almost always classified as public officials. *See, e.g., Time, Inc. v. Pape*, 401 U.S. 279, 291 – 92 (1971). The sheriff and the deputies here are public officials. The publications at issue concern the discharge of their public duties and do not relate to private affairs. Therefore, plaintiffs have no claim for false light invasion of privacy.

We affirm the trial court's dismissal of the false light claim. Because we disagree with the court of appeals' reasoning, we vacate that opinion and remand to the trial court for further proceedings consistent with this opinion.

Review Questions

1. What are the common elements for the various intentional torts?
2. Does a plaintiff need to prove damage to establish an intentional tort case?
3. What are the differences between battery and assault?
4. Does the distinction between libel and slander affect the rules of law governing the tort of deformation?
5. How different are the four types of invasion of privacy?
6. What are the defenses and privileges to each kind of intentional torts?

CHAPTER 7
TORTS OF NEGLIGENCE

尽管前一章介绍了英美侵权法中的重要内容——故意侵权,但事实上大多数侵权赔偿请求涉及的是非由故意过错造成的无心伤害或事故。这种非故意造成的损害假如在行为人像一个理性且谨慎的人一样行事就可以避免时,这种行为叫做过失。当被告违反了其对原告所负有的义务并使得原告从事实上和法律上两个角度看都因被告违反义务的行为而遭受了损害,则被告构成过失侵权。过失侵权责任的基础是行为人对他人造成了不合理的损害风险。为了证明被告过失侵权,必须证明被告的行为与其所能带来的利益相比,可能造成比社会愿意接受的损害风险更大的风险,亦即不合理的风险。初步证明一个过失侵权案件,原告必须证明被告对其负有注意义务却违背了该义务,原告因此遭受损害,且原告的损害与被告的过失行为之间有因果关系。本章从这几点出发介绍英美侵权法中的过失侵权类型。

1. Duty

Duty is the first element the plaintiff needs to prove in order to establish a *prima facie* case of negligence. No duty, no liability.

1.1 The General Duty

Generally speaking, any person has a duty to exercise reasonable care toward other people. When a person engages in an activity, he is under a legal duty to act as an ordinary, prudent, reasonable person. The presumption is that an ordinary, prudent, reasonable person will take precautions against creating unreasonable risks of injury to other persons. The reasonable person always does what is right under the circumstances by exercising prudent care, skill, and judgment.

1.2 To Whom the Duty of Care Owed

The duty of care is generally owed to any foreseeable plaintiffs. Problems arise when A breaches a duty to B and also causes injury thereby to C to whom a foreseeable risk of injury might or might not have been created at the time of the original negligent act. Courts have different solutions to this problem. In the case reprinted later in this chapter *Palsgraf v. Long Island Railroad Co.*, Justice Cardozo and Justice Andrews had different views. Cardozo would grant C recoveries only if C could establish that a reasonable person would have foreseen a risk of injury to him in the circumstances, *i.e.*, that he was located in a foreseeable "zone of danger." However, Andrews held that C might establish the existence of a duty extending from A to C by showing that A had breached a duty he owed B. If so, A owed a duty of care to anyone who suffered injuries as a proximate result of his breach of duty to someone.

Rescuers generally are regarded as foreseeable plaintiffs as long as the rescue is not wanton; hence, the defendant is liable if he negligently puts himself or

rescuer 营救者，援救者

a third person in peril and the plaintiff is injured in attempting a rescue. Intended beneficiaries of economic transactions are also foreseeable plaintiffs. For example, a third person for whose economic benefit a legal or business transaction is made (e. g. , the beneficiary of a will) is owed a duty of care if the defendant could reasonably foresee harm to that party if the transaction is done negligently.

1.3 Standard of Care

The general standard of conduct to which one must conform to avoid being negligent is that of a reasonable person under like circumstances. It is measured by an objective standard. It is actually a sliding standard that is tapered to a person's age, training, and profession. Generally, the courts will presume the reasonable person with the same physical characteristics as the defendant, with the average mental ability, and with the same knowledge as average member of community.

The courts refuse to consider mental deficiencies of actors in assessing conduct. Average mental ability is the general standard. The only exception to this general rule is that children are to be judged according to what might be expected of children of similar age and experience. So a child is required to conform to the standard of care of a child of like age, education, intelligence, and experience, which is a subjective evaluation. In most states, the minimum age for a child to be liable for negligence is four. There is an exception to the above exception though: if a child is engaged in adult activities, then the child is required to conform to the same standard of care as an adult in such an activity. Thus, a child driving an automobile, flying an airplane, or driving a motorboat will be judged by the general standard of care an adult should apply with.

However, the courts have adopted a more subjective, individualized approach to the question of defendants' physical disabilities. Thus, if the defendant was blind at the time of the allegedly negligent conduct, the jury is to measure his conduct against that of a reasonably prudent blind person under

in peril 处于危险之中

a sliding standard 浮动标准
taper 逐渐变弱

physical characteristics 生理特征
mental ability 精神状态

similar circumstances.

Nevertheless, some persons are held to a standard of conduct different from that of the ordinary person. For example, a person who is a professional or has special skills (e.g., doctor, lawyer, airplane mechanic, etc.) is required to possess and exercise the knowledge and skill of a member of the profession or occupation in good standing in similar communities. Thus, a specialist might be held liable where a general practitioner would not. Common carriers and innkeepers are required to exercise a very high degree of care toward their passengers and guests while an automobile driver owes a lower degree of care to a nonpaying guest. The duties owed by owners and occupiers of land also vary, which are to be discussed below.

1.4 Duty Owed by Owners and Occupiers of Land

The general standard of care may be modified if it is between an owner, occupier, or possessor of land and entrants on the land, The possessors of land owe different duties toward the trespassers, licensees, or invitees.

A trespasser is a person who enters or remains upon land in the possession of another without a privilege or permission to do so. Generally, the landowner owes no duty to an undiscovered trespasser, but owes duty of ordinary care to warn the discovered trespasser of, or to make safe, artificial conditions known to the landowner that involve a risk of death or serious bodily harm and that the trespasser is unlikely to discover. It does not apply to natural conditions on the land though. In general, the duty of the possessor toward trespassers is to refrain from wanton and willful conduct. However, if the trespasser is on the land for the purpose of committing a crime, the possessor may be liable only for intentionally injuring the trespasser.

A higher duty may be owed to young trespassers under the "attractive nuisance doctrine," which requires a landowner to be subject to liability for physical harm to children trespassing thereon caused by an artificial condition upon the land if the place

---

profession 职业
occupation 行业,职业
in good standing 声誉良好的
specialist 专家
practitioner 从业者
common carrier 公共运输商
innkeeper 旅馆主人;客栈掌柜
nonpaying guest 免费乘客,搭便车者

entrant 进入者
trespasser 侵入他人土地者
licensee (获得所有者同意可进入其地界的)被许可人
invitee 受邀进入他人土地者;被邀请者

ordinary care 普通注意,一般注意
artificial conditions 人为条件,非自然条件

attractive nuisance doctrine 保护儿童免受危险物品伤害原则(指在自己或他人的处所或公共场所置放会危及儿童的物品时,如果能合理预见到这些物品将诱使儿童来到该场所,则行为人应当尽到合理注意,保护儿童免受其害的义务)

where the condition exists is one upon which the landowner knows or has reason to know that children are likely to trespass, and the condition is one of which the landowner knows or has reason to know and which he realizes or should realize will involve an unreasonable risk of death or serious bodily harm to such children, and the children because of their youth do not discover the condition or realize the risk involved in intermeddling with it or in coming within the area made dangerous by it, and the utility to the possessor of maintaining the condition and the burden of eliminating the danger are slight as compared with the risk to children involved, and the landowner fails to exercise reasonable care to eliminate the danger or otherwise to protect the children.

A licensee is a person who enters on the land of another with the landowner's permission for his own purpose or business rather than for the landowner's benefit, e.g., social guests. The landowner owes a duty to warn the licensee of a dangerous condition known to the owner that creates an unreasonable risk of harm to the licensee and that the licensee is unlikely to discover. However, the landowner has no duty to inspect.

An invitee is a person who enters onto the premises in response to an express or implied invitation of the landowner. The invitee may be either a public invitee or a business visitor. A public invitee is a person who is invited to enter or remain on land as a member of the public for a purpose for which the land is held open to the public, such as museums, churches, airports, etc. A business visitor is a person who is invited to enter or remain on land for a purpose directly or indirectly connected with business dealings with the possessor of the land, such as the store customers and persons accompanying them, employees, persons making deliveries, etc. The duty owed to an invitee is one of reasonable care under the circumstances. The possessor of land has a general duty to use reasonable and ordinary care in keeping the property reasonably safe for the benefit of the invitee. He has all the duties owed by the landowner to a licensee, as well as the duty to inspect and repair. It should be noted that the landowner has no duty to warn of any obvious danger to anyone.

1.5 Affirmative Duty to Act

Generally, there is no legal duty imposed on any person to affirmatively act for the benefit of others. However, there are exceptions to this rule. First, one could assume the duty by gratuitously acting for the benefit of another, although under no duty to do so in the first instance; then he is under a duty to act like an ordinary, prudent, reasonable person and continue the assistance. Second, one whose negligence places another in a position of peril is under a duty to use reasonable care to aid or assist that person. Third, if the defendant has a special relationship to the plaintiff, e. g., parent-child, employer-employee, etc., he or she may be liable for failure to act if the plaintiff is in peril. Fourth, the common carriers have to use reasonable care to aid or assist passengers, and the innkeepers, restaurateurs, shopkeepers, and others who gather the public for profit have a duty to use reasonable care to aid or assist their patrons and to prevent injury to them from third persons.

1.6 Case 26: Tubbs v. Argus

Appellate Court of Indiana, Division 2
Lillian C. Tubbs v. Anna A. Argus
140 Ind. App. 695, 225 N. E. 2d 841
May 9, 1967

Praff, Presiding Justice.

This appeal arises as a result of demurrer to appellant's Second Amended Complaint which was sustained and judgment entered thereon upon the failure and refusal of the appellant to plead over.

The facts material to a determination of the issues raised on this appeal may be summarized as follows:

On January 28, 1959 at approximately 12:00 noon, the appellant was riding as a guest passenger in the right front seat of an automobile owned and operated by the appellee in the 100 block west of West Hampton Drive in the City of Indianapolis, Indiana.

While traveling in an easterly direction the automobile was driven over the south curb of West Hampton Drive and into a tree, resulting in injury to the appellant. After the said collision, the appellee abandoned the automobile and did not render reasonable aid and assistance to the injured appellant. Appellant alleges that she suffered additional injuries as a result of appellee's failure to <u>render</u> reasonable <u>aid and assistance</u> and seeks to recover only for these additional injuries.

render aid/assistance 提供帮助、协助

In her assignment of errors, the appellant <u>avers</u> that the trial court erred in sustaining the demurrer to appellant's Second Amended Complaint. More specifically, the appellant alleges that appellee's failure to render reasonable aid and assistance constituted a breach of a common law duty.

aver（在诉状中）宣称，断言,主张,陈述

The appellee contends that throughout the appellant's occupancy of the said motor vehicle, she was a guest as defined under the "Guest Statute," which limited liability to those injuries resulting from wanton and willful misconduct and thus precluded liability for negligence. *See* BURNS IND. STAT. ANNO. §47‑1021 (1965 Replacement), which reads as follows:

> 47‑1021 (10142.1). Guest of owner or operator — Right to damages. The owner, operator, or person responsible for the operation of a motor vehicle shall not be liable for loss or damage arising from injuries to or death of a guest, while being transported without payment therefore, in or upon such motor vehicle, resulting from the operation thereof, unless such injuries or death are caused by the wanton or willful misconduct of such operator, owner, or person responsible for the operation of such motor vehicle. (Acts 1929, ch. 201, §1, p.679; 1937, ch. 259, §1, p.1229.)

A <u>literal interpretation</u> of this statute leads this court to the conclusion that the motor vehicle operator is not liable for injuries resulting from the operation of said vehicle, unless caused by his wanton and willful

literal interpretation 按字面解释

misconduct.

Before the appellee in the case at bar can invoke this statute to preclude herself from liability for negligence, the injuries must result from the operation of said motor vehicle.

The appellant herein is seeking recovery for additional injuries arising from the appellee's failure to render reasonable aid and assistance, and not for the initial injuries which resulted from the operation of the automobile. It is the opinion of this Court that appellant's cause of action for additional injuries is outside the scope of Sec. 47 - 1021 because these additional injuries did not arise until after the operation of the said automobile had ceased. Sec. 47 - 1021 is only applicable to those injuries resulting from the operation of the said vehicle. Thus the appellee cannot invoke Sec. 47 - 1021, *supra*, to limit his liability for these additional injuries to acts of wanton and willful misconduct.

At common law, there is no general duty to aid a person who is in peril. *L. S. Ayres & Company v. Hicks* (1941), 220 Ind. 86, 40 N.E.2d 334; *Hurley Adm. v. Eddingfield* (1900), 156 Ind. 416, 59 N.E. 1058. However, in *L. S. Ayres & Company*, *supra*, page 94, 40 N.E.2d page 337, the Supreme Court of Indiana held that "under some circumstances, moral and humanitarian considerations may require one to render assistance to another who has been injured, even though the injury was not due to negligence on his part and may have been caused by the negligence of the injured person. Failure to render assistance in such a situation may constitute actionable negligence if the injury is aggravated through lack of due care." *Tippecanoe Loan*, etc., *Co. v. Cleveland*, etc. *R. Co.* (1915), 57 Ind. App. 644, 104 N.E. 866; *Depue v. Flatau* (1907), 100 Minn. 299, 111 N.W. 1.

In *Tippecanoe Loan*, etc., *Co. v. Cleveland*, etc. *R. Co.*, *supra*, this court held that a railroad company was liable for failing to provide medical assistance to an employee who was injured through no fault of the railroad company, but who was rendered helpless and by reason of which the employee's injuries were aggravated.

humanitarian 人道主义的

The Supreme Court of Indiana in *L. S. Ayres*, *supra*, found the appellant liable for aggravation of injuries when it failed to extricate the appellee, a six year old boy, whose fingers were caught in the moving parts of an escalator, even though the jury conclusively established that the appellant was not negligent with respect to the choice, construction, or manner of operating the elevator. In so holding, the Supreme Court stated that it may be deduced from *Tippecanoe Loan, etc. Co. v. Cleveland, etc. R. Co., supra*, "that there may be a legal obligation to take positive or affirmative steps to effect the rescue of a person who is helpless and in a situation of peril, when the one proceeded against is a master or an invitor or when the injury resulted from use of an instrumentality under the control of the defendant."

The doctrine of law as set forth in Restatement (Second) of Torts, § 322, p. 133, adds credence to these two Indiana cases. "... If the actor knows or has reason to know that by his conduct, whether tortious or innocent, he has caused such bodily harm to another as to make him helpless and in danger of future harm, the actor is under a duty to exercise reasonable care to prevent such further harm."

One distinction between the *Ayres, supra* and *Tippecanoe, supra* cases and the case at bar is that both of the former cases involve situations where an economic advantage flows to the defendant, while the case at bar does not. It is the opinion of this Court that an affirmative duty to render reasonable aid and assistance is not limited to those cases involving the flow of an economic advantage to the alleged defendant. The court, in both the above mentioned cases, stated that other relationship may impose a like obligation and it is the opinion of the Court that the case at bar presents a situation in which an affirmative duty arises to render reasonable aid and assistance to one who is helpless and in a situation of peril, when the injury resulted from use of an instrumentality under the control of the defendant.

In the case at bar, the appellant received her injuries from an instrumentality under the control of the appellee. Under the rule stated above and on the

extricate 使解脱,救出

escalator 电动扶梯

elevator 电梯
deduce 推论

credence 信任,可信性,可靠性

authority of the cases cited, this was a sufficient relationship to impose a duty to render reasonable aid and assistance, a duty for the breach of which the appellee is liable for the additional injuries suffered.

We are of the opinion that the court below erred in sustaining the demurrer to appellant's Second Amended Complaint.

This cause is reversed and remanded for proceedings not inconsistent with this opinion.

Judgment reversed.

2. Breach

The second element of a *prima facie* case of negligence is the breach of the duty by the defendant because of negligence. Where the defendant's conduct falls short of that level required by the applicable standard of care owed to the plaintiff, he has breached his duty. Therefore, a breach of duty is a failure to act in a manner that a reasonable person would have acted under the same or similar circumstance, or when action was necessary to protect or help another person and a reasonable person would have done so.

There must be reasonable evidence of negligence. Custom or usage may be introduced to establish the standard of care in a given case, while the violation of statutes can also evidence the breach of the duty. But where the thing is shown to be under the management of the defendant or his servants, and the accident is such as in the ordinary course of things does not happen if those who have the management use proper care, it affords reasonable evidence, in the absence of explanation by the defendants, that the accident arose from want of care. This is the circumstantial evidence doctrine called "*Res Ipsa Loquitur*," meaning that "the thing speaks for itself." It deals with those situations where the fact that a particular injury occurred may itself establish or tend to establish a breach of duty owed. Where the facts are such as to strongly indicate that the plaintiff's injuries resulted from the defendant's negligence, the trier of fact may be permitted to infer the defendant's liability.

In order to apply *res ipsa loquitur* doctrine, first,

the plaintiff must show <u>inference</u> of negligence, *i.e.*, the plaintiff must establish that the accident causing his injury is the type that would not normally occur unless someone was negligent. For example, a windowpane fell from a second story window in the defendant's building, landing on the plaintiff. *Res Ipsa Loquitur* may apply to this situation. Second, the plaintiff must establish evidence connecting the defendant with the negligence in order to support a finding of liability. This requirement can be satisfied by showing that the instrumentality that caused the injury was in the sole control of the defendant. It is enough to show that the power of control and opportunity to exercise that power are with the defendant; actual possession of the instrumentality is not necessary. Third, the plaintiff must also prove that the injury was not <u>attributable to</u> him, but may do so by his own testimony.

The doctrine of *Res Ipsa Loquitur* allows plaintiffs to win some of the cases in which a gap in the evidence prevents them from proving the specifics of the defendants' negligent conduct.

Case 27: Boyer v. Iowa High School Athletic Association

Supreme Court of Iowa
Marian Boyer v. Iowa High School Athletic Association
260 Iowa 1061, 152 N.W.2d 293
July 11, 1967

Garfield, Chief Justice.

This is a law action by plaintiff, a paid <u>spectator</u> at a <u>tournament</u> basketball game under the management, supervision and direction of defendant Iowa High School Athletic Association, to recover for personal injuries from collapse of <u>bleachers</u>. Defendant appeals from judgment on jury verdict for plaintiff.

The tournament was held at Roosevelt Junior High School <u>fieldhouse</u> in Mason City under a written contract between the school and defendant. Plaintiff, her husband and a Mr. and Mrs. Garland sat together at the game on the top row of seats. The bleachers were of wood and steel in sections 16 feet long and seven rows high. Below each row of seats above the bottom one was a wood footrest. The top row of seats was eight or nine feet above the gymnasium floor.

When the bleachers are not in use they are pushed back toward the wall with the seats and footrests in a near-vertical, rather than horizontal, position. Normally it takes three men to pull the bleachers out from their folded or collapsed position ready for occupancy and to push them back toward the wall to make added floor space. There are handholes in the vertical board between the bottom seat and the floor for use in pulling the bleachers out. "They push in kind of hard." During the school year the bleachers are pulled out and pushed back two to four times a week.

The tournament game, between teams from Mason City and a nearby town, was close and exciting. Near the end of the game the spectators seated in front of those on the top row stood up on the seats or footrests "like they do at all exciting games," and plaintiff, her husband and the Garlands were forced to do likewise in order to see the finish of the game.

As the game ended and the spectators were leaving their position in the section occupied by plaintiff and those with her, the seats and footrests collapsed or folded back toward the wall, with the boards in more of a vertical position. Plaintiff and Mr. Garland were thrown onto the floor, plaintiff's husband was left hanging by one foot on the bleachers, head down. Mrs. Gerland had stepped back from the top footrest to the seat on which she had been sitting and which was left intact. She did not fall. Plaintiff's injuries are not an issue on this appeal.

Only the one section of bleachers collapsed. Everyone in it was standing toward the end of the game. The Boyers and Garlands had been directed to the seats they occupied. There were no aisles or spaces unoccupied by spectators in the bleachers. The spectators ordinarily left the bleachers, as they attempted to do this time, by stepping from their seats or footrests to those below.

I. Plaintiff pleaded her case in two counts or

divisions, one charging specific acts of negligence, the other in reliance on the doctrine of *Res Ipsa Loquitur*. We have frequently held this is permissible provided, of course, the doctrine is properly applicable. *Eaves v. City of Ottumwa*, 240 Iowa 956, 968, 38 N.W. 2d 761; *Ruud v. Grimm*, 252 Iowa 1266, 1274, 110 N. W. 2d 321, 325.

The trial court ruled there was no evidence to support the charges of specific negligence and withdrew them from jury consideration. The case was submitted to the jury on the doctrine of *Res Ipsa Loquitur*.

II. Defendant first assigns error in the court's refusal to withdraw from the jury the division based on *Res Ipsa Loquitur*.

"Under the doctrine referred to, where injury occurs by an instrumentality under the exclusive control and management of defendant and the occurrence is such as in the ordinary course of things would not happen if reasonable care had been used, the happening of the injury permits but does not compel an inference that defendant was negligent." *Shinofield v. Curtis*, 245 Iowa 1352, 1360, 66 N.W. 2d 465, 470.

"... In considering the applicability of *Res Ipsa Loquitur*, the question whether the particular occurrence is such as would not happen if reasonable care had been used rests on common experience and not at all on evidence in the particular case that tends in itself to show such occurrence was in facts the result of negligence. *Shinofield v. Curtis, supra.*" *Smith v. Ullerich*, Iowa, 145 N.W. 2d 1, 5.

Thus the two foundation facts for application of the *res ipsa* doctrine, which permits an inference of defendant's negligence from happening of the injury, are: (1) exclusive control and management by defendant of the instrumentality which causes the injury, and (2) the occurrence is such as in the ordinary course of things would not happen if reasonable care had been used.

We think the jury could properly find these foundation facts existed and infer therefrom plaintiff's injury was caused by defendant's negligence. Bleachers designed for use by spectators at athletic events do not ordinarily collapse, when used as they normally are, without negligence of those having control and management thereof.

Defendant asserts the *res ipsa* doctrine does not apply, first, because it is said the evidence of the cause of the collapse was accessible to plaintiff and not peculiarly accessible to defendant. As plaintiff admits in argument, under our decisions the underlying reason for the *res ipsa* rule is that the chief evidence of the true cause of the injury is practically accessible to defendant but inaccessible to the injured person. See *Smith v. Ullerich*, supra, 145 N. W. 2d 1, 6; *Shinofield v. Curtis*, supra, 245 Iowa 1352, 1360, 66 N. W. 2d 465, 470; *Eaves v. City of Ottumwa*, supra, 240 Iowa 956, 972, 38 N. W. 2d 761, 770. See also *Sample v. Schwenck*, 243 Iowa 1189, 1198, 54 N. W. 2d 527, 532.

In these precedents one or both of the foundation facts above referred to were lacking and the absence of what we have said is the underlying reason for the rule was given as an added reason why it was not applicable to the particular case. We have never held presence of this "underlying reason" is an indispensable requirement for application of the doctrine.

Nor are we persuaded evidence of the true cause of the collapse or partial collapse of the bleachers was not peculiarly accessible to defendant rather than to plaintiff. The athletic director of the Mason City schools was acting manager of the tournament. He and the head custodian at Roosevelt Junior High School must be deemed, under the contract between the school and defendant, to have been acting under the management, supervision, and direction of defendant. They had the exclusive control and management of the bleachers at least until game time and had the best opportunity to then discover any defect in them which may have caused the collapse.

We are told plaintiff had as much access to the bleachers immediately after the accident as defendant did and could discover any defect in them. A seriously injured person could hardly be expected to then examine the bleachers for defects rather than to be concerned with proper treatment of her injuries.

Argument that so far as shown no part of the bleachers was broken or out of place merely indicates absence of specific acts of negligence and does not negative applicability of the *res ipsa* doctrine. Indeed where the precise cause of the injury clearly appears or is beyond dispute there is no room for inference and the *res ipsa* rule has no application. *Eaves v. City of Ottumwa, supra,* 240 Iowa 956, 968, 38 N. W. 2d 761, 768; *Schneider v. Swaney Motor Car Co.,* 257 Iowa 1177, 1185, 136 N. W. 2d 338, 343.

The argument that the only permissible conclusion to be drawn from the evidence is that the movement of the spectators at the end of the game caused the bleachers to collapse cannot be accepted. Such a conclusion would rest wholly on speculation or conjecture. There is no evidence to support it. Assuming, but not deciding, this would be a defense to the *res ipsa* doctrine, it was defendant's burden to rebut the inference of negligence. *Thompson v. Burke Engin. Sales Co.,* 252 Iowa 146, 152, 106 N. W. 2d 351, 355; *Hall v. Town of Keota,* 248 Iowa 131, 143, 79 N. W. 2d 784, 791; *Larrabee v. Des Moines Tent & A. Co.,* 189 Iowa 319, 325, 178 N. W. 373.

conjecture 猜测，假设，推测

Such limited control of the bleachers as plaintiff and other spectators may have had during and immediately following the game did not, as a matter of law, render the doctrine of *Res Ipsa Loquitur* inapplicable. The jury could find defendant and its agents were in control of the bleachers at the time of the negligent act, as failure to inspect, which subsequently resulted in injury to plaintiff and that she and the other spectators did nothing improper or unusual during their occupancy of them. *See* precedents last above, also *Benedict v. Eppley Hotel Co.,* 159 Neb. 23, 65 N. W. 2d 224, 229 – 230; *Van Stavaren v. F. W. Woolworth Co.,* 29 N. J. Super. 197, 102 A. 2d 59.

Defendant seeks to distinguish most of the decisions cited by plaintiff as to applicability of *res ipsa* on the ground evidence was there received of some defect which may have caused collapse of the

detract 减损,使分心	seat on which the injured person was sitting. In our view this does not detract from their weight as precedents. Introduction of evidence of specific negligence does not deprive a plaintiff of the right to have the *res ipsa* doctrine submitted to the jury in support of a general allegation of negligence in another count. Eaves v. City of Ottumwa, supra, 240 Iowa 956, 967-968, 38 N.W.2d 761, 768; Schneider v. Swaney Motor Car Co., supra, 257 Iowa 1177, 1185, 136 N.W.2d 338, 343.
deprive somebody of something 剥夺某人某物	
direct verdict 直接裁断	III. Defendant assigns error in the overruling of its motion to direct verdict on the ground there is no sufficient evidence to show ordinary prudence would have suggested to defendant that any negligence on its part would probably result in injury to someone. We find the assignment without merit.
	In argument on this point it seems to be assumed cause of collapse of the bleachers was movement of the spectators as the game ended. As stated in the preceding division, we think this does not appear. The precedents cited consider the liability of a proprietor of a place of amusement or entertainment for sudden, isolated acts of third persons which could not reasonably be anticipated. A long quotation from Foust v. Kinley, 254 Iowa 690, 117 N.W.2d 843, constitutes the principal part of the argument. We regard these cases as not pertinent to the issues submitted to the jury.
amusement 娱乐,娱乐活动,消遣	
entertainment 娱乐	
isolate 使孤立	
anticipate 预期,预料	
quotation 引证(指向法庭或法官提出成文法、法庭意见、判例或其他权威言论的准确语句,以支持所提出的论点或主张)	
tenant 土地保有人(指依任何权利占有或持有土地的人,无论这些保有是因上下级的封赠,还是依不动产租赁合同而产生)	IV. Instruction 7 told the jury defendant was the tenant or possessor of the premises where the game was played, including the bleachers, and was required to use reasonable care to protect from injury those who came there at its invitation. Defendant objected to the instruction on the ground the construction of the contract between defendant and the school was for the jury, not the court. Overruling the objection is assigned as error.
construct (construction) 解释(合同条款的释义)	Defendant also requested instruction 9 which would have told the jurors it was for them to determine whether, under the contract between defendant and the school, the responsibility to use

reasonable care to maintain the bleachers in a reasonably safe condition was upon defendant or the school. The request was refused.

Defendant's assignment of error in the giving of instruction 7 and refusal of its ninth request is that it was for the jury, not the court, to determine what rights and duties, if any, defendant had toward the maintenance and care of the physical plant. Defendant's first brief point under this assignment is that the interpretation of an ambiguous or uncertain contract is for the jury. Plaintiff, in effect, admits this brief point as an abstract proposition. The arguments center about whether the contract is ambiguous or uncertain as defendant asserts or clear and unambiguous as plaintiff contends. We find no error in the respect asserted.

A contract is ambiguous when, after application of pertinent rules of interpretation to the face of the instrument, a genuine uncertainty exists as to which of two or more meanings is the proper one. The question of interpretation, *i.e.*, the meaning to be given the words of a contract, is one of fact which may or may not be for the judge or the jury.

Construction of a contract means determination of its legal operation — its legal effect upon the action of courts. Construction is always a matter of law for the court. *Morris Plan Leasing Co. v. Bingham Feed and Grain Co.*, 259 Iowa 404, 143 N. W. 2d 404, 412; *Fetters v. City of Des Moines*, Iowa, 149 N. W. 2d 815, 818.

Section one of the contract between defendant and the school provides:

> The School agrees that the ... Association's DISTRICT Tournament shall be conducted and played in the School gymnasium on the following dates ... and for such purpose to make available and furnish its gymnasium, necessary equipment other than that furnished by the Association as herein provided, door men, ushers, announcers, scorers, timekeepers, and to have its superintendent or principal act as active manager thereof and conduct the tournament Subject to the management,

doormen 门卫
usher 引座员
announcer 报幕员,广播员
scorer 记录员,记分员
timekeeper 计时员
superintendent 监督人,负责人

supervision and direction of the Association in accordance with its rules and regulations.

Section seven of the contract provides defendant agrees to pay and the school agrees to accept as full compensation For the use of all facilities, equipment, personnel and services to be furnished by the school twenty per cent of the tournament receipts, not exceeding an average of $200 per night.

These provisions seem clearly to constitute defendant tenant or possessor of the gymnasium and equipment therein and to place the personnel and services to be furnished by the school under defendant's management, supervision and direction, for the duration of the tournament. There was no need for extrinsic evidence as an aid to interpretation of the contract nor do we find such evidence was offered.

It seems to us a rule applicable here is that presumptively the law regards the tenant of property as the owner for the time-being and subject to all the responsibilities of one in possession to one who enters upon it by invitation. See Fetters v. City of Des Moines, supra, Iowa, 149 N.W.2d 815, 819–820.

"Presumptively the one who occupies premises is liable to one who is negligently injured while rightfully thereon." Burner v. Higman & Skinner Co., 127 Iowa 580, 585, 103 N.W. 802, 804; Fetters case, supra.

It is perhaps unnecessary to this division to quote one of the rules and regulations referred to in section one of the contract between defendant and the school. However item 16 thereof has a distinct bearing on the case and may be set out. It provides:

Item 16 — CHECKING BLEACHERS AND OVERCROWDING OF GYMNASIUMS

Your attention is called to the importance of checking your bleachers, to avoid overcrowding of them.

As you probably remember, several years ago a section of bleachers collapsed at the Purdue University Field House. Two students were killed and scores hospitalized. This is a serious matter and you are urged to check carefully your bleachers to ascertain that they are in good condition, well-supported and do not permit overcrowding of these bleachers. An announcement might well be made at each game urging those people on the bleachers to sit quietly. Every effort should be made <u>to see to it</u> that no concerted swaying movement of fans is permitted. Check your bleachers before each session. Above everything else, do not overcrowd the bleachers and do not permit crowding in the exits and aisles. High School tournaments have had a good record in Iowa. Let's keep the record <u>untarnished</u>.

to see to it 务必

untarnished 无污点的

cautionary 警告的

This language must be deemed <u>cautionary</u> instructions to persons, as above indicated, under defendant's management, supervision, and direction during the tournament.

V. Error is assigned in the refusal of defendant's first requested instruction which stated the user of a manufactured product is not required to take added precautionary measures to make it safer but is authorized to use it in the condition as purchased from the manufacturer, <u>ordinary wear and tear</u> excepted, provided it is used in the manner and for the purpose for which it was manufactured. Also that the jury could not find defendant negligent for failing to make the bleachers safer by adding something thereto if they were being used in the manner and for the purpose for which they were manufactured.

ordinary wear and tear 通常的损耗

Defendant's objection to the refusal of this request asserted it allowed the jury to speculate as to a duty on defendant to improve a manufactured product whereas it was under no such duty.

The request appears to be based on language in *Wagner v. Larson*, 257 Iowa 1202, 1211, 1212, 136 N. W. 2d 312, 318. Its abstract correctness may be assumed. However, we think the court was not required to so instruct and that to have done so would have injected into the case an issue not pleaded, as the case was submitted to the jury, and it might have led to confusion. Had the jury based recovery on defendant's failure to make the bleachers safer than when obtained from the manufacturer, it would have gone outside the court's instructions. See *Hart v. Hinkley*, 215 Iowa 915, 919, 247 N.W. 258; *Murphy v. City of Waterloo*, 255 Iowa 557, 566, 123 N.W.2d 49, 54.

VI. Defendant assigns error in the refusal of its second requested instruction which would have called attention to evidence there had been no prior similar incidents; such evidence tended to show absence of danger and, in effect, lack of knowledge of danger by defendant, and should be given such weight for such purpose as the jury saw fit to give it.

Defendant's objection to the refusal of this request includes the assertion that without it the jury would not know what weight to give to the testimony referred to.

The court properly refused this second request. Instructions should not ordinarily call attention to testimony favorable to one party because they give undue prominence thereto. *Eaves v. City of Ottumwa, supra*, 240 Iowa 956, 967, 38 N.W.2d 761, 768; *Vance v. Grohe*, 223 Iowa 1109, 1118, 274 N.W.2d 902. See also *Belle v. Iowa State Highway Comm.*, 256 Iowa 43, 50-51, 126 N.W.2d 311, 315-316.

VII. Defendant's final assignment is in failure to sustain its motion for directed verdict on the ground plaintiff did not prove negligence of defendant.

As stated in division I hereof, the court ruled there was no evidence to support the charges of specific negligence and withdrew them from jury consideration. Defendant argues it follows from this the count based on *Res Ipsa Loquitur* should also have been withdrawn since, we are told, there was no failure of the mechanism.

This final assertion is not quite accurate. The bleachers collapsed to a position where occupants were thrown to the floor. It is true there is no evidence of the specific cause of the collapse. But it does not appear, certainly not as a matter of law, there was no failure of the mechanism. In any event, we think this assigned error is answered by our holding in division II that absence of evidence of specific acts of negligence does not negative applicability of the *res ipsa* doctrine.

We find no reversible error in any respect assigned and argued.

Affirmed.

All justices concur except Mason, J., who takes no part and Becker and Rawlings, JJ., who concur specially in the result.

Becker, Justice (concurring in result).

I concur in result.

It seems both unnecessary and unwise to continue to cling to the exclusive control doctrine when we have decided cases where exclusive control was not in fact proved and yet approved the use of the doctrine of *res ipsa*, *Weidert v. Monahan Post Legionnaire Club*, 243 Iowa 643, 51 N. W. 2d 400; *Sutcliffe v. Fort Dodge Gas & Elec. Co.*, 218 Iowa 1386, 257 N. W. 406; *Thompson v. Burke Engin. Sales Co.*, 252 Iowa 146, 106 N. W. 2d 351, and *Larrabee v. Des Moines Tent & Awning Co.*, 189 Iowa 319, 178 N. W. 373. Many authorities on the subject indicate quite clearly that exclusive control is not, or should not be, a prerequisite to the application of the doctrine of *Res Ipsa Loquitur*.

Restatement, Second, Torts, section 238 D(g) p. 161, states: "Exclusive control is merely one fact which establishes the responsibility of the defendant; and if it can be established otherwise, exclusive control is not essential to a *Res Ipsa Loquitur* case. The essential question becomes one of whether the probable cause is one which the defendant is under a duty to the plaintiff to anticipate or guard against."

Harper and James, THE LAW OF TORTS, section 19.7, p. 1085, states: "Viewed in this light the requirement of proof of exclusive control is immediately seen to impose too strict a burden upon plaintiffs. Exclusive control may have the requisite logical tendency, but there are also many other ways (not involving exclusive control) in which the probable negligence can be attributed to defendant. And in fact the courts do not generally apply this requirement as it is literally stated, although

cling to 坚持

mechanical insistence upon it has brought about an occasional restrictive result. The requirement as it is generally applied is more accurately stated as one that the evidence must afford a rational basis for concluding that the cause of the accident was probably 'such that the defendant would be responsible for any negligence connected with it.'"

Other authorities might be cited for the proposition that while exclusive control is an element to be considered, it is not a prerequisite to the use of the doctrine.

3. Damage

A *prima facie* case of negligence also requires proof of damage. Negligent conduct alone is not tortuous. The negligence must cause some actual loss or damage; without injury, there is no recovery. The damages recoverable in a negligence action include personal injury and property damage. Generally, the plaintiff is entitled to compensation for all his damages, past, present, and prospective; both special and general. This includes fair and adequate compensation for medical expenses and lost earnings plus amounts for pain and suffering (including emotional distress), together with compensation for impaired future earning capacity. The latter will be discounted to present value so as to avoid an excess award; *i.e.*, the plaintiff receives an amount that, if securely invested, would produce the income that the jury wishes him to have. The measure of damages for property damage is the reasonable cost of repair, or, if the property has been almost or completely destroyed, its fair market value at the time of the accident. If the defendant's conduct was "wanton and willful," reckless, or malicious, then punitive damages may be granted to the plaintiff.

In order to get damages, the plaintiff must exercise his duty to take reasonable steps to mitigate damages. In property damage cases, the plaintiff has a duty to preserve and safeguard the property; and in personal injury cases he has a duty to seek appropriate treatment to effect a cure or healing and to prevent

personal injury 人身伤害

property damage 财产损失

aggravation. Failure to mitigate precludes recovery of any additional damages caused by aggravation of the injury.

Damages are not reduced or mitigated by reason of benefits received by the plaintiff from other sources, e. g., health insurance, sick-pay from employer. Hence, at trial, the defendant may not introduce evidence relating to any such financial aid from other sources. This is called "collateral source rule." A growing number of states have made exceptions to this rule in certain types of actions (e.g. medical malpractice actions), allowing the defendant to introduce evidence of insurance awards or disability benefits.

sick-pay 病假工资

collateral source rule 平行来源规则（指受害人从与侵权行为人完全无关的来源获得的赔偿，不能从侵权行为人所应负担的赔偿中扣除）

medical malpractice 医疗责任事故，医疗失职

4. Causation

The final element in an action for negligence is a close causal connection between the defendant's conduct and the injury that occurred. Causation has two components: cause in fact and proximate cause.

The law determines whether A is the cause in fact of B by raising the question of "whether, but for A, B would not have happened." This is called the "but for" test, which will determine that an act or omission to act is the cause in fact of an injury when the injury would not have occurred but for the act. For example, failure to provide a fire escape is a cause of death of one who was thereby unable to flee a fire, but it is not a cause of death of one who suffocated in bed.

In addition to being a cause in fact, the defendant's conduct must also be a proximate cause of the injury. Not all injuries "actually" caused by the defendant will be deemed to have been proximately caused by his acts. Thus, the doctrine of proximate causation is a limitation of liability and deals with liability or nonliability for unforeseeable or unusual consequences of one's acts. One important element of proximate cause is foreseeability: Would the defendant reasonably foresee the injurious results of his or her action? The law limits the defendant's responsibility to immediate or foreseeable harm as opposed to remote or unforeseeable harm. The rules of proximate cause

cause in fact 事实（上的）原因

proximate cause 近因；实质性原因

suffocate 窒息，闷死

sometimes permit a defendant to escape liability even if all the other elements of the *prima facie* case — cause-in-fact, negligence, and harm — have been established.

However, causation is different from the duty issue, even though both involve notions of foreseeability. The duty element of negligence focuses on whether the defendant's conduct foreseeably creates a broader "zone of risk" that poses a general threat of harm to others. The proximate causation element, on the other hand, is concerned with whether and to what extent the defendant's conduct foreseeably and substantially causes the specific injury that actually occurred.

Causation issue is also different from liability issue. Once the proximate cause is found, the defendant is liable for all harmful results that are the normal incidents of and within the increased risk caused by his acts. This is called "eggshell skull rule" which is illustrated in the context of a battery case in *Vosburg v. Putney*, reprinted in Section 2.1.1 of Chapter 6 of this book. For example, the original tortfeasor is usually liable for the aggravation of the plaintiff's condition caused by the malpractice of the plaintiff's treating physician.

Causation is a very complicated issue in the tort of negligence. This section just briefly introduces the concept, and the readers may want to read more books and articles discussing this issue. Below are some cases dealing with the causation issue.

4.1 Case 28: **Lyons v. Midnight Sun Transportation Services, Inc.**

Supreme Court of Alaska
David Lyons v. Midnight Sun
Transportation Services, Inc.
928 P.2d 1202
Dec. 27, 1996

Per Curiam.

I. Facts and Proceedings
Esther Hunter-Lyons was killed when her Volkswagen

van was struck broadside by a truck driven by David Jette and owned by Midnight Sun Transportation Services, Inc. When the accident occurred, Jette was driving south in the right-hand lane of Arctic Boulevard in Anchorage. Hunter-Lyons pulled out of a parking lot in front of him. Jette braked and steered to the left, but Hunter-Lyons continued to pull out further into the traffic lane. Jette's truck collided with Hunter-Lyons's vehicle. David Lyons, the deceased's husband, filed suit, asserting that Jette had been speeding and driving negligently.

At trial, conflicting testimony was introduced regarding Jette's speed before the collision. Lyons's expert witness testified that Jette may have been driving as fast as 53 miles per hour. Midnight Sun's expert testified that Jette probably had been driving significantly slower and that the collision could have occurred even if Jette had been driving at the speed limit, 35 miles per hour. Lyons's expert later testified that if Jette had stayed in his own lane, and had not steered to the left, there would have been no collision. Midnight Sun's expert contended that steering to the left when a vehicle pulls out onto the roadway from the right is a normal response and is generally the safest course of action to follow.

Over Lyons's objection, the jury was given an instruction on the sudden emergency doctrine.① The jury found that Jette, in fact, had been negligent, but his negligence was not a legal cause of the accident.

broadside 侧面

lane 车道,街巷,小路,狭窄的通道

brake 刹车
steer 驾驶,操纵

sudden emergency doctrine 紧迫事件原则(根据该原则,有主要过失的被告,在有突发的危险且该危险系由对方的过失所造成的情况下,不负法律责任)

---

① Jury Instruction #17 read in its entirety:
  Midnight Sun claims that it is not liable for plaintiffs' harm because David Jette acted with reasonable care in an emergency situation.
  In an emergency, a person is not expected or required to use the same judgment and care that is required in calmer and more deliberate moments. If, in an emergency, a person acts as a reasonably careful person would act in a similar emergency, there is no negligence even though afterwards it might appear that a different course of action would have been better and safer.
  For Midnight Sun to win on this claim, you must decide that it is more likely true than not true that:
  1. there was an emergency situation which was a sudden and unexpected peril presenting actual or apparent imminent danger to someone;
  2. David Jette did not cause the emergency; and
  3. David Jette acted as a reasonably careful person would have acted in similar circumstances.
  If you do not find all of these three facts, then you should decide whether Midnight Sun was negligent on the basis of the other instructions.

Lyons appeals, arguing that the court should not have given the jury the sudden emergency instruction.

II. Analysis and Discussion

The sudden emergency doctrine is a rule of law which states that a person confronted with a sudden and unexpected peril, not resulting from that person's own negligence, is not expected to exercise the same judgment and prudence the law requires of a person in calmer and more deliberate moments. The person confronted with the imminent peril must, however, act as a reasonable person would under the same conditions. *Beaumaster v. Crandall*, 576 P. 2d 988, 991 (Alaska 1978).

Lyons argues that it was error for the trial court to give the sudden emergency instruction to the jury in this case; that the sudden emergency instruction is never appropriate in an automobile accident case; and that the instruction is incompatible with Alaska's comparative negligence system of apportioning tort liability.

Midnight Sun maintains that the sudden emergency instruction was warranted by the facts and is not incompatible with the comparative fault system.

A. Any Error Was Harmless

We find that Lyons has little cause to complain of the sudden emergency instruction because the jury decided the issue in his favor. To the question "Was Midnight Sun's employee, David Jette, negligent?" the jury answered "YES." The jury finding of negligence indicates that the jury concluded David Jette was driving negligently or responded inappropriately when Ms. Hunter-Lyons entered the traffic lane and, thus, did not exercise the care and prudence a reasonable person would have exercised under the circumstances.

However, Lyons's claims were defeated on the basis of lack of causation. Although the jury found Jette to have been negligent, it also found that this negligence was not the legal cause of the accident. Duty, breach of duty, causation, and harm are the separate and distinct elements of a negligence claim, all of which must be proven before a defendant can be held liable for the plaintiff's injuries. See *Alvey v. Pioneer Oilfield Servs., Inc.*, 648 P. 2d 599, 600 (Alaska 1982) (listing elements of negligence in context of motion for summary judgment as duty, breach of duty, injury, and cause). The sudden emergency instruction addresses only the standard of care imposed on all people to act as a reasonable person would under the circumstances. The instruction could not have infected the jury's finding that Jette was not the legal cause of Ms. Hunter-Lyons's death.

 Further, we cannot say that the jury's finding of lack of causation was unreasonable. There was evidence presented at trial from which the jury could reasonably have drawn the conclusion that even though Jette was driving negligently, his negligence was not the proximate cause of the accident. Midnight Sun introduced expert testimony to the effect that the primary cause of the accident was Ms. Hunter-Lyons's action in pulling out of the parking lot in front of an oncoming truck. Terry Day, an accident reconstruction specialist testified that, depending on how fast Ms. Hunter-Lyons was moving, the accident could have happened even if Jette had been driving within the speed limit. Midnight Sun also introduced expert testimony to the effect that Jette responded properly to the unexpected introduction of an automobile in his traffic lane. Although all of this testimony was disputed by Lyons, a reasonable jury could have concluded that Ms. Hunter-Lyons caused the accident by abruptly pulling out in front of an oncoming truck, and that David Jette's negligence was not a contributing factor. With the element of causation lacking, even the most egregious negligence cannot result in liability.

infect 使受影响

egregious 惊人的,过分的

B. Sudden Emergency Instruction Disapproved
 Although any possible error resulting from the use of the sudden emergency instruction was rendered harmless by the jury finding that Jette's negligence was not a legal cause of the accident, we take this opportunity to disapprove of the instruction's further use. It adds nothing to the established law that the duty of care, which all must exercise, is to act

reasonably under the circumstances. The instruction is potentially confusing. Although we cannot say that the instruction is never appropriate, we discourage its employment. In support of this admonition, we offer the following background.

The sudden emergency doctrine arose as a method of <u>ameliorating</u> the, sometimes <u>harsh</u>, "all or nothing" rule in <u>contributory negligence</u> systems. For example, in *Stokes v. Saltonstall*, 38 U. S. 181（1839）, the United States Supreme Court approved the use of an early version of the sudden emergency instruction. *Id*. at 193. In that case, the plaintiff and his wife were injured while leaping from a <u>careening coach</u> <u>piloted</u> by a drunken driver. *Id*. at 182. The defendant claimed contributory negligence on the part of the plaintiffs which would have barred all recovery. *Id*. at 187 – 88. The court <u>endorsed</u> the doctrine wholeheartedly, stating:

> [T]o enable the plaintiff to sustain the action it is not necessary that he should have been thrown off the coach; it is sufficient if he were placed by the misconduct of the defendant, in such a situation as obliged him to adopt the alternative of a dangerous leap, or to remain at certain peril; if that position was occasioned by the fault of the defendant, the action may be supported. On the other hand, if the plaintiff's act resulted from a <u>rash</u> apprehension of danger, which did not exist, and the injury which he sustained is to be attributed to <u>rashness</u> and <u>imprudence</u>, he is not entitled to recover.

Id. at 193.

Although the doctrine came out of the <u>contributory negligence</u> regime, there is nothing about it which is inherently incompatible with a comparative fault system. Comparative negligence is a method of apportioning liability for a particular accident among the various parties who have been deemed negligent. The sudden emergency doctrine, in turn, is an expression of the applicable standard of care against which particular actions are judged in order to determine whether they were negligent in character. The fault of one person, determined in the light of a sudden emergency instruction, can be compared to the fault of another person, whose negligence may have created the emergency, with no logical inconsistency. Other courts have rejected the contention that the instruction cannot be used in a jurisdiction which has adopted a system of comparative negligence. *Young v. Clark*, 814 P. 2d 364, 368 (Colo. 1991); *Weiss v. Bal*, 501 N. W. 2d 478, 481 (Iowa 1993) ("[W]e reject plaintiffs' argument that such an instruction has no place in a comparative fault scheme."); *Ebach v. Ralston*, 510 N. W. 2d 604, 610 (N. D. 1994).

Although not inherently inconsistent with modern methods of apportioning liability, the sudden emergency instruction has, nevertheless, come under criticism, and some states have limited or abolished it. Reasoning that because the standard of care is expressed in terms of a reasonable person under the circumstances, several courts have concluded that the instruction is wholly redundant. Mississippi eliminated the instruction in *Knapp v. Stanford*, 392 So. 2d 196 (Miss. 1980), because the court believed the instruction only served to obfuscate the operation of the comparative negligence statute, and was often interpreted as requiring a higher standard of proof for a finding of negligence. *Id*. at 198. The justices ruled that the wiser policy would be to apply the general rules of negligence to all situations, and the jury should be left to consider only what a reasonable person would have done under the circumstances of a given case. *Id*. at 199. Likewise, Nebraska's highest court found that the instruction served no useful purpose. In *McClymont v. Morgan*, 238 Neb. 390, 470 N. W. 2d 768 (1991), the trial court refused to give the plaintiff's proposed instruction on the effect of an emergency. The supreme court affirmed, stating that the sudden emergency instruction gives undue emphasis to one aspect of the standard of care, and to one party's argument. *Id*. 470 N. W. 2d at 770. The effect of the emergency on the standard of care might still be argued to the jury. *Id*.

Other courts, while not banning the instruction

redundant (redundancy) 多余的(多余;冗长)

obfuscate 使迷乱,使模糊

altogether, have strongly discouraged its use. *Ellwood v. Peters*, 182 So. 2d 281 (Fla. App.), *cert. denied*, 188 So. 2d 814 (Fla. 1966); *DiCenzo v. Izawa*, 68 Haw. 528, 723 P. 2d 171 (1986); *Keel v. Compton*, 120 Ill. App. 2d 248, 256 N. E. 2d 848 (1970); *Gagnon v. Crane*, 126 N. H. 781, 498 A. 2d 718 (1985); *McKee v. Evans*, 380 Pa. Super. 120, 551 A. 2d 260, *app. denied*, 522 Pa. 600, 562 A. 2d 824 (1988).

Several courts have forbidden giving the instruction in automobile accident cases. Montana's supreme court, in *Simonson v. White*, 220 Mont. 14, 713 P. 2d 983 (1986), found no reason to give the sudden emergency instruction in an automobile accident case stating that the instruction adds nothing to the applicable law in any negligence case, that a driver must exercise due care under the circumstances, and that it tends to leave jurors with the impression that an emergency somehow excuses the driver from the ordinary standard of care. *Id*. 713 P. 2d at 989. An Oregon court has also expressed reservations about the use of the instruction in automobile cases. *Templeton v. Smith*, 88 Or. App. 266, 744 P. 2d 1325 (1987), *review denied*, 305 Or. 45, 749 P. 2d 1182 (1988).

In *Finley v. Wiley*, 103 N. J. Super. 95, 246 A. 2d 715 (App. Div. 1968), a New Jersey court stated it "entertain[ed] grave doubt as to whether a sudden emergency charge should ever be given in an ordinary automobile accident case." *Id*. 246 A. 2d at 719. The *Finley* court felt that the unexpected hazards of driving are, in fact, to be expected. *Id*. Quoting Prosser, TORTS, pp. 172 – 73 (3d ed. 1964) it said, "[U]nder present day traffic conditions, any driver of an automobile must be prepared for the sudden appearance of obstacles in the street ..." See also *Paiva v. Pfeiffer*, 229 N. J. Super. 276, 551 A. 2d 201, 204 – 05 (App. Div. 1988).

We believe that the sudden emergency instruction is a generally useless <u>appendage</u> to the law of negligence. With or without an emergency, the standard of care a person must exercise is still that of a reasonable person under the circumstances. With or without the instruction, parties are still entitled to

appendage 附属物

present evidence at trial which will establish what the circumstances were, and are also entitled to argue to the jury that they acted as a reasonable person would have in light of those circumstances. Thus, barring circumstances that we cannot at the moment hypothesize, a sudden emergency instruction serves no positive function. Further, the instruction may cause confusion by appearing to imply that one party is less blameworthy than the other. Therefore, we hold that it should not be used unless a court finds that the particular and peculiar facts of a case warrant more explanation of the standard of care than is generally required.

hypothesize 假设,假定

blameworthy 该受责备的,应受谴责的

III. Conclusion

Based on the above, we conclude that any error in giving the instruction was harmless. However, given the redundancy of the instruction and its potential for sowing confusion, we discourage its use in future cases.

Affirmed.

4.2 Case 29: Palsgraf v. The Long Island Railroad Co.

Palsgraf v. The Long island Railroad Co.
Court of Appeals of New York
248 N. Y. 339, 162 N. E. 99
May 29, 1928

Cardozo, Ch. J.

Plaintiff was standing on a platform of defendant's railroad after buying a ticket to go to Rockaway Beach. A train stopped at the station, bound for another place. Two men ran forward to catch it. One of the men reached the platform of the car without mishap, though the train was already moving. The other man, carrying a package, jumped aboard the car, but seemed unsteady as if about to fall. A guard on the car, who had held the door open, reached forward to help him in, and another guard on the platform pushed him from behind. In this act, the package was dislodged, and fell upon the rails. It was a package of small size, about fifteen inches long, and was covered by a newspaper. In fact it contained

mishap 不幸之事,灾祸

dislodge 使移动,离开原位

fireworks, but there was nothing in its appearance to give notice of its contents. The fireworks when they fell exploded. The shock of the explosion threw down some scales at the other end of the platform, many feet away. The scales struck the plaintiff, causing injuries for which she sues.

The conduct of the defendant's guard, if a wrong in its relation to the holder of the package, was not a wrong in its relation to the plaintiff, standing far away. Relatively to her it was not negligence at all. Nothing in the situation gave notice that the falling package had in it the potency of peril to persons thus removed. Negligence is not actionable unless it involves the invasion of a legally protected interest, the violation of a right. "Proof of negligence in the air, so to speak, will not do." Pollock, TORTS (11th ed.) 455; *Martin v. Herzog*, 228 N. Y. 164, 170; *cf. Salmond*, TORTS (6th ed.) 24. "Negligence is the absence of care, according to the circumstances" Willes, J., in *Vaughan v. Taff Vale Ry. Co.*, 5 H. & N. 679, 688; 1 Beven, NEGLIGENCE (4th ed.) 7; *Paul v. Consol. Fireworks Co.*, 212 N. Y. 117; *Adams v. Bullock*, 227 N. Y. 208, 211; *Parrott v. Wells-Fargo Co.*, 15 Wall. [U. S.] 524. The plaintiff as she stood upon the platform of the station might claim to be protected against intentional invasion of her bodily security. Such invasion is not charged. She might claim to be protected against unintentional invasion by conduct involving in the thought of reasonable men an unreasonable hazard that such invasion would ensue. These, from the point of view of the law, were the bounds of her immunity, with perhaps some rare exceptions, survivals for the most part of ancient forms of liability, where conduct is held to be at the peril of the actor. *Sullivan v. Dunham*, 161 N. Y. 290. If no hazard was apparent to the eye of ordinary vigilance, an act innocent and harmless, at least to outward seeming, with reference to her, did not take to itself the quality of a tort because it happened to be a wrong, though apparently not one involving the risk of bodily insecurity, with reference to some one else. "In every instance, before negligence can be predicated of a given act, back of the act must be sought and found a duty to the individual complaining, the observance of which would have averted or avoided the injury." (McSherry, C. J., in *W. Va. Central R. Co. v. State*, 96 Md. 652, 666; *cf. Norfolk & Western Ry. Co. v. Wood*, 99 Va. 156, 158, 159; *Hughes v. Boston & Maine R. R. Co.*, 71 N. H. 279, 284; *U. S. Express Co. v. Everest*, 72 Kan. 517; *Emry v. Roanoke Nav. Co.*, 111 N. C. 94, 95; *Vaughan v. Transit Dev. Co.*, 222 N. Y. 79; *Losee v. Clute*, 51 N. Y. 494; *DiCaprio v. N. Y. C. R. R. Co.*, 231 N. Y. 94; 1 SHEARMAN & REDFIELD ON NEGLIGENCE, § 8, and cases cited; COOLEY ON TORTS (3d ed.) 1411; JAGGARD ON TORTS, VOL. 2, p. 826; WHARTON, NEGLIGENCE, § 24; Bohlen, STUDIES IN THE LAW OF TORTS, p.601). "The ideas of negligence and duty are strictly correlative."(Bowen, L. J., in *Thomas v. Quartermaine*, 18 Q. B. D. 685, 694) The plaintiff sues in her own right for a wrong personal to her, and not as the vicarious beneficiary of a breach of duty to another.

  A different conclusion will involve us, and swiftly too, in a maze of contradictions. A guard stumbles over a package which has been left upon a platform. It seems to be a bundle of newspapers. It turns out to be a can of dynamite. To the eye of ordinary vigilance, the bundle is abandoned waste, which may be kicked or trod on with impunity. Is a passenger at the other end of the platform protected by the law against the unsuspected hazard concealed beneath the waste? If not, is the result to be any different, so far as the distant passenger is concerned, when the guard stumbles over a valise which a truckman or a porter has left upon the walk? The passenger far away, if the victim of a wrong at all, has a cause of action, not derivative, but original and primary. His claim to be protected against invasion of his bodily security is neither greater nor less because the act resulting in the invasion is a wrong to another far removed. In this case, the rights that are said to have been violated, the interests said to have been invaded, are not even of the same order. The man was not injured in his person nor even put in danger. The purpose of the act, as well as its effect, was to make his person safe. If there was a wrong to him at all, which may very well be doubted, it was a wrong to a property interest only, the safety of his package. Out of this wrong to property, which threatened injury to nothing else, there has passed, we are told, to the plaintiff by derivation or succession a right of action for the invasion of an interest of another order, the right to bodily security. The diversity of interests emphasizes the futility of the effort to build the plaintiff's right upon the basis of a wrong to someone else. The gain is one of emphasis, for a like result would follow if the interests were the same. Even then, the orbit of the danger as disclosed to the eye of reasonable vigilance would be the orbit of the duty. One who jostles one's neighbor in a crowd does not invade the rights of others standing at the outer fringe when the unintended contact casts a bomb upon the ground. The wrongdoer as to them is the man who carries the bomb, not the one who explodes it without suspicion of the danger. Life will have to be made over, and human nature transformed, before prevision so extravagant can be accepted as the norm of conduct, the customary standard to which behavior must conform.

The argument for the plaintiff is built upon the shifting meanings of such words as "wrong" and "wrongful," and shares their instability. What the plaintiff must show is "a wrong" to herself, i.e., a violation of her own right, and not merely a wrong to someone else, nor conduct "wrongful" because unsocial, but not "a wrong" to anyone. We are told that one who drives at reckless speed through a crowded city street is guilty of a negligent act and, therefore, of a wrongful one irrespective of the consequences. Negligent the act is, and wrongful in the sense that it is unsocial, but wrongful and unsocial in relation to other travelers, only because the eye of vigilance perceives the risk of damage. If the same act were to be committed on a speedway or a race course, it would lose its wrongful quality. The risk reasonably to be perceived defines the duty to be obeyed, and risk imports relation; it is risk to another or to others within the range of apprehension. Seavey, *Negligence, Subjective or Objective*, 41 H. L. Rv. 6; *Boronkay v. Robinson & Carpenter*, 247 N. Y. 365. This does not mean, of course, that one who launches a destructive force is always relieved of liability if the force, though known to be destructive, pursues an unexpected path. "It was not necessary that the defendant should have had notice of the particular method in which an accident would occur, if the possibility of an accident was clear to the ordinarily prudent eye." *Munsey v. Webb*, 231 U. S. 150, 156; *Condran v. Park & Tilford*, 213 N. Y. 341, 345; *Robert v. U. S. E. F. Corp.*, 240 N. Y. 474, 477. Some acts, such as shooting, are so imminently dangerous to anyone who may come within reach of the missile, however unexpectedly, as to impose a duty of prevision not far from that of an insurer. Even today, and much oftener in earlier stages of the law, one acts sometimes at one's peril. Jeremiah Smith, *Tort and Absolute Liability*, 30 H. L. Rv. 328; Street, FOUNDATIONS OF LEGAL LIABILITY, VOL. 1, pp. 77, 78. Under this head, it may be, fall certain cases of what is known as transferred intent, an act willfully dangerous to A resulting by misadventure in injury to B (*Talmage v. Smith*, 101 Mich. 370, 374). These cases aside, wrong is defined in terms of the natural or probable, at least when unintentional. *Parrot v. Wells-Fargo Co.* (*The Nitro-Glycerine Case*), 15 Wall. [U. S.] 524. The range of reasonable apprehension is at times a question for the court, and at times, if varying inferences are possible, a question for the jury. Here, by concession, there was nothing in the situation to suggest to the most cautious mind that the parcel wrapped in newspaper would spread wreckage through the station. If the guard had thrown it down knowingly and willfully, he would not have threatened the plaintiff's safety, so far as appearances could warn him. His conduct would not have involved, even then, an unreasonable probability of invasion of her bodily security. Liability can be no greater where the act is inadvertent.

Negligence, like risk, is thus a term of relation. Negligence in the abstract, apart from things related,

apprehension 忧虑,恐惧,担心

at one's peril 自担风险

misadventure 意外事故

concession 认可,让步

affront 有意冒犯,公开侮辱

offshoot 分支,支流

trespass on the case 间接侵害之诉(普通法的侵害诉讼形式之一,指一方的侵害行为与另一方的损失或伤害之间有间接而非直接的因果关系,是现代法中过失损害侵权之诉的前身)

right of subrogation 代位权

is surely not a tort, if indeed it is understandable at all (Bowen, L. J., in *Thomas v. Quartermaine*, 18 Q. B. D. 685, 694). Negligence is not a tort unless it results in the commission of a wrong, and the commission of a wrong imports the violation of a right, in this case, we are told, the right to be protected against interference with one's bodily security. But bodily security is protected, not against all forms of interference or aggression, but only against some. One who seeks redress at law does not make out a cause of action by showing without more that there has been damage to his person. If the harm was not willful, he must show that the act as to him had possibilities of danger so many and apparent as to entitle him to be protected against the doing of it though the harm was unintended. Affront to personality is still the keynote of the wrong. Confirmation of this view will be found in the history and development of the action on the case. Negligence as a basis of civil liability was unknown to mediaeval law. 8 Holdsworth, HISTORY OF ENGLISH LAW, p. 449; Street, FOUNDATIONS OF LEGAL LIABILITY, VOL. 1, pp. 189, 190). For damage to the person, the sole remedy was trespass, and trespass did not lie in the absence of aggression, and that direct and personal. Holdsworth, op. cit. p. 453; Street, op. cit. vol. 3, pp. 258, 260, vol. 1, pp. 71, 74. Liability for other damage, as where a servant without orders from the master does or omits something to the damage of another, is a plant of later growth. Holdsworth, op. cit. 450, 457; Wigmore, *Responsibility for Tortious Acts*, VOL. 3, ESSAYS IN ANGLO-AMERICAN LEGAL HISTORY, 520, 523, 526, 533. When it emerged out of the legal soil, it was thought of as a variant of trespass, an offshoot of the parent stock. This appears in the form of action, which was known as trespass on the case. Holdsworth, op. cit. p. 449; cf. *Scott v. Shepard*, 2 Wm. Black. 892; Green, RATIONALE OF PROXIMATE CAUSE, p. 19. The victim does not sue derivatively, or by right of subrogation, to vindicate an interest invaded in the person of another. Thus to view his cause of action is to ignore the fundamental difference between tort and crime. Holland, JURISPRUDENCE (12th ed.), p. 328.

He sues for breach of a duty owing to himself.

The law of causation, remote or proximate, is thus foreign to the case before us. The question of liability is always anterior to the question of the measure of the consequences that go with liability. If there is no tort to be redressed, there is no occasion to consider what damage might be recovered if there were a finding of a tort. We may assume, without deciding, that negligence, not at large or in the abstract, but in relation to the plaintiff, would entail liability for any and all consequences, however novel or extraordinary. *Bird v. St. Paul F. & M. Ins. Co.*, 224 N. Y. 47, 54; *Ehrgott v. Mayor, etc., of N. Y.*, 96 N. Y. 264; *Smith v. London & S. W. Ry. Co.*, L. R. 6 C. P. 14; 1 Beven, NEGLIGENCE, 106; Street, op. cit. vol. 1, p. 90; Green, RATIONALE OF PROXIMATE CAUSE, pp. 88, 118; *cf. Matter of Polemis*, L. R. 1921, 3 K. B. 560; 44 Law Quarterly Review, 142. There is room for argument that a distinction is to be drawn according to the diversity of interests invaded by the act, as where conduct negligent in that it threatens an insignificant invasion of an interest in property results in an unforeseeable invasion of an interest of another order, as, e.g., one of bodily security. Perhaps other distinctions may be necessary. We do not go into the question now. The consequences to be followed must first be rooted in a wrong.

The judgment of the Appellate Division and that of the Trial Term should be reversed, and the complaint dismissed, with costs in all courts.

Andrews, J. (dissenting)

Assisting a passenger to board a train, the defendant's servant negligently knocked a package from his arms. It fell between the platform and the cars. Of its contents the servant knew and could know nothing. A violent explosion followed. The concussion broke some scales standing a considerable distance away. In falling they injured the plaintiff, an intending passenger.

Upon these facts may she recover the damages she

anterior 在前的

at large 大多数的;整个的
entail 使承担,带来
novel 新奇的,异常的

concussion 震荡,冲击

has suffered in an action brought against the master? The result we shall reach depends upon our theory as to the nature of negligence. Is it a relative concept — the breach of some duty owing to a particular person or to particular persons? Or where there is an act which unreasonably threatens the safety of others, is the doer liable for all its proximate consequences, even where they result in injury to one who would generally be thought to be outside the radius of danger? This is not a mere dispute as to words. We might not believe that to the average mind the dropping of the bundle would seem to involve the probability of harm to the plaintiff standing many feet away whatever might be the case as to the owner or to one so near as to be likely to be struck by its fall. If, however, we adopt the second hypothesis we have to inquire only as to the relation between cause and effect. We deal in terms of proximate cause, not of negligence.

Negligence may be defined roughly as an act or omission which unreasonably does or may affect the rights of others, or which unreasonably fails to protect oneself from the dangers resulting from such acts. Here I confine myself to the first branch of the definition. Nor do I comment on the word "unreasonable." For present purposes it sufficiently describes that average of conduct that society requires of its members.

There must be both the act or the omission, and the right. It is the act itself, not the intent of the actor, that is important. *Hover v. Barkhoof*, 44 N. Y. 113; *Mertz v. Connecticut Co.*, 217 N. Y. 475. In criminal law both the intent and the result are to be considered. Intent again is material in tort actions, where punitive damages are sought, dependent on actual malice — not on merely reckless conduct. But here neither insanity nor infancy lessens responsibility. *Williams v. Hays*, 143 N. Y. 442.

As has been said, except in cases of contributory negligence, there must be rights which are or may be affected. Often though injury has occurred, no rights of him who suffers have been touched. A licensee or trespasser upon my land has no claim to affirmative care on my part that the land be made safe. *Meiers v. Koch Brewery*, 229 N. Y. 10. Where a railroad is required to fence its tracks against cattle, no man's rights are injured should he wander upon the road because such fence is absent. *Di Caprio v. N. Y. C. R. R.*, 231 N. Y. 94. An unborn child may not demand immunity from personal harm. *Drobner v. Peters*, 232 N. Y. 220.

But we are told that "there is no negligence unless there is in the particular case a legal duty to take care, and this duty must be one which is owed to the plaintiff himself and not merely to others." SALMOND TORTS (6th ed.) 24. This, I think, is too narrow a conception. Where there is the unreasonable act, and some right that may be affected there is negligence whether damage does or does not result. That is <u>immaterial</u>. Should we drive down Broadway at a reckless speed, we are negligent whether we strike an approaching car or miss it by an inch. The act itself is wrongful. It is a wrong not only to those who happen to be within the radius of danger but to all who might have been there — a wrong to the public at large. Such is the language of the street. Such the language of the courts when speaking of contributory negligence. Such again and again their language in speaking of the duty of some defendant and discussing proximate cause in cases where such a discussion is wholly irrelevant on any other theory. *Perry v. Rochester Line Co.*, 219 N. Y. 60. As was said by Mr. Justice Holmes many years ago, "the measure of the defendant's duty in determining whether a wrong has been committed is one thing, the measure of liability when a wrong has been committed is another." *Spade v. Lynn & Boston R. R. Co.*, 172 Mass. 488. <u>Due care</u> is a duty imposed on each one of us to protect society from unnecessary danger, not to protect A, B, or C alone.

It may well be that there is no such thing as negligence in the abstract. "Proof of negligence in the air, so to speak, will not do." In an empty world negligence would not exist. It does involve a relationship between man and his fellows. But not merely a relationship between man and those whom he might reasonably expect his act would injure. Rather, a relationship between him and those whom he does in fact injure. If his act has a tendency to harm someone,

immaterial 无关紧要

due care 适当注意（义务）

it harms him a mile away as surely as it does those on the scene. We now permit children to recover for the negligent killing of the father. It was never prevented on the theory that no duty was owing to them. A husband may be compensated for the loss of his wife's services. To say that the wrongdoer was negligent as to the husband as well as to the wife is merely an attempt to fit facts to theory. An insurance company paying a fire loss recovers its payment of the negligent incendiary. We speak of subrogation — of suing in the right of the insured. Behind the cloud of words is the fact they hide, that the act, wrongful as to the insured, has also injured the company. Even if it be true that the fault of father, wife, or insured will prevent recovery, it is because we consider the original negligence not the proximate cause of the injury. Pollock, TORTS (12th ed.) 463.

In the well-known *Polemis Case* (1921, 3 K. B. 560), Scrutton, L. J., said that the dropping of a plank was negligent for it might injure "workman or cargo or ship." Because of either possibility the owner of the vessel was to be made good for his loss. The act being wrongful the doer was liable for its proximate results. Criticized and explained as this statement may have been, I think it states the law as it should be and as it is. *Smith v. London & Southwestern Ry. Co.*, [1870-71] 6 C. P. 14; *Anthony v. Slaid*, 52 Mass. 290; *Wood v. Penn. R. R. Co.*, 177 Penn. St. 306; *Trashansky v. Hershkovitz*, 239 N. Y. 452.

The proposition is this. Every one owes to the world at large the duty of refraining from those acts that may unreasonably threaten the safety of others. Such an act occurs. Not only is he wronged to whom harm might reasonably be expected to result, but he also who is in fact injured, even if he be outside what would generally be thought the danger zone. There needs be duty due the one complaining but this is not a duty to a particular individual because as to him harm might be expected. Harm to someone being the natural result of the act, not only that one alone, but all those in fact injured may complain. We have never, I think, held otherwise. Indeed in the *Di Caprio* case we said that a breach of a general ordinance defining the degree of care to be exercised in one's calling is evidence of negligence as to everyone. We did not limit this statement to those who might be expected to be exposed to danger. Unreasonable risk being taken, its consequences are not confined to those who might probably be hurt.

If this be so, we do not have a plaintiff suing by "derivation or succession." Her action is original and primary. Her claim is for a breach of duty to herself — not that she is subrogated to any right of action of the owner of the parcel or of a passenger standing at the scene of the explosion.

The right to recover damages rests on additional considerations. The plaintiff's rights must be injured, and this injury must be caused by the negligence. We build a dam, but are negligent as to its foundations. Breaking, it injures property down stream. We are not liable if all this happened because of some reason other than the insecure foundation. But when injuries do result from our unlawful act we are liable for the consequences. It does not matter that they are unusual, unexpected, unforeseen and unforeseeable. But there is one limitation. The damages must be so connected with the negligence that the latter may be said to be the proximate cause of the former.

insecure 不安全的,有危险的

These two words have never been given an inclusive definition. What is a cause in a legal sense, still more what is a proximate cause, depend in each case upon many considerations, as does the existence of negligence itself. Any philosophical doctrine of causation does not help us. A boy throws a stone into a pond. The ripples spread. The water level rises. The history of that pond is altered to all eternity. It will be altered by other causes also. Yet it will be forever the resultant of all causes combined. Each one will have an influence. How great only omniscience can say. You may speak of a chain, or if you please, a net. An analogy is of little aid. Each cause brings about future events. Without each the future would not be the same. Each is proximate in the sense it is essential. But that is not what we mean by the word. Nor on the other hand do we mean sole cause. There is no such thing.

ripple 涟漪,细浪
to all eternity 直到永远

omniscience 上帝,全知者

tributary 支流	Should analogy be thought helpful, however, I prefer that of a stream. The spring, starting on its journey, is joined by <u>tributary</u> after tributary. The river, reaching the ocean, comes from a hundred sources. No man may say <u>whence</u> any drop of water is derived. Yet for a time distinction may be possible. Into the clear creek, brown <u>swamp</u> water flows from the left. Later, from the right comes water <u>stained</u> by its clay bed. The three may remain for a space, sharply divided. But at last, inevitably no trace of separation remains. They are so <u>commingled</u> that all distinction is lost.

Should analogy be thought helpful, however, I prefer that of a stream. The spring, starting on its journey, is joined by <u>tributary</u> after tributary. The river, reaching the ocean, comes from a hundred sources. No man may say <u>whence</u> any drop of water is derived. Yet for a time distinction may be possible. Into the clear creek, brown <u>swamp</u> water flows from the left. Later, from the right comes water <u>stained</u> by its clay bed. The three may remain for a space, sharply divided. But at last, inevitably no trace of separation remains. They are so <u>commingled</u> that all distinction is lost.

As we have said, we cannot trace the effect of an act to the end, if end there is. Again, however, we may trace it part of the way. A murder at Sarajevo may be the necessary <u>antecedent</u> to an <u>assassination</u> in London twenty years hence. An overturned lantern may burn all Chicago. We may follow the fire from the <u>shed</u> to the last building. We rightly say the fire started by the lantern caused its destruction.

A cause, but not the proximate cause. What we do mean by the word "proximate" is, that because of convenience, of public policy, of a rough sense of justice, the law arbitrarily declines to trace a series of events beyond a certain point. This is not logic. It is practical politics. Take our rule as to fires. Sparks from my burning <u>haystack</u> set on fire my house and my neighbor's. I may recover from a negligent railroad. He may not. Yet the wrongful act as directly harmed the one as the other. We may regret that the line was drawn just where it was, but drawn somewhere it had to be. We said the act of the railroad was not the proximate cause of our neighbor's fire. Cause it surely was. The words we used were simply indicative of our notions of public policy. Other courts think differently. But somewhere they reach the point where they cannot say the stream comes from any one source.

Take the illustration given in an unpublished <u>manuscript</u> by a distinguished and helpful writer on the law of torts. A <u>chauffeur</u> negligently collides with another car which is filled with dynamite, although he could not know it. An explosion follows. A, walking

---

Margin glossary:

tributary 支流

whence 从何处

swamp 沼泽
stain 沾污, 变脏

commingle 混合

antecedent 前事, 前情
assassination 暗杀, 刺杀
shed 棚, 小屋, 库房, 堆房, 车库

haystack 干草堆

manuscript 手稿
chauffeur 司机

on the sidewalk nearby, is killed. B, sitting in a window of a building opposite, is cut by flying glass. C, likewise sitting in a window a block away, is similarly injured. And a further illustration. A nursemaid, ten blocks away, <u>startled</u> by the noise, involuntarily drops a baby from her arms to the walk. We are told that C may not recover while A may. As to B it is a question for court or jury. We will all agree that the baby might not. Because, we are again told, the chauffeur had no reason to believe his conduct involved any risk of injuring either C or the baby. As to them he was not negligent.

startle 吃惊

But the chauffeur, being negligent in risking the collision, his belief that the scope of the harm he might do would be limited is immaterial. His act unreasonably <u>jeopardized</u> the safety of any one who might be affected by it. C's injury and that of the baby were directly <u>traceable</u> to the collision. Without that, the injury would not have happened. C had the right to sit in his office, secure from such dangers. The baby was entitled to use the sidewalk with reasonable safety.

jeopardize 危害,使陷危地,使受危困

traceable 可追踪的,起源于

The true theory is, it seems to me, that the injury to C, if in truth he is to be denied recovery, and the injury to the baby is that their several injuries were not the proximate result of the negligence. And here not what the chauffeur had reason to believe would be the result of his conduct, but what the prudent would foresee, may have a bearing. May have some bearing, for the problem of proximate cause is not to be solved by any one consideration.

It is all a question of <u>expediency</u>. There are no fixed rules to govern our judgment. There are simply matters of which we may take account. We have in a somewhat different connection spoken of "the stream of events." We have asked whether that stream was <u>deflected</u> — whether it was forced into new and unexpected channels. *Donnelly v. Piercy Contracting Co.*, 222 N. Y. 210. This is <u>rhetoric</u> rather than law. There is in truth little to guide us other than common sense.

expediency 方便

deflect 使偏斜,使转向

rhetoric 花言巧语,巧辩,虚夸

There are some <u>hints</u> that may help us. The proximate cause, involved as it may be with many

hint 暗示,提示

other causes, must be, at least, something without which the event would not happen. The court must ask itself whether there was a natural and continuous <u>sequence</u> between cause and effect. Was the one a substantial factor in producing the other? Was there a direct connection between them, without too many intervening causes? Is the effect of cause on result not too <u>attenuated</u>? Is the cause likely, in the usual judgment of mankind, to produce the result? Or by the exercise of prudent <u>foresight</u> could the result be foreseen? Is the result too remote from the cause, and here we consider <u>remoteness</u> in time and space. *Bird v. St. Paul F. & M. Ins. Co.*, 224 N. Y. 47, where we passed upon the construction of a contract — but something was also said on this subject. Clearly we must so consider, for the greater the distance either in time or space, the more surely do other causes intervene to affect the result. When a lantern is overturned the firing of a shed is a fairly direct consequence. Many things contribute to the spread of the <u>conflagration</u> — the force of the wind, the direction and width of streets, the character of intervening structures, other factors. We draw an uncertain and <u>wavering line</u>, but draw it we must as best we can.

Once again, it is all a question of fair judgment, always keeping in mind the fact that we endeavor to make a rule in each case that will be practical and in keeping with the general understanding of mankind.

Here another question must be answered. In the case supposed it is said, and said correctly, that the chauffeur is liable for the direct effect of the explosion although he had no reason to suppose it would follow a collision. "The fact that the injury occurred in a different manner than that which might have been expected does not prevent the chauffeur's negligence from being in law the cause of the injury." But the natural results of a negligent act — the results which a prudent man would or should foresee — do have a bearing upon the decision as to proximate cause. We have said so repeatedly. What should be foreseen? No human foresight would suggest that a collision itself might injure one a block away. On the contrary, given an explosion, such a possibility might be reasonably expected. I think the direct connection, the foresight of which the courts speak, assumes prevision of the explosion, for the immediate results of which, at least, the chauffeur is responsible.

It may be said this is unjust. Why? In fairness he should make good every injury flowing from his negligence. Not because of tenderness toward him we say he need not answer for all that follows his wrong. We look back to the catastrophe, the fire kindled by the spark, or the explosion. We trace the consequences — not indefinitely, but to a certain point. And to aid us in fixing that point we ask what might ordinarily be expected to follow the fire or the explosion.

This last suggestion is the factor which must determine the case before us. The act upon which defendant's liability rests is knocking an apparently harmless package onto the platform. The act was negligent. For its proximate consequences the defendant is liable. If its contents were broken, to the owner; if it fell upon and crushed a passenger's foot, then to him. If it exploded and injured one in the immediate vicinity, to him also as to A in the illustration. Mrs. Palsgraf was standing some distance away. How far cannot be told from the record — apparently twenty-five or thirty feet. Perhaps less. Except for the explosion, she would not have been injured. We are told by the appellant in his brief "it cannot be denied that the explosion was the direct cause of the plaintiff's injuries." So it was a substantial factor in producing the result — there was here a natural and continuous sequence — direct connection. The only intervening cause was that instead of blowing her to the ground the concussion smashed the weighing machine which in turn fell upon her. There was no remoteness in time, little in space. And surely, given such an explosion as here it needed no great foresight to predict that the natural result would be to injure one on the platform at no greater distance from its scene than was the plaintiff. Just how no one might be able to predict. Whether by flying fragments, by broken glass, by wreckage of machines or structures no one could say. But injury in some form was most probable.

unjust 不公平的

catastrophe 重大灾难
kindle 点燃,燃起
indefinitely 不确定地

vicinity 邻近,接近,附近

smash 打碎,粉碎

predict 预言
fragment 碎片,断片,破片
wreckage 残骸

Under these circumstances I cannot say as a matter of law that the plaintiff's injuries were not the proximate result of the negligence. That is all we have before us. The court refused to so charge. No request was made to submit the matter to the jury as a question of fact, even would that have been proper upon the record before us.

The judgment appealed from should be affirmed, with costs.

5. Defenses to Negligence

There are three main defenses to an action in negligence: contributory negligence, comparative negligence, and assumption of risk. In most states, the burden is on the defendant to establish the defense.

Contributory negligence occurs when the plaintiff's own negligence is successfully asserted. At common law, the plaintiff's contributory negligence completely barred his right to recover, even though the degree of the defendant's negligence was much greater than that of plaintiff.

Recently, most courts have rejected entirely the "all or nothing" approach of contributory negligence in favor of a comparative negligence system, whereby the plaintiff's recovery is diminished by the percentage he or she has contributed to the injury. Where contributory negligence is shown, the trier of fact weighs the plaintiff's negligence against that of the defendant and reduces the plaintiff's damages accordingly. For example, A negligently drove through a stop sign and collided with B, who was contributorily negligent by driving inattentively. B suffers damages of $100,000. If a jury finds that B was 30% negligent and A was 70% negligent, B will recover $70,000.

Another defense to negligence is assumption of risk, under which the defendant will win if it can be proved that the plaintiff assumed the risk. Assumption of risk completely bars the plaintiff's recovery. Assumption of risk can be either express or implied. Express assumption of risk occurs when the plaintiff

CHAPTER 7　TORTS OF NEGLIGENCE

agrees in advance that the defendant is not liable for negligent conduct that will injure the plaintiff. These types of agreements are often referred to as exculpatory clauses or waivers. They may be void as against public policy. For example, common carriers and public utilities are not permitted to limit their liability for personal injury by a disclaimer on, e.g., a ticket, a posted sign, etc. Implied assumption of risk rises when the plaintiff, with knowledge and appreciation of a particular risk, nevertheless voluntarily chooses to remain exposed to the risk. The plaintiff must have known of the risk and voluntarily assumed it. It is irrelevant that the plaintiff's choice is unreasonable.

in advance 预先

exculpatory clause 免责条款

disclaimer 免责声明

appreciation 了解,知道
expose 使面临,使遭受

Case 30: Knight v. Jewett

Supreme Court of California
Kendra Knight v. Michael Jewett
3 Cal. 4th 296, 834 P. 2d 696
Aug. 24, 1992

George, Justice.

In this case, and in the companion case of *Ford v. Gouin*, 3 Cal. 4th 339, 834 P. 2d 724, we face the question of the proper application of the "assumption of risk" doctrine in light of this court's adoption of comparative fault principles in *Li v. Yellow Cab Co.* (1975) 13 Cal. 3d 804, 532 P. 2d 1226. Although the *Li* decision itself addressed this issue, subsequent Court of Appeal decisions have differed in their interpretation of *Li*'s discussion of this point. We granted review to resolve the conflict among the Courts of Appeal.

I

We begin with a summary of the facts of this case, as set forth in the declarations and deposition transcripts submitted in support of and in opposition to defendant's motion for summary judgment.

On January 25, 1987, the day of the 1987 Super Bowl football game, plaintiff Kendra Knight and defendant Michael Jewett, together with a number of other social acquaintances, attended a Super Bowl

in support of 维护,支持,拥护
in opposition to 反对,与……相对

acquaintance 熟人

party at the home of a mutual friend. During half time of the Super Bowl, several guests decided to play an informal game of touch football on an adjoining dirt lot, using a "peewee" football. Each team had four or five players and included both women and men; plaintiff and defendant were on opposing teams. No rules were explicitly discussed before the game.

Five to ten minutes into the game, defendant ran into plaintiff during a play. According to plaintiff, at that point she told defendant "not to play so rough or I was going to have to stop playing." Her declaration stated that "[defendant] seemed to acknowledge my statement and left me with the impression that he would play less rough prospectively." In his deposition, defendant recalled that plaintiff had asked him to "be careful," but did not remember plaintiff saying that she would stop playing.

On the very next play, plaintiff sustained the injuries that gave rise to the present lawsuit. As defendant recalled the incident, his team was on defense on that play, and he jumped up in an attempt to intercept a pass. He touched the ball but did not catch it, and in coming down he collided with plaintiff, knocking her over. When he landed, he stepped backward onto plaintiff's right hand, injuring her hand and little finger.

Both plaintiff and Andrea Starr, another participant in the game who was on the same team as plaintiff, recalled the incident differently from defendant. According to their declarations, at the time plaintiff was injured, Starr already had caught the pass. Defendant was running toward Starr, when he ran into plaintiff from behind, knocked her down, and stepped on her hand. Starr also stated that, after knocking plaintiff down, defendant continued running until he tagged Starr, "which tag was hard enough to cause me to lose my balance, resulting in a twisting or spraining of my ankle."

The game ended with plaintiff's injury, and plaintiff sought treatment shortly thereafter. After three operations failed to restore the movement in her little finger or to relieve the ongoing pain of the injury, plaintiff's finger was amputated. Plaintiff then instituted the present proceeding, seeking damages from defendant on theories of negligence and assault and battery.

After filing an answer, defendant moved for summary judgment. Relying on the Court of Appeal decision in *Ordway v. Superior Court* (1988) 198 Cal. App. 3d 98,, defendant maintained that "reasonable implied assumption of risk" continues to operate as a complete defense after *Li v. Yellow Cab Co.*, *supra*, 13 Cal. 3d 804, 532 P. 2d 1226 (hereafter *Li*), and that plaintiff's action was barred under that doctrine. In this regard, defendant asserted that "[b]y participating in [the touch football game that resulted in her injury], plaintiff ... impliedly agreed to reduce the duty of care owed to her by defendant ... to only a duty to avoid reckless or intentionally harmful conduct," and that the undisputed facts established both that he did not intend to injure plaintiff and that the acts of defendant which resulted in plaintiff's injury were not reckless. In support of his motion, defendant submitted his own declaration setting forth his version of the incident, as summarized above, and specifically stating that he did not intend to step on plaintiff's hand or to injure her. Defendant also attached a copy of plaintiff's deposition in which plaintiff acknowledged that she frequently watched professional football on television and thus was generally familiar with the risks associated with the sport of football, and in which she conceded that she had no reason to believe defendant had any intention of stepping on her hand or injuring her.

In opposing the summary judgment motion, plaintiff first noted that, in contrast to the *Ordway* decision, the Court of Appeal decision in *Segoviano v. Housing Authority* (1983) 143 Cal. App. 3d 162 specifically held that the doctrine of "reasonable implied assumption of risk" had been eliminated by the adoption of comparative fault principles, and thus under *Segoviano* the basic premise of defendant's summary judgment motion was untenable and plaintiff was entitled to have the lawsuit proceed under comparative fault principles.

Furthermore, plaintiff maintained that even the

---

institute the proceeding
开始诉讼程序

untenable 不能维持的，站不住脚的

trial court inclined to follow the *Ordway* decision, there were numerous disputed material facts that precluded the granting of summary judgment in favor of defendant. First, plaintiff noted there was a clear dispute between defendant's and plaintiff's recollection of the specific facts of the play in which plaintiff was injured, and, in particular, of the details of defendant's conduct that caused plaintiff's injury. She claimed that under the facts as described by plaintiff and Starr, defendant's conduct was at least reckless.

Second, plaintiff vigorously disputed defendant's claim that, by participating in the game in question, she impliedly had agreed to reduce the duty of care, owed to her by defendant, to only a duty to avoid reckless or intentionally harmful conduct. Plaintiff maintained in her declaration that in view of the casual, social setting, the circumstance that women and men were joint participants in the game, and the rough dirt surface on which the game was played, she anticipated from the outset that it was the kind of "mock" football game in which there would be no forceful pushing or hard hitting or shoving. Plaintiff also asserted that the declarations and depositions of other players in the game, included in her opposition papers, demonstrated that the other participants, including defendant, shared her expectations and assumptions that the game was to be a "mellow" one and not a serious, competitive athletic event.① Plaintiff claimed that there had been no injuries during touch football games in which she had participated on previous occasions, and that in view of the circumstances under which the game was played, "[t]he only type of injury which I reasonably anticipated would have been

---

① The portion of defendant's deposition attached to plaintiff's opposition included the following passage:
"Q: ... [F]rom your perspective — and I asked this same question of both of your friends yesterday — is the standard of care in which you were going to be dealing with people out there in the play field different, in your opinion, when you're playing in that kind of a game, that is, the one that happened on that day versus if you're out there playing in the exact same place and with a bunch of guys and no girls."
"A: Yeah, it would be different. Yes."
"Q: So, theoretically, you should be much more careful when the women are out there than if it was a bunch of guys?"
"A: Right."

something in the nature of a bruise or bump."

In addition, in further support of her claim that there was at least a factual dispute as to whether she impliedly had agreed to assume the risk of injury from the type of rough play defendant assertedly engaged in, plaintiff relied on the portion of her declaration in which she stated that (1) she specifically had told defendant, immediately prior to the play in question, that defendant was playing too rough and that she would not continue to play in the game if he was going to continue such conduct, and (2) defendant had given plaintiff the impression he would refrain from such conduct. Plaintiff maintained that her statement during the game established that a disputed factual issue existed as to whether she voluntarily had chosen to assume the risks of the type of conduct allegedly engaged in by defendant.

In his reply to plaintiff's opposition, defendant acknowledged there were some factual details — "who ran where, when and how" — that were in dispute. He contended, however, that the material facts were not in dispute, stating those facts were "that plaintiff was injured in the context of playing touch football."

After considering the parties' submissions, the trial court granted defendant's motion for summary judgment. On appeal, the Court of Appeal, recognizing the existing conflict in appellate court decisions with regard to the so-called "reasonable implied assumption of risk" doctrine, concluded that *Ordway v. Superior Court*, supra, 198 Cal. App. 3d 98, rather than *Segoviano v. Housing Authority*, supra, 143 Cal. App. 3d 162, should be followed, and further concluded that under the *Ordway* decision there were no disputed material facts to be determined. The Court of Appeal, holding that the trial court properly had granted summary judgment in favor of defendant, affirmed the judgment.

As noted, we granted review to resolve the conflict among Court of Appeal decisions as to the proper application of the assumption of risk doctrine in light of the adoption of comparative fault principles in *Li*, supra, 13 Cal. 3d 804, 532 P. 2d 1226.

bruise 伤痕,擦伤,碰伤
bump 肿块

submission（向法官或陪审团提出的）意见

II

treatise 论文,论述

As every leading tort treatise has explained, the assumption of risk doctrine long has caused confusion both in definition and application, because the phrase "assumption of risk" traditionally has been used in a number of very different factual settings involving analytically distinct legal concepts. See, e.g., PROSSER & KEETON ON TORTS (5th ed. 1984) § 68, pp. 480 - 481; 4 Harper et al., THE LAW OF TORTS (2d ed. 1986) § 21.0, pp. 187 - 189; Schwartz, COMPARATIVE NEGLIGENCE (2d ed. 1986) § 9.1, p. 154; 3 Speiser et al., THE AMERICAN LAW OF TORTS (1986) §§ 12: 46 - 12: 47, pp. 636 - 640. Indeed, almost a half-century ago, Justice Frankfurter described the term "assumption of risk" as a classic example of a felicitous phrase, "undiscriminatingly used to express different and sometimes contradictory ideas," and whose uncritical use "bedevils the law." Tiller v. Atlantic Coast Line R. Co. (1943) 318 U. S. 54, 68 (conc. opn. of Frankfurter, J.).

felicitous 巧妙的,极为适当的
undiscriminatingly 不加区别地
uncritical 不严厉的,不加批判的
bedevil 使痛苦,使苦恼

In some settings — for example, most cases involving sports-related injuries — past assumption of risk decisions largely have been concerned with defining the contours of the legal duty that a given class of defendants — for example, owners of baseball stadiums or ice hockey rinks— owed to an injured plaintiff. (See, e. g., Quinn v. Recreation Park Assn. (1935) 3 Cal. 2d 725, 729, 46 P. 2d 144 [baseball stadium owner]; Shurman v. Fresno Ice Rink (1949) 91 Cal. App. 2d 469, 474 - 477, 205 P. 2d 77 [hockey rink owner].) In other settings, the assumption of risk terminology historically was applied to situations in which it was clear that the defendant had breached a legal duty of care to the plaintiff, and the inquiry focused on whether the plaintiff knowingly and voluntarily had chosen to encounter the specific risk of harm posed by the defendant's breach of duty. See, e. g., Vierra v. Fifth Avenue Rental Service (1963) 60 Cal. 2d 266, 271, 383 P. 2d 777 [plaintiff hit in eye by flying piece of metal in area adjacent to drilling]; Prescott v. Ralphs Grocery Co. (1954) 42 Cal. 2d 158, 161 - 162, 265 P. 2d 904 [plaintiff injured

contour 轮廓

baseball stadium 棒球场
ice hockey rink 冰球场

terminology 术语

on wet sidewalk on store premises].

Prior to the adoption of comparative fault principles of liability, there often was no need to distinguish between the different categories of assumption of risk cases, because if a case fell into either category, the plaintiff's recovery was totally barred. With the adoption of comparative fault, however, it became essential to <u>differentiate between</u> the distinct categories of cases that traditionally had been <u>lumped</u> together under the rubric of assumption of risk. This court's <u>seminal</u> comparative fault decision in *Li*, *supra*, 13 Cal. 3d 804, 532 P. 2d 1226, explicitly recognized the need for such <u>differentiation</u>, and attempted to explain which <u>category</u> of assumption of risk cases should be merged into the comparative fault system and which category should not. Accordingly, in considering the current <u>viability</u> of the assumption of risk doctrine in California, our analysis necessarily begins with the *Li* decision.

In *Li*, our court undertook a basic reexamination of the common law doctrine of contributory negligence. As *Li* noted, contributory negligence generally has been defined as "conduct on the part of the plaintiff which falls below the standard to which he should conform for his own protection, and which is a legally contributing cause cooperating with the negligence of the defendant in bringing about the plaintiff's harm." *Li*, *supra*, 13 Cal. 3d at p. 809, 532 P. 2d 1226, quoting REST. 2D TORTS, § 463. Prior to *Li*, the common law rule was that "[e]xcept where the defendant has the last clear chance, the plaintiff's contributory negligence bars recovery against a defendant whose negligent conduct would otherwise make him liable to the plaintiff for the harm sustained by him." *Li*, *supra*, at pp. 809 - 810, 532 P. 2d 1226, quoting REST. 2D TORTS, § 467.

In *Li*, *supra*, 13 Cal. 3d 804, 532 P. 2d 1226, we observed that "[i]t is unnecessary for us to catalogue the enormous amount of critical comment that has been directed over the years against the 'all-or-nothing' approach of the doctrine of contributory negligence. The <u>essence</u> of that <u>criticism</u> has been <u>constant</u> and clear: the doctrine is <u>inequitable</u> in its

differentiate between 辨别
lump 把……归并到一起
seminal 创新的,影响深远的
differentiation 区别
catalogue 类型

viability 可行性

essence 本质
criticism 评论,批评
constant 不变的,坚决的,持续的
inequitable 不公正的,不合乎衡平原则的

operation because it fails to distribute responsibility in proportion to fault ... The basic objection to the doctrine — grounded in the primal concept that in a system in which liability is based on fault, the extent of fault should govern the extent of liability — remains irresistible to reason and all intelligent notions of fairness." Id. at pp. 810 - 811, 532 P. 2d 1226. After taking additional note of the untoward practical consequences of the doctrine in the litigation of cases and the increasing rejection of the doctrine in other jurisdictions, the Li court concluded that "[w]e are likewise persuaded that logic, practical experience, and fundamental justice counsel against the retention of the doctrine rendering contributory negligence a complete bar to recovery — and that it should be replaced in this state by a system under which liability for damage will be borne by those whose negligence caused it in direct proportion to their respective fault." Id. at pp. 812 - 813, 532 P. 2d 1226.

After determining that the "all-or-nothing" contributory negligence doctrine should be replaced by a system of comparative negligence, the Li court went on to undertake a rather extensive discussion of the effect that the adoption of comparative negligence would have on a number of related tort doctrines, including the doctrines of last clear chance and assumption of risk. Li, supra, 13 Cal. 3d at pp. 823 - 826, 532 P. 2d 1226.

Under the last clear chance doctrine, a defendant was rendered totally liable for an injury, even though the plaintiff's contributory negligence had played a role in the accident, when the defendant had the "last clear chance" to avoid the accident. With regard to that doctrine, the Li decision, supra, 13 Cal. 3d 804, 532 P. 2d 1226, observed: "Although several states which apply comparative negligence concepts retain the last clear chance doctrine [citation], the better reasoned position seems to be that when true comparative negligence is adopted, the need for last clear chance as a palliative of the hardships of the 'all-or-nothing' rule disappears and its retention results only in a windfall to the plaintiff in direct contravention of the principle of liability in proportion to fault.

[*Citations.*]" *Id*. at p. 824, 532 P. 2d 1226. Accordingly, the court concluded that the doctrine should be "subsumed under the general process of assessing liability in proportion to fault." *Id*. at p. 826, 532 P. 2d 1226.

  subsume 把……归入,
纳入,把……包括在内,包含

  With respect to the effect of the adoption of comparative negligence on the assumption of risk doctrine — the issue before us today — the *Li* decision, *supra*, 13 Cal. 3d 804, 532 P. 2d 1226, stated as follows: "As for assumption of risk, we have recognized in this state that this defense overlaps that of contributory negligence to some extent and in fact is madeup of at least two distinct defenses. 'To simplify greatly, it has been observed ... that in one kind of situation, to wit, where a plaintiff unreasonably undertakes to encounter a specific known risk imposed by a defendant's negligence, plaintiff's conduct, although he may encounter that risk in a prudent manner, is in reality a form of contributory negligence ... Other kinds of situations within the doctrine of assumption of risk are those, for example, where plaintiff is held to agree to relieve defendant of an obligation of reasonable conduct toward him. Such a situation would not involve contributory negligence, but rather a reduction of defendant's duty of care.'" *Grey v. Fibreboard Paper Products Co*. (1966) 65 Cal. 2d 240, 245 – 246, 418 P. 2d 153; *see also Fonseca v. County of Orange* (1972) 28 Cal. App. 3d 361, 368 – 369; *see generally*, 4 Witkin, SUMMARY OF CAL. LAW (8th ed. 1974), TORTS, § 723, pp. 3013 – 3014; 2 Harper & James, THE LAW OF TORTS (1st ed. 1956) § 21. 1, pp. 1162 – 1168; *cf*. Prosser, TORTS (4th ed. 1971) § 68, pp. 439 – 441. We think it clear that the adoption of a system of comparative negligence should entail the merger of the defense of assumption of risk into the general scheme of assessment of liability in proportion to fault in those particular cases in which the form of assumption of risk involved is no more than a variant of contributory negligence. *See generally*, Schwartz, COMPARATIVE NEGLIGENCE (1st ed. 1974) ch. 9, pp. 153 – 175." *Li*, *supra*, 13 Cal. 3d at pp. 824 – 825, 532 P. 2d 1226.

  entail 使必需

  As this passage indicates, the *Li* decision, *supra*,

13 Cal. 3d 804 532 P. 2d 1226, clearly contemplated that the assumption of risk doctrine was to be partially merged or subsumed into the comparative negligence scheme. Subsequent Court of Appeal decisions have disagreed, however, in interpreting *Li*, as to what category of assumption of risk cases would be merged into the comparative negligence scheme.

A number of appellate decisions, focusing on the language in *Li* indicating that assumption of risk is in reality a form of contributory negligence "where a plaintiff unreasonably undertakes to encounter a specific known risk imposed by a defendant's negligence." 13 Cal. 3d at p. 824, 532 P. 2d 1226, have concluded that *Li* properly should be interpreted as drawing a distinction between those assumption of risk cases in which a plaintiff "unreasonably" encounters a known risk imposed by a defendant's negligence and those assumption of risk cases in which a plaintiff "reasonably" encounters a known risk imposed by a defendant's negligence. See, e. g., *Ordway v. Superior Court*, supra, 198 Cal. App. 3d 98, 103 – 105. These decisions interpret *Li* as subsuming into the comparative fault scheme those cases in which the plaintiff acts unreasonably in encountering a specific known risk, but retaining the assumption of risk doctrine as a complete bar to recovery in those cases in which the plaintiff acts reasonably in encountering such a risk. Although aware of the apparent <u>anomaly</u> of a rule under which a plaintiff who acts reasonably is completely barred from recovery while a plaintiff who acts unreasonably only has his or her recovery reduced, these decisions nonetheless have concluded that this distinction and consequence were intended by the *Li* court.①

anomaly 异常,不规则

---

① In *Ordway v. Superior Court*, supra, 198 Cal. App. 3d 98, the court suggested that the differentiation in the treatment accorded reasonable and unreasonable plaintiffs under an approach viewing "reasonable implied assumption of risk" as a complete bar to recovery was only "superficially anomalous," *Id*. at p. 104, and could be explained by reference to "the expectation of the defendant. He or she is permitted to ignore reasonably assumed risks and is not required to take extraordinary precautions with respect to them. The defendant must, however, anticipate that some risks will be unreasonably undertaken, and a failure to guard against these may result in liability." *Id*. at p. 105.

Even when the matter is viewed from the defendant's perspective, however, this suggested dichotomy is illogical and untenable. From the standpoint of a potential defendant, it is far more logical to require that the defendant take precautions with respect to risks that the defendant reasonably can foresee being undertaken, than it would be to impose liability only for risks that the defendant is less likely to anticipate will be encountered.

Ordway also attempted to explain the anomaly by reformulating the distinction between reasonable and unreasonable assumption of risk as one between plaintiffs who make a "knowing and intelligent" choice and those who act "negligent[ly] or careless[ly]." *Ordway v. Superior Court*, *supra*, 198 Cal. App. 3d 98, 105, and the dissenting opinion cites this reformulated terminology with approval. See dis. opn. by Kennard, J., post, p. 25 of 11 Cal. Rptr. 2d, p. 719 of 834 P. 2d. The *Li* decision, however, specifically subsumed within comparative fault those assumption of risk cases in which a defendant "unreasonably undertakes to encounter a specific known risk." *Li*, *supra*, 13 Cal. 3d 804, 824, 532 P. 2d 1226, *i.e.*, cases in which a defendant makes a knowing, but unreasonable, choice to undertake a risk. Indeed, in recasting the "unreasonable" assumption of risk category to include only those cases in which the plaintiff merely was careless and did not act with actual knowledge of the risk, *Ordway* inadvertently redefined the unreasonable assumption of risk category out of existence. The pre-*Li* decisions clearly held that where a plaintiff was injured as the result of a defendant's breach of duty, the assumption of risk doctrine applied only to those instances in which the plaintiff actually knew of and appreciated the specific risk and nonetheless chose to encounter the risk. See, e.g., *Vierra v. Fifth Avenue Rental Service*, *supra*, 60 Cal. 2d 266, 271, 383 P. 2d 777. ("Actual, and not merely constructive, knowledge of the danger is required.")

In our view, these decisions — regardless whether they reached the correct result on the facts at issue — have misinterpreted *Li* by suggesting that our decision contemplated less favorable legal treatment for a

dichotomy 分歧,二分法
standpoint 立场,看法,观点

precaution 预防措施

anticipate 预期,预料

reformulate 再次系统地阐述;再次表述

encounter 遭遇

recast 重作

constructive knowledge 推定知道,应当知道

plaintiff who reasonably encounters a known risk than for a plaintiff who unreasonably encounters such a risk. Although the relevant passage in *Li* indicates that the assumption of risk doctrine would be merged into the comparative fault scheme in instances in which a plaintiff "unreasonably undertakes to encounter a specific known risk imposed by a defendant's negligence" (13 Cal. 3d at p. 824, 532 P. 2d 1226), nothing in this passage suggests that the assumption of risk doctrine should survive as a total bar to the plaintiff's recovery whenever a plaintiff acts reasonably in encountering such a risk. Instead, this portion of our opinion expressly contrasts the category of assumption of risk cases which "involve contributory negligence" (and which therefore should be merged into the comparative fault scheme) with those assumption of risk cases which involve "a reduction of defendant's duty of care." *Id.* at p. 825, 532 P. 2d 1226.

Indeed, particularly when the relevant passage in *Li*, *supra*, 13 Cal. 3d at pp. 824‐825, 532 P. 2d 1226, is read as a whole and in conjunction with the authorities it cites, we believe it becomes clear that the distinction in assumption of risk cases to which the *Li* court referred in this passage was not a distinction between instances in which a plaintiff unreasonably encounters a known risk imposed by a defendant's negligence and instances in which a plaintiff reasonably encounters such a risk. Rather, the distinction to which the *Li* court referred was between (1) those instances in which the assumption of risk doctrine embodies a legal conclusion that there is "no duty" on the part of the defendant to protect the plaintiff from a particular risk — the category of assumption of risk that the legal commentators generally refer to as "primary assumption of risk" and (2) those instances in which the defendant does owe a duty of care to the plaintiff but the plaintiff knowingly encounters a risk of injury caused by the defendant's breach of that duty — what most commentators have termed "secondary

as a whole 作为一个整体
in conjunction with 连同,共同
authority 这里指判例

commentator 释评家, 评论者

assumption of risk."① Properly interpreted, the relevant passage in *Li* provides that the category of assumption of risk cases that is not merged into the comparative negligence system and in which the plaintiff's recovery continues to be completely barred involves those cases in which the defendant's conduct did not breach a legal duty of care to the plaintiff, *i.e.*, "primary assumption of risk" cases, whereas cases involving "secondary assumption of risk" properly are merged into the comprehensive comparative fault system adopted in *Li*.②

Since *Li*, California cases uniformly have recognized that so long as an express assumption of risk agreement does not violate public policy (*see*, *e.g.*, *Tunkl v. Regents of University of California* (1963) 60 Cal. 2d 92, 95 – 101, 383 P. 2d 441), such an agreement

volenti non fit injuria
自担风险者不能因此起诉他人

---

① The introductory passage from the Harper and James treatise on THE LAW OF TORTS, that was cited with approval in *Li*, stated in this regard: "The term assumption of risk has led to no little confusion because it is used to refer to at least two different concepts, which largely overlap, have a common cultural background, and often produce the same legal result. But these concepts are nevertheless quite distinct rules involving slightly different policies and different conditions for their application. (1) In its primary sense the plaintiff's assumption of a risk is only the counterpart of the defendant's lack of duty to protect the plaintiff from that risk. In such a case plaintiff may not recover for his injury even though he was quite reasonable in encountering the risk that caused it. *Volenti non fit injuria*. (2) A plaintiff may also be said to assume a risk created by defendant's breach of duty towards him, when he deliberately chooses to encounter that risk. In such a case, except possibly in master and servant cases, plaintiff will be barred from recovery only if he was unreasonable in encountering the risk under the circumstances. This is a form of contributory negligence. Hereafter we shall call this 'assumption of risk in a secondary sense.'" 2 Harper & James, THE LAW OF TORTS (1st ed. 1956) § 21.1, p. 1162, fns. omitted, cited in *Li*, *supra*, 13 Cal. 3d 804, 825, 532 P. 2d 1226.

② Although in the academic literature "express assumption of risk" often has been designated as a separate, contract-based species of assumption of risk distinct from both primary and secondary assumption of risk (*see*, *e.g.*, PROSSER & KEETON ON TORTS (5th ed. 1984) § 68, p. 496), cases involving express assumption of risk are concerned with instances in which, as the result of an express agreement, the defendant owes no duty to protect the plaintiff from an injury-causing risk. Thus in this respect express assumption of risk properly can be viewed as analogous to primary assumption of risk. One leading treatise describes express assumption of risk in the following terms: "In its most basic sense, assumption of risk means that the plaintiff, in advance, has given his express consent to relieve the defendant of an obligation of conduct toward him, and to take his chances of injury from a known risk arising from what the defendant is to do or leave undone... The result is that the defendant is relieved of legal duty to the plaintiff; and being under no duty, he cannot be charged with negligence." PROSSER & KEETON ON TORTS, *supra*, § 68, pp. 480 – 481, fn. omitted.

operates to relieve the defendant of a legal duty to the plaintiff with respect to the risks encompassed by the agreement and, where applicable, to bar completely the plaintiff's cause of action. See, e.g., *Madison v. Superior Court* (1988) 203 Cal. App. 3d 589, 597-602.

Although the difference between the "primary assumption of risk"/"secondary assumption of risk" nomenclature and the "reasonable implied assumption of risk"/"unreasonable implied assumption of risk" terminology embraced in many of the recent Court of Appeal decisions may appear at first blush to be only semantic, the significance extends beyond mere rhetoric. First, in "primary assumption of risk" cases — where the defendant owes no duty to protect the plaintiff from a particular risk of harm — a plaintiff who has suffered such harm is not entitled to recover from the defendant, whether the plaintiff's conduct in undertaking the activity was reasonable or unreasonable. Second, in "secondary assumption of risk" cases — involving instances in which the defendant has breached the duty of care owed to the plaintiff — the defendant is not entitled to be entirely relieved of liability for an injury proximately caused by such breach, simply because the plaintiff's conduct in encountering the risk of such an injury was reasonable rather than unreasonable. Third and finally, the question whether the defendant owed a legal duty to protect the plaintiff from a particular risk of harm does not turn on the reasonableness or unreasonableness of the plaintiff's conduct, but rather on the nature of the activity or sport in which the defendant is engaged and the relationship of the defendant and the plaintiff to that activity or sport. For these reasons, use of the "reasonable implied assumption of risk"/"unreasonable implied assumption of risk" terminology, as a means of differentiating between the cases in which a plaintiff is barred from bringing an action and those in which he or she is not barred, is more misleading than helpful. ①

Our reading of *Li*, *supra*, 13 Cal. 3d 804, 532 P. 2d 1226, insofar as it draws a distinction between assumption of risk cases in which the defendant has not breached any legal duty to the plaintiff and those in which the defendant has breached a legal duty, is supported not only by the language of *Li* itself and the authorities it cites, but also, and perhaps most significantly, by the fundamental principle that led the *Li* court to replace the all-or-nothing contributory negligence defense with a comparative fault scheme. In "primary assumption of risk" cases, it is consistent with comparative fault principles totally to bar a plaintiff from pursuing a cause of action, because when the defendant has not breached a legal duty of care to the plaintiff, the defendant has not committed any conduct which would warrant the imposition of any liability whatsoever, and thus there is no occasion at all for invoking comparative fault principles. See PROSSER & KEETON ON TORTS, *supra*, § 68, at pp. 496 – 497. By contrast, in the "secondary assumption of risk" context, the defendant has breached a duty of care owed to the plaintiff. When a risk of harm is created or imposed by a defendant's breach of duty, and a plaintiff who chose to encounter the risk is injured, comparative fault principles preclude

---

① In addition to the sports setting, the primary assumption of risk doctrine also comes into play in the category of cases often described as involving the "firefighter's rule." (*See Terhell v. American Commonwealth Associates* (1985) 172 Cal. App. 3d 434, 437.) In its most classic form, the firefighter's rule involves the question whether a person who negligently has started a fire is liable for an injury sustained by a firefighter who is summoned to fight the fire; the rule provides that the person who started the fire is not liable under such circumstances. (*See*, *e. g.*, *Walters v. Sloan* (1977) 20 Cal. 3d 199, 202, 571 P. 2d 609.) Although a number of theories have been cited to support this conclusion, the most persuasive explanation is that the party who negligently started the fire had no legal duty to protect the firefighter from the very danger that the firefighter is employed to confront. *See*, *e. g.*, *Baker v. Superior Court* (1982) 129 Cal. App. 3d 710, 719 – 721; *Nelson v. Hall* (1985) 165 Cal. App. 3d 709, 714. *See generally* 6 Witkin, SUMMARY OF CAL. LAW (9th ed. 1988) TORTS, § 739, pp. 69 – 70 [discussing rule as one illustration of duty approach]; *Anicet v. Gant* (Fla. Dist. Ct. App. 1991) 580 So. 2d 273, 276 ["a person specifically hired to encounter and combat particular dangers is owed no independent tort duty by those who have created those dangers ..."]. Because the defendant in such a case owes no duty to protect the firefighter from such risks, the firefighter has no cause of action even if the risk created by the fire was so great that a trier of fact could find it was unreasonable for the firefighter to choose to encounter the risk. This example again demonstrates that primary assumption of risk is not the same as "reasonable implied assumption of risk."

automatically placing all of the loss on the plaintiff, because the injury in such a case may have been caused by the combined effect of the defendant's and the plaintiff's culpable conduct. To retain assumption of risk as a complete defense in such a case would fly in the face of *Li*'s basic holding that when both parties are partially at fault for an injury, a rule which places all of the loss on one of the parties is inherently inequitable. See *Id.* at pp. 497-498.

Thus, just as the court in *Li* reasoned it would be improper to retain the last clear chance doctrine as a means of imposing all liability on a defendant in cases in which the defendant is aware of the risk of harm created by the plaintiff's negligence but fails to take the "last clear chance" to avoid the injury. *Li*, *supra*, 13 Cal. 3d at p. 824, 532 P. 2d 1226, we believe the *Li* court similarly recognized that, in the assumption of risk context, it would be improper to impose all responsibility on a plaintiff who is aware of a risk of harm created by the defendant's breach of duty but fails to avert the harm. In both instances, comparative fault principles call for a sharing of the burden of liability.

The dissenting opinion suggests, however, that, even when a defendant has breached its duty of care to the plaintiff, a plaintiff who reasonably has chosen to encounter a known risk of harm imposed by such a breach may be totally precluded from recovering any damages, without doing violence to comparative fault principles, on the theory that the plaintiff, by proceeding in the face of a known risk, has "impliedly consented" to any harm. See dis. opn. by Kennard, J., post, p. 25-26 of 11 Cal. Rptr. 2d, p. 719-720 of 834 P. 2d. For a number of reasons, we conclude this contention does not withstand analysis.

First, the argument that a plaintiff who proceeds to encounter a known risk has "impliedly consented" to absolve a negligent defendant of liability for any ensuing harm logically would apply as much to a plaintiff who unreasonably has chosen to encounter a known risk, as to a plaintiff who reasonably has chosen to encounter such a risk. As we have seen, however, *Li* explicitly held that a plaintiff who "unreasonably undertakes to encounter a specific known risk imposed by a defendant's negligence" *Li*, *supra*, 13 Cal. 3d at p. 824, 532 P. 2d 1226 is not completely barred from recovery; instead, the recovery of such a plaintiff simply is reduced under comparative fault principles. Thus, the dissenting opinion's implied consent argument is irreconcilable with *Li* itself.

irreconcilable 矛盾的

Second, the implied consent rationale rests on a legal fiction that is untenable, at least as applied to conduct that represents a breach of the defendant's duty of care to the plaintiff. It may be accurate to suggest that an individual who voluntarily engages in a potentially dangerous activity or sport "consents to" or "agrees to assume" the risks inherent in the activity or sport itself, such as the risks posed to a snow skier by moguls on a ski slope or the risks posed to a water skier by wind-whipped waves on a lake. But it is thoroughly unrealistic to suggest that, by engaging in a potentially dangerous activity or sport, an individual consents to (or agrees to excuse) a breach of duty by others that increases the risks inevitably posed by the activity or sport itself, even where the participating individual is aware of the possibility that such misconduct may occur.

snow skier 滑雪者
mogul 雪墩
ski slope 滑雪坡
water skier 滑水者
wind-whipped waves 被风吹卷起的海浪

A familiar example may help demonstrate this point. Although every driver of an automobile is aware that driving is a potentially hazardous activity and that inherent in the act of driving is the risk that he or she will be injured by the negligent driving of another, a person who voluntarily chooses to drive does not thereby "impliedly consent" to being injured by the negligence of another, nor has such a person "impliedly excused" others from performing their duty to use due care for the driver's safety. Instead, the driver reasonably expects that if he or she is injured by another's negligence, *i.e.*, by the breach of the other person's duty to use due care, the driver will be entitled to compensation for his or her injuries. Similarly, although a patient who undergoes elective surgery is aware that inherent in such an operation is the risk of injury in the event the surgeon is negligent, the patient, by voluntarily encountering such a risk,

elective surgery 非急需施行的手术,选择性外科手术

surgeon 外科医生

does not "impliedly consent" to negligently inflicted injury or "impliedly agree" to excuse the surgeon from a normal duty of care, but rather justifiably expects that the surgeon will be liable in the event of medical malpractice.

Thus, there is no merit to the dissenting opinion's general claim that simply because a person is aware an activity involves a risk of harm that may arise from another's negligence and voluntarily proceeds to participate in that activity despite such knowledge, that person should be barred from obtaining any recovery on the theory that he or she impliedly consented to the risk of harm. As we shall discuss in part III, legal liability for an injury which occurs during a sporting event is significantly affected by the assumption of risk doctrine, but only because the doctrine has been utilized in framing the duty of care owed by a defendant in the context of a sporting event, and not because the plaintiff in such a case has, in any realistic sense of the term, "consented" to relieve the defendant of liability.

Third, the dissenting opinion's claim that the category of cases in which the assumption of risk doctrine operates to bar a plaintiff's cause of action after *Li* properly should be gauged on the basis of an implied consent analysis, rather than on the duty analysis we have described above, is, in our view, untenable for another reason. In support of its implied consent theory, the dissenting opinion relies on a number of pre-*Li* cases, which arose in the "secondary assumption of risk" context, and which held that, in such a context, application of the assumption of risk doctrine was dependent on proof that the particular plaintiff subjectively knew, rather than simply should have known, of both the existence and magnitude of the specific risk of harm imposed by the defendant's negligence. See *Vierra v. Fifth Avenue Rental Service*, supra, 60 Cal. 2d 266, 271 - 275, 383 P. 2d 777; *Prescott v. Ralphs Grocery Co.*, supra, 42 Cal. 2d 158, 161 - 162, 265 P. 2d 904. Consequently, as the dissenting opinion acknowledges, were its implied consent theory to govern application of the assumption of risk doctrine in the sports setting, the basic liability of a defendant who engages in a sport would depend on variable factors that the defendant frequently would have no way of ascertaining (for example, the particular plaintiff's subjective knowledge and expectations), rather than on the nature of the sport itself. As a result, there would be drastic <u>disparities</u> in the manner in which the law would treat defendants who engaged in precisely the same conduct, based on the often unknown, subjective expectations of the particular plaintiff who happened to be injured by the defendant's conduct.

disparity 不一致

Such an approach not only would be inconsistent with the principles of fairness underlying the *Li* decision, but also would be <u>inimical</u> to the fair and efficient administration of justice. If the application of the assumption of risk doctrine in a sports setting turned on the particular plaintiff's subjective knowledge and awareness, summary judgment rarely would be available in such cases, for, as the present case reveals, it frequently will be easy to raise factual questions with regard to a particular plaintiff's subjective expectations as to the existence and magnitude of the risks the plaintiff voluntarily chose to encounter. By contrast, the question of the existence and scope of a defendant's duty of care is a legal question which depends on the nature of the sport or activity in question and on the parties' general relationship to the activity, and is an issue to be decided by the court, rather than the jury. *See*, *e.g.*, 6 Witkin, SUMMARY OF CAL. LAW, *supra*, TORTS, § 748, pp. 83–86 and cases cited. Thus, the question of assumption of risk is much more amenable to resolution by summary judgment under a duty analysis than under the dissenting opinion's suggested implied consent approach.

inimical 抵触的

An <u>*amicus curiae*</u> in the companion case has questioned, on a separate ground, the duty approach to the post-*Li* assumption of risk doctrine, suggesting that if a plaintiff's action may go forward whenever a defendant's breach of duty has played some role, however minor, in a plaintiff's injury, a plaintiff who voluntarily engages in a highly dangerous sport — for example, skydiving or mountain climbing — will

amicus curiae 法院之友（对案件中的疑难法律问题陈述意见并善意提醒法院注意某些法律问题的临时法律顾问, 协助法庭解决问题的人）

escape any responsibility for the injury so long as a jury finds that the plaintiff was not "unreasonable" in engaging in the sport. This argument rests on the premise that, under comparative fault principles, a jury may assign some portion of the responsibility for an injury to a plaintiff only if the jury finds that the plaintiff acted unreasonably, but not if the jury finds that the plaintiff knowingly and voluntarily, but reasonably, chose to engage in a dangerous activity. *Amicus curiae* contends that such a rule frequently would permit voluntary risk takers to avoid all responsibility for their own actions, and would impose an improper and undue burden on other participants.

Although we agree with the general thesis of *amicus curiae*'s argument that persons generally should bear personal responsibility for their own actions, the suggestion that a duty approach to the doctrine of assumption of risk is inconsistent with this thesis rests on a mistaken premise. Past California cases have made it clear that the "comparative fault" doctrine is a flexible, commonsense concept, under which a jury properly may consider and evaluate the relative responsibility of various parties for an injury (whether their responsibility for the injury rests on negligence, strict liability, or other theories of responsibility), in order to arrive at an "equitable apportionment or allocation of loss." See *Daly v. General Motors Corp.* (1978) 20 Cal. 3d 725, 734 – 742, 575 P. 2d 1162; *Safeway Stores, Inc. v. Nest-Kart* (1978) 21 Cal. 3d 322, 328 – 332, 579 P. 2d 441; *Far West Financial Corp. v. D & S Co.* (1988) 46 Cal. 3d 796, 804, fn. 7, 760 P. 2d 399.

Accordingly, contrary to *amicus curiae*'s assumption, we believe that under California's comparative fault doctrine, a jury in a "secondary assumption of risk" case would be entitled to take into consideration a plaintiff's voluntary action in choosing to engage in an unusually risky sport, whether or not the plaintiff's decision to encounter the risk should be characterized as unreasonable, in determining whether the plaintiff properly should bear some share of responsibility for the injuries he or she suffered. See, e. g., *Kirk v. Washington State University* (1987) 109 Wash. 2d 448,

746 P. 2d 285, 290 – 291. *See generally* Schwartz, COMPARATIVE NEGLIGENCE, *supra*, § 9. 5, p. 180; Diamond, *Assumption of Risk After Comparative Negligence: Integrating Contract Theory into Tort Doctrine* (1991) 52 OHIO ST. L. J. 717, 748 – 749. Thus, in a case in which an injury has been caused by both a defendant's breach of a legal duty to the plaintiff and the plaintiff's voluntary decision to engage in an unusually risky sport, application of comparative fault principles will not operate to relieve either individual of responsibility for his or her actions, but rather will ensure that neither party will escape such responsibility.

It may be helpful at this point to summarize our general conclusions as to the current state of the doctrine of assumption of risk in light of the adoption of comparative fault principles in *Li*, *supra*, 13 Cal. 3d 804, 119 Cal. Rptr. 858, 532 P. 2d 1226, general conclusions that reflect the view of a majority of the justices of the court [*i.e.*, the three justices who have signed this opinion and Justice Mosk (*see* conc. and dis. opn. by Mosk, J., ante, p. 18 of 11 Cal. Rptr. 2d, p. 712 of 834 P. 2d)]. ① In cases involving "primary assumption of risk" — where, by virtue of the nature of the activity and the parties' relationship to the activity, the defendant owes no legal duty to protect the plaintiff from the particular risk of harm that caused the injury — the doctrine continues to operate as a complete bar to the plaintiff's recovery. In cases involving "secondary assumption of risk" — where the defendant does owe a duty of care to the plaintiff, but the plaintiff proceeds to encounter a known risk imposed by the defendant's breach of duty — the doctrine is merged into the comparative fault scheme,

---

① Although Justice Mosk agrees that, in this context, a defendant's liability should be analyzed under a duty analysis, he is of the view that the "primary" and "secondary" assumption of risk terminology is potentially confusing and would prefer entirely to eliminate the doctrine of implied assumption of risk as a bar to recovery and simply to apply comparative fault principles to determine liability. (*See* conc. and dis. opn. by Mosk, J., *ante*, pp. 18 – 19 of 11 Cal. Rptr. 2d, pp. 712 – 713 of 834 P. 2d.) Because the *Li* decision, *supra*, 13 Cal. 3d 804, 824 – 825, 532 P. 2d 1226, indicated that the preexisting assumption of risk doctrine was to be only partially merged into the comparative fault system, the analysis set forth in the present opinion (distinguishing between primary and secondary assumption of risk) in our view more closely reflects the *Li* holding than does Justice Mosk's proposal.

and the trier of fact, in apportioning the loss resulting from the injury, may consider the relative responsibility of the parties.

Accordingly, in determining the propriety of the trial court's grant of summary judgment in favor of the defendant in this case, our inquiry does not turn on the reasonableness or unreasonableness of plaintiff's conduct in choosing to subject herself to the risks of touch football or in continuing to participate in the game after she became aware of defendant's allegedly rough play. Nor do we focus upon whether there is a factual dispute with regard to whether plaintiff subjectively knew of, and voluntarily chose to encounter, the risk of defendant's conduct, or impliedly consented to relieve or excuse defendant from any duty of care to her. Instead, our resolution of this issue turns on whether, in light of the nature of the sporting activity in which defendant and plaintiff were engaged, defendant's conduct breached a legal duty of care to plaintiff. We now turn to that question.

III

As a general rule, persons have a duty to use due care to avoid injury to others, and may be held liable if their careless conduct injures another person. See Civ. Code, § 1714. Thus, for example, a property owner ordinarily is required to use due care to eliminate dangerous conditions on his or her property. See, e.g., Rowland v. Christian (1968) 69 Cal. 2d 108, 443 P. 2d 561. In the sports setting, however, conditions or conduct that otherwise might be viewed as dangerous often are an integral part of the sport itself. Thus, although moguls on a ski run pose a risk of harm to skiers that might not exist were these configurations removed, the challenge and risks posed by the moguls are part of the sport of skiing, and a ski resort has no duty to eliminate them. See generally Annot. (1987) 55 A. L. R. 4th 632. In this respect, the nature of a sport is highly relevant in defining the duty of care owed by the particular defendant.

Although defendants generally have no legal duty to eliminate (or protect a plaintiff against) risks inherent in the sport itself, it is well established that defendants generally do have a duty to use due care not to increase the risks to a participant over and above those inherent in the sport. Thus, although a ski resort has no duty to remove moguls from a ski run, it clearly does have a duty to use due care to maintain its towropes in a safe, working condition so as not to expose skiers to an increased risk of harm. The cases establish that the latter type of risk, posed by a ski resort's negligence, clearly is not a risk (inherent in the sport) that is assumed by a participant. *See generally* Annot. (1979) 95 A. L. R. 3d 203.

towrope 拖曳缆

In some situations, however, the careless conduct of others is treated as an "inherent risk" of a sport, thus barring recovery by the plaintiff. For example, numerous cases recognize that in a game of baseball, a player generally cannot recover if he or she is hit and injured by a carelessly thrown ball (*see, e.g., Mann v. Nutrilite, Inc.* (1955) 136 Cal. App. 2d 729, 734 – 735, 289 P. 2d 282), and that in a game of basketball, recovery is not permitted for an injury caused by a carelessly extended elbow (*see, e.g., Thomas v. Barlow* (1927) 5 N. J. Misc. 764, 138 A. 208). The divergent results of the foregoing cases lead naturally to the question how courts are to determine when careless conduct of another properly should be considered an "inherent risk" of the sport that (as a matter of law) is assumed by the injured participant.

divergent 分歧的
foregoing 前面的,前述的,先前的

Contrary to the implied consent approach to the doctrine of assumption of risk, discussed above, the duty approach provides an answer which does not depend on the particular plaintiff's subjective knowledge or appreciation of the potential risk. Even where the plaintiff, who falls while skiing over a mogul, is a total novice and lacks any knowledge of skiing whatsoever, the ski resort would not be liable for his or her injuries. *See Brown v. San Francisco Baseball Club* (1950) 99 Cal. App. 2d 484, 488 – 492, 222 P. 2d 19 [baseball spectator's alleged ignorance of the game did not warrant imposing liability on stadium owner for injury caused by a carelessly thrown ball]. And, on the other hand, even where the plaintiff actually is aware that a particular ski resort on

novice 新手

occasion has been negligent in maintaining its towropes, that knowledge would not preclude the skier from recovering if he or she were injured as a result of the resort's repetition of such deficient conduct. In the latter context, although the plaintiff may have acted with knowledge of the potential negligence, he or she did not consent to such negligent conduct or agree to excuse the resort from liability in the event of such negligence.

Rather than being dependent on the knowledge or consent of the particular plaintiff, resolution of the question of the defendant's liability in such cases turns on whether the defendant has a legal duty to avoid such conduct or to protect the plaintiff against a particular risk of harm. As already noted, the nature of a defendant's duty in the sports context depends heavily on the nature of the sport itself. Additionally, the scope of the legal duty owed by a defendant frequently will also depend on the defendant's role in, or relationship to, the sport.

The latter point is demonstrated by a review of one of the numerous cases involving an injury sustained by a spectator at a baseball game. In *Ratcliff v. San Diego Baseball Club* (1938) 27 Cal.App.2d 733, 81 P.2d 625, a baseball spectator was injured when, walking in the stands between home plate and first base during a game, she was hit by an accidentally thrown bat. She sued both the player who threw the bat and the baseball stadium owner. The jury returned a verdict in favor of the player, but found the stadium owner liable. On appeal, the Court of Appeal affirmed.

Had the *Ratcliff* court utilized an implied consent analysis, the court would have looked only to the knowledge of the particular plaintiff (the spectator) to determine whether the risk of being hit by an accidentally thrown bat was an inherent risk of the sport of baseball assumed by the plaintiff, and would have treated the plaintiff's action against both defendants similarly with regard to such risk. The Ratcliff court did not analyze the case in that manner, however. Instead, the court implicitly recognized that two different potential duties were at issue — (1) the duty of the ballplayer to play the game without carelessly throwing his bat, and (2) the duty of the stadium owner to provide a reasonably safe stadium with regard to the relatively common (but particularly dangerous) hazard of a thrown bat. Because each defendant's liability rested on a separate duty, there was no inconsistency in the jury verdict absolving the batter of liability but imposing liability on the stadium owner for its failure to provide the patron"protection from flying bats, at least in the area where the greatest danger exists and where such an occurrence is reasonably to be expected." *Ratcliff v. San Diego Baseball Club*, supra, 27 Cal. App. 2d at p. 736, 81 P. 2d 625.

batter 击球手
patron 主顾

Other cases also have analyzed in a similar fashion the duty of the owner of a ballpark or ski resort, in the process defining the risks inherent in the sport not only by virtue of the nature of the sport itself, but also by reference to the steps the sponsoring business entity reasonably should be obligated to take in order to minimize the risks without altering the nature of the sport. See, e.g., *Quinn v. Recreation Park Assn.*, supra, 3 Cal. 2d 725, 728 - 729, 46 P. 2d 144 [discussing separately the potential liability of a player and a baseball stadium owner for injury to a spectator]; *Shurman v. Fresno Ice Rink*, supra, 91 Cal. App. 2d 469, 474 - 477, 205 P. 2d 77 [discussing duty owed by owner of ice hockey rink to spectators].

ballpark 棒球场

ice hockey rink 冰球场
cursory 匆匆忙忙的,粗略的,草率的

Even a cursory review of the numerous sports injury cases reveals the diverse categories of defendants whose alleged misconduct may be at issue in such cases. Thus, for example, suits have been brought against owners of sports facilities such as baseball stadiums and ski resorts(see, e.g., *Quinn v. Recreation Park Assn.*, supra, 3 Cal. 2d 725, 46 P. 2d 144; *Danieley v. Goldmine Ski Associates, Inc.* (1990) 218 Cal. App. 3d 111), against manufacturers and reconditioners of sporting equipment (see, e.g., *Holdsworth v. Nash Mfg., Inc.* (1987) 161 Mich. App. 139, 409 N. W. 2d 764; *Gentile v. MacGregor Mfg. Co.* (1985) 201 N. J. Super. 612, 493 A. 2d 647), against sports instructors and coaches (see, e.g., *Scroggs v. Coast Community College Dist.* (1987) 193

resort 度假胜地

reconditioner 调整者,调整机

Cal. App. 3d 1399; *Morris v. Union High School Dist. A* (1931) 160 Wash. 121, 294 P. 998), and against coparticipants (see, e.g., *Tavernier v. Maes* (1966) 242 Cal. App. 2d 532), alleging that such persons, either by affirmative misconduct or by a failure to act, caused or contributed to the plaintiff's injuries. These cases demonstrate that in the sports setting, as elsewhere, the nature of the applicable duty or standard of care frequently varies with the role of the defendant whose conduct is at issue in a given case.

In the present case, defendant was a participant in the touch football game in which plaintiff was engaged at the time of her injury, and thus the question before us involves the circumstances under which a participant in such a sport may be held liable for an injury sustained by another participant.

The overwhelming majority of the cases, both within and outside California, that have addressed the issue of coparticipant liability in such a sport, have concluded that it is improper to hold a sports participant liable to a coparticipant for ordinary careless conduct committed during the sport — for example, for an injury resulting from a carelessly thrown ball or bat during a baseball game — and that liability properly may be imposed on a participant only when he or she intentionally injures another player or engages in reckless conduct that is totally outside the range of the ordinary activity involved in the sport. See, e.g., *Gauvin v. Clark* (1989) 404 Mass. 450, 537 N.E. 2d 94, 96-97.

In reaching the conclusion that a coparticipant's duty of care should be limited in this fashion, the cases have explained that, in the heat of an active sporting event like baseball or football, a participant's normal energetic conduct often includes accidentally careless behavior. The courts have concluded that vigorous participation in such sporting events likely would be chilled if legal liability were to be imposed on a participant on the basis of his or her ordinary careless conduct. The cases have recognized that, in such a sport, even when a participant's conduct violates a rule of the game and may subject the violator to internal sanctions prescribed by the sport itself, imposition of legal liability for such conduct might well alter fundamentally the nature of the sport by deterring participants from vigorously engaging in activity that falls close to, but on the permissible side of, a prescribed rule.

A sampling of the cases that have dealt with the question of the potential tort liability of such sports participants is instructive. In *Tavernier v. Maes*, *supra*, 242 Cal. App. 2d 532, for example, the Court of Appeal upheld a verdict denying recovery for an injury sustained by the plaintiff second baseman as an unintended consequence of the defendant baserunner's hard slide into second base during a family picnic softball game. Similarly, in *Gaspard v. Grain Dealers Mutual Insurance Company* (La. Ct. App. 1961) 131 So. 2d 831, the plaintiff baseball player was denied recovery when he was struck on the head by a bat which accidentally flew out of the hands of the defendant batter during a school game. *See also Gauvin v. Clark*, *supra*, 404 Mass. 450, 537 N. E. 2d 94, 96 - 97 [plaintiff hockey player injured when hit with hockey stick by opposing player; court held that defendant's liability should be determined by whether he acted "with reckless disregard of safety"]; *Marchetti v. Kalish* (1990) 53 Ohio St. 3d 95, 559 N. E. 2d 699, 703 [child injured while playing "kick the can"; "we join the weight of authority ... and require that before a party may proceed with a cause of action involving injury resulting from recreational or sports activity, reckless or intentional conduct must exist"]; *Kabella v. Bouschelle* (Ct. App. 1983) 100 N. M. 461, 465, 672 P. 2d 290, 294 [plaintiff injured in informal tackle football game; court held that "a cause of action for personal injuries between participants incurred during athletic competition must be predicated upon recklessness or intentional conduct, ' not mere negligence'"]; *Ross v. Clouser* (Mo. 1982) 637 S. W. 2d 11, 13 - 14 [plaintiff third baseman injured in collision with baserunner; court held that "a cause of action for personal injuries incurred during athletic competition must be predicated on recklessness, not mere negligence"]; *Moe v. Steenberg* (1966) 275 Minn. 448, 147 N. W. 2d 587 [plaintiff ice skater

baseman 垒手

tackle football 橄榄球

predicate 作出论断,断言

ice skater 溜冰人

denied recovery for injury incurred when another skater, who was skating backwards, accidentally tripped over her after she had fallen on the ice]; *Thomas v. Barlow*, *supra*, 5 N.J. Misc. 764, 138 A. 208 [recovery denied when appellate court concluded that plaintiff's injury, incurred during a basketball game, resulted from an accidental contact with a member of the opposing team].

By contrast, in *Griggas v. Clauson* (1955) 6 Ill. App. 2d 412, 128 N. E. 2d 363, the court upheld liability imposed on the defendant basketball player who, during a game, wantonly assaulted a player on the opposing team, apparently out of frustration with the progress of the game. And, in *Bourque v. Duplechin* (La. Ct. App. 1976) 331 So. 2d 40, the court affirmed a judgment imposing liability for an injury incurred during a baseball game when the defendant baserunner, in an <u>ostensible</u> attempt to break up a double play, ran into the plaintiff second baseman at full speed, without sliding, after the second baseman had thrown the ball to first base and was standing four to five feet away from second base toward the <u>pitcher's mound</u>; in upholding the judgment, the court stated that defendant "was under a duty to play softball in the ordinary fashion without <u>unsportsmanlike</u> conduct or wanton injury to his fellow players." (*Id.* at p. 42.) See also *Averill v. Luttrell* (1957) 44 Tenn. App. 56, 311 S. W. 2d 812 [defendant baseball catcher properly held liable when, deliberately and without warning, he hit a batter in the head with his fist]; *Hackbart v. Cincinnati Bengals, Inc.* (10th Cir. 1979) 601 F. 2d 516 [trial court erred in absolving defendant football player of liability when, acting out of anger and frustration, he <u>struck a blow</u> with his <u>forearm</u> to the back of the head of an opposing player, who was <u>kneeling on the ground</u> watching the end of a pass interception play]; *Overall v. Kadella* (1984) 138 Mich. App. 351, 361 N. W. 2d 352 [hockey player permitted to recover when defendant player intentionally <u>punched</u> him in the face at the conclusion of the game].

In our view, the reasoning of the foregoing cases is sound. Accordingly, we conclude that a participant in an active sport breaches a legal duty of care to other participants — i.e., engages in conduct that properly may subject him or her to financial liability — only if the participant intentionally injures another player or engages in conduct that is so reckless as to be totally outside the range of the ordinary activity involved in the sport. ①

As applied to the present case, the foregoing legal principle clearly supports the trial court's entry of summary judgment in favor of defendant. The declarations filed in support of and in opposition to the summary judgment motion establish that defendant was, at most, careless or negligent in knocking over plaintiff, stepping on her hand, and injuring her finger. Although plaintiff maintains that defendant's rough play as described in her declaration and the declaration of Andrea Starr properly can be characterized as "reckless," the conduct alleged in those declarations is not even closely comparable to the kind of conduct — conduct so reckless as to be totally outside the range of the ordinary activity involved in the sport — that is a prerequisite to the imposition of legal liability upon a participant in such a sport.

Therefore, we conclude that defendant's conduct in the course of the touch football game did not breach any legal duty of care owed to plaintiff. Accordingly, this case falls within the primary assumption of risk doctrine, and thus the trial court properly granted summary judgment in favor of defendant. Because plaintiff's action is barred under the primary assumption of risk doctrine, comparative fault principles do not come into play.

The judgment of the Court of Appeal, upholding the summary judgment entered by the trial court, is

---

① As suggested by the cases described in the text, the limited duty of care applicable to coparticipants has been applied in situations involving a wide variety of active sports, ranging from baseball to ice hockey and skating. Because the touch football game at issue in this case clearly falls within the rationale of this rule, we have no occasion to decide whether a comparable limited duty of care appropriately should be applied to other less active sports, such as archery or golf. We note that because of the special danger to others posed by the sport of hunting, past cases generally have found the ordinary duty of care to be applicable to hunting accidents. See, e.g., *Summers v. Tice* (1948) 33 Cal. 2d 80, 83, 199 P. 2d 1.

affirmed.

Lucas, C.J., and Arabian, J., concur.

Mosk, Justice, concurring and dissenting.

Because I agreed with the substance of the majority opinion in *Li v. Yellow Cab Co.* (1975) 13 Cal.3d 804, 532 P.2d 1226 (*see id.* at p.830, 532 P.2d 1226), I concur generally with Justice George's analysis as set forth in part II of the lead opinion. And like the lead opinion, I conclude that the liability of sports participants should be limited to those cases in which their misconduct falls outside the range of the ordinary activity involved in the sport. As part I of the lead opinion explains, the kind of overexuberant conduct that is alleged here was not of that nature. I therefore agree that defendant was entitled to summary judgment, for the reasons set forth in part III of the lead opinion.

But I would go farther than does the lead opinion. Though the opinion's interpretation of *Li v. Yellow Cab Co.*, *supra*, 13 Cal.3d 804, 532 P.2d 1226 is reasonable, I believe the time has come to eliminate implied assumption of risk entirely. The all-or-nothing aspect of assumption of risk is as anachronistic as the all-or-nothing aspect of contributory negligence. As commentators have pointed out, the elements of assumption of risk "are accounted for already in the negligence *prima facie* case and existing comparative fault defense." Wildman & Barker, *Time to Abolish Implied Assumption of a Reasonable Risk in California*, (1991) 25 U.S.F. L. REV. 647, 679. Plaintiffs' behavior can be analyzed under comparative fault principles; no separate defense is needed. (*See id.*) Wildman and Barker explain cogently that numerous California cases invoke both a duty analysis — which I prefer — and an unnecessary implied assumption of risk analysis in deciding a defendant's liability. (*See id.* at p.657 & fn. 58.) In the case before us, too, the invocation of assumption of risk is superfluous; far better to limit the analysis to concluding that a participant owes no duty to avoid conduct of the type ordinarily involved in the sport.

Were we to eliminate the doctrine of assumption

of risk, we would put an end to the doctrinal confusion that now surrounds apportionment of fault in such cases. Assumption of risk now stands for so many different legal concepts that its utility has diminished. A great deal of the confusion surrounding the concept "stems from the fact that the term 'assumption of risk' has several different meanings and is often applied without recognizing these different meanings." *Rini v. Oaklawn Jockey Club* (8th Cir. 1988) 861 F. 2d 502, 504–505. Courts vainly attempt to analyze conduct in such esoteric terms as primary assumption of risk, secondary assumption of risk, reasonable implied assumption of risk, unreasonable implied assumption of risk, *etc*. Since courts have difficulty in assessing facts under the rubric of such abstruse distinctions, it is unlikely that juries can comprehend such distinctions.

Justice Frankfurter explained in a slightly different context, "The phrase 'assumption of risk' is an excellent illustration of the extent to which uncritical use of words bedevils the law. A phrase begins life as a literary expression; its felicity leads to its lazy repetition; and repetition soon establishes it as a legal formula, undiscriminatingly used to express different and sometimes contradictory ideas." *Tiller v. Atlantic Coast Line R. Co.* (1943) 318 U.S. 54, 68 (conc. opn. of Frankfurter, J.). Thus the *Rini* court, in attempting to determine the viability of assumption of risk in light of the Arkansas comparative fault law, was forced to identify "four types of assumption of risk ..." *Rini v. Oaklawn Jockey Club*, *supra*, 861 F. 2d at p. 505. These included "implied secondary reasonable assumption of risk" and "implied secondary unreasonable assumption of risk." *Id*. at p. 506.

I would eliminate the confusion that continued reliance on implied assumption of risk appears to cause, and would simply apply comparative fault principles to determine liability.

Panelli, justice, concurring and dissenting.

I concur in the majority opinion solely with respect to the result reached. The majority correctly affirms the judgment of the Court of Appeal, which upheld the summary judgment entered by the trial

doctrinal confusion 学理的混乱

diminish 缩减
surround 包围,环绕

vainly 徒劳地,自负地
esoteric 奥秘的

abstruse 难懂的,深奥的

uncritical 不加批判的

felicity 恰当
formula （普通法）诉讼中所用的一套程式化语句

viability 可行性

court. I dissent, however, from the reasoning of the majority opinion. Instead, I reach a like result by adopting and applying the "consent-based" analysis set forth in the dissenting opinion by Justice Kennard. While I subscribe to the analysis of the dissenting opinion with respect to the doctrine of implied assumption of the risk, I am not in accord with how it would dispose of this case. I believe that defendant met the burden of demonstrating that plaintiff assumed the risk of injury by her participation in the touch football game.

  As the dissenting opinion explains: "To establish the defense [of implied assumption of the risk], a defendant must prove that the plaintiff voluntarily accepted a risk with knowledge and appreciation of that risk. *Prescott v. Ralphs Grocery Co.*, (1954) 42 Cal. 2d 158, 161, 265 P. 2d 904." (Dis. opn., ante, p. 21 of 11 Cal. Rptr. 2d, p. 715 of 834 P. 2d.) As the dissenting opinion further explains: "A defendant need not prove, however, that the plaintiff 'had the prescience to foresee the exact accident and injury which in fact occurred.' *Sperling v. Hatch* (1970) 10 Cal. App. 3d 54, 61." *Id*.

  There is no question that plaintiff voluntarily chose to play touch football. ① The undisputed facts in this case also show that plaintiff knew of and accepted the risks associated with the game. Plaintiff was an avid football fan. She had participated in games of touch football in the past. She was aware of the fact that in touch football players try to deflect the ball from receiving players. Plaintiff admitted that the players in the game in question could expect to receive "bumps" and "bruises." These facts indicate that plaintiff knew and appreciated that physical injury resulting from contact, such as being knocked to the ground, was possible when playing touch football.

---

① Plaintiff points to her request to the defendant during the game to temper his roughness to demonstrate that she did not assume the risk of being injured. She claims that defendant "seemed to acknowledge [her] statement" and "left [her] with the impression that he would play less rough." Plaintiff's reported request to defendant does not defeat summary judgment. She continued to play the game. As demonstrated below, she knew that physical contact and resulting injury could occur during a touch football game.

Defendant was not required to prove more, such as that plaintiff knew or appreciated that a "serious injury" or her particular injury could result from the expected physical contact.

To support the conclusion that summary judgment be reversed under the consent-based approach, the dissenting opinion stresses the broad range of activities that can be part of a "touch football game" and that few rules were delineated for the particular game in which plaintiff was injured. I find these facts to be irrelevant to the question at hand. The risk of physical contact and the possibility of resulting injury is inherent in the game of football, no matter who is playing the game or how it is played. While the players who participated in the game in question may have wanted a "mellow" and "noncompetitive" game, such expectations do not alter the fact that anyone who has observed or played any form of football understands that it is a contact sport and that physical injury can result from such physical contact.

The undisputed facts of this case amply support awarding defendant summary judgment based upon plaintiff's implied assumption of the risk. I, therefore, concur in affirming the judgment of the Court of Appeal.

Baxter, J., concurs.

Kennard, Justice, dissenting.

I disagree with the plurality opinion both in its decision to affirm summary judgment for defendant and in its analytic approach to the defense of assumption of risk.

We granted review in this case and its companion, *Ford v. Gouin*, 3 Cal. 4th 339, 834 P. 2d 724, to resolve a lopsided conflict in the Courts of Appeal on whether our adoption 17 years ago of a system of comparative fault in *Li v. Yellow Cab Co.* (1975) 13 Cal. 3d 804, 532 P. 2d 1226 (hereafter *Li*) necessarily abolished the affirmative defense of implied assumption of risk.① When confronted with this issue,

delineate 描述

mellow 柔和的

amply 充足地

plurality 多数

analytic approach 分析法

lopsided conflict 不平衡的冲突

---

① Of the several Court of Appeal decisions that considered this issue, only one concluded that our adoption in *Li* of a system of comparative fault necessarily abolished the traditional defense of assumption of risk.

the overwhelming majority of appellate courts in this state have held that, except to the extent it was subsumed within the former doctrine of contributory negligence this court abolished in *Li*, implied assumption of risk continues as a complete defense. I would so hold in this case, adhering to the traditional analysis of implied assumption of risk established by a long line of California cases, both before and after *Li*.

Not content with deciding the straightforward issue before us — whether the defense of implied assumption of risk survived *Li* — the plurality opinion uses this case as a forum to advocate a <u>radical transformation</u> of tort law. The plurality proposes to recast the analysis of implied assumption of risk from a subjective evaluation of what a particular plaintiff knew and appreciated about the encountered risk into a determination of the presence or absence of duty legally imposed on the defendant. By thus transforming an affirmative defense into an element of the plaintiff's negligence action, the plurality would abolish the defense without acknowledging that it is doing so.

The plurality opinion also announces a rule that those who engage in active sports do not owe coparticipants the usual duty of care — as measured by the standard of a reasonable person in like or similar circumstances — to avoid inflicting physical injury. According to the plurality, a sports participant has no duty to avoid conduct inherent in a particular sport. Although I agree that in organized sports contests played under well-established rules participants have no duty to avoid the very conduct that constitutes the sport, I cannot accept the plurality's nearly <u>boundless</u> expansion of this general principle to eliminate altogether the "reasonable person" standard as the measure of duty actually owed between sports participants.

The ultimate question posed by this case is whether the trial court properly granted summary judgment for defendant. Deriving the facts from the evidence that the parties presented to the trial court on defendant's motion for summary judgment, and relying on well-established summary judgment principles, I conclude that defendant is not entitled to summary judgment.

---

radical transformation 根本转变

boundless 没有限制的

In reaching a contrary conclusion, the plurality mischaracterizes the nature of the athletic contest during which plaintiff incurred her injury. The evidence reveals that rather than an organized match with well-defined rules, it was an impromptu and informal game among casual acquaintances who entertained divergent views about how it would be played. This inconclusive record simply does not permit a pretrial determination that plaintiff knew and appreciated the risks she faced or that her injury resulted from a risk inherent in the game.

mischaracterize 曲解

athletic contest 体育竞赛

impromptu 即席的

I

To explain my conclusion that implied assumption of risk survives as an affirmative defense under the system of comparative fault this court adopted in *Li* in 1975, I first summarize the main features of the defense as established by decisions published before *Li*.

In California, the affirmative defense of assumption of risk has traditionally been defined as the voluntary acceptance of a specific, known and appreciated risk that is or may have been caused or contributed to by the negligence of another. *Prescott v. Ralphs Grocery Co.* (1954) 42 Cal. 2d 158, 162, 265 P. 2d 904; *see Hayes v. Richfield Oil Corp.* (1952) 38 Cal. 2d 375, 384 - 385, 240 P. 2d 580. Assumption of risk may be proved either by the plaintiff's spoken or written words (express assumption of risk), or by inference from the plaintiff's conduct (implied assumption of risk). Whether the plaintiff knew and appreciated the specific risk, and voluntarily chose to encounter it, has generally been a jury question. *See* 6 Witkin, SUMMARY OF CAL. LAW (9th ed. 1988) TORTS, § 1110, p. 523.

The defense of assumption of risk, whether the risk is assumed expressly or by implication, is based on consent. (*Vierra v. Fifth Avenue Rental Service* (1963) 60 Cal. 2d 266, 271, 383 P. 2d 777; *see* Prosser & Keeton, TORTS (5th ed. 1984) § 68, p. 484.) Thus, in both the express and implied forms, the defense is a specific application of the maxim that one "who consents to an act is not wronged by it." CIV. CODE,

maxim 法律格言,法律原则,法律准则

§3515. This consent, we have explained, "will negative liability." *Prescott v. Ralphs Grocery Co.*, *supra*, 42 Cal. 2d 158, 161, 265 P. 2d 904; see also *Gyerman v. United States Lines Co.* (1972) 7 Cal. 3d 488, 498, fn. 10, 498 P. 2d 1043 ["In assumption of the risk the negligent party's liability is negated..."], and thus provides a complete defense to an action for negligence.

The elements of implied assumption of risk deserve some explanation. To establish the defense, a defendant must prove that the plaintiff voluntarily accepted a risk with knowledge and appreciation of that risk. *Prescott v. Ralphs Grocery Co.*, *supra*, 42 Cal. 2d 158, 161, 265 P. 2d 904. The normal risks inherent in everyday life, such as the chance that one who uses a public highway will be injured by the negligence of another motorist, are not subject to the defense, however, because they are general rather than specific risks. See *Hook v. Point Montara Fire Protection Dist.* (1963) 213 Cal. App. 2d 96, 101.

The defense of implied assumption of risk depends on the plaintiff's "actual knowledge of the specific danger involved." *Vierra v. Fifth Avenue Rental Service*, *supra*, 60 Cal. 2d 266, 274, 383 P. 2d 777. Thus, one who "knew of the general danger in riding in a bucket of the mine owner's aerial tramway, did not assume the risk, of which he had no specific knowledge, that the traction cable was improperly spliced." *Id.* at p. 272, 383 P. 2d 777, referring to *Bee v. Tungstar Corp.* (1944) 65 Cal. App. 2d 729, 733, 151 P. 2d 537; see also *Carr v. Pacific Tel. Co.* (1972) 26 Cal. App. 3d 537, 542-543. A defendant need not prove, however, that the plaintiff "had the clairvoyance to foresee the exact accident and injury which in fact occurred." *Sperling v. Hatch* (1970) 10 Cal. App. 3d 54, 61. "Where the facts are such that the plaintiff must have had knowledge of the hazard, the situation is equivalent to actual knowledge and there may be an assumption of the risk..." *Prescott v. Ralphs Grocery Co.*, *supra*, 42 Cal. 2d at 162, 265 P. 2d 904. Indeed, certain well-known risks of harm may be within the general "common knowledge." *Tavernier v. Maes* (1966) 242 Cal. App. 2d 532, 546.

As set forth earlier, a person's assumption of risk must be voluntary. "The plaintiff's acceptance of a risk is not voluntary if the defendant's tortious conduct has left him [or her] no reasonable alternative course of conduct in order to [¶] (a) avert harm to himself [or herself] or another, or [¶] (b) exercise or protect a right or privilege of which the defendant has no right to deprive him [or her]." REST. 2D TORTS, § 496E, subd. (2); see also *Curran v. Green Hills Country Club* (1972) 24 Cal. App. 3d 501, 505 - 506.

This requirement of voluntariness precludes assertion of the defense of assumption of risk by a defendant who has negligently caused injury to another through conduct that violates certain safety statutes or ordinances such as those designed to protect a class of persons unable to provide for their own safety for reasons of inequality of bargaining power or lack of knowledge. See *Finnegan v. Royal Realty Co.* (1950) 35 Cal. 2d 409, 430 - 431, 218 P. 2d 17 [violation of fire-safety ordinance]; *Fonseca v. County of Orange* (1972) 28 Cal. App. 3d 361, 366, 368 [violation of safety order requiring <u>scaffolding</u> and <u>railings</u> at bridge construction site]; see also *Mason v. Case* (1963) 220 Cal. App. 2d 170, 177. Thus, a worker who, to avoid loss of livelihood, continues to work in the face of safety violations does not thereby assume the risk of injury as a result of those violations. See, e.g., LAB. CODE, § 2801; *Fonseca v. County of Orange*, supra, 28 Cal. App. 3d 361. In such cases, the implied agreement upon which the defense is based is contrary to public policy and therefore unenforceable.

Our 1975 decision in *Li*, supra, 13 Cal. 3d 804, 532 P. 2d 1226, marked a fundamental change in California law governing tort liability based on negligence. Before *Li*, a person's own lack of due care for his or her safety, known as contributory negligence, completely barred that person from recovering damages for injuries inflicted by the negligent conduct of another. In *Li*, we held that a lack of care for one's own safety would no longer entirely bar recovery, and that juries thereafter should compare the fault or negligence of the plaintiff with that of the defendant to apportion loss between the

scaffolding 脚手架,建筑架

railing 扶手,栏杆

two. *Id.* at pp. 828 – 829, 532 P. 2d 1226.

Before it was abolished by *Li*, *supra*, 13 Cal. 3d 804, 532 P. 2d 1226, the defense of contributory negligence was sometimes confused with the defense of implied assumption of risk. Although this court had acknowledged that the two defenses may "arise from the same set of facts and frequently overlap," *Vierra v. Fifth Avenue Rental Service*, *supra*, 60 Cal. 2d 266, 271, 383 P. 2d 777, we had emphasized that they were nonetheless "essentially different" (*id.*) because they were "based on different theories" *Prescott v. Ralphs Grocery Co.*, *supra*, 42 Cal. 2d 158, 161, 265 P. 2d 904. Contributory negligence was premised on a lack of due care or, stated another way, a departure from the reasonable person standard, whereas implied assumption of risk has always depended on a voluntary acceptance of a risk with knowledge and appreciation of that risk. *Id.* at pp. 161 – 162, 265 P. 2d 904; *Gonzalez v. Garcia* (1977) 75 Cal. App. 3d 874, 878.

The standards for evaluating a plaintiff's conduct under the two defenses were entirely different. Under contributory negligence, the plaintiff's conduct was measured against the objective standard of a hypothetical reasonable person. *Gonzalez v. Garcia*, *supra*, 75 Cal. App. 3d 874, 879. Implied assumption of risk, in contrast, has always depended upon the plaintiff's subjective mental state; the relevant inquiry is whether the plaintiff actually knew, appreciated, and voluntarily consented to assume a specific risk of injury. *Grey v. Fibreboard Paper Products Co.* (1966) 65 Cal. 2d 240, 243 – 245, 418 P. 2d 153.

We said in *Li*, <u>albeit</u> in <u>dictum</u>, that our adoption of a system of comparative fault would to some extent necessarily impact the defense of implied assumption of risk. *Li*, *supra*, 13 Cal. 3d 804, 826, 532 P. 2d 1226. We explained: "As for assumption of risk, we have recognized in this state that this defense overlaps that of contributory negligence to some extent and in fact is made up of at least two distinct defenses. 'To simplify greatly, it has been observed … that in one kind of situation, *to wit*, where a plaintiff unreasonably undertakes to encounter a specific known risk imposed by a defendant's negligence, plaintiff's conduct,

albeit 尽管，虽然
dictum 法官个人意见，附带意见

CHAPTER 7   TORTS OF NEGLIGENCE   **359**

although he [or she] may encounter that risk in a prudent manner, is in reality a form of contributory negligence ... Other kinds of situations within the doctrine of assumption of risk are those, for example, where plaintiff is held to agree to relieve defendant of an obligation of reasonable conduct toward him [or her]. Such a situation would not involve contributory negligence, but rather a reduction of defendant's duty of care.' [Citations.] We think it clear that the adoption of a system of comparative negligence should entail the merger of the defense of assumption of risk into the general scheme of assessment of liability in proportion to fault in those particular cases in which the form of assumption of risk involved is no more than a variant of contributory negligence." *Li*, *supra*, 13 Cal. 3d 804, 824 – 825, 532 P. 2d 1226.

Although our adoption in *Li* of a system of comparative fault eliminated contributory negligence as a separate defense, it did not alter the basic attributes of the implied assumption of risk defense or call into question its theoretical foundations, as we affirmed in several cases decided after *Li*. For example, in *Walters v. Sloan* (1977) 20 Cal. 3d 199, 571 P. 2d 609, we said that "one who has knowingly and voluntarily confronted a hazard cannot recover for injuries sustained thereby." At p. 204, 571 P. 2d 609; see also *Ewing v. Cloverleaf Bowl* (1978) 20 Cal. 3d 389, 406, 572 P. 2d 1155 [acknowledging the continued viability of the assumption of risk defense after the adoption of comparative fault]. Thereafter, in *Lipson v. Superior Court* (1982) 31 Cal. 3d 362, 644 P. 2d 822, we reiterated that "the defense of assumption of risk arises when the plaintiff voluntarily undertakes to encounter a specific known risk imposed by defendant's conduct." At p. 375, fn. 8, 644 P. 2d 822.

The Courts of Appeal directly addressed this issue in several cases, which were decided after *Li*, *supra*, 13 Cal. 3d 804, 532 P. 2d 1226, and which considered whether, and to what extent, implied assumption of risk as a complete defense survived our adoption in *Li* of a system of comparative fault. The first of these cases was *Segoviano v. Housing Authority* (1983) 143

attribute 特质,特性

reiterate 重申

Cal. App. 3d 162 (hereafter *Segoviano*).

In *Segoviano*, the plaintiff was injured during a flag football game when an opposing player pushed him to the ground as the plaintiff was running along the sidelines trying to score a touchdown. Although the jury found that the opposing player was negligent, and that this negligence was a legal cause of the plaintiff's injury, it also found that the plaintiff's participation in the game was a negligent act that contributed to the injury. Applying the instructions it had been given on comparative negligence, the jury apportioned fault for the injury between the two players and reduced the plaintiff's award in accord with that apportionment. 143 Cal. App. 3d at p. 166.

To determine whether the jury had acted properly in making a comparative fault apportionment, the *Segoviano* court began its analysis by distinguishing those cases in which the plaintiff's decision to encounter a known risk was "unreasonable" from those in which it was "reasonable." *Segoviano*, *supra*, 143 Cal. App. 3d 162, 164. In so doing, *Segoviano* relied on this court's language in *Li*, which I have quoted on page 23 of 11 Cal. Rptr. 2d, page 717 of 834 P. 2d, ante that a plaintiff's conduct in "unreasonably" undertaking to encounter a specific known risk was "a form of contributory negligence" that would be merged "into the general scheme of assessment of liability in proportion to fault." *Li*, *supra*, 13 Cal. 3d 804, 824 – 825, 532 P. 2d 1226.

The *Segoviano* court defined an "unreasonable" decision to encounter a known risk as one that "falls below the standard of care which a person of ordinary prudence would exercise to avoid injury to himself or herself under the circumstances." *Segoviano*, *supra*, 143 Cal. App. 3d 162, 175, citing REST. 2D TORTS, § 463. The *Segoviano* court cited a person's voluntary choice to ride with a drunk driver as an example of an "unreasonable" decision. *Id*. at p. 175; see *Gonzalez v. Garcia*, *supra*, 75 Cal. App. 3d 874, 881; *Paula v. Gagnon* (1978) 81 Cal. App. 3d 680, 685. Because an "unreasonable" decision to risk injury is neglect for one's own safety, the *Segoviano* court observed, a jury can appropriately compare the negligent plaintiff's fault with that of the negligent defendant and apportion responsibility for the injury, applying comparative fault principles to determine the extent of the defendant's liability. *Segoviano, supra,* at pp. 164, 170.

By contrast, the plaintiff's decision to play flag football was, in the *Segoviano* court's view, an example of a "reasonable" decision to encounter a known risk of injury. Although the risk of being injured during a flag football game could be avoided altogether by choosing not to play, this did not render the plaintiff's decision to play "unreasonable." *Segoviano, supra,* 143 Cal. App. 3d 162, 175. Rather, the court said, a person who participates in a game of flag football is not negligent in doing so, because the choice does not fall below the standard of care that a person of ordinary prudence would exercise to avoid being injured. The *Segoviano* court concluded that such cases, in which there is no negligence of the plaintiff to compare with the negligence of the defendant, cannot be resolved by comparative fault apportionment of the plaintiff's damages. *Id.* at pp. 174 – 175.

The *Segoviano* court next considered whether the defense of implied assumption of risk, to the extent it had not merged into comparative fault, continued to provide a complete defense to an action for negligence following our decision in *Li, supra,* 13 Cal. 3d 804, 532 P. 2d 1226. The court asked, in other words, whether a plaintiff's voluntary and nonnegligent decision to encounter a specific known risk was still a complete bar to recovery, or no bar at all.

In resolving this issue, the court found persuasive a commentator's suggestion that "it would be whimsical to treat one who has unreasonably assumed the risk more favorably ... than one who reasonably assumed the risk ..." *Segoviano, supra,* 143 Cal. App. 3d 162, 169, quoting Fleming, *The Supreme Court of California 1974 – 1975, Forward: Comparative Negligence at Last — By Judicial Choice* (1976) 64 CAL. L. REV. 239, 262. To avoid this "whimsical" result, in which "unreasonable" plaintiffs were allowed partial recovery by way of a comparative fault apportionment while "reasonable"

whimsical 古怪的

plaintiffs were entirely barred from recovery of damages, the *Segoviano* court concluded that our decision in *Li*, *supra*, 13 Cal. 3d 804, 532 P. 2d 1226, must mean that the defense of implied assumption of risk had been abolished in all those instances in which it had not merged into the system of comparative fault, and that only express assumption of risk survived as a complete defense to an action for negligence. *Segoviano*, *supra*, 143 Cal. App. 3d 162, 169 – 170. The *Segoviano* court thus held that the defense of implied assumption of risk "plays no part in the comparative negligence system of California." *Id*. at p. 164. Various Court of Appeal decisions soon challenged this holding of *Segoviano*.

One decision characterized *Segovian's* analysis as "suspect." *Rudnick v. Golden West Broadcasters* (1984) 156 Cal. App. 3d 793, 800, *fn*. 4. Another case disregarded it entirely in reaching a contrary result (*Nelson v. Hall* (1985) 165 Cal. App. 3d 709, 714 ["Where assumption of the risk is not merely a form of contributory negligence," it remains "a complete defense."]; *accord*, *Neinstein v. Los Angeles Dodgers, Inc*. (1986) 185 Cal. App. 3d 176, 183; *Willenberg v. Superior Court* (1986) 185 Cal. App. 3d 185, 186 – 187). And in *Ordway v. Superior Court* (1988) 198 Cal. App. 3d 98, 104 (hereafter *Ordway*), the court rejected *Segoviano* outright, holding instead that "reasonable" implied assumption of risk continued as a complete defense under the newly adopted system of comparative fault.

The Court of Appeal that decided *Ordway*, *supra*, interpreted *Li*'s reference to a form of assumption of risk under which "plaintiff is held to agree to relieve defendant of an obligation of reasonable conduct toward him [or her]" (*Li*, *supra*, 13 Cal. 3d at 824, 532 P. 2d 1226) as describing a doctrine that the *Ordway* court termed "reasonable" implied assumption of risk. This doctrine, the *Ordway* court concluded, was unaffected by *Li*'s adoption of a system of comparative negligence and remained a complete defense after *Li*. *Ordway*, *supra*, 198 Cal. App. 3d 98, 103 – 104. According to *Ordway*, a plaintiff who voluntarily and reasonably assumes a risk, "whether

outright 率直地,一直向前,立刻地

for recreational enjoyment, economic reward, or some similar purpose," is deemed thereby to have agreed to reduce the defendant's duty of care and "cannot prevail." *Id*. at p. 104.

After concluding that the defense of implied assumption of risk remained viable after this court's decision in *Li*, *supra*, 13 Cal. 3d 804, 532 P. 2d 1226, the *Ordway* court discussed the preclusive impact of the defense on the facts of the case before it. *Ordway* involved a negligence action brought by a professional jockey who had been injured in a horse race when another jockey, violating a rule of the California Horse Racing Board, crossed into the plaintiff's lane. The court first noted that professional jockeys must be aware that injury-causing accidents are both possible and common in horse racing, as in other sports activities. *Ordway*, *supra*, 198 Cal. App. 3d 98, 111. The court observed that although the degree of risk to be anticipated would vary with the particular sport involved, a plaintiff may not recover from a coparticipant for a sports injury if the coparticipant's injury-causing actions fell within the ordinary expectations of those engaged in the sport. *Id*. at pp. 111 – 112. On this basis, the *Ordway* court held that the plaintiff jockey's action was barred.

Other decisions by the Courts of Appeal that have addressed implied assumption of risk have followed *Ordway*, *supra*, 198 Cal. App. 3d 98. *Nunez v. R'Bibo* (1989) 211 Cal. App. 3d 559, 562 – 563; *Von Beltz v. Stuntman, Inc.* (1989) 207 Cal. App. 3d 1467, 1477 – 1478; *King v. Magnolia Homeowners Assn.* (1988) 205 Cal. App. 3d 1312, 1316. In my view, *Ordway* was correct in its conclusions that the defense of implied assumption of risk survived this court's adoption in *Li*, *supra*, 13 Cal. 3d 804, 532 P. 2d 1226, of a system of comparative fault, and that the defense remains a complete bar to recovery in negligence cases in which the plaintiff has knowingly and voluntarily consented to encounter a specific risk.

Ordway was also correct in its observation that the terms "unreasonable" and "reasonable" are confusing when used to distinguish the form of implied assumption of risk that has merged into the system of

recreational enjoyment 休闲娱乐

preclusive 除外的，妨碍的

jockey 赛马的骑师

comparative fault from the form that has not so merged. As *Ordway* suggested, the reasonable/unreasonable labels would be more easily understood by substituting the terms "knowing and intelligent" for "reasonable," and "negligent or careless" for "unreasonable." *Ordway*, *supra*, 198 Cal. App. 3d 98, 105.

The defense of implied assumption of risk is never based on the "reasonableness" of the plaintiff's conduct, as such, but rather on a recognition that a person generally should be required to accept responsibility for the normal consequences of a freely chosen course of conduct. *See* Simons, *Assumption of Risk and Consent in the Law of Torts: A Theory of Full Preference* (1987) 67 B. U. L. Rev. 213, 258 ["consent is neither reasonable nor unreasonable[;] [i]t simply expresses what plaintiff wants or prefers"]. In implied assumption of risk situations, the plaintiff's conduct often defies legal characterization as either reasonable or unreasonable. Even when this is not so, and a court or jury could appropriately determine whether the plaintiff's conduct was reasonable, the distinction to be drawn is not so much between reasonable and unreasonable conduct. Rather, the essential distinction is between conduct that is deliberate and conduct that is merely careless. Referring to "reasonable" implied assumption of risk lends unwarranted credence to the charge that the law is "whimsical" in treating unreasonable behavior more favorably than behavior that is reasonable. There is nothing arbitrary or whimsical in requiring plaintiffs to accept responsibility for the consequences of their considered and deliberate choices, while at the same time apportioning liability between a plaintiff and a defendant who have both exhibited carelessness.

In those cases that have merged into comparative fault, partial recovery is permitted, not because the plaintiff has acted unreasonably, but because the unreasonableness of the plaintiff's apparent choice provides compelling evidence that the plaintiff was merely careless and could not have truly appreciated and voluntarily consented to the risk, or because enforcement of the implied agreement on which the defense is based would be contrary to sound public policy. In these cases, implied assumption of risk is simply not available as a defense, although comparative negligence may be.

In those cases in which a plaintiff's decision to encounter a specific known risk was not the result of carelessness (that is, when the plaintiff's conduct is not merely a form of contributory negligence), nothing in this court's adoption in *Li*, *supra*, 13 Cal. 3d 804, 532 P. 2d 1226 of a system of comparative fault suggests that implied assumption of risk must or should be eliminated as a complete defense to an action for negligence. I would hold, therefore, that the defense continues to exist in such situations unaffected by this court's adoption in *Li* of a comparative fault system.

II

The plurality opinion approaches the viability of implied assumption of risk after *Li*, *supra*, 13 Cal. 3d 804, 532 P. 2d 1226, in a fashion altogether different from the traditional consent analysis I have described. It begins by conceding that *Li* effected only a partial merger of the assumption of risk defense into the system of comparative fault. It then concludes, with no foundational support in California law, that the actual effect of this partial merger was to bifurcate implied assumption of risk into two subcategories that the plurality calls "primary" and "secondary" assumption of risk.

bifurcate 分成两部分
subcategory 子范畴,亚类

The plurality's "secondary assumption of risk" category includes those situations in which assumption of risk is merely a variant of contributory negligence. In those situations, under the plurality approach, implied assumption of risk merges into comparative fault; a trial court presented with a "secondary" case would therefore instruct the jury only on the principles of damage apportionment based on comparative fault, but not on implied assumption of risk as a separate and complete defense. Thus, implied assumption of risk does not survive as a separate and complete defense in these "secondary" cases.

variant 变体,异体

Under the plurality's approach, implied assumption of risk fares no better in the "primary assumption of risk" cases. That category includes only those cases in

fare 进展

which the defendant owes no duty to the plaintiff. Without duty, of course, there is no basis for a negligence action and thus no need for an affirmative defense to negligence. Consequently, implied assumption of risk ceases to operate as an affirmative defense in these "primary" cases.

The plurality purports to interpret *Li*, *supra*, 13 Cal. 3d 804, 532 P. 2d 1226, but instead works a <u>sleight-of-hand switch</u> on the assumption of risk defense.

In those situations in which implied assumption of risk does not merge into comparative fault, the plurality recasts what has always been a question of the plaintiff's implied consent into a question of the defendant's duty. This fundamental alteration of well-established tort principles was not <u>preordained</u> by *Li* nor was it a logical evolution of California law either before or after this court's decision in *Li*. <u>Seizing</u> on *Li*'s statement that a plaintiff who assumes the risk thereby reduces a defendant's duty of care, the plurality concludes that defendants had no duty of care in the first place. The plurality presents its analysis as merely an integration of the defense of implied assumption of risk into the system of comparative fault, but this "integration" is in truth a complete abolition of a defense that California courts have adhered to for more than 50 years. I see no need or justification for this drastic revision of California law.

III

On a motion for summary judgment, a defendant can establish implied assumption of risk as a complete defense to negligence by submitting uncontroverted evidence that the plaintiff sustained the injury while engaged in voluntarily chosen activity under circumstances showing that the plaintiff knew or must have known that the specific risks of the chosen activity included the injury suffered. See Code Civ. Proc., § 437c, subds. (a), (c), (f); *Garcia v. Rockwell Internat. Corp.* (1986) 187 Cal. App. 3d 1556, 1560; *Fireman's Fund Ins. Co. v. City of Turlock* (1985) 170 Cal. App. 3d 988, 994. In this case, the trial court entered summary judgment for defendant, ruling that the evidence supporting the motion established assumption of risk under the traditional consent analysis.

The undisputed, material facts are as follows: Plaintiff, defendant, and six or eight other guests gathered at the home of a mutual friend to watch a television broadcast of the 1987 Super Bowl football game. During the game's half time, the group went to an adjacent dirt lot for an informal game of touch football. The participants divided into two teams, each including men as well as women. They used a child's soft, "peewee-size" football for the game. The players expected the game to be "mellow" and "noncompetitive," without any "forceful pushing, hard hitting or hard shoving."

Plaintiff and defendant were on opposing teams. Plaintiff was an avid fan of televised professional football, but she had played touch football only rarely and never with this particular group. When defendant ran into her early in the game, plaintiff objected, stating that he was playing too roughly and if he continued, she would not play. Plaintiff stated in her declaration that defendant "seemed to acknowledge [her] statement" and "left [her] with the impression that he would play less rough." On the very next play, defendant knocked plaintiff down and inflicted the injury for which she seeks recovery.

We have held that summary judgment "is a drastic measure" that should "be used with caution." *Molko v. Holy Spirit Assn.* (1988) 46 Cal.3d 1092, 1107, 762 P.2d 46. On appeal from a summary judgment, well-settled rules dictate that the moving party's evidence supporting the motion be strictly construed and that doubts about granting the motion be resolved in favor of the party that opposed the motion. *Id.* Applying those rules here, I conclude that defendant has not established implied assumption of risk as a complete defense to plaintiff's action for negligence.

Notably missing from the undisputed facts is any evidence that plaintiff either knew or must have known that by participating in this particular game she would be engaging in a sport that would subject players to being knocked to the ground. She had played touch football only rarely, never with these players, and just before her injury had expressly told defendant that her

drastic 激烈的

dictate 命令,要求,规定

participation in the touch football game was conditioned on him not being so rough. Moreover, the game was not even a regular game of touch football. When deposed, defendant conceded that this touch football game was highly unusual because the teams consisted of both men and women and the players used a child's peewee ball. He agreed that the game was not "regulation football," but was more of a "mock" football game.

"Touch football" is less the name of a game than it is a generic description that encompasses a broad spectrum of activity. At one end of the spectrum is the "traditional" aggressive sandlot game, in which the risk of being knocked down and injured should be immediately apparent to even the most casual observer. At the other end is the game that a parent gently plays with young children, really little more than a game of catch. Here, defendant may prevail on his summary judgment motion only if the undisputed facts show that plaintiff knew this to be the type of game that involved a risk of being knocked to the ground. As explained above, such knowledge by the plaintiff was not established. Accordingly, the trial court erred in granting summary judgment for defendant on the ground that plaintiff had assumed the risk of injury.

IV

To uphold the grant of summary judgment for defendant, the plurality relies on a form of analysis virtually without precedent in this state. As an offshoot of its advocacy of the primary/secondary approach to implied assumption of risk, the plurality endorses a categorical rule under which coparticipants in active sports have no duty to avoid conduct "inherent" in the sport, and thus no liability for injuries resulting from such conduct. Applying the rule to the facts shown here, the plurality concludes that plaintiff's injury resulted from a risk "inherent" in the sport she played and that defendant owed her no duty to avoid the conduct that caused this injury.

Generally, a person is under a legal duty to use ordinary care, measured by the conduct of a hypothetical reasonable person in like or similar circumstances, to avoid injury to others. CIV. CODE, § 1714, subd. (a). Judicially fashioned exceptions to this general duty rule must be clearly supported by public policy. *Burgess v. Superior Court* (1992) 2 Cal. 4th 1064, 1079, 831 P. 2d 1197. The plurality's no-duty-for-sports rule is such a judicially fashioned exception to the general duty rule. Under the plurality's rule, a sports participant's conduct is not evaluated by the "reasonable person" standard. Rather, the player is exempted from negligence liability for all injuries resulting from conduct that is "inherent" in the sport.

The plurality's no-duty-for-sports rule derives from cases in a few jurisdictions concluding that a participant's liability for injuries to a coparticipant during competitive sports must be based on reckless or intentional conduct. See *Gauvin v. Clark* (1989) 404 Mass. 450, 537 N. E. 2d 94; *Kabella v. Bouschelle* (Ct. App. 1983) 100 N. M. 461, 672 P. 2d 290; *Ross v. Clouser* (Mo. 1982) 637 S. W. 2d 11; *Nabozny v. Barnhill* (1975) 31 Ill. App. 3d 212, 334 N. E. 2d 258. Although these courts have chosen to explain the rule in terms of the absence of duty, the consent analysis of implied assumption of risk would provide an equally satisfactory explanation. See *Ordway*, *supra*, 198 Cal. App. 3d 98, 110 – 112. The reason no duty exists in these competitive sports situations is that, as the Massachusetts Supreme Court has explained in *Gauvin*, each participant has a right to infer that the others have agreed to <u>undergo</u> a type of physical contact that would otherwise constitute assault and battery. ① *Gauvin v. Clark*, *supra*, 537 N. E. 2d at p. 96. Without some reference to mutual consent or implied agreement among coparticipants, the no-duty-for-sports rule would be difficult to explain and justify. Thus, the rationale of the rule, even in no-duty <u>garb</u>, is harmonious with the traditional logic of implied assumption of risk.

undergo 遭受,忍受,经历

garb 外表,装扮

---

① In adopting a rule of no duty for organized competitive sports, the Massachusetts court candidly acknowledged that legislative abolition of the assumption of risk defense had forced it to shift the focus of analysis from the plaintiff's knowing confrontation of risk to the scope of the defendant's duty of care. *Gauvin v. Clark*, *supra*, 537 N. E. 2d at p. 97, *fn.* 5.

Although there is nothing inherently wrong with the plurality's no-duty rule as applied to organized, competitive, contact sports with well-established modes of play, it should not be extended to other, more casual sports activities, such as the informal "mock" football game shown by the evidence in this case. Outside the context of organized and well-defined sports, the policy basis for the duty limitation — that the law should permit and encourage vigorous athletic competition (*Gauvin v. Clark, supra*, 537 N. E. 2d at p. 96) — is considerably weakened or entirely absent. Thus, the no-duty-for-sports rule logically applies only to organized sports contests played under well-settled, official rules (*Gauvin v. Clark, supra*, 537 N. E. 2d 94 [college varsity hockey game]; *Ross v. Clouser, supra*, 637 S. W. 2d 11 [church league softball game]; *Nabozny v. Barnhill, supra*, 334 N. E. 2d 258 [organized, amateur soccer game]), or on unequivocal evidence that the sport as played involved the kind of physical contact that generally could be expected to result in injury (*Kabella v. Bouschelle, supra*, 100 N.M. 461, 672 P. 2d 290).

The plurality may believe that its no-duty rule for sports participants will facilitate early resolution of personal injury actions by demurrer or motions for summary judgment and thus provide relief to overburdened trial courts by eliminating the need for jury trials in many of these cases. But the plurality fails to explain just how trial courts will be able to discern, at an early stage in the proceedings, which risks are inherent in a given sport.

Under the plurality's no-duty-for-sports rule, a sports participant is exempted from negligence liability for all injuries resulting from conduct that is within "the range of ordinary activity involved in the sport." Plur. opn., *ante*, at p. 17 of 11 Cal. Rptr. 2d, p. 711 of 834 P. 2d. Under this approach, as the plurality acknowledges, "the nature of a defendant's duty in the sports context depends heavily on the nature of the sport itself." *Id*. at p. 15 of 11 Cal. Rptr. 2d, p. 709 of 834 P. 2d.

The issue framed by the plurality's no-duty approach

varsity 大学运动代表队

amateur 业余的
soccer game 英式足球比赛

unequivocal 清楚的,明白的,不会出错的,毫无疑问的,确定的(用于证明责任方面时,意指达到最高可能性的和确定无疑的证明)

discern 分辨,识别

can be decided on demurrer only if the plaintiff has alleged in the complaint that the injury resulted from a risk inherent in an injury-causing sport, something careful pleaders are unlikely to do. And because summary judgment depends on uncontroverted material facts, early adjudication of the duty issue by summary judgment is equally doubtful. In cases involving all but the most well-known professional sports, plaintiffs will usually be able to counter defense evidence seeking to establish what risks are inherent in the sport. Cases that cannot be resolved by demurrer or summary judgment will, under the plurality's approach, proceed to trial solely under comparative fault, leaving the jury no opportunity to decide whether the plaintiff made a knowing and voluntary decision to assume the risk.

adjudication（法院的）宣判,裁定

The plurality's resolution of this case amply illustrates the difficulty of attempting to decide the question of duty by motion for summary judgment. To sustain summary judgment under the plurality's approach, the defendant must have conclusively negated the element of duty necessary to the plaintiff's negligence case. *Molko v. Holy Spirit Assn.*, *supra*, 46 Cal.3d 1092, 1107, 762 P.2d 46. Therefore, under the plurality approach, defendant here is entitled to summary judgment only if he negated the element of duty by presenting undisputed evidence showing that his injury-causing conduct was within the range of activity ordinarily involved in the sport he was then playing.

sustain 认可,确认

But what is "the range of the ordinary activity" involved in touch football? As I have previously explained, the generic term "touch football" encompasses such a broad range of activity that it is difficult to conceive of an "ordinary" game. Even if such a game could be identified, defendant offered no evidence in support of his motion for summary judgment to show that players are knocked to the ground in the "ordinary" game. In the absence of uncontroverted evidence on this material fact, defendant was not entitled to summary judgment.

conceive of 设想

As mentioned earlier, defendant admitted at his deposition that this was not a "regulation football" game, and that it was more of a "mock" game because it was played by both men and women using a child's peewee ball. Given the spontaneous and irregular form of the game, it is not surprising that the participants demonstrated uncertainty about the bounds of appropriate conduct. One participant, asked at deposition whether defendant had done anything "out of the normal," touched the nub of the problem by replying with this query: "Who's [sic; whose] normal? My normal?"

Defendant did not present uncontroverted evidence that his own rough level of play was "inherent" in or normal to the particular game being played. In the view of one of the players, defendant was playing "considerably rougher than was necessary." Other players described defendant as a fast runner and thought he might have been playing too hard. Absent uncontroverted evidence that defendant's aggressive style of play was appropriate, there is no basis for the plurality's conclusion that his injury-causing conduct in knocking plaintiff to the ground was within the range of ordinary and acceptable behavior for the ill-defined sports activity in which plaintiff was injured. Defendant did not meet his burden to establish by undisputed evidence a legal entitlement to summary judgment. The record fails to support summary judgment under either the traditional consent approach to the defense of assumption of risk or the plurality's no-duty approach. Thus, the trial court erred in granting defendant's motion for summary judgment, and the Court of Appeal erred in affirming that judgment. I would reverse.

spontaneous 自发的

nub 要点
query 疑问,质问

Review Questions

1. What are the basic elements of the tort of negligence?
2. Do the courts use objective standard or subjective standard in evaluating the duties owed by the defendant?
3. If the plaintiff cannot find sufficient evidence to prove that the defendant breached the duty, how does common law court protect the plaintiff's interests?
4. What is the cause in fact, what is the cause in law?
5. Do you think the comparative negligence doctrine is a better one than the contributory negligence doctrine? Why or why not?
6. How to understand the foreseeability issue in the tort of negligence?

CHAPTER 8
STRICT LIABILITY

　　根据英美侵权法,基于公共利益和公共政策等原因,行为人还可能需要在没有任何过错时承担侵权责任,即严格责任。一旦严格责任制被采纳,即使行为人的行为并非故意或者没有过失,行为人也应承担法律责任。本章简要介绍英美侵权法中的严格责任理论、其初步证明要件以及抗辩理由。

1. A *Prima Facie* Case

The elements of a *prima facie* case of strict liability tort are: the existence of an absolute duty on the part of the defendant to make safe; breach of that duty by the defendant; the breach of the duty was the actual and proximate cause of the plaintiff's injury; and damage to the plaintiff's person or property.

Strict liability was first applied in the United States to the keeping of dangerous animals such as lions, tigers, elephants, and wolves. Owners of those animals who injure another are strictly liable. Another group of cases of strict liability hold people accountable for any damages connected with ultrahazardous or abnormally dangerous activities, such as blasting at a construction site, even when they were not at fault. Activities are considered to be ultrahazardous or abnormally dangerous if they involve a substantial risk of serious harm to person or property no matter how much care is exercised. Whether an activity is ultrahazardous or abnormally dangerous is a question of law to be determined by the judge. To be an ultrahazardous or abnormally dangerous, the activity must involve a risk of serious harm to persons or property, it must be one that cannot be performed without risk of serious harm no matter how much care is taken, and it must not be a commonly engaged-in activity by persons in the community. For example, a mill owner was strictly liable when a neighbor's mines were flooded by water escaping from the mill owner's reservoir. ①

2. Products Liability

Recently a great deal of attention has been given to cases involving products liability, which is the liability of a supplier of a product to one injured by the

---

① For more cases illustrating the origin and development of the strict liability rule, *see* LINGYUN GAO, UNDERSTANDING THE COMMON LAW ANALYZING & WRITING AS A LAWYER (SHANGHAI JIAOTONG UNIVERSITY PRESS, 2012).

product. Several theories of liability may be applied to these cases: intent (*e.g.*, battery), negligence (duty to care), strict liability, implied warranties of merchantability and fitness for a particular purpose, and representation theories (express warranty and misrepresentation).

When applied to these cases, the doctrine of strict liability holds one liable for injuries caused by a defective, unreasonably dangerous product that he has placed on the market. A number of states have passed products liability legislation. Many statutes alter to some extent the doctrine of strict liability when it is applied to manufacturers and limit its application in the case of retailers and wholesalers.

In order to apply the strict liability rule to the products liability cases, the plaintiff must first prove the existence of a defect. There are two types of defects: manufacturing defects and design defects. Manufacturing defects exist when a product emerges from a manufacturing process not only different from the other products, but also more dangerous than if it had been made the way it should have been, and the product may be so "unreasonably dangerous" as to be defective because of the manufacturing process. Design defects refer to the situation that when all the products of a line are made identically according to manufacturing specifications, but have dangerous propensities because of their mechanical features or packaging, the entire line may be found to be defective because of poor design. Inadequate warnings can be analyzed as a type of design defect. A product must have clear and complete warnings of any dangers that may not be apparent to users. The defendant must be a "commercial supplier" (manufacturer, retailer, assembler, or wholesaler) of the product in question, as distinguished from a casual seller(*e.g.*, a homemaker who sells a jar of jam to a neighbor).

Then the plaintiff must prove the breach of duty on the part of the defendant. He does not need to prove that the defendant was at fault in selling or producing a defective product — only that the product in fact is so defective as to be "unreasonably dangerous." A retailer in a strict liability action may be liable for a

implied warranty 默示担保
merchantability 适销性
representation 事实陈述,陈述(指以言词或行为所作的事实表述,以使他人与之订立合同或实施其他行为)
express warranty 明示担保
misrepresentation 虚假陈述
defective (产品)有瑕疵的
alter 修改,变更
manufacturer 生产商,制造商
retailer 零售商
wholesaler 批发商
manufacturing defect 制造缺陷,制造瑕疵
design defect 设计瑕疵,设计缺陷
emerge 形成

specification 说明书
propensity 倾向

warning 警示

assembler 装配工

casual seller 偶然做一次生意的卖方,临时出售物品的一方

manufacturing or design defect simply because it was a commercial supplier of a defective product — even if it had no opportunity to inspect the manufacturer's product before selling it.

The next thing the plaintiff must prove is the causation issue. The plaintiff must trace the harm suffered to a defect in the product that existed when the product left the defendant's control, and that the product has not been substantially altered thereafter. The negligent failure of an intermediary to discover the defect does not void the supplier's strict liability.

It is to be noted that there is no requirement of contractual privity between the plaintiff and the defendant. Most courts extend this strict duty to any supplier in the chain of distribution and extend the protection not only to buyers, but also to members of the buyer's family, guests, friends, and employees of the buyer, and foreseeable bystanders. However, most states deny recovery under strict liability when the sole claim is for economic loss.

3. Defenses to Strict Liability

Since the doctrine of strict liability is not based on fault, the defense of contributory negligence is not usually available to a defendant sued on this theory. So contributory negligence is no defense if the plaintiff merely failed to discover the defect or guard against its existence, or where the plaintiff's misuse was reasonably foreseeable. But, if a person knowingly places himself in a place of danger or engages in a dangerous activity, then a defendant may use the fact that the plaintiff has assumed the risk of injury as a defense. Of course, the plaintiff who sues on the theory of strict liability must show that the activity subject to the doctrine has a causal relationship to his injury. Disclaimers of liability are ineffective if personal injury or property damage has occurred. Comparative negligence can be a valid defense to strict liability.

Review Questions
1. Do you think the strict liability rule is better than the negligence theory?
2. What are the elements of a *prima facie* case of strict liability?
3. Why is strict liability applied to products liability cases?
4. Do you think it is reasonable to hold a manufacturer liable for the injuries suffered by a person who has no privity with the manufacturer?

REFERENCES

American Bar Association Section of Litigation, MODEL JURY INSTRUCTIONS FOR BUSINESS TORT LITIGATION Ch. 1 (1980).

Harry Sabbath Bodin, *Opening the Trial*, SELECTING A JURY, OPENING THE TRIAL, OPENING TO THE COURT OR JURY (Practising Law Institute 1954).

Harry Sabbath Bodin, *Selecting a Jury*, SELECTING A JURY, OPENING THE TRIAL, OPENING TO THE COURT OR JURY (Practising Law Institute 1954).

Qingbai Chen, ENGLISH LANGUAGE OF THE FOREIGN ECONOMIC LAW (Publishing House of Law 1994).

Jay M. Feinman, EVERYTHING YOU NEED TO KNOW ABOUT THE AMERICAN LEGAL SYSTEM (Law Press China 2004).

Lingyun Gao, COMMON LAW CASE ANALYSIS & LEGAL WRITING (SHANGHAI PEOPLE'S PUBLISHING HOUSE 2005).

Mark F. Grady, TORTS (WEST PUBLISHING CO. 1994).

Robert W. Hamilton, Alan Scott Rau, & Russell J. Weintraub, CONTRACTS CASES AND MATERIALS (2ND ED.) (West Publishing Co. 1992).

James A. Henderson, Jr., Richard N. Pearon, & John A. Siliciano, THE TORTS PROCESS (5TH ED.) (Aspen Law & Business, 1999).

Vincent R. Johnson, AMERICAN TORT LAW (China Renmin University Publishing House 2004).

Martin W. Littleton, *Opening to the Court or Jury*, SELECTING A JURY, OPENING THE TRIAL, OPENING TO THE COURT OR JURY (Practising Law Institute 1954).

Thomas A. Mauet, FUNDAMENTALS OF TRIAL TECHNIQUES (3RD ED.) (Little, Brown & Co. 1992).

James W. McElhaney, TRIAL NOTEBOOK (ABA Section of Litigation 1981).

Alan E. Morrill & Leroy J. Tornquist, TRIAL DIPLOMACY (3RD ED.) (Willamette Univ. 2001).

John Edward Murray, Jr., CONTRACTS: CASE AND MATERIALS 8 – 9 (5TH ED., LEXIS Publishing 2000).

Robert L. Rabin, PERSPECTIVES ON TROT LAW (2ND ED.) (Little, Brown & Co.) 1983.

John W. Strong, MCCORMICK ON EVIDENCE (5TH ED.) (West Publishing Co. 1999).

G. H. Treitel, THE LAW OF CONTRACT (9TH ED.) (Sweet & Mexwell 1995).

Jian Zhao & Guozuo Xia, A COURSE IN LAW-BASED ENGLISH (China Renmin University Publishing House 2000).

图书在版编目(CIP)数据

英美合同侵权法/高凌云编著. —2版. —上海：复旦大学出版社,2016.7(2018.9重印)
(复旦博学·法学系列)
ISBN 978-7-309-12376-0

Ⅰ.英… Ⅱ.高… Ⅲ.①合同-侵权行为-研究-英国②合同-侵权行为-研究-美国 Ⅳ.①D956.13②D971.23

中国版本图书馆 CIP 数据核字(2016)第 141147 号

英美合同侵权法(第二版)
高凌云　编著
责任编辑/张　炼

复旦大学出版社有限公司出版发行
上海市国权路 579 号　邮编：200433
网址：fupnet@ fudanpress.com　http://www.fudanpress.com
门市零售：86-21-65642857　团体订购：86-21-65118853
外埠邮购：86-21-65109143　出版部电话：86-21-65642845
上海春秋印刷厂

开本 787×960　1/16　印张 24.25　字数 554 千
2018 年 9 月第 2 版第 2 次印刷

ISBN 978-7-309-12376-0/D·829
定价：45.00 元

如有印装质量问题，请向复旦大学出版社有限公司出版部调换。
版权所有　　侵权必究